D0914095

The 32 hours of interviews that Minister Mentor Lee Kuan Yew gave are unprecedented in their candour and in the variety of issues discussed. The publication of these interviews gives Americans a unique opportunity to understand how this exceptional statesman brought a minor city-state, robbed of opportunity by its colonial past and devastated by the Japanese invasion in World War II, to the global economic powerhouse and first-rank nation it is today.

I have known Lee Kuan Yew well for some 45 years, ever since he came to Harvard for a lecture. I have huge admiration and respect for him and can state without equivocation that I consider him one of the most able, foresighted and analytical global leaders of the last half century. With his eye still on the future, Lee consented to the publication of these very personal interviews in order to educate the rising generation, too young to have experienced Singapore's difficult history, about the hard choices he made, ones they, too, will have to confront. There are valuable lessons for all nations in this interesting and illuminating book.

– Dr Henry A. Kissinger, US Secretary of State, 1973–1977

Among the political leaders in Asia, Minister Mentor Lee Kuan Yew is an especially dear friend and someone for whom I have utmost respect. Prior to attending G7 meetings as Japan's prime minister, I would meet with Prime Minister Lee Kuan Yew to gather his insight and opinions on issues facing Asia for use as reference in the meetings. His astute observations and analysis of Asian politics are always extremely meaningful and valuable.

– Yasuhiro Nakasone, Japanese Prime Minister, 1982–1987

Lee Kuan Yew: Hard Truths to Keep Singapore Going offers rare and compelling access into the mind of a remarkable leader and statesman. In this engaging series of new interviews, Minister Mentor Lee Kuan Yew candidly imparts his wisdom, as well as his fears, as he contemplates Singapore's role in a rapidly changing, and profoundly challenging, global society. An important addition to Lee Kuan Yew's legacy, *Lee Kuan Yew: Hard Truths to Keep Singapore Going* illuminates his conviction that a prosperous, sustainable future must be built upon the lessons of the past.

– Bill Clinton, US President, 1993–2001

Lee Kuan Yew remains, as always, passionate about Singapore, its citizens, its future and its relationship with its neighbours. That passion has driven him to make Singapore vibrant and relevant, and towards this he is committed to shaping the minds of young Singaporeans. This latest book illuminates his thinking that is bound to raise discussions about the future of Singapore.

– Tun Daim Zainuddin, Malaysian Finance Minister,
1984–1991 and 1999–2001

Lee Kuan Yew is the very symbol of the Singaporean success story, who transformed a backward trading port into a thriving nation with global reach far exceeding its size. His inspiring and pragmatic ideas have provided nations of the world with invaluable reference for their development. Lee speaks out his mind with clear, candid and forceful words that will surely have strong and lasting impact on the readers.

– Lee Myung-bak, President of the Republic of Korea, 2008–

I have extraordinarily high regard for former Prime Minister Lee Kuan Yew. He is one of the brightest and most effective world leaders that I have ever known. Besides, he is a valued friend. Minister Mentor Lee has done a wonderful job for Singapore and, further, his views are so respected outside of Singapore that he is a true world leader.

– George H.W. Bush, US President, 1989–1993

I met Lee Kuan Yew, whom his friends call simply Harry, the first time in the seventies. When I talk to Harry or read his speeches, interviews or letters I am always impressed because of his straight overview of world policy and world economy and of his firm judgment. And often I am amazed by his perspicacity. I am also fascinated by Lee's growing strong reference to Asian values and especially to the cultural traditions of Confucianism. The older Lee Kuan Yew gets, the more he declares himself to Confucian philosophy of state. It was

Lee Kuan Yew who initiated me to occupying myself with the teachings of Confucianism.

Last but not least, I do admire that Lee Kuan Yew has brought unbelievable and great economic success to Singapore within the last decades. My wife and I have enormous respect and admiration for my friend's lifetime achievements.

– Helmut Schmidt, German Chancellor, 1974–1982

I have the highest regard for Mr Lee Kuan Yew. He embodies, at the highest level, the values that make a great statesman. I often describe him as a sage. He is someone you will always be able to learn from, no matter the level of your responsibility. After my election as President of France in May 1995, it was Singapore, in February 1996, that I chose to make as my first official visit to Asia. I very much wanted to acknowledge the extraordinary achievement of the Minister Mentor, who had made the city-state of Singapore a centre of prosperity and stability for all of Asia. I see Lee Kuan Yew regularly. We have pursued a dialogue over the years, from which I have gained much, and continue to gain. I salute him with my friendship and respect.

– Jacques Chirac, French President, 1995–2007

Lee Kuan Yew is a beacon drawing you to Singapore to see its breathtaking achievements, but even more, if you're lucky enough to spend some time with a legendary human being. Whenever he speaks, whether the meeting is large or small, you can hear a pin drop. The reason for all the attention given to Lee Kuan Yew is the universal recognition of his powerful intellect, his good judgment, and his strong leadership. He believes in accountability, including accountability for himself. He says what he means and he means what he says.

He sets high standards for himself and has caused Singapore to do so, too. In Singapore, the object is to do everything well. As a small city-state, Singapore has succeeded in carefully selecting enterprises, be they local or global in nature, in which it can excel. It runs the world's best airline. It has a superb health system. Its orchid garden sets the bar for the world. Singapore also looks to its own defence by supporting a small but powerful military, thereby creating a clear deterrent capability.

I welcome this opportunity to express my admiration for an old friend from whom I have learned so much and whose friendship has been a source of inspiration for so many years.

– George P. Shultz, US Secretary of State, 1982–1989

Lee Kuan Yew's actions have proven that he is one of the great leaders of our time. But he is also extremely sagacious. Whenever we meet, even when I disagree, I never cease to learn from him. This book is a great example.

– Dr Joseph S. Nye, Jr, University Distinguished Service Professor, Harvard University, and author of The Powers to Lead

What Younger Singaporeans say

The book gives the clearest insight yet, into the deeper foundations of a man many regard as one of the finest statesmen in history. It is easy to place MM Lee in one-dimensional terms, but fault lies with those who don't look closely enough – this book offers everyone a retake on MM Lee, and for those discerning enough, a second appraisal on the Singaporean psyche. This looks to be the most insightful piece of work on him yet.

– Leon Tham, 27, banking professional

To someone who has grown up abroad, this is a fascinating introduction to MM Lee's life and ideas. The dialogue made me feel a part of the conversation. MM makes a sincere attempt to share the truth of his life with us – this generation for whom he is more icon than man. And though the words of warning are many, the decision to heed them is ours.

– Julia Chan-Lee, 30, Assistant HR Manager

This book stands out from others on MM Lee precisely due to the refreshingly candid and probing questions posed to the elder statesman. From opening up our political system to press freedom, MM in his characteristic candour defends his position like a quintessential ideologue, despite all the tough questions. Definitely worth a read.

– Muhammad Farouq Osman, 21, NUS undergraduate

MM recognises that our generation is full of individuals who are not afraid to express themselves through their choice of music, clothing, or sexuality. He seems to have softened with age and the understanding that the times change, inevitably so.

– Chan Yuping, 23, NUS undergraduate

I was struck by the fire that Lee still has in his belly and the thought that perhaps it is Lee's lack of allegiance to any one school of political or economic thought that allowed him to steer Singapore from third world to first. Lee's ethos of doing whatever it takes to lead Singapore comes out very strongly and it makes me wonder whether there are leaders with such formidability, drive and ambition for Singapore in the current generation.

– Mahesh Rai, 26, lawyer

The Q&A style somewhat reminded me of a recent Charlie Rose interview with Lee Kuan Yew which I found to be candid, genuine, and more importantly, a live dialogue. Particularly, the focus on income inequality and his views on egalitarianism and foreign talent strike a very hot spot, especially among Singapore's youth.

– David Zhang, 24, co-founder of an Internet start-up

The interviews cast him as a seer or futurist and his views are frank, decided and interesting to read. They give a good flavour of what is in his and the government's mind. But a lot of statements are sweeping and it's hard to believe in them unconditionally.

– Chew Xiang, 27, student

The book reminds us of the balancing act that MM had to manage as a public figure as well as a family man. He may seem like the typical father of a certain generation, in speaking of his children's achievements, but it takes a certain kind of love to give his children (and grandchildren) the space to develop according to their abilities, and it takes a certain kind of tenderness to maintain the love with his wife.

– Kay Chewlin, 28, self-employed

It's an absorbing read. The writers weave in MM's personal anecdotes to reflect his own vulnerability as a person. There's a human quality to the copy that I did not quite expect an MM memoir to have.

– Nanny Eliana, 32, PR consultant

The book displays a rarely-seen side of him: what he's like as a person, as compared to a leader, or a politician, or a thinker. The chapter on family made me laugh and cry, sometimes on the same page. Contrary to what MM Lee says in the book about a politician's personal life having no bearing on his ability to lead a country, I think people are eager to know their leaders' real personalities so they can form a more complete judgment of them. I wish this book had been available earlier, and I'm glad it is now.

– Fiona Chan, 28, journalist

My family will always remember that Singapore has given so many opportunities even to those suffering from most tragic circumstances, the way my parents did. They could never have imagined that they would be able to afford sending both my brother and me abroad for an education that they missed. Their love for this nation and their pride in our governance has remained imprinted in my heart.

– Michelle Joycelyn Tan Huiling, 22, student at the
University of New South Wales

I have always been proud to call Singapore my home and although we are a small island nation, we have a burgeoning industry and a youthful identity. Singapore has a very special place in my heart and the connection that has developed between me and my country has only grown stronger with each year, as I learn more about our humble beginnings and our struggle for independence.

– Alethea Tan, 15, Raffles Girls' School

LEE KUAN YEW
HARD TRUTHS
TO KEEP SINGAPORE GOING

HAN FOOK KWANG   ZURAIDAH IBRAHIM

CHUA MUI HOONG   LYDIA LIM   IGNATIUS LOW

RACHEL LIN   ROBIN CHAN

Straits Times Press

Lee Kuan Yew: Hard Truths to Keep Singapore Going

Published by Straits Times Press
(a subsidiary of Singapore Press Holdings)
Mezzanine Floor, Information Resource Centre
Level 3, Podium Block, Singapore Press Holdings
1000 Toa Payoh North, News Centre
Singapore 318994
Tel: (65) 6319 6319 Fax: (65) 6319 8258
stpressbooks@sph.com.sg
Online bookstore: www.stpressbooks.com.sg

First printed January 2011
5th impression April 2011

National Library Board Singapore Cataloguing in Publication Data

Lee Kuan Yew : hard truths to keep Singapore going / Han Fook
Kwang ... [et al.]. – Singapore : Straits Times Press, c2011.
p. cm.
Includes bibliographical references and index.
ISBN: 978-981-4266-72-7

1. Lee, Kuan Yew, 1923- – Interviews. 2. Lee, Kuan Yew, 1923-
– Political and social views. 3. Prime ministers – Singapore –
Interviews. 4. Singapore – Politics and government – 21st century.
5. Singapore – Social conditions – 21st century. I. Lee, Kuan Yew,
1923- II. Han, Fook Kwang.

DS610.73
959.5705092 — dc22   OCN662551098

In memory of
Kwa Geok Choo

CONTENTS

Preface

The reader, upon picking up this volume, might well ask: "Why another book on Lee Kuan Yew?" Many volumes on Singapore's most famous leader already line the shelves, including his two-part memoirs published in 1998 and 2000. His fans have burnished his legacy in their books; his foes have tried to bury it in theirs. There seems to be scant space for yet another book on the Minister Mentor.

We embarked on this project mainly because, even as there is a broad consensus on governance in Singapore, several issues continue to provoke debate. In previous books, we felt many of these hot-button issues had not been dealt with extensively. Hence, we decided to focus selectively on the more controversial topics, allowing us to examine with closer scrutiny those ideas of Lee's that provoke the most doubt and dissension.

Indeed, Lee himself had become aware that a younger generation of Singaporeans no longer regarded his views with the same weight and relevance as older citizens who had rallied around him unwaveringly in the country's tumultuous journey to nationhood. He wanted to find a way to engage them. He called *The Straits Times* editor Han Fook Kwang one evening in late August 2008 and told him he was writing a book. It would be like a Part 3 to his two-volume memoirs. He sought Han's views on an early draft of a few chapters he had written. As much of what he wanted to discuss centred on ideas and insights, Han and a group of colleagues suggested an alternative to memoir-writing: why not hold a series of interviews with him on key ideas that had influenced his leadership of Singapore? A cut-and-thrust approach would throw those ideas into sharper relief. We could also focus on issues upon which the established consensus of the past seemed to be shifting, we told him. Lee agreed readily. Such was his enthusiasm that when Han took a week to mull over the details of the proposal, Lee urged speed in an email. "Don't let the grass grow under your feet," he wrote.

Lee allowed an unprecedented degree of access to his time. The writers – seven journalists with *The Straits Times* – met him face-to-face in 16 lengthy sittings between December 2008 and October 2009. Every session was videotaped in its entirety. We were conscious that this was a rare opportunity to probe him on his views. To hone our questions, we not only examined what previous writers had said but also conducted a series of interviews and focus group dialogues with observers of Singapore.

The interviews with Lee were challenging, with discussions often at a deadlock and lasting hours. Lee held on to his opinions tenaciously and at times took our more critical questions as evidence that we were biased critics of his legacy. At those times, he would get combative. Exploratory questions were better received. Throughout, though, he was candid and frank. Even as he pulled no punches, he also gamely took on all manner of questions, from political theory to personal trivia. ("Do you believe in fengshui?" is one example.) In an email to the authors, he wrote, "Do not fear putting hard questions. I agreed with your proposal because you said this (cut-and-thrust approach) is what many will read. I want my views born of 50 years of experience read and understood, whether or not they agree with me."

The material was then synthesised into 11 chapters, with the interviews excerpted in their original question-and-answer format but edited for clarity and flow. The idea was to let Lee speak in his own words. For those who want not only to read him but also to hear him, we have included a DVD covering two hours of the ebb and flow of the conversations we had at dusk in the quiet echoing rooms of the Istana.

We have also attempted to introduce a younger perspective to Lee's ideas, to reflect the generation too young to remember Lee as Prime Minister – in other words, his inheritors.

This is not meant to be an academic work; nor does it claim to be exhaustive. It aims to be a dispassionate record of Lee's views in his own words. It also tries to reflect the global changes that have taken place since the publication of Lee's memoirs ten years ago. In that regard, this book picks up where his memoirs left off. We challenged Lee with new issues that have taken the world by storm, such as climate change, the rise of China and the problem of radical religion. These questions had not captured the public imagination ten years ago, but are of great importance now. Similarly, the conventional wisdom on certain issues – such as economic growth, Singapore's welfare framework and the growing presence of foreigners – has shifted. Lee's views have to be examined and interrogated in this new context.

Some of his answers may come as a shock. Others are different iterations of well-known, firmly-held convictions. Lee is unshakeable in his core beliefs.

To him, it is patently obvious that Singapore's vulnerability as a nation-state makes strong government essential for its existence. To him, it is also obvious that too strong a reliance on the state discourages personal effort and erodes the drive to succeed. Hence, the state must not over-provide, but must always have policies that keep the competitive edge keen. These are the "hard truths" that undergird Singapore's policy choices; and are the facts of life that a young generation must come to grips with, to keep Singapore going.

Overall, however, the reader should find his ideas thought-provoking, contentious even. The book will also unearth the personal side of Lee, as he speaks frankly about his family life. By bringing the controversial aspects of Lee's ideas to the fore and by highlighting, at the same time, the man behind the politician, the book offers a unique inroad into Lee's life and opinions.

Finally, there is another more important reason to read this book: to understand Lee is to understand Singapore's past and present, and, dare we conjecture, its future too.

Acknowledgments

This book is a collaboration that extends well beyond the seven authors. It includes more than 200 Singaporeans who gave willingly their time and energy to debate with and engage us on the issues that they believe ought to matter in Singapore today. They were thoughtful and enthusiastic and candid. Their commitment augurs well for Singapore. We would like to thank all of them, including the young people whom Rachel and Robin approached for questions for Lee Kuan Yew.

We are grateful to Singapore Press Holdings for supporting this project. We are especially appreciative of the sacrifices our colleagues made in helping us shoulder the responsibilities at *The Straits Times* while we spent time away from the newsroom to focus on the book. Several of them read earlier drafts and gave helpful comments, especially Sonny Yap, Rachel Chang, Peh Shing Huei and Janadas Devan. Our former editor-in-chief Cheong Yip Seng, who was involved in the Lee Kuan Yew memoirs, gave us his perspective on how our book could still tread new ground.

Our heartfelt gratitude goes to our indefatigable behind-the-scenes team of designer Sally Lam, photo editor Stephanie Yeow, copy editor Linda Collins and cameramen Kemburaju Thangarajan and T. Kumar. Our thanks also go to the Straits Times Press team, Shirley Hew and Shova Loh, for doing this project in double quick time.

We would like to thank Lee Wei Ling for lending us family albums and allowing us exclusive use of family photographs never before made public.

Most of all, this project would not have been possible if Minister Mentor Lee Kuan Yew had not taken a leap of faith and agreed to our proposal to do this book as a dialogue in a question-and-answer format.

Collaboration or not, the responsibility for the book's shortcomings lies entirely with the authors.

Foreword

My abiding concern for Singapore arises from my belief that the younger generation, especially those below 35, had never seen the harsh economic conditions. They therefore do not know the threats we face from neighbouring countries. For example, on our National Day, 9 August 1991, the Malaysian and the Indonesian armed forces held joint exercises at Kota Tinggi with parachute drops. Hence we mobilised our forces, in addition to forces parading for the National Day celebrations. I did not believe they wanted to invade us, but they wanted to intimidate and con us, so that we know our place at the bottom of the pecking order in the region. We need a sturdy, strong and capable SAF, not only to defend Singapore but return blow for blow when necessary. If we do not have this strong SAF, we are vulnerable to all kinds of pressures, from both Malaysia and Indonesia.

To have such an SAF, we need a robust economy that is not easily put off-course by external shocks. The economy needs constant renewal of its structure and of the type of industries and services it attracts, those that require higher skills to match a better-educated population. We have been successful for the present in attracting investments. So we have had to bring in immigrants and foreign workers from Malaysia, China, India and the region. If we do not have these immigrants and foreign workers, the economic opportunities will pass us by. To miss these investments would be stupid. Every major investment strengthens and expands the base of our economy and makes it less likely that we will be badly affected by a downturn in any particular sector.

The economy and defence are closely interlinked. Without strong economic growth, we cannot keep up the kind of 3G SAF, one that every few years has to renew its equipment with new-generation missiles, ships, aircraft and submarines. We need the sea lanes to Singapore to be open; hence a capable navy is crucial.

These are sensitive subjects that we cannot talk freely about because they would provoke our neighbours. But never forget that the more prosperous and vibrant we are, the more the angst of the people in our region. Our city skyline is ever-changing. We now have one of the most splendid city centres in the world, a marina equivalent to the Piazza in Venice. That is what two famous city planners advised us to do – Kenzo Tange of Japan, and I.M. Pei of China (and United States). Because of their separate and independent advice, we reclaimed the bay and made the marina smaller so that each side can see the other side and so it becomes an attractive piazza, and not a huge bay.

I wrote a few chapters for a third volume of my memoirs to convince the younger generation that if we are weak, either in our economy or in our armed forces, we are at risk. We are safe because we are sturdy and robust.

I sent these few chapters I had written to Han Fook Kwang. He replied that if I write my thoughts in that way, the younger generation will say, "Ah, it is the same old tune." He and his colleagues suggested that they put hard questions to me, the kind of doubts and disbeliefs that they have gathered in feedback from a younger generation, and some that they themselves had. They suggested they confront me with these hard questions and get my answers on them.

I hope this book has achieved that purpose. I spent many hours spread over several months. The authors have put them in question-and-answer format so that they do not paraphrase my words. My main message is: If you think I am just playing a broken record, you may live to regret it. I have lived through many economic and political crises in the region and the world. These have crystallised some fundamental truths for me that we forget or ignore at our peril.

Without a strong economy, there can be no strong defence. Without a strong defence, there will be no Singapore. It will become a satellite, cowed and intimidated by its neighbours. To maintain a strong economy and a strong defence all on a narrow base of a small island with over four

PART 1
FACING
THE HARD
TRUTHS

1 AN 80-STOREY BUILDING ON MARSHY LAND

ON THE VERDANT grounds of the Istana stands an empty house with arches and deep verandahs hugging its sides. Hardly palatial but set on an estate unmatched by any millionaire's mansion in Singapore, Sri Temasek is the official residence of the Prime Minister. None of Singapore's three Prime Ministers, however, has ever called it home.

Lee Kuan Yew thought about moving in when he became the country's first Prime Minister in 1959. His three children were then aged seven, four and two. "The place was full of butlers and orderlies," he recalled. "So, ball rolls down the hill in the drains and the butler will run, pick it up. So my wife said, 'No, no, they will pick it up. Let's not move in here.

They'll get a false sense of life.' That, you play with the ball and it is okay, somebody will fetch it back."

The family stayed put in their Oxley Road home. They visited the Istana house often though, spending afternoons there studying or swimming while Lee practised his golf on the pristine nine-hole course. Except for a few weeks in 1965 when they moved into Sri Temasek for security reasons following Singapore's expulsion from Malaysia, the children grew up in their own home.

Built as the governor's residence in 1869, the Istana complex now houses the office of the President, the Prime Minister's Office and Cabinet Room. It is the setting for state functions and its immaculate gardens are a much-loved spot for photo-taking among Singaporeans when the grounds are opened on public holidays. It was also the venue for a series of interviews with Lee Kuan Yew, over 32 hours throughout 2009, for a better grasp of the mind of the man who has made a deeper imprint on Singapore than any other.

During those meetings, held in the fading hours of the day and often slipping past nightfall, Lee would cover topics and terrain as breathtakingly wide-ranging as one would expect from a leader who had, for 50 years, considered it his job to think of everything from macro-economic competitiveness to social habits, marriage and procreation. He also revealed sides of himself rarely seen. As he recounted his days, there appeared the doting husband trying to repay the debt of a lifetime of loving companionship of the wife then in her waning days. At times, he would be the old-world grandfather befuddled by the ambitions and youthful angst of his seven grandchildren. At others, he would be the loyal friend still penning comforting words to ailing companions from an age long passed. There was also Lee the hardnosed geopolitical realist, a statesman with an astute sense of the forces underlying world history and politics. And then there was Lee the unflinching analyst of social dynamics, offering unvarnished views on race and intelligence that would horrify polite company.

Whatever their original trajectory, however, the conversations would invariably bounce back to what was emerging to be his central obsession as the 86-year-old patriarch of a stable and successful city state: how to make Singaporeans understand that the good life is not theirs by right. That in the real world of nation-states, there are no butlers to pick up after them. "No, you are going to fetch your own ball back or you lose it," he said. He was referring to his children's sojourn at Sri Temasek, but he could have as easily been talking about his fears for Singapore.

Our questions covered the gamut, from his opinions about his successors to the festering accusations that he was a dictator. He fielded them all. However, it became obvious that the main reason he had agreed to this unprecedented series of interviews was to help strengthen in Singaporeans the survival instinct that he feared would be threatened by the very success of his work. Singapore was a First World country but would always remain vulnerable – "an 80-storey building standing on marshy land", as he put it. It was, of course, a subject that he had delved into countless times before, but in 2009 there seemed to be a heightened sense of resolve and urgency in wanting Singaporeans to understand their country's exceptional vulnerability.

Although Singapore was in recession at the time, Lee's concern was not sparked by the global financial crisis. Indeed, that year, the annual World Competitiveness Yearbook found that Singapore ranked second only to Denmark in being best prepared to withstand the economic stresses during a recession, out of 57 countries surveyed. The government had the resources to soften the blow, barely even needing to dip into its massive reserves. Taking the long view, the Singapore story was still one of miraculous progress. With a GDP per capita of US$36,537, it was and remains one of the top 10 richest countries in the world, once purchasing power has been taken into account. Almost 90 per cent of its households live in their own homes, with nearly three-quarters housed in four-room or larger public flats and private homes. Its two sovereign wealth funds are the top seventh and eleventh in the world. It is a thriving city attracting migrants at record levels, and from such a diversity of places that you could find in some schools as many as 30 nationalities being represented. No, Lee's obsession with Singapore's vulnerability was not as fickle as the stock market or tied to quarterly growth rates. The origins of this book predate the Lehman Brothers collapse and the Singapore government's realisation that the country could not escape the contagion.

In discussions over the book with *The Straits Times* editor Han Fook Kwang in late August 2008, Lee said he wanted to "concentrate Singaporean minds on what we must aim for to achieve the quality of government and high standards of governance that have been the foundation of Singapore's growth and transformation". He said matter-of-factly that he did not know how many years he had left. When Han suggested a concept for the book, Lee agreed readily. Barely a week later, he prodded Han to hurry: "Don't let the grass grow under your feet." The task of "concentrating minds" was urgent.

For Lee, one fundamental truth behind the importance of top quality government is vulnerability. It is the inescapable, permanent condition of Singapore as an independent republic. Singapore's multiethnic population, jostling for resources on what former Indonesian President B.J. Habibie called a little red dot on the map, meant that communal peace could never be taken for granted. Beyond its borders, its neighbours were wary of its success and, even when relations were at their fraternal best, were unable to think of Singapore as anything other than a kid brother who needed to be reminded of his place. Lee put it more bluntly – tiny yet tenacious Singapore was seen as the "interloper" in the region.

Singapore's dependence on Malaysia for its water was, for decades, the most tangible symbol of the island's vulnerability. The development of recycled "NEWater" was a turning point that Lee would mention with satisfaction in our meetings. In a media interview, government engineer Harry Seah, who was involved in the NEWater project, expressed the import of that breakthrough this way: "We knew with this, we can be free."

That freedom was underwritten by massive investments in defence and security, as Lee would point out to us. Still, symptoms of Singapore's vulnerability periodically surfaced. Its need for sand for construction work and its land reclamation programme proved to be another Achilles' heel that neighbours could exploit. Its miniscule mass also meant limited airspace that was further conscribed by neighbours unwilling to allow Singapore's air force the use of certain flight zones.

Singapore is not New Zealand, as Lee would say. He recounted how New Zealand had shrunk its air force to just over 50 aircraft mostly for maritime patrol and transport, because of spending cutbacks and strategic realignments. It is now without a fighting air force. In contrast, the Republic of Singapore Air Force has over 400 aircraft to protect 710 sq km of land. New Zealand politicians had explained to him that anyone with designs on their country would have to cross the Tasman Sea, and therefore take on Australia first. "They've opted out," said Lee of New Zealand's ability to use its geographical isolation as a defensive strength.

Singapore's geography affords it no such security. While its strategic location had helped it become one of the busiest ports in the world and turned it into the region's commercial hub, this blessing also proved a burden. "In Singapore, we are in a very turbulent region," he would remind us. "If we do not have a government and a people that differentiate themselves from the rest of the neighbourhood ... Singapore will cease to exist." He recounted commenting to his Australian hosts in 1988 after a visit to New Zealand, that "I could come back here in 100 years and I'd be sure to find this place, still green grass, still sheep and cows and wheat and fruit trees ... When I project myself forward 100 years for Singapore, I cannot tell you that it will exist."

When one of us moaned that he found such a view rather depressing, Lee's eyes widened, pausing in realisation that he needed to offer hope as well. "Yes, we are in the midst of a volatile region but we are in the centre of the world's fastest-growing region with India and China, and if we don't grow, we are stupid," he said by way of reassurance.

Singapore's multiethnic composition is another source of concern. With Chinese comprising 74 per cent of the population, Malays at 13 per cent and Indians and others making up the rest, managing social harmony has always been a preoccupation of government. The challenge has become more complex in recent years with the arrival of waves of immigrants from China, India and elsewhere. When an Islamic terror cell was discovered in 2001, it was yet another reminder of the high stakes in the unremitting effort to preserve interethnic peace. On the whole, Lee was less optimistic than recent surveys about Singaporeans' attitudes towards multiracial integration. At one of our sessions, he recounted how he had just attended a constituency event featuring multiracial performances. He found them contrived, a target to aspire to rather than a reflection of reality. It was "an ideal which we may never completely reach, but because we have this ideal, we will continue to make progress", he said. On surveys that showed Singaporeans had no qualms about having a non-Chinese as prime minister, Lee was incredulous. "Utter rubbish," he said of an S. Rajaratnam School of International Studies survey on race and religion in 2007, in which more than 90 per cent of Chinese polled said they could accept an Indian or Malay as a prime minister. "You believe these polls? They say what is politically correct."

Taken together, Singapore's size and geographical location and multiracial, multireligious composition require an exceptional approach to governance. "I'm concerned that Singaporeans assume that Singapore is a normal country, that we can be compared to Denmark or New Zealand or even Liechtenstein or Luxembourg," he told us several times. Singapore could not afford complacency or wide latitude for experimentation, he argued. "If we ignore those circumstances, we'll go down the drain," he said.

A Denmark or Sweden could make do with a mediocre government but for Singapore mediocrity meant the slippery slope to failure and irrelevance. For Lee, having exceptional talent in charge is critical. Without men of integrity and ability helming key institutions and government, the place would go down. "Once you have weaker people on top, the whole system slowly goes down. It's inevitable."

Was this concern about vulnerability ultimately a way to justify the PAP's monopoly on power and the lack of political competition? Lee bristled at the suggestion. If others could offer a better alternative to the

PAP, they were welcome to take over. He was not interested in the PAP's future. He was interested in the country's future and consolidating it any way he could. "Whether it's the PAP or any other government does not interest me. I'm beyond that phase," he said. "If any serious man turns up and forms an alternative equal to us, I say, 'Good.' Then we are getting a proper alternative."

Over the years, Singapore's security has been the subject of scholarly inquiry. Singapore-Malaysia dynamics are much more than a matter of neighbourly relations; they have affected domestic politics because each looms large in the other's sense of identity. Singapore gained independence after a traumatic merger of 23 months with Malaysia ended on 9 August 1965. It was a time fraught with racial tensions. Singaporean political scientist Bilveer Singh viewed Singapore's relations with Malaysia as tinged by a "Holocaust syndrome" or an "enemy on the doorstep" mentality. British scholar Michael Leifer observed that the emotional baggage of the founding generation of leaders on both sides had possibly become "political mythology" and that "the departure of those most intimately associated with the events of 1965 and its aftermath could help to reduce the emotive element in bilateral relations".

The suggestion that the country's vulnerability was exaggerated made Lee visibly angry. "Two years of every young man's life, 5 to 6 per cent of GDP and a frugal government that builds up reserves? We do this because of hallucinations?" he exclaimed, referring to Singapore's hard-nosed policies on national service, defence spending and fiscal prudence. "So when you tell me we're not vulnerable, I say, 'God!'"

The most parsimonious explanation for Lee's preoccupation with Singapore's vulnerability in these interviews is that he sensed he had yet to convince Singaporeans, especially the young, of this immutable reality. While much could be entrenched and institutionalised, certain instincts were difficult to pass on to generations with totally different life experiences. And time was running out. At 86, he was acutely aware of his own mortality. His closest colleagues and confidants from the old guard generation had died, even as he remained in good health and in command of his faculties. By 2010, his inner circle had long disappeared. He was almost alone.

On October 2, 2010, his wife and confidante of more than 60 years died. Her illness began much earlier, in 2003, when she suffered a stroke while on a visit to London. Although she recovered and continued her outings with him at home and abroad, other episodes followed. In 2008, she became bedridden and had great difficulty communicating. During our interviews, Lee would tell us that he read to her in the evenings the latest news and her favourite poems. He would mention in passing how her illness had changed his own routine, such as having to attend to the mundane minutiae of running a household – like paying the maids their salaries – and eating his meals alone. While he showed little emotion when revealing the private details of their life together, there was no doubting the void he felt and the palpable sense of reaching the final stretch of a long and eventful life.

In 2006, he referred to the knowledge that he had accumulated: "There's a databank here that I think a younger minister will take some time to equal. Supposing I can – like a computer – put it into a thumb drive and then they can access it, then I say, all right, call it quits." If even his Cabinet colleagues cannot instantly download his experience, what more other young Singaporeans outside of government – Singaporeans for whom the struggles of the past are just facts in textbooks?

As part of the research for this book, the younger collaborators interviewed 150 young people and found that many regarded Lee as a mythological figure from another era. Distant and detached, feared and revered all at once were the adjectives that came to mind. He was a figure they heard stories about from their elders but never encountered or needed to know in their lives. Lee would acknowledge in our meetings the stark generational differences between Singaporeans. His own generation's experiences could not be reproduced. They understood Singapore's special circumstances. So should the younger generation. That understanding would galvanise them to work hard and be prepared to serve the country. Recognising the limited options before the country would also foster a modicum of circumspection before they considered supporting alternative Western models of society.

At some points in the interview, Lee mused aloud whether new crises, such as the ongoing financial downturn, would help to forge that sense of reality, of Singapore's unique circumstances. But in the same breath, he accepted that the government had to act and was actually cushioning the impact of the crisis rather well. This was the government's Catch-22. It was intent on serving Singapore's interests, but its sustained success made it more likely that citizens would take for granted the special conditions which enabled the government to function effectively. Lee was determined to do his part, using his moral authority to bring home to Singaporeans that the country's choices would always be constrained by its unique circumstances.

Lee was hardly the easiest person to interview. He was blunt at times, and often cantankerous and combative. Although he had agreed to a no-holds-barred interview format, he did not conceal his annoyance when he felt that the questions reflected perspectives that he had no patience for. The journalists before him then seemed to become, in his eyes, surrogates for his ideological opponents and were dressed down accordingly. On other occasions, though, he seemed to relish the exercise, sometimes prefacing an extended discourse with "Have I told you this story?" or coming prepared with a clutch of anecdotes and a choice phrase for the week.

Visible too were the signs of a man coping with the frailties of age. One day, he shuffled in wearing sandals. His toes had an infection. After a trip to Malaysia, where he had fallen off an exercise bicycle in his hotel in Kuantan, he appeared with an improvised therapeutic device: a heating pad strapped to his leg with neon-coloured skipping ropes. After converting to a floor bike, his stiffness moved to his back and the pad followed. Several times, he would use a spritzer to moisten his parched throat. Once, during a trip to Armenia, he developed pneumonia as he was having problems swallowing and food had gone down his windpipe.

Not once, however, did he lament about being tired or weary. The interviews drew not only from his surfeit of memories, but also from the latest developments in Asia and the world. He was obviously keeping abreast of things, whether it was China's green energy ambitions or the elections in Japan. While he was less in command of the specific details of domestic policies, he was more than familiar with their general thrust. He kept himself scrupulously up to date on world events. He read the papers every day and in the office, his radio would always be tuned to the BBC World News Service.

At the final interview, we asked him about the leaders he admired the most. In past speeches and his memoirs he had mentioned Deng Xiaoping. This time, he also named Charles de Gaulle, the president of the French Fifth Republic, and Winston Churchill, Britain's wartime Prime Minister. He quoted Churchill's famous "We shall fight on the beaches" speech. He recounted how de Gaulle had fought the odds to rouse and rally his people at times of near-defeat. As he talked, his eyes gleamed, he gritted his teeth. He clenched both his hands into fists and his voice curdled in his throat before spilling forth. In that moment, the same fierce determination he showed as a young leader in the 1950s and 1960s when rallying his own people flashed across his face. One remembered all over again that Lee was born a fighter. In that moment too, one could see the scale of the terrain that he pictured himself battling in. Not for him the quotidian concerns of a country content with its creature comforts. This was a leader who had overseen events unfold in grand terms, life and death, danger and escape, success and failure – of a people, of a country. Singapore is not in that moment of epic change. Will it have in its sinews the same fighting spirit as its founding father when that time comes? It is a question only the young can answer.

"If we are not vulnerable, why do
we spend 5 to 6 per cent of
GDP year after year on defence?
Are we mad?"

$Q:$ *Some commentators say that you have created Singapore in your image, including "always living in fear of a catastrophe". Why are you so worried that it could all fail?*

$A:$ I'm concerned that Singaporeans assume that Singapore is a normal country, that we can be compared to Denmark or New Zealand or even Liechtenstein or Luxembourg. We are in a very turbulent region. If we do not have a government and a people that differentiate themselves from the rest of the neighbourhood in a positive way and can defend ourselves, Singapore will cease to exist. It's not the view of just my generation but also those who have come into Defence, Foreign Affairs Ministries and those who have studied the position. Whether it's Ng Eng Hen, who was a surgeon, or Raymond Lim, formerly an academic and a lawyer by training, or Vivian Balakrishnan, an eye surgeon, they all understand now the circumstances that conscribe us. If we ignore those circumstances, we'll go down the drain.

We have not got neighbours who want to help us prosper. When we prospered, they for many years believed we were living off their resources. It was only when they became aware that our economic policy of welcoming foreign investments made the difference that they were sufficiently convinced to also do likewise. We are an upstart in this region because we survived for so long and I believe we can survive easily another 50–100 years given the international environment, provided we have a strong system that enables us to maximise our chances.

$Q:$ *What do you mean by a "strong system"? Is it another phrase for PAP continuing to be in power?*

$A:$ Whether it's the PAP or any other government does not interest me. I'm beyond that phase. I'm not out here to justify the PAP or the present government. I want to get across just how profound is this question of leadership and people and the ethical and philosophical beliefs of the leadership and the people.

Q: *Not many people can understand that we're not a normal country.*

A: Denmark, Sweden can get by with mediocre governments, Singapore cannot. The civil service will go down. If at the core centre quality goes down, then in all the subsidiary organisations quality will also go down. You will no longer inspire. Because no man can judge a person accurately if that person is superior than he is. So we never ask somebody who's inferior to judge. Very seldom does an inferior person say, "He's better than me." Once you have weak people on top, the whole system slowly goes down. It's inevitable.

Q: *Are we really as vulnerable as you suggest? Critics would say you make things seem so dire that so many things practised elsewhere, including in small countries, such as political competition, will not be available here.*

A: No, we are not preventing competition. What we are preventing is duds getting into Parliament and government. Any person of quality, we welcome him but we don't want duds. We don't want Chee Soon Juan, or J.B. Jeyaretnam. They're not going to build the country. But if any serious man turns up and forms an alternative equal to us, I say, "Good." Then we are getting a proper alternative. But look at the candidates they put up.

Now, are we not vulnerable? If we are not vulnerable, why do we spend 5 to 6 per cent of GDP year after year on defence? Are we mad? This is a frugal government, you know that well.

We dug a deep tunnel for the sewers at the cost of $3.65 billion in order to use the sewage water for NEWater, to be independent.

We are not vulnerable? They can besiege you. You'll be dead. Your sea lanes are cut off and your business comes to a halt. What is our reply? Security Council, plus defence capabilities of our own, plus the Security Framework Agreement with the Americans.

They stopped sand.[1] Why? To conscribe us. As Mahathir[2] says, "Even at their present size they are trouble, you let them grow some more they will be more trouble." We've got friendly neighbours? Grow up.

Why would we put a strong Minister in Defence if it's not important? He's the strongest Minister in the Cabinet next to the PM, toughest, most capable. We have always put a strong man there. Do we parade our vulnerabilities? We are living in an adult world. Why do we have peace? Because it is not cost-free if you hit us. If you hit us we will hit you and the damage may be more on your side.

Q: *But this point about not being a normal country...*

A: Forgive me for saying this: Assuming that I'm just nearly as intelligent as you are, but I've lived more than 85 years and I've been through all these ups and downs and I've spent all my life since the age of 32 figuring out how to make this place work, right? First, I believed and said the only way it could work was to join Malaya because otherwise we cannot live. Our water, our raw materials, imports, much of the exports come from Malaya. That was at that time. We couldn't get to Malaya because the Tunku didn't want the Chinese population. We worked around that and we joined Malaysia. Then we found ourselves trapped, from a communist Singapore to a Malay-ultra Malaysia. Has Malaysia changed? How has it changed?

Why did I break down when we got out on the 9th of August?[3] Because I left behind tens of thousands of people who had joined our rallies, and I knew that they were going to be handicapped, again a minority and leaderless. We provided the leadership. So when you tell me we're not vulnerable, I say, "Oh, God!"

You speak to the SAF (Singapore Armed Forces) commanders. Why do they do this – two years of every young man's life,[4] 5 to 6 per cent of GDP and a frugal government that builds up reserves? We do this because of hallucinations? Or because that's the only way we can be left alone to survive and prosper?

Why do you think we spent all this effort to solve our water problem until we became specialists in water? Mahathir knew we needed Johor water. So when the water agreement was going to end in 2011 for Tebrau and Skudai, we knew we would be short.[5] Then we discovered NEWater. He thought we were bluffing. You say we're not vulnerable?

We should not gloss over our worries. They are real problems. And we are what we are because we can stand up for ourselves. If we can't, we've had it. The Security Council passes resolutions. So what? Who goes to Kuwait's rescue? The US. Why? Because of oil. Why? Because next stop would be Saudi Arabia.[6] Who's coming to our rescue because of water? The US? No. We rescue ourselves. Either the media grows up, especially the young reporters, or we're going to bring up a generation that lives in a dream world of security when none exists.

Q: *Don't you think that how Malaysia wants to run its domestic affairs will have less and less bearing on what it feels about Singapore's success compared to now when there is still the baggage of separation and envy?*

A: Do you really believe that? Look, they want to take over the hub status of our airport. We were awarded possession of Pedra Branca by the International Court of Justice. Malaysia got Middle Rocks. They have yet to draw the boundaries.[7] I cannot forget what a Malay student in Raffles College from Kedah told me in 1941. He said, "You Chinese are too much. Too many of you." The Chinese dominate all the shops. And he's from Kedah where there were few Chinese.

I thought logic would overcome this prejudice when we joined Malaysia, the logic of the altered demography. I was wrong. The Tunku had no intention, none whatever. He was a nice man, he had Chinese friends. But he and the Malays had to be on top. That's his vision of social balance.

Q: *So you are saying that this state of affairs will not change? Some people say that this wish by others to put us down will diminish over time because you have a younger generation of leaders.*

A: Will the fundamental basis on which any generation of Malaysian leaders organise their country change?

Q: *It will forever not change?*

A: Forever is a very long time. But do you really see the basis on which Malaysia is organised changing any time soon? Singapore is organised on a totally different basis. We are a multiracial meritocracy, we've found a balance between the races, and between social and economic classes. Can we change?

All my relatives in Kuala Lumpur have migrated to Australia; they have given up. But we are here in Singapore and we intend to be permanently here. As long as we're strong enough and we have an international balance, we will be secure.

Now, I am not arguing that because of this fundamental difference between our societies and political structures, we cannot work together. We can and do cooperate, bilaterally and in Asean too. We agreed to go to the ICJ over Pedra Branca and did not come to blows. I signed several agreements with Dr Mahathir that still hold today. Why? Because they are also in Malaysia's interests.

That is how rational and pragmatic countries operate. We don't have to love each other to work with each other. A convergence of interests does not erase emotions but can temper them. Prime Minister Najib Razak is a rational leader. He wants to cooperate with us because he sees the benefits for Malaysia. But he has to deal with the emotions of his domestic ground, just like politicians everywhere. So will the Malay ground allow cooperation with Singapore? To what extent will they support projects which while they benefit Malaysia, will also help Singapore to prosper? Every Malaysian leader must remember these questions. We should not forget this.

Q: *But if the gap between Singapore and Malaysia widens, as it has, and we become stronger relative to them, will this issue become more manageable for us?*

A: Yes and no. Yes, in that they're less able to bully us. No, they will get more resentful. They already say, "We shouldn't have let them out." You read this in their Malay papers. Every now and again, they openly express great regret that Tunku let Singapore off. Singapore was part of their land.

Did I know this when we started? In 1952, when I was so light-hearted, I thought, yes, I'll go into politics, we get independence, I'll make a bit of money in the law and carry on. Then I got involved. I found I was captured by the communists. So we went into Malaysia where the communists could not operate. Then we were captured by the Malay "ultras". Within two years, we were asked to leave. We had to make independent Singapore work.

If I'd known all this turmoil, I might never have entered politics. If you ask me to repeat what we've done from 1959 until now – I say no, no, we cannot repeat the outcome. It was a confluence of many factors: my relationship with the British Labour government that bought me time when I needed it in 1971, and then my relationship with the Conservative government that bought me more time in 1975 before British forces withdrew.[8] By then, we had stabilised our relationship with President Suharto. Suharto understood that if we live and let live, Indonesia and Singapore would do better. He decided he could trust me.

Then I tried to stabilise things with Razak. He died. Hussein Onn, he didn't last long.[9] Then Mahathir. He knew he couldn't put me down because we had clashed before in the Malaysian Parliament where I was not intimidated. But when Goh Chok Tong took over, Mahathir wanted to alter several agreements with me. I told Chok Tong if he agreed to changing it, he would have no end of trouble. What's agreed is agreed and closed. So Mahathir became angry. So Chok Tong said, "You want to change this and that, we do a package deal." You extend the water for another hundred years, because at that time we had not found NEWater. Then Mahathir upped the price from 3 sen per 1,000 gallons to 3 ringgit, because Hong Kong paid RM8 per 1,000 gallons to China.[10]

Technology progressed, our water team worked hard and with NEWater, we could be self-sufficient. That disappointed Mahathir. His plan to squeeze us and get any price was over.

Q: *The Malaysians I meet tell me that Singapore is an irritation and that the politicians and media there may kick you now and then but it makes no sense for Malaysia to go to war with Singapore.*

A: That's good.

Q: *So that should give us some comfort.*

A: Because the assumption is, Singapore is strong enough to defend itself.

Q: *No, that Singapore is quite irrelevant to their worldview. They see us as a minor irritation and then some.*

A: Just see what the Malaysian Labour Minister said: "We are preparing for jobs for 300,000 redundant Malaysian workers from Singapore – before any redundancy takes place."[11] But where are the jobs? They say this to show that "I'm a big country, no trouble at all, I'll take my people back." Why do they take such a superior attitude?

Q: *They put it to me that the obsession with Malaysia is yours. They are less obsessed with Singapore.*

A: No, but we have not said anything that displayed obsession. We just keep our thoughts to ourselves. They come out every other day, especially in the Malay press and sometimes also in the English papers.

Q: *I grew up thinking that really the economic miracle was actually quite fragile, not politics and our neighbours as the key imperative.*

A: They are two sides of the same question. You cannot have a strong defence unless you have a strong finance. And you cannot have strong defence and strong finance unless you have a strong, unified, well-educated and increasingly cohesive society. They are all part of one whole.

Without a strong economy, how do you have a strong defence? So, how do you have a strong economy? By maximising your human resources. Your people, the way they are trained, organised, educated to serve the world's needs, which means infrastructure, connections, linkages with those parts of the world which will add value to our lives. Second, we leapfrogged the region because they wanted to squeeze us. We brought in multinationals.

I went to America in 1968 and I saw, oh, Europe was retreating but the Americans were expanding, transplanting their factories abroad. That was how we started on semi-conductors. With the Cultural Revolution in China, Taiwan and Hong Kong became risky, so they chose Singapore. We succeeded in giving them the conditions so more came and finally we became the computer centre and the hard disk centre for the world. From there we went into petrochemicals.

So all these things added up to create the economy that we now have which Mahathir wanted to overwhelm. Ports, for example: he started Tanjung Pelepas to undercut us.[12] He wanted to stop the railway line. We built a railway line to connect Jurong Port and Tanjong Pagar for export of iron ore from Terengganu. After 1992, operations on this line ceased. They go to Port Klang. Now they go to Tanjung Pelepas. His win-win is: "I win, you lose." Similarly, the Indonesians. When they wanted to privatise Tanjung Priok, a seaport near Jakarta, they said no, not Singapore. They gave it to Hutchison's from Hong Kong.[13] They developed Batam to eat into our container port. It did not reduce our throughput.

There is this drive to put us down because we are interlopers. The world is full of interlopers. The whites are in South America, in Africa, in Australia, in New Zealand, in Canada. The history of human civilisation is one of unending human migration.

The third factor is our people. Suppose we are quarrelling amongst ourselves, can we advance? Why did we choose English? When we became independent, the Chinese Chamber of Commerce – I have written that in my memoirs – wanted Chinese as our major language. They were convinced that China would be a great country and Chinese would be the important language. I looked at them to say, any such trouble from you, I'll have to act against you. I do not want a Ceylon position where with one stroke of the pen, they abolished English, made Sinhalese their official language, crippled the Tamils who had learnt English well. Endless troubles thereafter.

My reasons were quite simple. First, internal stability. Everybody on an equal basis: we all have to learn English, a foreign language. Nobody gets an advantage. Second, it's the language of international commerce. Chinese? What was Chinese trade in the 1960s? Imports and exports of Chinese products, medicine, herbs were piffling. Then English blossomed and America spread it on TV and now Internet around the world. We have become an education centre. The rest of Asean wants to learn English. That's an advantage for us. What motivated me? Internal stability and peace. We treat everybody equally. We judge you on your merits. This is a level playing field. We do not discriminate our people on race, language, religion. If you can perform, you get the job.

And I decided this for our own reasons. Two years ago, Gallup did an analysis of what made a country grow. They decided it is talent. They noted that in the 1980s, economists projected that Japan and Germany would overtake America. They did not. The reason? America was attracting talent from all over the world. So whether China will be the most powerful nation will depend on whether it can attract foreign talent and retain its own talent.

We must attract and retain talent. Talent does not mean only bright academics. Talent includes football stars, tennis stars, singers, rock stars, whatever. Then we have vibrancy. A country grows by building one city at a time. A city grows by building one sector at a time. They analysed four categories of talent: innovators, entrepreneurs, mentors, super-mentors. Americans beat the others because the Americans have all four types. They have developed a culture that brings in the talented.

I didn't understand all this when I started. I was British-trained and the British were structured in a different way. They don't go for change, but stick to tradition. The Americans innovated. Why did I learn? Because I had to make this society produce results, then we will become prosperous, then we can have a strong defence, and the world has a place for us. If you believe we're like Norway or Sweden or Denmark, then we won't survive. Singapore is an 80-storey building on marshy land. We've learnt how to put in stakes and floats so we can go up for another 20, maybe over a hundred storeys. Provided you understand and ensure that the foundation is strong. Crucial is interracial, interreligious harmony. Without that, quarrelling with one another, we are doomed.

Q: *When you say that we shouldn't quarrel among ourselves, is that an excuse to stifle dissent?*

A: No, no, we must not have the kind of conflicts between races, religions, cultures, languages. Political dissent is another matter. If you have racial or religious conflicts, we will degenerate to a Beirut. I have no doubt in my mind that if we did not give the Malays and less-educated Indians a sense that they are sharing in this society – that they also have their own flats, they also have a job, they also have a place in similar schools for their children – we're going to have a Beirut situation.[14] Bombs will go off.

Q: *Can a vulnerable country afford political dissent?*

A: When you say I should loosen up and then allow an opposition, just look around you and see, which country in Southeast Asia or South Asia has reached a steady state where they swop governments and life goes on? You show one to me.

My purpose is not to burnish the PAP or to burnish myself or any leader. My purpose is to secure Singapore's future and anything that consolidates or increases the stability and security for Singapore. No, I've finished my work. I don't need more achievements for Singapore.

What is it I can do? Crystallise my experience, what I think would help Singapore and Singaporeans to continue in a secure condition. Can that be forever? I cannot say that. Can we be different from other countries in Southeast Asia? So far, yes, we are different. We have to position ourselves and encourage the major powers to be in a balance of influence and power in the region, to give us maximum freedom of movement and freedom of choice. Are we as safe as New Zealand and can we dispense with our air force? No. Would I like to be New Zealand? Not really. I think it's not an exciting, happening economy. Yes, they grow the world's best grasses, good for horses and cows and sheep. But a dull life. We are in the centre of the world's fastest-growing region with India and China. If we don't grow, we must be stupid.

Q: *One of the things that strike me when I listen to you talk about the existential facts about Singapore is how little we hear that kind of perspective in public. Also, to what extent do you think you have been able to imbue this thinking in your own colleagues?*

A: Oh absolutely, they understand this.

Q: *What about the general public?*

A: You have to decide how much and how often you can remind people of our lack of depth and vulnerability. It is likely to unnecessarily affect morale. These are my fears. Will these fears come true in 10 years? I'd say, "No, we are secure." Twenty years also I would say "No." But people who come here to strike roots are not going to stay just for 20 years. They are here to stay forever, right? And their children are here to stay too. Suppose I were to underline our need to always fight outside Singapore. The Chinese and Indian immigrants will think, "Better go back, or hop on to America or Australia, because Australia is further away from this volatile area. Best of all, go to America." Even Singaporeans may start thinking like this.

Q: *Do you worry about this place after you are no longer around?*

A: After I'm dead?

Q: *I mean, all these calculations...*

A: No, all these calculations have been discussed and re-discussed.

Q: *But they originate from you.*

A: Yes, but every member of the Cabinet and definitely every Defence Minister and all the critical ministers understand exactly what our position is.

Q: *But the external situation will change. There will be new challenges and new calculations will have to be done. Original thinking will be required.*

A: But they have the capabilities. They may not be found all in one man. But it wasn't in me alone. I had a group of men who together had multi-sided perspectives, like a Rubik's Cube.

Q: *It's not tested, their capacity for original thinking.*

A: How can you say it's not tested? They are getting out of this recession with great skill. They are handling it with great skill. I'm just standing by seeing that this is all right. They worked out the solution. I did not, I cannot read the facts and figures of the Ministry of Finance and MTI (Ministry of Trade and Industry) and EDB (Economic Development Board) in detail. I had to read them when I was Prime Minister, but I'm not any longer. I look ahead for over-the-horizon problems and opportunities.

I said, look, let's build up relations with China, and let's build up relations with India, let's increase ties with the Gulf. Russia, that's far away but we try to get closer, they have oil. These are going to be additional motors to drive us forward. Recently, I told the Malaysians I've got those opportunities, so do not believe that I have no choice but to invest in Malaysia. You want Singaporeans to invest here, you've got to be constant, you cannot be fair weather today, rain tomorrow and stormy the day after, and then back again to fair. These are long-term investments. They understood me.

Mahathir, of course, has a different mindset, but the *menteri besars* and ministers understood me. So Mahathir said, the Iskandar region, they'll be taken over by the Chinese from Singapore, they'll exclude the Malays![15] That does not make sense to Singaporeans.

Look at the URA (Urban Redevelopment Authority) plans that will come to fruition in the next 10 years. The Marina, Singapore river, Collyer Quay, Boat Quay, Orchard Road, F1, two integrated resorts. Investors have absolute confidence in us. Confident that this place is stable, the government is stable, the labour and industrial situation is stable. Across the board, in the next 10 years, maybe even the next 20 years, we can make a quantum leap. The Western media no longer talk about Singapore as a sterile place. It's a fun place, a buzzing commercial and economic centre. We'll have become more cosmopolitan, with people from other regions, China, India, US, Europe, Australia and New Zealand. It's our destiny.

Endnotes

1   Malaysia banned all sand exports to Singapore in 1997, saying that it needed to conserve resources and protect sea and river beds. Indonesia banned sand exports to Singapore in 2007, citing environmental concerns. Singapore uses sand in construction and land reclamation; Indonesia's ban caused construction activities to grind to a halt as sand prices trebled in 2007. Singapore now buys sand from further afield.

2   Prime Minister of Malaysia from 1981 to 2003.

3   Lee is referring to the press conference he held announcing Singapore's separation from Malaysia. Singapore obtained independence on 9 August 1965.

4   Lee is referring to the conscription of all male citizens and second-generation permanent residents. They serve two years of full-time national service in either the Singapore Armed Forces, the Singapore Police Force or the Singapore Civil Defence Force.

5   This is the 1961 water agreement, which set aside land in Gunong Pulai, Sungei Tebrau and Sungei Skudai and gave Singapore "the right to draw off and take all water available in, under or upon any part of the land" or "any river in, under or upon" the specified area until 2011. Under the agreement, Singapore pays 3 sen for every 1,000 gallons of raw water it draws.

6   The United States led a coalition force in the First Gulf War to expel Iraqi invaders in Kuwait. Iraq had accused Kuwait of drilling into its oil supplies and exceeding oil cartel OPEC's quotas, thus bringing down oil prices.

7   Singapore and Malaysia had both claimed Pedra Branca and two nearby maritime formations, Middle Rocks and South Ledge, as their own territory. Arbitration by the International Court of Justice awarded the island to Singapore in May 2008. Middle Rocks was awarded to Malaysia and the Court determined that South Ledge belonged to whoever owns the territorial waters in which the outcrop sits. However, the exact boundaries of their territorial waters in the Pedra Branca and Middle Rocks area have yet to be determined and Singapore and Malaysia have formed a joint technical committee to discuss these boundaries.

8   The exact date on which the British would withdraw their troops was a source of much anxiety to Lee. In 1967, the British had initially set a withdrawal date in the mid-1970s, but brought it forward to 1971 due to economic problems. Negotiations with the British government then delayed

withdrawal from March 1971 to December 1971. Most of the British troops had left by 1971, but a token force remained until 1976.

9 Tun Abdul Razak and Tun Hussein bin Dato' Onn were the second and third Prime Ministers of Malaysia respectively. The former was premier from 1970 to 1976 and the latter from 1976 to 1981.

10 Dr Mahathir first raised the comparison between Hong Kong and Singapore in January 2002, against a backdrop of thorny negotiations between Singapore and Malaysia over a package of bilateral issues including the price and provision of water, railway land, use of airspace and the construction of another bridge linking both countries.

11 A statement issued in October 2008 by Malaysian Human Resources Minister S. Subramaniam said that his ministry would help Malaysians laid off in Singapore to find new jobs. He was also reported as saying: "There are some 300,000 Malaysians working in the Republic ... They can contact the Labour Department in Johor Bahru for help in getting jobs in the state."

12 The Port of Tanjung Pelepas was launched in 2000. Two of PSA's biggest customers, Danish shipping line Maersk and Taiwan's Evergreen Marine Corp, relocated there.

13 Tanjung Priok is Jakarta's international seaport, run by Hong Kong port operator Hutchison.

14 Sectarian tensions between Christian and Muslim groups lay behind the Lebanese Civil War, which lasted from 1975 to 1990.

15 Mahathir's comments on the matter were publicised in the Singapore press in September 2007. He was quoted as saying: "The Iskandar Development Region will ... be filled with Singapore Chinese and Malaysian Chinese who can afford it. What if their numbers exceed the Malay population? We will once again lose Malay territory to the Chinese, as had happened with Singapore previously."

2 WILL THE PAP LAST?

A MUFFLED PING from the lift door inside the Cabinet Room signalled an arrival from the offices on the upper floors. Lee Kuan Yew stepped out of it, armed with two black folders and a trace of a smile. As he took his seat, he nudged the files across the long teak table towards us. The folders contained letters from all over the world in praise of Singapore and its Minister Mentor. To Lee, the fan mail – or "submissions", as he called them, revealing his legal bent – provided independent, unsolicited endorsement of his approach. "I didn't contrive them," he said.

That unexpected "evidence" was how our first meeting for this book began. There were more surprises to come. With the submissions, Lee had wanted to set the context right for our interviews. We were about to scrutinise a system that worked and was admired globally, contrary to the stereotypes purveyed by the Western media: an antiseptic island peopled by a passive citizenry and governed by paranoia, Disneyland with the death penalty.

Yet the very fact that Lee came prepared with such a dossier was a recognition that Singapore's critics cannot be simply wished away. The global dominance of the United States means that liberal democracy has emerged as the standard against which all countries are most commonly measured. By that standard, Singapore will always be found wanting in the eyes of liberal democracy advocates. Some leaders might be inclined to pander to global public opinion by mouthing democratic platitudes. But that kind of white flag has never flown over Lee's ideological ramparts. In our meetings, he was as disdainful as ever of Western liberal democracy. Never mind the fact the ballot box has endorsed him and his party and resoundingly and repeatedly.

In other democracies the test of consolidation is the two-turnover rule or two changes of government. In Singapore, one party, the PAP, has held power for 51 uninterrupted years. The test of stability for Singapore will be whether the system can survive Lee. So far, it has endured with Lee no longer in central charge of government, but playing the role of mentor.

After stepping down in 1990, Lee has remained in Cabinet, as Senior Minister and then Minister Mentor. Throughout his 31 years in the top office, he was the principal architect of modifications to the political system to suit what he saw were Singapore's unique circumstances of a small, densely populated country in an unfriendly neighbourhood, with no hinterland and natural resources, and an electorate of diverse racial and religious backgrounds. Lee and his successors have shown that a one-party dominant state with free elections – and not all the other accoutrements of democracy like a freewheeling media – can enjoy legitimacy. Yet critics like American political scientist Samuel Huntington have warned that what Lee has built is founded not on sound institutions but his own power. The system will follow him to his grave, Huntington once predicted. Others, like Nobel Prize-winning economist Amartya Sen, have dismissed Lee's view that not all societies take well to democracy, saying that Lee is being selective in identifying cultural traits resistant to democracy.

Lee maintains that critics fail to grasp Singapore's unique vulnerabilities and the responsibilities of governing the country. He also sees a more sinister reason for Western diatribes against Singapore – an unspoken fear that it could prove to be a viable alternative model for emerging countries, especially China. Indeed, in the burgeoning cities of southern China, governance manuals, such as *Why Can Singapore Do It?* by Shenzhen University politics professor Lu Yuanli, are bestsellers. Campaigns by party leaders there to learn from Singapore are just the latest echo of the late paramount leader Deng Xiaoping's clarion call. During his fabled 1992 tour of the south, Deng threw down this gauntlet to the party: Study and surpass Singapore.

Lu's book, for example, catalogues the secrets of Singapore's success: incorruptible government, able and honest leaders, a disciplined workforce, and policy-making focused on long-term good rather than short-term gain. Lu likened the PAP's longevity to well-worn shoes: "One can widen the shoe, make it softer, replace the sole and make repairs – and it'll still be more comfortable than a new pair of shoes."

Others are sceptical. Contrast Lu's effusiveness with Indian-born American scholar Fareed Zakaria's critique: "All liberalising autocrats have believed that they can, like Lee, achieve modernity but delay democracy. But they can't. Other than the oil-rich Gulf states, Singapore is the only country with a per capita GDP of over $10,000 that is not a democracy ... It is an obvious exception to the rule and one that will not last."

Admirers and critics alike though agree that Lee's imprint on Singapore politics, as in many other spheres, is indelible. Said Zakaria, "Richard Nixon once compared him to legendary statesmen like Disraeli, Bismarck and Churchill. But, Nixon said, he occupies a small stage. That stage doesn't look so small anymore. Lee Kuan Yew took a small spit of land in Southeast Asia, which became independent in 1965 after great struggle and anguish, with no resources and a polyglot population of Chinese, Malaysian and Indian workers, and turned it into one of the economic centres of the world."

Michael Barr, Australian academic and author of some of the most critical analyses of Lee's rule, wrote, "Who other than Mr Lee could have delivered stability and prosperity out of the mayhem of the 1950s and 1960s? No other candidates combined Mr Lee's intelligence, courage and hard-headed ruthlessness with his ability to win people's trust and loyalty."

By 2009, Lee had stepped down as Prime Minister for almost 20 years. Hence, our interviews would be a golden opportunity for a stock-take on what he thought of the political system and the challenges ahead, or so we believed. We booked two interview dates to discuss "politics" and sent him a list of questions a week ahead.

At the appointed hour, Lee walked in and whipped out another "submission". He read aloud a collective response from his younger Cabinet colleagues to our questions, which he had forwarded to them. The younger ministers found our queries to be "standard" fare from critics.

Lee dropped another bombshell. He was not interested in talking about politics, he said emphatically, as he tossed our printout of questions back across the table at us. "I am no longer in charge," he declared. Pose those queries to the younger ministers, he said with a dismissive wave of the hand. He inhaled deeply and puffed out his cheeks. Lips pursed, silence. He glared at us through narrowed eyes. But there was a flicker of amusement on his face, as if he too realised the irony of the guru, the master strategist, the mentor, muzzling himself from, of all things, talking politics.

We tried to press on. Younger Singaporeans deserved to know what he thought of the current system and the leadership, one of us said. "No, no, I cannot in any way be condescending on the younger ministers. My job is to support them," he replied.

So it was that Lee remained reticent on political leadership and liberalisation throughout the two sessions. Even when he did relent, he never strayed from talking about just his own role in the past and what he considered to be Singapore's perennial fundamentals.

Lee then surprised us again, now not only with what he omitted, but also with what he stressed repeatedly. Time and again he returned to this unexpected theme: the inevitability of the PAP someday losing power. This is despite the absence of any apparent cracks in Singapore's dominant-party system. While the PAP has never regained the monopoly of Parliament that it enjoyed until 1981 when J.B. Jeyaretnam won the Anson by-election, the opposition has not gone beyond the record four seats it won in 1991 and today only has two seats. The PAP's share of the valid vote has ranged from a decent 61 per cent to a thumping 75.3 per cent in the five general elections since 1984.

Yet Lee refuses to take the PAP's continued success for granted. He does not care whether the PAP exists in perpetuity, he said. What is important is that Singapore perpetuates itself. He is not interested in seeing the PAP victorious at all costs, he told us. If the party lost the voters' trust and let another more capable group take over, so be it. To Lee, the PAP would sow the seeds of its own destruction if it deterred the best people from rising to the top or failed to deliver what the electorate needed.

Lee also sticks to his government's line that it is not its job to ease Singapore towards a two-party system and ensure a less traumatic handover if that came to pass. After all, his party had clawed its way up from the ranks of a rowdy opposition, succeeding against the colonialists and leftists in its own nest.

Lee believes that the same kind of pitched battle is possible in today's Singapore. Any opposition party can challenge the PAP and knuckleduster its way into power. The worthy will prove themselves in conflict. Contrary to what the critics claim, the opposition's main problem has nothing to do with the state of civil liberties. It is that the PAP has left no stone unturned. Any credible opposition would not be able to come up with a truly alternative platform because if it were made up of smart people who want to do what is best for Singapore, it would arrive at similar conclusions to that of the PAP's, he said.

While others may be troubled by whether Singapore is a full-fledged democracy and if people enjoy full civil liberties, Lee is seized by more pragmatic concerns: Are people's lives improving from year to year, election to election? Is Singapore continuing to attract investments and create well-paying jobs for its citizens? Do people have opportunities to make it in life?

The current system of government may evolve, but not towards a Western-style liberal democracy. Of this Lee is adamant: Democracy as practised by the West is not a universal good.

Is there any virtue at all in democracy, then? Only one, he replied: It allows governments to be thrown out without violence.

Over the years, commentators have described how Lee's own personality has left a mark on Singapore politics – hard, combative and unforgiving of the vanquished. He is who he is, he told us. He might have said and done "some sharp things", but his battles were never about the person but what he stood for, he is certain.

Even if he revealed little about the current leadership, perhaps his pithiest lines are about them and future generations of leaders. What does it take to be a politician, we asked. His answer, without a moment's thought: "You must have convictions. If you don't have convictions, you are going in for personal glory or honour or publicity or popularity, forget it."

Lee should know. Throughout his years in office, he sought to do the best for his people. But he also seemed driven by the need to win two epic battles. First, against the West, he wanted to show that independent Singapore could chart its own way forward; it did not have to swallow any form of post-colonial condescension or the liberal agenda preached by the Western media or messianic foreign governments.

But there was another bigger argument he had to win. Singapore, including its political system, would be everything that Malaysia was not.

The explicit and implicit references to Malaysia surface when one studies Lee's speeches over the years, especially in validating meritocracy, multiracialism and the protection of minorities. Singapore was and is what Malaysia could have been had it forsaken racial politics and made their aborted union work.

But at this point in his life, as he told us later, he is not interested in proving himself. He is, after all, merely a mentor. In the Cabinet Room where we sat for our first few meetings, Lee has been known to hold forth on political tutorials he believes the younger leaders need. As he would tell us, his job is no longer to make decisions, but to warn his younger colleagues of "sidetracks" when they make decisions.

He would repeat, in different ways, that he would not be there to guide Singapore 15 to 20 years down the road. His central concern now is persuading the younger generation that the future is uncertain, and can be secured only if they take to heart Singapore's need for able and committed leaders. "This place is like a chronometer," he said. "You drop it, you break it, it's finished. Some countries, you get a second chance, you buy spare parts, you put it back again. I'm not sure we'll ever get a second chance."

Making sure that the one chance was not squandered has been his life's calling. He put it more plainly: "Singapore is my concern till the end of my life."

That, no one doubts.

"If liberal democracy is so
superior it will take over the
world just like the
market economy…"

Q: *You've been instrumental in shaping the political system here. What did you set out to achieve?*

A: How we've developed is in part an accident of history when the Barisan withdrew and left Parliament to us on our own. What has followed is a result of the forecasts we made as to what is best for Singapore, what will maximise its capabilities. We started out with the British-made constitution and we had to amend it in several respects to suit ourselves. The key features we have kept are, first, separation between the bureaucracy and Parliament and the political leadership. Second, every five years, there's a free vote. So if any party comes in, it will find itself with a functioning system. We have created a system whereby if Singaporeans believe we're unfit to govern, they vote us out. That's their choice. But should we contrive that? It doesn't make sense to set Singapore back.

During my time, I progressively adjusted to the changing mood of the country. The Non-Constituency MPs was my creation. The Nominated MPs was the creation of Goh Chok Tong. The latest amendments being proposed are the thinking of Lee Hsien Loong and his younger ministers. (See section on "Evolving the Political System", page 91.)

So a gradual adjustment. The duty of the government is to allow the change in such a way that it does not demolish the system, which will bring down the country.

Q: *You started out as a socialist and very quickly became a realist and pragmatist. What shaped your political beliefs?*

A: By nature I'm not a person who's tied to theories. Theories should evolve from practice. A theory has to be tested. I don't believe that democracy is the best form of government for all countries and will spread throughout the world. If it is, why are the Western countries so keen to force it down people's throats? If liberal democracy is so superior, it will take over the world just like the market economy is definitely superior to planned economies and has taken over the whole world.

My fundamental belief is that whatever your background, you should have an equal chance in life, in education, in health, in nutrition. So you may not be as well-fed with all the meat and vitamins as a wealthier person, but you should have enough to make sure that you're not stunted, so you can perform and achieve your best in life. That's the only way a society can grow. I am against a society which has no sense of nurturing its best to rise to the top. I'm against a feudal society where your birth decides where you stay in the pecking order. The example, par excellence, of that is India's caste system. They've settled you for generations. So you're Brahmin, you're a priest of a temple and your children are Brahmin, you marry Brahmins. It's division of labour by caste. If you're born an untouchable, you'll stay an untouchable. It's predestined, for life.

The Chinese have a different position, more in keeping with what happens in the animal kingdom. I'm successful, I'm powerful, I multiply. You're weak, you're no good, you're sterile. You have no women, I have a harem. The net result is, the next generation, many get their genes from the bright and the energetic. The Chinese emperor at the end of every imperial examination, once in three years, chose the top scholar, the *zhuang yuan*, to marry his daughter. It didn't matter whether the scholar married any number of concubines after that. The emperor wanted the royal family to be infused with good genes.

It is the unspoken truth that if you want better durians all the time, you bud graft and you choose the best durian for that. It is selective breeding. I believe the same happens with human beings. But of course this is repulsive to Western liberals. They want to pretend that all men are equal.

But you're not a geneticist, nor can you change the genes. So what I tell the people is, "I'm not God. God has made you what you are. I cannot change you but I can help you do better." All men should be given equal chances in life, but we should not expect equal outcomes.

Q: *You've worked the political system, elections and one man, one vote, for 50 years now. How difficult has it been to make it succeed in Singapore?*

A: If I had not been a good persuader it would not have worked. Two things helped me. One, the severity of the crisis we were in. So I said, we either change or we die.

So we changed the labour laws, the Employment Act, the Trade Unions Act, and we changed the framework within which populist pressures could operate. The unions got to take a vote before they can go on strike and not just a small cabal in the leadership, which was what the communists did regardless of what the members wanted or didn't want. They decided when they're going on strike and if you didn't join them, they fixed you. The crisis enabled me to reformat the playing field.

Secondly, within that reformatted playing field, I had the capacity to persuade people that this is the way forward. If we do this, they will get homes, they will get schools, they will get help and so on. And we delivered.

Q: *It's unlikely we would have as effective a persuader as you in future. So would it be more difficult to work the system?*

A: Of course. But it's not only about having a persuader like me. It's because the electorate is now more stratified into working class, upper working class, lower middle class, middle class, upper middle class and the entrepreneurs and the very wealthy. So their interests are more variegated. But back then, survival was key. So

I was able to change the laws. I decided, for example, all sea fronts can be reclaimed without compensation to your land, otherwise we wouldn't have had the reclamations that we had. If we had to pay compensation to the owners, our development would have been aborted. I changed the rules. I knew enough about the law to know that this was a chance to reformat the framework and give us scope to rebuild Singapore and give everybody a stake. It was social and legal engineering that we did. And there was no squeak from the landowners because either they allowed this and their land eventually rises in value, or the place will collapse and their land becomes valueless. They knew that and they were praying for my success.

Q: *Was the absence of an effective opposition in Singapore during that period a big factor?*

A: It made it easier but even if the Barisan were there, what would have been Barisan's counter-argument? That I'm favouring the landlords against the poor? Or that I'm favouring the poor against the landlords? Of course they would have muddied the field just to oppose for the sake of opposing. So time would have been lost arguing over just words.

But when we became more developed, we had to change the Land Acquisition Act and pay full compensation.[1] It has become more expensive to acquire land for public purposes. So infrastructure development costs and HDB (Housing and Development Board) land prices must go up because we are now acquiring properties at market price.

Q: *It's a fairer system.*

A: Is it? Without the basic stability of everybody having a home and a stake, would your property be worth anything in a situation of infractions and contentions, and would we get new investments? But you get an emergent middle class and they lobby the MPs. For one middle class family, how many non-middle class families do we have? I think at least two. Now a working class family will have to pay more because the land costs more. So we make up to new buyers by giving them a grant, up to $80,000 for their first HDB flat, to lower the cost.

Q: *Among your early Cabinet colleagues, who challenged you the most?*

A: There's Goh Keng Swee, Raja, Toh Chin Chye. Toh Chin Chye challenged me ideologically. He is the man who says, "No, we don't want hospital fees. Look at China, all equal." I said, rubbish. You believe that a farmer has the same access to medicines as the people in the Politburo? But he believed it. He is ideologically that way and he never changed. He did not want to face reality.

Doubts over democracy

As a realist, Lee's views on democracy are informed by its complicated history and cultural relativism. It's not a universal good, he argues. Fundamentally, he believes that liberal democracy is not workable in Singapore's multicultural context.

Q: *What's your view of democracy?*

A: (American political scientist) Samuel Huntington says some cultures do not receive democracy well. He singled out the Orthodox Christians, the Muslims. He said Japan is an exception. But I'm not sure Japan is an exception. Their democracy is a very special democracy. It's father to son, very much the old samurai tradition. So the faction leaders are like the old samurai heads. I'm not sure that they are going to become, as he said, a liberal democracy which is à la America. We have built up a democratic system which suits us. In a liberal democracy, a man, once elected, is free from all party discipline. You have that in Singapore, you have unstable government. So we didn't say you cannot change sides. You can. But to join the other side you vacate the seat, and face a by-election. That prevents these musical chairs. Malaysia hasn't got this and now they are stuck. The opposition will not allow a change in the constitution.

Q: *When you say there is universal acceptance of market economy but no great rush for democracy...*

A: Yes, because it does not necessarily lead to better governance and stability and prosperity. You take Sri Lanka. The Sinhalese nationalists have beaten the Tamil Tigers. Whatever they wanted to offer to the Tamils is now off the table. One man, one vote puts the minorities in a captive position, as it could happen to minorities in Singapore. We understood that and we prevented that from happening constitutionally and by policies. Otherwise, we'll end up with the equivalent of the Tamil Tigers situation. The same has happened in Xinjiang too.

Q: *But at no point in history do we have so many democratically elected governments around the globe. Doesn't that suggest democracy has its attractions?*

A: No. The greatest attraction is, you can change governments without violence. In China, the greatest disadvantage was that you can only change governments by rebellion, *qi yi*. *Qi yi* means righteous uprising. That means the ruler has lost his mandate and deserves to be overthrown. Here, we can be voted out if we are no longer fit to govern. If we're voted out, the system is still working. It is our duty to ensure that. And the elected president is to add another layer of safeguard to give the country a chance for recovery.

Q: *How so?*

A: The new government cannot frivolously change the top men with its own sycophants nor spend the country's past reserves without the president's consent. They need to govern within these rules. If they can win a second election with an overwhelming majority of two-thirds, they might change the rules. But I don't think that's easy. And if they are incompetent, they will lose after one term.

If we do not envisage losing, we would not have to put these safeguards in place. I envisaged at some point, people will get tired of a stable government and say, let's try the opposition. It's bound to happen sometime. I don't know when. I don't think it will happen in the next five, 10 years because you've got a competent government. But supposing in this recession, we had an incompetent government and jobs were massively lost, then you're going to get a rebellion of some sort.

Q: *Huntington also has a theory that the political system can in turn influence the culture. Do you believe that the relationship works both ways?*

A: Marginally. Chinese culture has evolved over a period of 5,000 years. I don't see China having one man, one vote. Not possible. In our case, we are a transplanted society. So it's a slightly different environment where the people are prepared to adjust, because once you leave your country, you have to accept the different conditions of your new country.

Q: *If you met Huntington today, what would you say to him about that comment that your system will follow you to your grave?*

A: I'd say, "You're wrong." Look, I've been out of power from 1990. If we were going to go wrong, this is already 20 years, the system would have gone wrong. It has not. And it's because of the careful selection of people who are in charge, in the Cabinet, in Parliament, in anti-corruption, in the Presidency. We intend to keep it that way.

Q: *So, you agree with Huntington that some societies do not take well to democracy?*

A: Yes, he has laid out why multiculturalism will destroy America. He lays down the basic requirements for democracy. I quote: *The question of the conflict or convergence of cultures is a central issue confronting American society. Are we a country with one culture or many? If we are a country of many cultures, then what is the basis of national unity? Historically America has been a single dominant culture, the product of the original British settlers and successive waves of immigrants have assimilated into the culture while also modifying it. Its key elements have been European heritage, English language, Christian religion, Protestant values. Ethnic, regional, racial and other subcultures existed within this overarching dominant culture in which virtually all groups share. Now, however, the existence and the legitimacy of the core culture is under challenge by devotees of multiculturalism, by political figures including the President and Vice-President.* (He wrote in the time of Bill Clinton and Al Gore.) *President Clinton has explicitly stated that we need a great revolution to prove that we literally can live without a dominant European culture. VP Gore has despite his Harvard education mistranslated our national motto*, E Pluribus Unum, *from many one, to mean, from one many.*

This is his intellectual critique. He may be right, he may be wrong. But he believes sincerely enough to put it down in writing.

Huntington: *America is obviously a multiethnic and a multiracial society – I don't know what's the difference between that, multiethnic and multiracial – If it also becomes a multicultural society, lacking a common core culture, what will hold it together? The standard answer is that Americans are united in their commitment to political principles embodied in the Declaration of Independence, the Constitution and other documents and often referred to as the American Creed, liberty, enterprise. Most Americans do adhere to these values. Those values however are the product of an original unifying culture and if that culture disappears, can a set of abstract political principles hold this society together? The experience of other societies that were united only by political principles such as the Soviet Union and Yugoslavia is not reassuring. The issue for Americans is whether we will renew and strengthen the culture which has historically defined us as a nation or whether this country will be torn apart and fractured by those determined to undermine and destroy European Christian Protestant English culture that has been the source of our national wealth and power and the great principles of liberty, equality and democracy that have made this country the hope for people all over the world. That is a challenge confronting us in the first years of the 21st century.*[2]

He doesn't mention the Hispanics but he warning the Democrats, Al Gore and Clinton, "You're barking up the wrong tree. You must assimilate these peoples into your culture, not allow multicultures. Multicultures, they will outnumber you."

Now, what does it mean for us? Will we ever have one culture? I don't think so. Will we have one religion? No. Will we have common space, growing ever-larger but still remaining our private different selves? I think it'll take a very, very long time. So what will hold us together? I believe the economic necessity of peace and stability and growth. This is sinking into the people's minds. If you start quarrelling over different religions, different cultures, different races, the whole place will fall apart. So let's live and let live.

You sent me a draft question that says a (S. Rajaratnam School of International Studies) poll says 90 per cent of Chinese Singaporeans say they will elect a non-Chinese as PM. Yes, this is the ideal. You believe these polls? Utter rubbish. They say what is politically correct. We field Chinese candidates in every single-member constituency. Ask Low Thia Khiang (opposition MP for Hougang, a single-member constituency). Right at the bottom, what is your gut feeling? You know you will lose if you don't.

Q: *And you believe that will always be the case in Singapore?*

A: I cannot tell you if it will be forever because forever is a very long time. But I will tell you for my lifetime, and probably your lifetime, it will not happen.

Q: *The survey you mentioned appears to show that the younger generation of Singaporeans are more hopeful.*

A: You believe that?

Q: *Doesn't the fact that they gave politically correct answers give you hope that they aspire to this multiracial ideal that you yourself have set out?*

A: You know as well as I do that there are certain areas where you say one thing as a principle, it's another problem when you have to make a choice. It's not easy.

Q: *J.B. Jeyaretnam was able to contest an election in a single-*

seat constituency and win. People will also cite PAP minority candidates who were able to win seats on their own.

A: I don't know whether you're old enough to remember. But why did we switch? In the early days they will vote for the PAP regardless of the candidate. Then after a while the electors got wise and they say we're going to have a PAP government anyway, so "I prefer a candidate who is more like me". I could sense that and I knew that we're going to have trouble. I mean we had trouble with some of our Malay candidates. I don't want to mention names. We had to switch him at the last moment to another constituency because he couldn't handle his Chinese constituents and we knew that they're going to not vote for him. So we switched him to another constituency. We dropped him after that.

Today the system has been fine-tuned to such an extent that we're able to get quality Malays into the political system. Will they join the opposition and be in the wilderness? No, I don't think so. Not when they can join the PAP, right? And we look for them strenuously because we want to get more Malays of quality to join the Cabinet.

Q: *After the fall of communism and the Soviet Union, you got involved in this debate about Asian values versus democratic values.*

A: Well, they were hammering us for not following their prescription of what a democracy should be: their liberal democracy in America. So I answered, there are many forms of democracy. We create a constitutional framework which suits us, the needs of our people and their basic values. I was talking of the Confucianist societies. In India, you criticise anybody and everybody. You read the newspapers, all the time there's contention. Two Indian litigants are in court and you can be sure they are there for a long time because it's part of the culture. You have two Chinese litigants for a one-week trial, by the second day they say, *"Suan le."* Settle it. So, in China if you can demean a leader, and that leader puts up with it, that means he's no good.

So, I did not start off as a man trained in Confucianism. I absorbed Confucianism at a lower level. I knew, I have to be respectful of my elders, be loyal to my family, what I should not do to my friends, that I should not denounce the government or the prince. But if they defame me, with our Chinese base, I will lose credit if I do not defend myself. But who are the people complaining? The Western media and people like Chee Soon Juan (secretary-general of the Singapore Democratic Party). Why does he complain? Because without telling lies, he has no way to dislodge us. But when we accuse him, we'll stick it on him. I call you a charlatan and a rogue. You sue me and I will prove it. He dares not sue me because he'll have to go into the witness box and we'll prove that he's a charlatan and a rogue.

"Are you intimidated?"

If anyone should know about the nuts and bolts of electoral politics in Singapore, it is Lee. He talks about what aspects of the system have worked, Singapore's constitutional and societal quirks and the chances of the opposition claiming more ground.

Q: *As we're talking about the opposition, may I ask, why are you reluctant to open up the system? You don't see any need for a two-party system?*

A: You're just reflecting the views of the Western-educated intelligentsia that we need an opposition so it can take over the government. There's no chance of the opposition having enough capable people to take over. It's as simple as that. We can't find enough good people to run the government, we are constantly looking for such candidates. You can see the quality of the people that Low Thia Khiang has found. He's tried very hard. We get the constant critics. I say, "Come on, form an opposition. Drive round the place. Go down and meet the people and see whether you can win them over." I took the draft questions you sent and I sent them to the other ministers for comments because I'm not making the changes now. This is their joint comment:

SPH have put down the standard issues which critics raise. They do not necessarily believe in all these criticisms but are raising them just to elicit your response. We're not claiming our present position is fixed and must never be changed. It will evolve over time with new generations of leaders and voters. Leaders and voters must work the system in their own way. The test of our election system is not whether there is an independent elections commission, but whether voting is honestly administered and whether it produces governments which enjoy legitimacy and govern the country well.

Q: *Yes, the call for an independent elections commission has been made by critics.*

A: There was no independent elections boundary commission in Britain.[3] We inherited that. So did Malaysia. We've done one tenth the gerrymandering others have done. All we did was to have more group constituency MPs, primarily because we had to get minority representation. There was a point reached when voters would no longer vote for a PAP minority candidate because they knew the PAP would be in government. The voter was saying, "I want a candidate who'll understand me – Chinese, dialect speaking." So getting an elections commission is not going to solve anything. Do you have legitimacy? That's what matters.

They're thinking of all the possible ways to break down a seemingly impregnable PAP. Open up the press, dissolve the NTUC, don't have the symbiosis. You'll end up dissolving institutions we have created that have made Singapore successful. Anybody who takes over should work those institutions. And I do not see any opposition team emerging in the next election that is capable enough remotely to do the job. I do not see it, neither does the present leadership.

Q: *Just in the next election or several more?*

A: This is the view of the younger ministers:

In recent GEs (general elections), many seats have been uncontested and the PAP has won an overwhelming majority in Parliament. We should not assume that this is a permanent state of affairs. For a start, the increase in the number of NCMPs will encourage more opposition candidates to stand, especially in the GRCs, and try their luck. If voters elect more opposition MPs, so be it. But we do not believe that helping to build an opposition, to buy insurance in case the PAP fails, will work. Instead it will lead to more party politicking and distraction from long-term issues.

That's their position. It's not very far removed from mine but then there's been osmosis all these years. They've been running the system, they have been going down to the ground. They have held the ground. Your questions should be put to them.

The future, I can only determine in my lifetime – and in this case my political lifetime. You may or may not believe me, but I'm no longer the decision-maker. Yes, I have influence. Yes, I make them pause and think again. But they make the decisions because it is they who will have to carry the ground and be responsible for the future. I tell them that I no longer have the same feel. In the past, I not only went down to the constituencies, but also visited new estates, visited the NTUC, and talked to them. Devan, then Ong Teng Cheong were there.[4] I was involved in everything. I knew what the ground feeling was.

Q: *How do you stay in touch now?*

A: Now I meet the NTUC once a year in an open dialogue with 2,000 people in Suntec City. It's not the same. You've to talk to them in small groups – and one to one – they tell you their problems before these become big. Not everybody can work with the NTUC and the grassroots leaders. We have to find MPs who can empathise with them. Lim Boon Heng developed empathy and they trusted him. Lim Swee Say is a natural.[5] He feels for them, he thinks with them, and he brings back their views to Cabinet, which influences our decision-making.

Do not believe for one moment that we'll always carry the workers. We only carry them if they feel they've had a fair deal whether in a downturn or an upturn. In this downturn, the NTUC was fully consulted. The unions knew what we were trying to do. There's no panic. This relationship needs to be nurtured and they must actually get benefits. So too with the overall ground. They say we give out goodies. Every government does what it can to win over the votes nearer election time. We don't want to do it too early because people forget. But if you do not give them a better life and their children the hope of a better future, we won't persuade them to support us. It's as simple as that.

Put these questions to the younger ministers, because what will happen in the future, they will decide. I can drop dead anytime. I've finished my tasks. My job now is to support the present team, to consolidate the gains for Singapore, that's all.

Q: *What are some of these areas where you've asked the ministers to pause and think again?*

A: No, they make the decisions. I tell them, there are these possibilities, unexpected obstacles and sidetracks that may hinder you. You've to prepare for it.

Q: *What are some of these sidetracks?*

A: My job is to support the younger ministers. I'm not going to be critical. I played a part when we selected them as MPs. I played no part when the Prime Minister, both Goh Chok Tong and Lee Hsien Loong, decided to make them ministers. In fact, in several cases I said, "No, I don't think we should make this person a minister, he doesn't measure up." But they went ahead. But these people didn't have the temperament. One shook hands with fishmongers and then washed her hands. You're going campaigning, you have to go to hawker centres, shake hands.[6] At the end of the day, you wash your hands with soap and water. But if you do that in public, you lose that sense of empathy.

Q: *But as the architect of the system, what are some of its weaknesses that you may want to warn the ministers about?*

A: The weak point is that there are not enough good people willing to go into politics. But for the inflow of foreign talent, we haven't got enough good people to run the economy. You have about one thousand in each cohort to spread over in the administrative service, defence, police and professional services. They are spread very thin. What counts? First, integrity. Second, commitment. Third, ability. And fourth, most important, a capacity to expound and carry people with you.

We've had to take out doctors to join politics. There's a fellow, Dr Janil Puthucheary. The Duke University dean said, "I see this man as the dean of this medical college." He's done medicine for 15 years already in Ireland, England, Australia. He's quite outstanding. He's in KK (Women's and Children's Hospital) now. Do we take him out? We took Balaji out. He didn't quite make it. But he said, "I'll carry on." We took Ng Eng Hen and Vivian Balakrishnan out. They're a success. But what a waste. They spent many years as a cancer surgeon and as an eye surgeon. So much better if they had from the beginning done economics and business administration.

Look down the road 15, 20 years, and we got an old age problem. It's a serious problem. If we don't have the economy going, the burden on Singaporeans who are working will be so heavy that many of the talented will migrate.

The opposition, a thinking opposition, will find Singapore's choices finite. We're not America or Australia in ratio of population to resources.

Q: *So, you don't see any opposition being able to offer an alternative?*

A: Is there an alternative? I don't see it. One way is for the PAP to break up into two parts. Will that help? For one, two elections? Then what? And then the opposition that doesn't get into power will say, I want to come back to the PAP. I don't want to sit out in the opposition benches. Makes no sense, right? We're going to tap the same limited talent pool.

Q: *What aspects of the political system do you think should not change?*

A: The basic ones: upholding of multiracialism, equality of opportunity, not equality of rewards but equality of opportunity in education, housing, health and so on. And a system based on meritocracy. That's the basis on which we have had intercommunal harmony and interreligious tolerance.

Q: *Are there values you would consider sacrosanct?*

A: That you must have the minorities elected. You can achieve it in two ways: proportional representation, in which case you're encouraging parties playing to Malay sentiments and rights to emerge. That's divisive. Or, you allow them to become the swing vote, which I think is a smarter way out. It's not the way Malaysia is going because they are allowing illegal immigrants, Muslims, to come in so that the Malays outnumber the Chinese and Indians and then they appeal only to the Malay voters. Many of their Chinese and Indians have left the country and won't go back.

We have not done that. And to make sure that meritocracy will prevail in the opposition, we've given the President reserve powers to veto any change which affects the position. We're limiting choices for ourselves.

But we're also preparing for a contingency where for some reason or the other, the electorate says okay, let's try the others. So be it, if the opposition comes in for two, three, four years without collapsing the economy. But it will cause great disquiet in the investment community. Even if the new government doesn't deviate from our policies, it will not be able to produce the same kind of solutions, like when we meet a crisis for example. It needs very careful, very able people to sit down and say, okay, this recession, we don't know how long it'll last, what is the most important thing? Jobs. If they have jobs, they've got pay, it's okay. So how do we help Singaporeans keep their jobs? We have the reserves. So we support them, tide them over in this period. We can do it for one, two, three years, if necessary. Is it the civil service who takes these things up? No. It's the ministers. They then discuss it with Lim Swee Say, with union leaders. Will this work? Will this reassure the workers? Go back, think it over. Test it out on the ground. They say, let's do it. All right, you're displaced, retrain, and we pay for the retraining. At the end of the day, we get a better work force. You think any ordinary team can do that? Not a chance.

Q: *So you believe Singapore cannot have an alternative set of leaders because of a lack of talented people rather than what the PAP has done to fix the system, as it were?*

A: Because the talent is not there. In the opposition you ask questions and you vote no and so on, just posturing. What's the alternative? They can come up with an alternative? Rubbish. They know that. Sylvia Lim (Non-Constituency MP) acknowledges that they're in no position to run the government.

Q: *You have described the political changes in Malaysia as a tectonic shift and we know part of that shift was because more young people voted for the opposition. Worldwide, too, you've had this wave of young people desiring change. Do you see that sort of tide sweeping over Singapore?*

A: In Singapore, change to what? It comes with time. If there's a change, a plausible alternative, yes. But you can see the alternative is not plausible. People come back from abroad – I've read all these reports – they say, "Absurd to pay the ministers so much." But they cool down very soon. Why? You're making this much in the private sector. You expect these ministers to stay for 20 years and sacrifice their families? Sacrifice themselves? Maybe they're prepared to. But sacrifice their families? They need to provide for their families. We have to be practical. We are living in a different era, my generation cannot be reproduced.

Q: *You mentioned that as society becomes more fragmented, it will be more difficult to work one man, one vote in Singapore.*

A: We have been holding the middle ground which means a large part of the working class, the unions and so on, and a large part of the middle class and even the upper middle class who see that this is advantageous to them. As long as that prevails, it will carry on. And there could come a time when the interest of the upper middle class will be divergent, that they don't think they should subsidise the lower classes. They may well support a party which says, "No, I don't think this taxation is right. Why should I support the people in the two-room and three-room and four-room flats?" We will widen the divide in our society. I don't know when, but it will come.

Q: *How so?*

A: It's a divide between the successful and the less successful which happens in every society. The successful have forgotten that without the peace and stability that made their education, their job or their business opportunities possible, they would never have made it. But having made it, they think they made it on their own. Some students from the top schools like Raffles Institution or Hwa Chong, they go abroad and they think that they had done it on their own. They don't owe the government or society anything. They are bright chaps, but how did they make it? Because we kept a balance in society. With peace, stability, we built up our education system and enabled the brightest to rise to the top. Even those who are less bright were given the opportunities to go as far as they can.

Q: *What do you mean when you said earlier that there will come a time when people will tire of the PAP government?*

A: There will come a time when eventually the public will say, look, let's try the other side, either because the PAP has declined in quality or the opposition has put up a team which is equal to the PAP and they say, let's try the other side. That day will come.

I mean, the Liberal Democratic Party in Japan carried on from 1950s until now. I think they took over in 1955.[7] That's four years before we did but they have come apart partly because they carried on with old ideas.

No system lasts forever, that's for sure. In the next 10 years to 20 years, I don't think it'll happen. Beyond that, I cannot tell. Will we always be able to get the most dedicated and the most capable, with integrity to devote their lives to this? I hope so, but forever, I don't know.

I can see the change in my grandchildren's generation. It's a change in values and attitudes of a different generation who feels that, you know, I'm not going to spend my life in public service like my father or my uncle. I see no reason for that. The place is running, let somebody else do it. Who is that somebody else? Have we got such a plethora of talent, capable, honest, dedicated? We haven't.

So, I can't tell you what it will be in 30 years. It could well be after it's broken up or threatens to break up, the people with a stake in it will either pack up and leave or take over and say, look, let's run this.

Q: *Is it just about opportunities or is there something that we have done in the way we've raised the younger generation that they don't feel the need to return to society?*

A: It's a change in the mood of the whole society. The generation that produced my sons and my daughter was a generation that understood that we could have lost it all.

I remember the master of Eliot House in Harvard who befriended me when I stayed there for two months. He said every three years we have a new generation, a change in mindset. That's America because it's a fast-changing society. In our case, probably every 10 years.

People take what they have as a new base. Ten years from now, they graduate, the marina is complete, IR (integrated resort) is there, the canals have become rivers, they take all these as a given. They believe that will always be there, they don't need to make any effort. I don't think they understand that there was a lot of hard work and planning before we got there, and a lot of effort has got to be put in to keep it like that.

Q: *Do we not have some enduring values already in what Singapore society ought to be – clean, incorruptible government, multiracialism, for example?*

A: How deep is it? Ask yourself how deep it is. Look, Americans went to war, two world wars. The blacks in the First World War were carriers of the ammo and so on. Second World War, they fought together. They came back to America, the blacks went back to the slums, the whites went back to the suburbs. Now, have they made enormous progress?

Q: *Don't you see it as beneficial to you to create the conditions for a more gradual evolution for the sake of the sustainability and stability of the system going forward?*

A: I do not believe for one moment that if we can get a small group of two or three, it will grow, because how are they going to grow? Chiam See Tong found Chee Soon Juan and it collapsed. Jeyaretnam found Francis Seow. Who else? Low Thia Khiang found who? Sylvia Lim.

Q: *Some people would say the barriers to contesting elections are so high.*

A: All you need is your deposit and a lot of sweat.

Q: *If you look at the political system today, are you satisfied with the level of competition that exists now?*

A: We'll be quite happy if we get a small group of equal calibre contesting against us. I mean, you look at the NMPs, they talk more sense than the opposition politicians. Would they fight an election? No. So? They have the brain power, they have the knowledge but they're not prepared to jump into the rough sea.

Q: *Many people say they are intimidated by the PAP. There is the climate of fear, crackdown on dissent and so on.*

A: No, no. Are you intimidated?

Q: *Since I'm asking you this question, obviously I'm not. But the fear is very real out there, when we interview people, they say it. The perception is fairly pervasive even among the professionals.*

A: Why should you, if you believe you're any good? This chap who stood up for gay rights, Siew Kum Hong, is not intimidated. We have no objections if he goes and joins the Workers' Party. He takes us on, we'll take him on. That's part of politics. You say that's intimidation? Well, George W. Bush survived the intimidation. He survived Al Gore. Second time he survived John Kerry. John Kerry and Al Gore both brighter than him but he had good coaches, Karl Rove.[8] So he got through.

Q: *How confident are you that the system you have set in place will survive that moment when people say yes, they've tired of the PAP government?*

A: It depends on when it happens and whether it's all of a sudden or it's gradually. If the decline in standards happens gradually, an opposition of quality will be launched. The public can sense it. If it is sudden, well, you're landed with an emergency, and unless a credible team emerges, the country will start to go down the drain.

Q: *How can it happen suddenly?*

A: I cannot say. You have a break-up in the leadership. They disagree profoundly, either for reasons of principle or personality and suddenly it breaks up. In 1961, it was doomed to happen with Barisan and the pro-communists. I cannot tell you what will happen in 20, 30, 40 years, not possible. We might have a genuine difference of perspective what the future should be, what kind of Singapore will survive and thrive in that future. We might have a clash. I don't know. Look, I've lived long enough to know that nobody settles the future of his country beyond more than a decade or so of his life. Stalin grabbed the whole of the eastern part of Europe, grabbed all the Asian republics in the south and in the east right up to Siberia; he took Mongolia which belonged to China under his wing. That's 1945. He died. The system later threw up a Gorbachev who never went through a revolution, who did not know that he was sitting on a boiling cauldron. Deng Xiaoping had been through a revolution and he knew that once China breaks up, it's finished. So he says, get them out or I shoot them (at Tiananmen). Why should he give up his lifetime's work for a few hundred agitators amongst the students fanned by agitators outside? Had the students won, do you think we will have today's China?

All I can say is, I think Singapore is safe for the next 10 years. No trouble because there's a team in place that will govern it competently. Whether that will continue for 15, 20, 30 years depends on them getting a capable team of successors in 10 years. Part of the team is in place but you need a leader. You need somebody who can communicate, who can mobilise people, move people. It's not enough to have good policies. You've got to convince people. That's one reason I am making fewer speeches. I want them to fill the gap.

Q: *Is the elected presidency the safeguard or the circuit-breaker if there is a sudden change in government?*

A: Yes, of course. I'm running a system where I'm hoping if the PAP loses, not everything will be lost for Singapore. And if you change all the permanent secretaries, military chiefs, commissioner of police, heads of statutory boards, then you'll ruin the system. For five years, the President can prevent that. And our past reserves cannot be raided. But if you're clever enough and you can win a second term with a two-thirds majority, you can change the constitution and unscramble the double-key safeguard. It will depend on an educated electorate to prevent such a disaster from happening.

So with these safeguards, it may be possible to salvage the situation for Singapore if it goes wrong in one or two elections. If we don't have this safety net, the country can go down after one freak election. It is a risk Singapore cannot afford to take.

Q: *That sounds quite a fragile mechanism. Could it have been stronger?*

A: You tell me how. You put it to the constitutional lawyers and ask them how you can prevent an elected government from undoing a constitution. If they get the two-thirds majority, they can do it and there are certain things that we require a referendum for but if they have the persuasive powers and carry through a referendum, they can change the rules. If we don't allow constitutional change, we will have a revolution. One of the first things I learnt when I was in London was listening to Harold Laski (English political theorist and Labour Party leader) who said you either have revolution by consent – at that time the Labour Party was just beginning its term and starting all this changing of the society – or you have a revolution by violence.

You take China and you compare it with India. They are two extremes. I do not see the Communist Party, however it transforms itself – unless a very unusual generation takes charge – considering losing power because China has never had an evolutionary change. Deng Xiaoping tried to formulate within the party an orderly change of leadership. Usually in China, as in Russia, it's skulduggery and violent struggle for succession. Under the existing circumstances, I do not see them surrendering power through either a referendum or elections. India is the other extreme. Every dissident province is allowed to go its own way. Boundaries of states are continually redrawn from British days to include people of the same language into the province. Any other way, India would have fallen apart.

Those are two extremes. We are somewhere in between. I see us either changing in an election or changing in a referendum. Why should you go and take up arms when you can change it by persuasion? If you believe your cause is right, we are not going to stop you. We're not going to stop you from publishing your newsletters, we're not going to stop you from holding indoor meetings.

"What have I given up? My life"

The true mettle of a leader is tested in crisis, Lee believes. He speaks candidly of his political experience, his guiding principles and his legacy.

Q: *What's your greatest fear for Singapore?*

A: I think a leadership and a people that have forgotten, that have lost their bearings and do not understand the constraints that we face. Small base, highly organised, very competent people, complete international confidence, an ability to engage the big countries. We lose that, we're down. And we can go down very rapidly.

Q: *After 57 years in politics, what are the most important lessons that you would distil for an aspiring politician in Singapore?*

A: You must have convictions. If you don't have convictions, you are going in for personal glory or honour or publicity or popularity, forget it. Do something else. When you want to go in, you take this job on like my original team did: "This is for life." We were putting our lives at stake taking on the communists. If you lose, they'll pull our fingernails out and brainwash us and we know that and they make no bones about it. That's number one, you must have the convictions to want to do it and do it not for glory but because you feel you have to do this.

Now, when I started I didn't imagine I'd do it for my life but having gone through that period, taking Singapore into Malaysia and seeing that we were ambushed, Tunku offered me a United Nations post as his ambassador, how could I do that? I would be running away from my responsibility. So I stuck on, he kicked me out. We had an island with no resources. How could I tell the people, "I'm tired, get somebody else to do this"? I was responsible for this. I had to see it through. I've done it and seen it through.

Did I expect we'll be so successful? No, because I could not predict how the world would develop, but I knew that if we seized every opportunity, we will progress with the world. If there is no outer world and we are dependent on the region, we'll be down several stages. But we leapfrogged, first by linking up with Britain, Europe, America, Japan.

Then in the 1980s we saw China. I was convinced they were going to grow big. By 1982–1983 I could say that with confidence. So we started to develop and cultivate our links with China. The effort has paid off. India too. It is a big country, we better have a balance. We cultivated the Indians and got them into the Asean Regional Forum and the East Asian Summit. We are the first country to have signed a free trade pact with them against the opposition of many of their ministers. So we got two extra boosters. Then we got the oil states in the Middle East and we have started engaging Russia in a small way. I don't think we can be what we are without all these external links.

Q: *But that strength of conviction, that can't be as strong with the present generation of leaders, right? It's not possible.*

A: You can't say. Look, I'm not sure what my grandchildren will be like. When Lee Hsien Loong was a little child, I took him campaigning with me. I had no quality time, so I said, you come along. He was interested, he came along, he heard all the speeches.

I think two riots must have struck him vividly. I was away September 1964, during the second riot that year after the Prophet Muhammad's Birthday riot in July. This is why I moved Toh Chin Chye. He panicked and called a curfew straightaway. So the whole city panicked. Suddenly all schools closed, buses ran over streets of confusion. My wife sent the driver with my father's Morris Minor to look for Hsien Loong but he was already walking the streets. They couldn't find him. He walked all the way home from Catholic High, which was behind St Joseph's. He was 12, old enough to understand what was happening.

They wanted him to stay on in Cambridge because he was an outstanding mathematician. So he wrote this letter to the tutor, said, "No, thank you, I've got to go back. This is my country and my obligation and I do not want to be somewhere where my contribution doesn't make much of a difference." And he came back to serve in the SAF. I never told him to join the SAF. He joined on his own will. I think his commitment is nearly as strong as mine. I mean, he hasn't gone through the same trials and tribulations but he's seen me go through them and he himself had tasted it, the disorder and the calamity that has struck us, the riots and so on. So because he has done it, my other son decided no, no, one is enough. We're not going to be a dynasty. So my daughter and my second son stayed away from politics.

Each generation faces a different milieu, a different backdrop, a different set of problems. If you don't have the conviction that you want to do this because you feel strongly you want to do something for the people, don't do it.

Q: *Were there ever times that you felt that you just had enough, when your convictions were really being tested?*

A: The more we're being tested, the more I have to be around to make sure we pass the test. No, no, this is a life-long commitment. What are the things important to me in my life? My family and my country. My family, my wife looked after. She brought up the children. I spent some time with them, trying to impart some values. Twice a year to hill stations, when I could go off on leave. I think they've grown up with the right values. But Singapore is an ever-going concern. Singapore is my concern till the end of my life. Why should I not want Singapore to continue to succeed?

A Western correspondent put it to former British PM John Major – he'd been here several times – "Margaret Thatcher on the sidelines made life difficult for you so you can say that you did not succeed because of her. But look at Lee Kuan Yew. He's in the government and the new PM is succeeding." You should see his answer. "He is making sure the new PM succeeds."

That was my intention. If the new PM fails, I have failed.

Mahathir never thought that way. He undermined his successors.

I have no regrets. I have spent my life, so much of it, building up this country. There's nothing more that I need to do. I can't worry about the fourth generation leadership except to advise the current ministers to get a team in because they need time to develop the new leaders. They can't just take a course in leadership for six months. They have to work together and understand this is the way it can work in Singapore. So there's no glitch when the leadership transition takes place. But I tell them frankly, they have to make the decisions in the light of the international situation that has changed and the domestic mood and a younger generation that's different.

Q: *Those may be your convictions but other people have not always seen you in that light.*

A: No, I'm not interested what other people see or don't see. That's irrelevant to me.

Q: *What are some of the most unfair things that have been said?*

A: I am not interested in that. If I allow myself to be affected by that, it will affect me in my job. I just ignore them. What do they know? What do they know of Singapore, what do they know of me? So when I meet them face to face, I say, how long have you been in Singapore, what do you know about Singapore? I was born and bred here, I live here. Are you better qualified than me to decide what works for this country? How many hours a day do you spend thinking of Singapore? I've said that once and after that, nobody wanted to take me on. No, I just chewed the interviewer up, without being rude. He was interested in a peripheral way, just to knock me down in the interview. This is my life and the lives of people who have entrusted me with this responsibility.

Whether you believe it, whether the London *Times* or *New York Times* or William Safire[9] believes it or not is irrelevant to me. But I know all the leaders who've met me have a regard for me because I give them straight answers. So they ask me about something, I give them a frank response. I don't waffle away. Why else should they see me, especially when I'm not the PM?

Q: *But how would you like history to judge you?*

A: I'm dead by then. There'll be different voices, different standpoints but I stand by my record. I did some sharp and hard things to get things right. Maybe some people disapproved of it. Too harsh, but a lot was at stake and I wanted the place to succeed, that's all. At the end of the day, what have I got? A successful Singapore. What have I given up? My life.

I'm lucky though. My wife was a very capable lawyer. I was not interested in money and anyway she had enough. She took good care of the children when they were growing up and now they are looking after themselves.

What am I doing this book for? I want your readers to know the hard truths. If you believe that this superstructure is the same as other countries in our range, you are dead wrong. Absolutely dead wrong. We will only be like this with an honest and capable government, capable of dealing with neighbours who do not want to see us succeed and capable enough to command the respect from the big countries with large numbers of able people and talk with them as equals. We choose our leaders carefully. Teo Chee Hean goes to the Munich Security Conference and I've met many defence ministers and correspondents who say he's a good man. They listened to him. He doesn't talk very much, but when he talks, they listen. And they say, this man knows what he's talking about because he's got a first-rate understanding of security issues. George Yeo too doesn't talk nonsense. So foreign leaders and ministers see him and they take him seriously.

Q: *Will you be contesting the next election? What are your plans for your role in politics after the next election and beyond?*

A: Yes, if I am fit and the PM thinks I can hold the ground. I take one election at a time. By the election after next I will be 93, unlikely to be able to go campaigning.

Q: *You have said that you will not retire. Does that mean you will continue to remain active in politics? Wouldn't it be better for you to play the role of an elder statesman in the mould of say Nelson Mandela, wielding moral authority and be above politics?*

A: To be an elder statesman you must be accepted by all that that is what you are. I am the founder of the PAP and do not pretend to be non-partisan.

A street fight: "Either you lose, or I lose"

"He has done a hell of a lot for the country," said one politician at a farewell for Lee Kuan Yew before he stepped down as Prime Minister in 1990. "Nobody can be a better teacher than Mr Lee – whom I consider to be one of the world's best speakers – as far as parliamentary debate is concerned," said another MP.

These words of praise for Lee were not from fans, but foes. The man at the farewell event was Lee Siew Choh, a nemesis of Lee who led the breakaway faction of the PAP in 1961 to form opposition party Barisan Sosialis. The man who improved his verbal sparring because of Lee was Chiam See Tong, veteran opposition MP. He received his first bruising lesson from Lee in his maiden parliamentary speech in 1984 when Lee lambasted him for not knowing land values. The two men fall into a long list of opponents Lee took on over the decades. They were hardly the toughest of enemies but he sought to demolish all of them with the same determination. Many often recoil at this streak of Lee to crush his opponents thoroughly and seemingly without mercy.

Q: *Over the years, you have dealt with many different political opponents. Has your basic approach to dealing with them changed at all or moderated in any way?*

A: Well, look at Low Thia Khiang. He's not ranting, he's not shouting, he's skilful, he wants to win over the ground, he's held Hougang. He attends every funeral, every wedding, and to every complaint. And he's always an observer, nibbling away at our policies, never meeting it head-to-head except when he came out with an alternative manifesto and we demolished it. That alternative manifesto says unscramble the NTUC, unscramble this, unscramble that, unscramble the quotas for housing, unscramble the GRCs.[10] All right, go to the electorate. When the election comes, does he say those things? No, it doesn't sell. What does he say? *Zheng hu wu ji, nang si bor ji* (Teochew for "The government has money, we have no money"). So, you know, he plays on emotions. That's all right if we counter him.

Q: *So you're saying that your approach has in fact shifted slightly depending on the nature of the opposition?*

A: Of course, yes. I have said if we have a credible First World opposition, we'll treat them with First World civility. That's that. But that doesn't mean we don't demolish you. I mean, you look at Tony Blair and David Cameron, each was trying to demolish the other, well, politely. And you look at Gordon Brown, he's been pummelled away by David Cameron every time he meets but in a polite way.

Q: *Some people will say that one factor behind the PAP's longevity is the fact that the PAP has very effectively and systematically demolished opposition.*

A: What political party helps an opposition to come into power? Why should we not demolish them before they get started? Once they get started it's more difficult to demolish them.

If you are polite to me, I'm polite to you but I'll demolish your policy. It is the job of every government to do that if you want to stay in power. Look at the LDP now in Japan, they are unable to demolish the opposition because they have lost credibility, they are not as good as their grandfathers or fathers.

Q: *But there had been instances in the past where you have felt that it was necessary to demolish the men, such as Jeyaretnam.*

A: Well yes, Jeyaretnam to begin with, Chee Soon Juan is another. I think they deserve to be demolished. I have no regrets. Jeyaretnam went nutty, selling things in the corner, how did that help him? And closing down his practice.[11] I mean, he thought, you know, Western-style, he's sacrificing for the country. No, it's his personal ambition to knock me down. I mean, I just laughed him off and brushed him aside, which annoyed him. No, I have no regrets. Chee Soon Juan, also no regrets.

Q: *Do you ever have any idea of the chilling effect that has on others who may be interested in politics but are frightened off?*

A: Well, if you do the same thing then you must expect the same treatment. Therefore you behave in a more civilised way, more political, like Low Thia Khiang or even Chiam. I've never been rough with Chiam. He's gentle, I'm gentle. He's a decent man and I respect him for that. He's able to hold his ground in spite of his physical infirmities.

Q: *Do the younger ministers share your killer instincts towards political opponents?*

A: Well, I don't know whether they do or they don't. They have not been called to account yet.

Q: *If there were an emerging opposition politician, who among the current ministers would be able to handle them the way you did?*

A: No, they may not deal with them in the way I do but they will deal with them effectively. Everybody has his style and that style is partly innate, partly the experiences you've gone through. I would not have been so robust or tough had I not had communists to contend with. I have met people who are utterly ruthless. I say, all right, it's a street fight, either you lose or I lose and that's that.

Cutting media critics down to size

The Singapore media scene as it exists today has been shaped by Lee Kuan Yew. The model is one of a regulated press that understands its job is not to be the fourth estate. It reports government news and sees itself as a positive agent in nation-building.

Lee defined the media's role early in office. In 1971, at the International Press Institute's annual conference in Helsinki, just weeks after he had closed down two newspapers and arrested the executives of a third, he said that the freedom of the media "must be subordinated to the overriding needs of Singapore, and to the primacy of purpose of an elected government".

In 1977, the press laws were amended to prevent any party from holding more than 3 per cent of the ordinary shares of a newspaper. This cap was raised to 5 per cent in 2002. Management shares were created in 1974 and given to the local banks. They were seen as politically neutral and interested in stability and growth. Newspapers were thus not subject to the whims of newspaper barons.

Today, the domestic media environment is more competitive than when his memoirs were published, partly because of the ubiquity of Internet access. How will the Internet affect the mainstream media? The man who shaped the media environment in Singapore gives his views.

Q: *How will new media change politics in Singapore and the way the government operates? Will government have to be more transparent?*

A: It's what the Chinese are now facing. So Sichuan earthquake, they came out immediately and during the Xinjiang riots, they came out immediately.[12] Images from cell phones, videos or photographs all go on the Internet immediately. They have to cope with it. But it doesn't mean that they're going to change their system fundamentally.

Q: *You have said that freedom of the press is subordinate to the primacy of purpose of an elected government, yet you never nationalised the press or, as in the case of Malaysia, taken control* *of ownership of media companies. Did you ever consider it?*

A: No. I don't think it's necessary to own the press. First, it'll become like Radio and Television Singapore and the whole media is controlled by the state which I don't think is good. In fact I wanted to allow the media, even the TV, some channels to be run by SPH, some by MediaCorp, and MediaCorp could eventually be privatised. I think there's value in having the press taking an independent view but within limits, knowing that we will not allow it to undermine government policies.

We started off on a fundamentally different basis from the Western media. First of all, the Western media never started in this way. It's the freedom of the owner to hire and fire people, to purvey his views. Even today, Rupert Murdoch, if you take a line which he doesn't agree with, you're fired.[13] So you find *The Wall Street Journal* slowly changing its stance. It's an exaggeration when they talk about a free and independent media. Rupert Murdoch decided to back Tony Blair because he was in favour of enterprise and against state control of enterprises. So all Murdoch's papers swung in favour of Tony Blair. That made the difference to the election results. Gordon Brown is more state-orientated and more socialist-minded. So I see the Murdoch Group – News Corp – taking a more neutral stance, no longer puffing the Labour government up. And when the election comes, I believe they'll puff up the Conservative Party because they will support the kind of policy Rupert Murdoch wants to promote.

We're not going to allow that in Singapore. We just want straightforward reporting of the hard facts as the news happens. And if you want to crusade there's the editorial and the commentary, which are clearly different from the news reports. I think there's value in that.

But now, we're going to get a lot of junk news and falsehoods on the Internet and I'm not sure how long it will be before the people get sophisticated enough to know what is rubbish and what is true. We've got to take the risk. It's already part of the media that Singaporeans are exposed to.

Q: *The new media has posed threats to governments, like in neighbouring Malaysia.*

A: I don't think we're going to have the same problems as Malaysia because their press lost credibility. The position of the media on television and in print was so divorced from reality that people look for alternative channels. So bloggers, Malaysiakini, Harakah, opposition newspapers fill up the space.

Q: *So you're quite happy with the balance that has been struck in Singapore?*

A: Yes, through the competition, whether it's *Today* by MediaCorp and the newspapers by SPH, they should be within those limits. They can compete for news but they keep political campaigning out of the newspapers and out of television.

Q: *Going forward, do you see pressures building up for a more open, liberal press?*

A: What is more open? Go on the Internet, you can publish your party's views, you can produce your party magazines, your newspapers, nothing to prevent you from doing all that. But if you commit anything libellous, we'll sue you. Anything which is untrue and defamatory, we will take action.

Q: *That position on defamation will never change.*

A: That position will never change because once you say you can speak untruths and go unpunished, you're going to have many untruths and they are referred to repeatedly until, like Goebbels[14] said, it begins to be believed.

Q: *Even though there're all sorts of things being said on the Internet? I mean it's a different situation today than it was 20 years ago.*

A: No. What is in the mainstream media should remain credible and should remain as it is. We're not going to shift away from that position. So people reading the newspapers, watching the news on TV or government websites will know this is the official position. These are facts we are stating. And over the long run, we'll gain credibility because we state the truth. We're not going to put anything on the mainstream media or government websites which is untrue. If we do that, we lose credibility.

Q: *You say that you value a credible media, yet the media here suffers from a perception that we are pro-government, that we lack credibility.*

A: The Western media will always take that line because they believe theirs is the acme of perfection and that anything that deviates from that and is successful must be knocked down. If we were failures, why do they worry? But we are successful. Our people are not deprived of the news, you can look at all the magazines available on the newsstands. But if they sell here and they state untruths, we have the right of reply and if it is defamatory, we'll sue them, which we have. At first they thought we were bluffing, so *The Economist, International Herald Tribune,* they thought they were big enough to get away with it. We sued them. They had to employ lawyers, they lost. So we have the right of reply and once you have the right of reply, then the journalists no longer appear so clever. If they write something and the other side cannot reply, they sound very clever. But when they write and they get rebutted in a succinct and acerbic manner, then they look very small.

Let's face facts. Whether it is a *Straits Times* commentary or whatever it is, if we think that's slanted and incorrect, we'll come out with a rebuttal. That rebuttal is designed to politely cut the writer down to size. So the next time he puts himself down in print, he'll be careful. Of course there are regular letter writers who just want to see their names in the press on trivia. We ignore them.

Q: *Do you think this perception of a lack of media freedom in Singapore will inhibit Singapore's ambitions as a global city?*

A: That's rubbish. The foreign media used to say we are dull, sterile, no fun, no buzz, now they're moving away from these descriptions. But we are not moving away from our base positions. We are not going to quail under their sustained attacks. If you quail, you're weak and a fool.

Q: *Just now you said that you value independence from the media in that it should not be campaigning against the government. So if the media campaigns for the government, is that lack of independence?*

A: We do not need the media to campaign for us, we do the campaigning ourselves. Why should we need the media to campaign for us? I won my first election in 1959 with the whole media against me. And I told *The Straits Times*, when I win I'll settle accounts with them. So they scooted off to KL. Then they found that the KL position was even more untenable, they came back here. So, we were not so bad.

You look at what's happened to *New Straits Times* and at *The Straits Times*. One has lost credibility, one has not. Whatever they say about *The Straits Times*, why are people from all over the world looking at it? Why are they? Because it's credible. What we say is happening in the region, in Singapore, Malaysia and so on, it's true. We're not propagating untruths. So they are looking at *The Straits Times* as a credible source of news. And the *Zaobao* is read widely in China, six million hits, not because we pander to them but we state facts and we report things which the Chinese newspapers do not.

Q: *I mean it's a very robust approach towards the foreign press. Some people say that only you can carry it off because you can take them on and you have the ability to take them on.*

A: No. The next generation is doing this. I'm no longer writing their replies, they are. The rules stay. You're wrong if you believe when I'm gone, all these things will be let loose. I think they understand the rules, what works and what doesn't work, what needs to be changed. It's their choice because they have to live with the consequences.

Q: *You talked earlier about how, you know, if the mainstream media continues to publish untruths you will go after them if it's libellous.*

A: Yes, of course.

Q: *But at the same time, what's already out there on the Internet is defamatory, far more damaging.*

A: What's out on the Internet everybody knows can be utterly scurrilous and no action can be taken, because it's very difficult.

Q: *Some of them are very open about their identity.*

A: But they are worthless people, they've got no money. You take them on, you waste money and then what will you get in compensation? Nothing.

Q: *But doesn't what they say chip away at the credibility and the integrity of government?*

A: No, I don't think so. After a while people understand it's just rambling and ranting on the Internet.

Q: *Precisely because people know the record of the PAP government, do you need to nail every lie to protect your reputation at all cost?*

A: Put that question to the new leaders. I defended my position tooth and nail. I succeeded. I fought against the media in Singapore and internationally. I won because I've persuasive powers. I can speak to the people over the blather of the media. In a way, I'm like a local Ronald Reagan. And I deliver. When I say I'll do something, they know I'm going to do it. So when I say I'm going to fix that guy, he will be fixed. Let's make no bones about it. I carry my own hatchet. If you take liberties with me, I'll deal with you. I look after myself because when you enter a blind alley with the communists, only one person comes out alive and I have come out alive. So, I'm not afraid of going into an alley with anybody, let alone the foreign press. What can they do to me? Can they influence my votes? They can't.

EVOLVING THE
POLITICAL
SYSTEM

The People's Action Party, founded by Lee Kuan Yew and his comrades in 1954, was elected to power in May 1959 when Singapore attained self-rule. Lee became Singapore's first Prime Minister.

The party's internal struggle with leftist elements led to a split in 1961, with the erstwhile comrades setting up Barisan Sosialis. A strategic mistake by Barisan's MPs to quit Parliament in 1966 to wage an extra-parliamentary struggle paved the way for the PAP's total control of the House by

From the early 1980s, the government engineered a series of modifications to the political system.

the 1968 general election. With carte blanche in Parliament and industrial peace after the taming of an unruly labour movement, the PAP government embarked unhindered on a strategy of attracting multinationals to Singapore to grow the economy and create jobs. In the general elections of 1968, 1972, 1976 and 1980, the PAP won between 70.4 and 86.7 per cent of the valid vote. For 13 years, it governed with no opposition in the House.

The monopoly was broken in 1981, when Joshua Benjamin Jeyaretnam of the Workers' Party won a by-election in Anson. In the 1984 general election, the opposition claimed a second seat, with Chiam See Tong winning Potong Pasir. If the Anson by-election shattered the myth of an invincible PAP, the 1984 polls confirmed it was not a fluke. The party also suffered a 12.9 percentage point drop in its share of the popular vote.

From the early 1980s, the government engineered a series of modifications to the political system. Two instincts guided the innovations. First, it began recognising better-educated voters' demands for consultation and alternative voices. Second, the rising tide of protest votes also convinced the ruling party that elections held an irrational element that exposed the country to unacceptable risk. So, Lee initiated a series of unprecedented constitutional changes, with the most far-reaching being in electoral politics.

In 1984, Parliament approved the Non-Constituency MP scheme, under which the "best loser" among the opposition candidates would get a seat in the House. Lee justified the scheme as one that would raise the quality of debate, improve transparency and persuade young voters that an opposition was unnecessary. Critics derided it as a "second-class MPs" scheme and a trick to perpetuate one-party dominance by persuading voters that the opposition didn't have to win for Parliament to become more plural.

Greater scope for "alternative views" was later introduced with the 1990 NMP Bill. Nominated MPs are drawn from the various professions and groups which are underrepresented. Again, critics saw this as a kind of faux-opposition, artificial and eminently controllable and a violation of the democratic principles of electoral competition and accountability.

The most controversial change, however, was the merging of single-member constituencies (SMCs) into group representation constituencies (GRCs), comprising teams of candidates with at least one ethnic minority in their ranks. This was to ensure that any party with designs on governing Singapore would have to field a multiracial slate. Its genesis was in the "Team MPs" idea first brought up by Lee in

July 1982, when he said that younger voters seemed unable to value having a racially-balanced mix of MPs. His fear: ethnic-based parties could exploit voters' primordial instincts.

Parliament approved the GRC bill in 1988; three months later when a general election was called, 39 SMCs were grouped into 13 newly-minted GRCs. The size of each GRC has risen steadily since, reaching six MPs in 1997. The GRC system effectively raises the barriers to contest, which critics claim is the real intent.

Accusations of gerrymandering have persisted, especially when marginal seats were absorbed into GRCs at successive elections. In the 1988 polls, for example, eight of the ten most hotly contested SMCs in the 1984 elections were absorbed into GRCs based on "safe" PAP seats.

In 2009, Prime Minister Lee Hsien Loong announced moves to shrink the average size of GRCs from 5.4 MPs to 5, saying that too big a GRC made it harder for voters to identify with the whole GRC or team. He also sought to increase the number of NCMPs to a maximum of nine, a change approved by Parliament in April 2010.

The political system has undergone other modifications. In 1984, Lee floated the idea of an elected president to ensure that a freak opposition takeover of government would not wreak irreparable harm. A constitutional change in 1991 then gave the president veto powers to block a government's use of past reserves and key public sector appointments. To increase the president's moral authority, it became a directly elected post. Critics saw it as a way to subvert a democratically elected Parliament and thwart a legitimate opposition regime. It did not help that candidates must be pre-approved by a committee comprising establishment members.

The first election in 1993 was won by the PAP's anointed candidate, former Deputy Prime Minister Ong Teng Cheong. The choice did not seem a formula for friction but Ong later openly accused the bureaucracy of stonewalling him. Lee said Ong misinterpreted his role. All subsequent polls have been uncontested.

THE SINGAPORE
PROMISE

Using personal lives to make a political point is a choice weapon in Lee's arsenal of persuasion, one he deployed to good effect when he turned to the camera crew during our interviews on politics and asked them:

"You have a home?"

Yes, said one cameraman. He had five years to his mortgage. This reply was not definitive enough proof that the property-owning democracy was a success, so Lee sought another target.

"You?"

It was the photographer Stephanie Yeow. This time, he'd hit the bullseye. She had 20 years of repayments left, but her CPF took care of monthly payments: no worries there. Even better, the flat she had been living in for nine years was in Sengkang, a new town brimming with improvement projects.

"What country in the world upgrades your property and increases your net worth? But we do it. Why? That's our political compass. Give every man or woman an asset."

Had the value of her flat appreciated? Yes, by $60,000. One of his security officers had his Sengkang flat go up in value by $200,000, Lee said.

Then the point was made: "What country in the world upgrades your property and increases your net worth? But we do it. Why? That's our political compass. Give every man or woman an asset."

Indeed, the PAP has created a nation of homeowners by providing means-tested grants for the purchase of subsidised public housing and allowing mortgage payments to be made from buyers' Central Provident Fund savings. In 2003, 93 per cent of Singaporean HDB dwellers owned their flats.

The theory behind the policy is simple: diffusing private property ownership gives citizens a stake in the country and a means to accumulate wealth without being dependent on the state. Estate upgrading – such as in our photographer's Sengkang town – sweetens the deal.

Lee had another housing success story to trade with us. One of his security officers, a mother of four, started with a three-room flat in Jurong West before moving twice and finally settling into a five-room flat in Yio Chu Kang, enjoying subsidies all three times. That privilege has since been clipped as buyers now get only two bites of the subsidy cherry. But here's the thing: She paid $7,000 for the Jurong West flat and sold it for $100,000.

That, said Lee, was the reason behind the PAP's success. "Now, if you want to know our longevity, what's it based on? Credibility. And everybody has a stake." The promise of affordable housing fulfilled in a nation of homeowners.

Endnotes

1   The Land Acquisition Act was amended in 2007 and allows owners of land that is acquired by the government to be paid the prevailing market rate.

2   Lee is quoting from Huntington's keynote address at Colorado College's 125th Anniversary Symposium in 1999, titled "Cultures in the 21st Century: Conflicts and Convergences".

3   Non-governmental boundary commissions were established in Britain in 1986.

4   Lee is referring to former Presidents Devan Nair and Ong Teng Cheong, who were both leaders of the National Trades Union Congress.

5   Lim Boon Heng was secretary-general of the National Trades Union Congress from 1993 to 2006. Lim Swee Say took over from him in 2007.

6   Lee is referring to Dr Seet Ai Mee. After she lost her Bukit Gombak seat in the 1991 general election, it was reported that Dr Seet had washed her hands after shaking the hand of a market fishmonger, possibly contributing to a negative perception of her. However, Dr Seet told PAP news magazine *Petir* in 2009 that she had washed her hands not after greeting fishmongers, but after shaking hands with several pork sellers. She did so because she did not want to cause offence if she were to shake the hand of a Muslim after that.

7   Japan's Liberal Democratic Party held power from 1955 to 2009, with an 11-month interruption from 1993 to 1994.

8   Political strategist and former top aide to President George W. Bush.

9   William Safire was a political columnist for the *New York Times* who criticised Lee and the "Singapore model" on many occasions.

10 This manifesto was advanced for the 2006 general election. Among other things, it called for the abolition of group representation constituencies, ethnic quotas in housing and delinking the labour unions from government.

11 Jeyaretnam was disbarred twice. The first occasion was in 1986, when he was found guilty of false declarations of Workers' Party accounts, but was reinstated by the London-based Privy Council in 1988 on the grounds that the convictions were wrong. The second was in 2001, when he was declared bankrupt after missing an instalment in his payment of defamation damages to several individuals, including then-Prime Minister Goh Chok Tong. He was reinstated in 2007.

12 The Sichuan earthquake happened in 2008; the Xinjiang riots in 2009.

13 Some of the newspapers and publications owned by Murdoch's News Corp are *The Times, The Wall Street Journal,* the *Far Eastern Economic Review, Dow Jones* and the *New York Post.*

14 This quote has been ascribed to Goebbels, the Nazi Propaganda Minister, and to Vladimir Lenin.

3 THE CREAM ON TOP

IN DECEMBER 2008, barely 48 hours after he had a pacemaker implanted, Lee Kuan Yew flew to Hong Kong for a dialogue on world issues. His host, former US President Bill Clinton, praised him to the top-drawer audience as "one of the wisest, most knowledgeable, most effective leaders in any part of the world for the last 50 years". But Lee was not there to be fêted. He had gone because he felt it was important for Singapore to maintain good ties with the former First Couple. Clinton's wife Hillary Rodham Clinton was then about to become secretary of state, the highest-ranking secretary in the US Cabinet.

As Lee had once declared his commitment towards Singapore was such that "even from my sickbed, even if you are going to lower me into the grave and I feel something is going wrong, I will get up", he probably felt the trip was all in a day's work. Since he stepped down as Prime Minister in 1990, Singaporeans had grown accustomed to Lee periodically inserting his larger-than-life presence in public affairs. This reassured them and foreign friends alike that the government continued to benefit from his experience, even as it made it harder for sceptics to shake off doubts about the completeness of Singapore's leadership succession.

But simply pointing to Lee's involvement as the key feature of leadership in the country is too simplistic. It ignores the fact that, for the past 30 years, he has been a man obsessed with finding new talent – and with the lack of it. This preoccupation was clear during our interviews on politics, and as told in the previous chapter, when he kept returning to the theme of the inevitability of the PAP someday losing power. One driving force behind that scenario would be a PAP that had become lax on quality or was confronted with an opposition that equalled it in talent.

Yet the political system banks on a much vaunted leadership renewal process that tries to ensure the best people in the prime of their lives are put in charge. Rejuvenation, in response to the inevitable ageing of leaders and the changing needs of the electorate, is the open secret of PAP's longevity. So, what might cause this strategy, and thus the PAP, to falter and fail? Are there warning signs to heed? Indeed, how does one define what makes for good quality political talent?

Lee's obsession with finding talented leaders stemmed from the belief that Singapore's unique circumstances, or vulnerabilities, require people of high calibre to manage or even overcome them. As he said in 1982, even when the quickening pace of retiring the first-generation leadership then was hurting his comrades, "leaving Singapore in the hands of mediocrities ... would be criminal". More than 25 years later, he put it to us again in our interviews: "If we do not have a government and a people who differentiate themselves from the rest of the neighbourhood in a positive way and can defend Singapore and its rights, it will cease to exist."

Lee started with some pragmatic assumptions about talent: Do the maths. The "talented tenth" of a population of three million throws up fewer outstanding individuals than the same proportion taken from a billion-strong nation. The Chinese, Lee argued, have scores of bright young hopefuls queuing up for government jobs, all of whom have impeccable academic pedigrees and technocratic mettle. Singapore has just one or two who make the cut. There is not enough talent to make even two teams of able ministers, a critical reason behind the lack of a credible opposition in Singapore, according to Lee. It is also why a suggestion once of creating an "internal opposition" within the PAP or splitting the party into two to engineer competition was never seriously pursued.

Another factor Lee cited for the talent shortfall is the tendency for younger Singaporeans to spurn public service. There is a deep generational ennui about politics, he felt, even in his own grandchildren. A successful professional would naturally gravitate towards a lucrative private sector career. Why take a chance on the political stage, when every move is subject to public scrutiny and criticism? Why, for that matter, take a pay cut to join a ministry? Lee even applied the same logic to himself; if he were a young lawyer now, there would be little reason for him to enter politics. His decision, like those of the other old guard ministers, was made in an age of revolution, a life-changing act forged in the fires of post-colonial struggle. Singaporeans of today, with comfortable lives and substantial pay cheques, see little need to pick up the leadership baton.

But the critical question is: What is this "talent" that Singapore's leaders must possess? Lee admitted right off the bat that it is not enough to find people who graduated summa cum laude from Ivy League universities, or top surgeons and lawyers. It is certainly not enough to be a good orator or popular at the polls. The government uses Shell's method of selecting its executives and looks for character, motivation and "helicopter quality", or the ability to assess situations through analysis, sense of reality and imagination. "Talent" therefore takes in not only raw academic or professional success, but also the fuzzier concept of having the "right" personality and outlook. Integrity and honesty are vital.

After the criteria comes the process. And here, even critics agree that the government's search for talent is rigorous and systematic, though the actual steps remain behind closed doors. High-flying professionals in the public and private sectors are handpicked and "invited to tea", a euphemism for the first step in a gruelling schedule of interviews that draw out the "inner core" of a person. Civil service candidates – typically stars who have succeeded after being given prestigious Public Service Commission scholarships – can short-cut the process if they have worked closely with top PAP leaders. Leadership hopefuls are brought before both Cabinet ministers and the party's Central Executive Committee – of which Lee is a member – to test their mettle. Hefty dossiers are compiled on all; some endure six-hour psychological tests and are probed on highly personal matters, such as their faith and marriage. They are pushed to say how they would grapple with moral dilemmas over their most deeply held values. The emotional interrogation was "very direct", one failed candidate said. It left him feeling "exposed".

It is a system designed to deter casual punters. But the high attrition rates could also make prospective leaders wary. Ross Worthington, public policy specialist and outspoken critic of Singapore politics, claimed that the process left the elite "littered with the metaphorical corpses of political discards and there was a heightened degree of passive hostility to involvement in government by much of the nation's elite."

After all the hoops they go through, are those who survive the kind of leaders that Singaporeans want? One crucial missing element for some is the electoral test, where candidates have to prove themselves before the voting public. Lee and his successors pride themselves on orderly succession with populist politics, ideological breaks and outward displays of backbiting kept to a minimum. The impetus for change comes from within, for example, as existing leaders age. Now, PAP politicians usually have a life span of three terms, with one-third retired at each election. In this orderly system, two prime ministers have stepped aside while in a position of electoral strength to make way for their heirs, tutoring them without wholly abandoning the scene. With a few exceptions, Singapore's first Cabinet cleared the stage quietly as their younger colleagues took over; the first "second generation" leaders, including future Prime Minister Goh Chok Tong, were recruited in 1976. Political scientist Diane Mauzy described it thus: "Singapore's systematic and painstakingly planned political succession sharply contrasts with succession in most of the Third World where, because of lack of political institutionalisation, political will and planning, succession changes often have been abrupt, disorderly and destabilising, with unpredictable outcomes."

Some argue, however, that political succession should not be just "business as usual". Pointing to US presidential election primaries, UK party conventions and other electoral devices, critics bemoan the lack of democratic selection in determining Singapore's future leaders. In the 2008 Cabinet, two out of the 20 ministers had not fought an election. Ng Eng Hen's and Vivian Balakrishnan's constituencies had gone uncontested in 2001 and 2006, which meant that they had gone from being medical doctors to PAP frontbenchers without needing to fight for their votes.

There is also the lingering criticism that the selection process favours stiff technocrats rather than sincere leaders who can empathise with people, a searing critique made most notably by writer Catherine Lim in her controversial 1994 article on The Great Affective Divide. An emotional estrangement, she felt, had arisen between the leaders and the led. Interviewed 15 years later, however, she conceded that Singapore's leaders are now "very visibly" friendlier and gentler with ordinary folk: "A kind of arrogance was their original stance when I wrote the article. No more now. Politically, it's no longer expedient to be so."

This is related to another criticism, that the policy of selecting professional high-flyers and government scholars produces leaders who are seen as elitist: upper-middle or upper-class public servants with impeccable academic grades but out of touch with the very people they are supposed to serve. Grassroots activists have never made it to the PAP's front bench, even if more of them have become MPs. At the time of our interviews, 12 out of the 20 Cabinet ministers were government scholars. In 2008, more than half of scholars lived in private property, compared to 20 per cent of the general population. Political scientist Kenneth Paul Tan warned that an elite class may develop "an exaggerated 'in-group' sense of superiority, a dismissive attitude towards the abilities of those who are excluded from this in-group".

Another concern of the PAP leadership renewal system is whether the selection process results in like choosing like, that affluent professionals are picking others who share their views and prejudices. Former outspoken personalities – such as Vivian Balakrishnan and Raymond Lim – who have joined the PAP are accused of being co-opted and having their wings clipped. Professor Joseph Nye of Harvard University's Kennedy School of Government, who is by his own admission "very impressed" by the Singapore leaders who have been at his faculty, felt that one weakness of the PAP selection system is that "dissenting and divergent views are not represented, and that is often important in a democracy". Former Nominated MP Geh Min remarked before the 2006 elections that, no matter how diverse the views of those whom the PAP had attracted into its ranks, "they undergo some kind of transformation into homo PAPsters".

Indeed, some in Lee's first Cabinet took issue with the nature and pace of renewal for just these reasons. They had wanted party activists who had rolled up their sleeves and done their time at the grassroots, not handpicked unknowns. Most were old party mobilisers such as Ong Pang Boon, Jek Yeun Thong and Fong Sip Chee, who had considerable grassroots experience, especially with the Chinese electorate. Former Senior Minister of State Lee Khoon Choy spoke out after the PAP's unexpected loss of four seats at the 1991 polls: "In the beginning, when we first participated in the 1959 elections, there were barbers, chee cheong fun sellers, hawkers, etc. They came from the grassroots. Later, there is an increasing tendency to walk the elitist line ... 80 per cent of our population speaks dialects and Mandarin. But as for the kind of elites selected: they are all English-educated, who cannot even speak Chinese. Some can speak but cannot write. Can such candidates communicate with the crowd?"

Chief dissenter was founding PAP member Toh Chin Chye, who was dropped from the Cabinet after the December 1980 general election. Lee said in his memoirs that the forced retirement was to "preempt any split in the leadership". Toh turned into a vocal backbencher and put a vastly different spin on the lack of prospective leaders, saying in a 1997 interview, "Today's generation has no culture and is averse to taking political risk ... But I cannot blame the present generation, because they see the heavy-handed response by the government to dissenting views."

Lee is clear though that political cream does not just rise to the top. It needs to be sieved and strained, from a much bigger vessel than the party cauldron. You need to do it systematically and you need to scour the professions for it. This way, you also deprive the opposition of this cream. You do not leave succession to chance, you plan. Lee draws an object lesson from the democratic disasters in neighbouring countries, where corruption, crass populism and deep divisions in the population have led to weak governments, policy flip-flops and, in some cases, total collapse. Contrast that with the high praise that Singapore's leaders have earned in international circles, Lee argued. This admiration is genuine and, it seems, fairly widely felt. Even writer Catherine Lim recounted her experiences with Western audiences whenever she criticised Singapore's leaders thus: "At one forum, a British businessman stood up and said, 'Please give us your Lee Kuan Yew, we'll give you our Tony Blair and throw in Cherie Blair as well.'"

Lee also has no patience for the litany of criticisms and showed his irritation at one particular charge: "The popular belief that we are an elitist lot is just stupid!" The PAP's leadership selection model is not a hypocritical system that pays lip service to being egalitarian, he argued. The reality as societies developed is that leaders often come from the same social circles, educational backgrounds and even family trees. Lee pointed to the experiences of other countries, where leadership selection is equally elitist but masquerades under the guise of egalitarianism. Oxbridge graduates stock Whitehall in the United Kingdom, Ivy Leaguers in the United States, graduates of the *grandes écoles* in France, powerful oligarchs elsewhere in the world. Even in China, which pays ideological lip service to egalitarianism, many second-generation leaders are relatives and acquaintances of the country's founding fathers. There is no truly egalitarian leadership anywhere in the world, Lee stated categorically.

Besides, he is adamant that having sterling academic grades or a good pedigree is not enough; even the most "elite" member of Singapore's leadership has to be tested in action. Ultimately, leaders have to deliver the economic goods and earn their legitimacy at the polls. There are also different definitions of success, depending on what the leader's mandate is: A grassroots leader has to be in touch with the ground, a prime minister has to be a good communicator. If they fail to govern, communicate or work the grassroots well, they are shown the door. Indeed, Australian academic Michael Barr described Lee's brand of elitism as one that seeks "to introduce an egalitarian society from above, whereby the elite rules as a benevolent leadership and identifies its interests with those of the poor and marginalised in society".

However, Lee did concede that a crucial part of the testing process for Singapore leaders is conflict. Their ideas need to be honed and the best way to do this is through the scrutiny of dissenters. With the absence of a strong opposition in Parliament, it is Cabinet that provides this debate, Lee said. He raised the example of the decision to allow casinos in Singapore, which had sharply divided the ministers. Although he was initially opposed to the idea, he was talked around to it. Another example is the issue of privatisation, on which Transport Minister Raymond Lim played a key role in persuading him.

But did he not feel that Singapore's leadership selection process risks producing groupthink? His retort: Ask the ministers themselves. The ministers reject the notion. Foreign Minister George Yeo, too, cited the example of the casino: "Despite MM's dogmatic view on this, it was raised by a few ministers, including me, when I was in the Ministry of Trade and Industry. MM listened and was eventually persuaded. Other ministers were still opposed, including the Prime Minister. Eventually, we reached consensus." It also helped that ministers mix with different groups and travel often, exposing them to experiences and ideas elsewhere, he said.

Health Minister Khaw Boon Wan also underscored the painstaking nature of policy formulation. Policy is not rubber-stamped by governmental yes-men, he said. It undergoes a long period of internal debate among civil servants and, often, across several ministries. "Ideas are a dime a dozen, but turning an idea into an effective policy that achieves its purpose takes many man-months of careful analysis, evaluation of options, critical assessment and many rounds of refinement," he said.

Some critics, however, take aim at a more personal target. Is the Minister Mentor still controlling things behind the scenes, nudging the current leaders towards his preferred policies? Why is it that, given all the rhetoric about leadership renewal and rejuvenation, given the total departure of his old guard colleagues from the stage, Lee is still in office? His answer was forthright: He is still of value and he cannot be anything other than himself, voicing his views and stirring debate.

Still, even within the ranks of the establishment, voices have emerged fearing for a system so successful that it atrophies from the lack of competition. Retired top civil servant Ngiam Tong Dow once called for an "alternative leadership" that would keep the current leaders on their toes and stave off inevitable decline. Accusing civil servants of "a particular brand of Singapore elite arrogance" and "believing our own propaganda", he said that unless Lee "allows serious political challenges to emerge from the alternative elite out there, the incumbent elite will just coast along. At the first sign of a grassroots revolt, they will probably collapse."

But Lee is unshakeable in his conviction that he and his successors have worked out the best – if not the only – way, for the present, to find the right people to run Singapore. PAP leaders point to their repeated success at 11 general elections and the country's sterling economic and social achievements as irrefutable proof.

"There just is no viable alternative programme for an island city state other than what we have empirically worked out in the last 30 years," Lee said in one speech. "This is why the able and talented have not come forward to form a credible alternative team and challenge the PAP."

In the end, it all boils down to that amorphous thing that both Shell and the PAP government look for in their leadership interviews: "sense of reality". Singapore's heirs are selected for having more or less the same sense of reality as the incumbent leadership. Therein lies the fundamental groupthink of which the PAP leadership selection stands accused. To Lee, this is not a problem. Singapore cannot afford to have leaders who do not share the same view on how to manage the country's existential realities: its ethnic fault lines, its geopolitical vulnerability and its open economy.

This too, perhaps, explains his "rise from the grave" speech. Lee's – and his successors' – search for new talented leaders could be seen as nothing less than an attempt to find a new generation which will lead Singapore almost as well as he and his old guard colleagues did, and with largely similar core beliefs. Those who disagree with the product of his talent-scouting system may need to come up with more than an alternative procedure. They may need to put forward a new "sense of reality", from which an alternative model of talent and leadership will flow.

"The popular belief that we are
an elitist lot is plain stupid."

Q: *What is the leadership challenge facing Singapore?*

A: We have a population of just over three million. Every year, we have about a hundred people of quality, with potential leadership qualities. Of them, you'll end up with 20, 30. We scour every profession, every business, but to succeed in politics, you've got to come in when you're still in your 30s or early 40s, when you're not too set in your ways or you cannot empathise with people – go canvassing, shake hands, kiss babies and so on.

We are so short that in 2001, we took three doctors; each of them was at the top of their profession: Ng Eng Hen, Vivian Balakrishnan, Balaji Sadasivan. Balaji was a top brain surgeon but he could not make the cut as a political leader.[1]

Q: *A criticism is that because yours is a top down approach, as you say you scour the country, you select leaders-to-be.*

A: No, we do not select who comes up as the top doctor or the top surgeon or the top accountant. It is the system that throws them up. We must go there and look at the top few.

Q: *That happens all the time in the corporate and military fields but do you see the political arena as being different in that you want greater involvement of the electorate in selecting the leaders?*

A: No, somebody's got to run the government and if you are lucky, the prime minister can not only run the government and choose the ministers, he's also able to persuade the people.

But within the party, you need all kinds of people. The people who spend time in the coffee shops are good grassroots leaders and you need them. Ong Ah Heng[2] was my branch secretary but he's a grassroots, hands-on man. So we sent him to the National Transport Workers' Union and we made him fight in Nee Soon

Central constituency. The other fellow is Ang Mong Seng.[3]

You need all types to make a party, but can he run a ministry? Founding PAP member Toh Chin Chye said, "No, don't worry, he will depend on his permanent secretary." That is nonsense. You can't do that.

Q: *Somehow, even though you say the party needs all types, people think you are overly focused on academic achievements.*

A: The idea that this government goes on academic qualifications is just wrong, dead wrong. Yes, we pay attention to that because that's the first cut. Over the years we found that whatever the field, whether it's General Electric, IBM, Microsoft, the leader is somebody who's got several basic qualities: high IQ, yes, necessary, but that's only one fragment. EQ (emotional quotient), leadership stamina, determination, resourcefulness, and a host of other features, which eventually manifest themselves in your success in your profession or your business.

So SIA's CEO, Chew Choon Seng, he was not a scholar though he earned a first class degree at the University of Singapore and a Masters from Imperial College. But a sound man, he understands people, leads them, understands the business, and SIA is doing well.

Q: *Even today, some Singaporeans are more inclined to Dr Toh's point of view. They want to see leaders rise up through the ranks through their own efforts, not handpicked and parachuted in to take on top posts.*

A: There's no leadership in the world which is all bottom up. You show me one. How is the American presidential candidate selected? From the bottom up? No. From within the elite of the Democratic Party and the elite of the Republican Party.

Barack Obama came in. He calculated carefully what his chances were. He charted his way through the primaries, concentrating on where they don't do polls but caucuses. He won in the caucuses. Hillary Clinton made the mistake of not taking him seriously. He got through, and won the nomination. Finally, Americans said, well, all right, let's try this black man, it might retrieve our image as a white nation. He's a very smart black man.

Take the Republican Party: Can you emerge from nowhere? No. John McCain is a war hero. His father was a four-star admiral. He won a Senate seat, fought against George W. Bush, lost, finally became the presidential candidate in 2008.

You take the leader of Britain's Conservative Party, David Cameron. He went to Eton and Oxford. Chosen by fellow Conservative MPs, many from the upper-middle class. Top down or bottom up?

In China's Communist Party, it's bottom up? The first generation of revolutionaries, yes, bottom up, but when Mao Zedong went into the Seventh National Congress of the Communist Party, he knocked out the others and became the sole leader after that. He decided every matter until he died.

Let's get the facts right. ANC (African National Congress), bottom up? The African masses decided? No. Nelson Mandela became the icon of their independence, the fighter who went to jail for over 20 years. When he retired, the group around him took over. Is that bottom up?

Q: *Yet one view is that when you talk about a dearth of talent, it's self-serving as far as the PAP is concerned because that justifies one-party rule in Singapore.*

A: Well then, find the talent and field them. That's my challenge. The only talent outside PAP MPs are in the Nominated Members of Parliament. We even considered fielding some of them as our candidates because they were good. But we decided against that. Not sure whether they will empathise with people.

Q: *Why are other countries with small populations, such as Denmark and Norway, able to support competitive, multi-party politics?*

A: If you believe we're just like Norway or Sweden or Denmark, then I think we won't survive. We are not. Denmark and Sweden can get by with mediocre governments, Singapore cannot. It will sink, the civil service will sink.

Once quality at the very core goes down, in all subsidiary organisations, quality will go down. No man can judge a person accurately if that latter person is superior to him.

Q: *Aren't political systems in which there is more intense competition for the top jobs stronger than Singapore's?*

A: We have three million people. You tell me where do we find the men with big-enough bottoms to sit on these big chairs? Temasek executive director Ho Ching says it's time for her to move on. Who's the successor? At this point, nobody from inside the organisation is ready to take over the job of managing this complex portfolio of companies. So Temasek had to look outside for a successor.

You take SingTel. My son (former CEO Lee Hsien Yang) says, "I'm leaving." Fortunately, his successor Chua Sock Koong is not doing badly. There's a dearth of people with leadership qualities.

We can't find a replacement for ambassador to China, Chin Siat Yoon, in Beijing. He says, "I've done enough." Where do you find a fellow who's Chinese-educated and bilingual in English, and has a keen sense of how to deal with people? Ng Ser Miang? But then we lose Ser Miang from the Olympics Committee.[4]

In China, when they have to promote a person as foreign minister, they have three or four candidates, all of equally great ability. But that's 1.3 billion people. The rejects of Beijing University could score a first class in our university.

Q: *The question then is, will you find in the Singapore system – because there's a lack of political competition – a different set of leaders compared with, say, China where they've risen up as a result of the competition?*

A: No, I don't think that's the difference. The Chinese system is even more selective and meritocratic than ours because they don't fight elections. So they ignore that EQ part. We have to get people who can fight elections and win. You can have all those qualities to lead, but if you can't fight an election and win, keep close to your constituents and win again, you're of not much value.

So you've got to come in early and learn how to get on with people. Our system is, we throw them in at the deep end of the pool. If they can't make it, we fish them out. In the private sector, you don't have to win elections. Once you satisfy your higher-ups, you're OK. The same applies in China. All those who've worked with us in Suzhou where they succeeded, are now in high positions in Beijing and other provincial governments. It is your performance that counts.

Q: *Many ordinary Singaporeans, even those who respect and admire the accomplishments of the PAP, cannot help but feel that your leadership selection system is elitist. It seems to exhibit a strong preference for those from privileged backgrounds, who studied at the top schools and won scholarships to brand-name universities.*

A: The popular belief that we are an elitist lot is plain stupid.

They don't understand. Experience pushed us slowly towards understanding that leadership is a conglomerate of qualities and leaders require the same qualities in almost any field, whether you are a general, a politician, a CEO or chief editor.

A reality is, however you start, however open and meritocratic the system is, as you develop, the population gets assorted and stratified. People get educated, the bright ones rise, they marry equally well-educated spouses. The result is their children are likely to be smarter than the children of those who are gardeners. Not that all of the children of gardeners or labourers are duds. Occasionally, two grey horses produce a white horse, but very few. If you have two white horses, the chances are you breed white horses.

It's seldom spoken publicly because those who are not white horses say, "You're degrading me." But it's a fact of life. You get a good mare, you don't want a dud stallion to breed with your good mare. You get a poor foal.

Your mental capacity and your EQ and the rest of you, 70 to 80 per cent of that is genetic. It takes time for you to mature, that's all. Twenty to 30 per cent is nurturing. That's life.

Q: *Putting aside the question of elitism and genetics, aren't you in any case concerned that with the current system of grooming, selecting and identifying leaders that you have fine-tuned to the degree that you have today, you may end up with people who are very similar in terms of their socioeconomic backgrounds?*

A: Once you are confined to Singaporeans and they all go through the same education system, the only differentiation is where they go to university abroad or in Singapore, and what profession they've chosen that exposes them to different environments, different experiences.

The French elite all go through the same schools. Everybody

goes through the national examinations. Again, the top people get into the *grandes écoles*.[5]

The German General Staff also all learn the same doctrines. One of the reasons the Germans believe their general staff is so successful is because any general you put in charge of a front, he will fit in with the other generals.

In Japan, Tokyo University is the top elite university. In Beijing, top quality people throughout the country compete fiercely to get into Beijing University or Qinghua, or failing that, Fudan.

The only differentiation you have is America. Because they've got west coast, midwest, south, north, east coast. In the old days, they all used to go to the east coast. Now they have built up Stanford, Texas, Northwestern, so on. They have different schools. Milton Friedman in Chicago has one economics school of thought, and Harvard, another school. It is the spread of their country and I think a deliberate diversity of schools of thought.

Q: *Are there very bright individuals who might have made great ministers except for the fact that they said, "I don't want to have anything to do with politics because if I join the PAP, I probably have to think like them and if I don't agree with them a hundred per cent, I won't survive in the system."*

A: No, that is completely untrue. Raymond Lim was under no constraint. You can speak to him now whether he has changed his views because we forced him to. Or Vivian Balakrishnan. Or whether when the facts were presented to him and he was given a task to do, he adjusted his thinking to meet that problem.

Q: *But do you encounter that kind of a concern when you first ask people to join politics?*

A: No, their concern is, "I'm happy where I am. Maybe in four years' time, when my children have grown up and gone to university." That is their concern. We tried to get Koh Boon Hwee[6] in 15, 20 years ago when he was with Wuthelam. I had lunch with him, so did Chok Tong. He told us frankly, "I want to be a successful corporate leader", and he has become one. That's his choice. He would have made a good minister, but now it's too late. Now, can't go down to a constituency and meet people and talk to them and so on. You have to start in your early 30s or early 40s. In your late 40s, you can't change.

Q: *Are you sure you have talent-scouted everyone out there who can be good political leaders? What about those who disagree with you strongly?*

A: Whether they agree with us or not, is not the criteria. Have you got what it takes? If you have, we want to meet you, we want to persuade you. That you disagree with us is irrelevant. You can change us. We're rational people. If we're wrong, you convince us, and we change.

Q: *Are there many good examples where younger ministers have changed your thinking on important fundamental issues, not just on peripheral matters?*

A: Since 1990, I've not been the PM, so I've not been in constant interaction with them. My interaction with them is socially in Parliament and in Cabinet. Their ministerial work goes to the PM, not me. I don't judge them.

Q: *Based on your interactions, can you give us examples where they've changed your thinking?*

A: Raymond Lim convinced me that we should privatise as

many of our companies as possible. But the problem is, how we find the men to take over. He said privatise SIA, privatise PSA. When you privatise, you have to give it to a majority shareholder who will be in charge of staff appointments – CEO, COO, CFO, who do you hand it to? OCBC, DBS, UOB or Temasek? That's the problem. There's a dearth of people.

Q: *Is there groupthink in Cabinet? Could you tell us how robust the debate is?*

A: We have independent minds. We're not people who have sold each other our ideas. Many of the difficult questions, we cogitate on them over several meetings and leave the decision open. You ask the younger ministers, no use asking me.

The other ministers meet without me. In order for me not to influence them, they meet first and decide what they're going to do, then they discuss with me. There are pre-Cabinet meetings over lunch and amongst themselves, where they talk freely. They started doing this with Goh Chok Tong, continued under Lee Hsien Loong. Please remember, I don't appoint ministers anymore, from 1990 when Goh Chok Tong became Prime Minister.

In the first few years, I'd say, "Well, I think the chap is better than that." But after the first few years, he decided who he needed, who he trusted to be in his team. I may not agree with him. In fact, in a few cases, I told him I would hesitate but he went ahead.

Q: *One view is that the pre-Cabinet meeting is proof that your influence is still so powerful and you're so dominant that they need to meet without you so that there is free and uninhibited discussion.*

A: Can I be other than myself? When I state an opinion, I don't just fire from my hip. It's something I've thought over and something influenced by my previous experience.

Who dares to tell me that my time is up? I'm on the JP Morgan Board, the (French oil giant) Total Board and a few other boards. When they reappointed me, I told them, "Look, the moment I'm slipping, please tell me. I'm already 80-plus."

Why did Bill Clinton want me to go to his dialogue in Hong Kong? He wanted me because he wanted to impress the Asian philanthropists to persuade them to donate to his charity. He asked me, because I'm prepared to contradict him. He's bright but I'm not stupid, and I've got experience. I'm prepared to say, "I disagree, this is my reason." That makes for a lively argument.

Although I just had an operation to insert a pacemaker a day before, I went. I had promised him that I would go before his wife became secretary of state. At the end of it, he said, "I owe you one." I replied, "I'll ask only for what's lawful."

As long as this ticker (points to his head) is going, I'm all right. This ticker (points to his heart) may stop first. What to do? That's life. We can't predict when we'll go but as long as I'm of value, my value is to try and consolidate what we've achieved in Singapore. I'm not interested in consolidating any leader or any system. Having seen this place rise, I do not want to see it fall, it's as simple as that.

Q: *Some would say you are the greatest innovator to have emerged from Singapore, and you emerged out of that time of intense political competition. In the present system, it is very unlikely that somebody as innovative will emerge.*

A: The pressures may not be the same, they're not life and death, they are not so imminent. But constant change also imposes enormous stress. Take this present situation (of the global credit crisis): If I were the prime minister, I'll be in the nitty-gritty, looking at the figures, saying, "Can we afford this?" Or, "If this carries on three, four years, what will happen? I've got to study the details." The immediate pressure is not the same anymore.

I lived with the stress of water from day one until NEWater.[7] I stayed focused on safeguarding our water supply until NEWater. Even when I wasn't prime minister, I insisted, every month, on a full report: What is the progress? Nobody knew the situation about water better than I did.

But I do not believe that the core members in the present team are intellectually inferior to my team. They may lack the out-of-the-box flashes of inspiration because they have never been under that severe a pressure.

Q: *Isn't that a problem?*

A: No, I can't say that. They've all gone to business school or studied public administration. There are few systems which they have not read up. But my lessons were learnt in the streets. This is a different generation, that's all. Gordon Brown is not going to be a Clement Attlee or a Hugh Gaitskell.[8] He's a different cut, different background, different situation. Winston Churchill's son and grandsons are not equal to him.

Q: *But in their history, leaders who went against the conventional grain have emerged, like Margaret Thatcher. Is there room for mavericks to rise in your selection system?*

A: You must be prepared to go against it when you are convinced that you are going in the wrong direction. You must be prepared to say, "No, this is wrong. We must reverse."

I don't see us going in any fundamentally wrong direction, or I would tell them, "Look, I think you are heading the wrong way." I don't see that. The options that we have, have been carefully worked out – internally, regionally and internationally. What may change will be the international and regional situation, then you've got to rethink the problem.

Cheaper than one F15 fighter aircraft

"This is to give you an idea of what my market value is worth," said Lee Kuan Yew as he handed us some papers. Listed in the printouts were his earnings from his memoirs, speaking engagements and appointments to various advisory boards since stepping down as Prime Minister in November 1990. He has donated all of it – without taking any tax deductions – to charity, with the bulk to three education endowment funds. Since 1991, he has donated almost S$13 million to charity (S$12.2 million and the rest in various currencies). "I don't have to go to Lee and Lee to be a rainmaker," he said, referring to the law firm he set up in 1955. The disclosure was also probably to disabuse anyone with the slightest inkling that money mattered to him. We were about to discuss the controversial policy on ministerial pay, a policy that he initiated.

In 1993, Lee proposed a formula to peg their pay to that of the private sector, meaning it would move up and down in tandem with the market. Parliament approved it in 1994. The benchmark salary for political office holders and top civil servants was set at two-thirds the median incomes of the top eight earners in six professions: lawyers, bankers, engineers, accountants, chiefs of multinationals and local manufacturers. In 2009, a minister's annual salary could top $1.5 million while the prime minister's exceeded $3 million.

The wisdom of the policy has been explained ad nauseam but the issue flares up periodically, especially when a top official stumbles. Many accept that ministers need to be paid well but disagree over how much and whether every minister is deserving of such pay. The opposition taps populist sentiments against it.

In the 2006 general election, the Workers' Party offered its own formula: Link ministers' pay to that of the bottom 20 per cent of income-earners and multiply it by 100.

Throughout, Lee has defended the policy stoutly, as one that deters corruption and makes up for the sacrifices of office-holders. As for the argument that public office is about honour, not money, he has one word for it: hypocrisy. Politicians in Britain and the United States positioned themselves to profit handsomely later with book deals, lectures and consultancy services. It often led to leaders preoccupied with crafting "exit strategies". "Do you want that system?" he asked.

Q: *Why is the debate on ministerial salaries still raging?*

A: On the question of salaries, I'm quite comfortable. What they're going to do in the future, the present leaders have to decide. But if I were them, I'd stick to the formula, maybe improve the formula. People know our system. If you're good, you are asked to stay. When you stay, then you do three, four, five terms. You become a really good minister because by then you have a wealth of experience, and seasoned judgment.

Do you make a good minister the first time you're a minister? No. You make a good minister after two terms. Then you understand Singapore, you understand the people, you understand the workings of government, you understand what is possible. Why do we pay them high wages? Because otherwise you serve half a term and you say, "I'm off."

In this environment, would they have come in? Would Vivian Balakrishnan have come in? Ng Eng Hen came in, he was earning $3 million a year as a cancer surgeon. Shanmugam was earning $5 million in good years. You pay him $300,000? You pay him a million-plus, he's satisfied because he's not after money, he wants to do a good job. He thinks he's made enough. But we want them to stay, learn and grow in a job and do two, three, four terms, then they become really experienced.

You will notice that I made an amendment in the law to enable the prime minister to pay a minister 90 per cent of the salaries in the private sector but he has not exercised that because it creates a certain disparity between ministers, where they came from, what they're earning well before they came in. So he tries to maintain a certain balance between them. They are not all paid the same because their contributions are not the same. I see it like this: The PM is a CEO of a team and he's got to make that team work. And the team costs less than 0.02 per cent of GDP or less than what Mindef has to pay for one F15 fighter aircraft.

Q: *Aren't you concerned that your ministerial pay policy remains deeply unpopular?*

A: It is people's expectations – office is for honour. It is not. To do it for one term is an honour. It's like Bob Rubin (former US Treasury secretary). He did one-and-a-half terms, called it a day. He joined Citigroup and drew US$100 million. Or Alan Greenspan (former Federal Reserve chairman) – he had made his fortune as a financial analyst. He did his three, four terms, made a tremendous name for himself. He's making a fortune outside because of his varied expertise and the network he made while he was Fed chairman.

So Hank Paulson (former US Treasury secretary) did the job for half a term. He was CEO of Goldman Sachs, he had to sell his shares or put them in an escrow. But his worth goes up or it goes down in accordance with his performance as Treasury secretary. And in the same way, Larry Summers or Tim Geithner.[9]

Paul Volcker (former chairman of the Federal Reserve, 1979–1987, chairman of the Economic Recovery Advisory Board under the Obama administration) is an unusual man. He's a very able man. He had a very small salary. I once asked him, "Why do you do this?" He said, "In Princeton, we were nurtured to be of value to our society." And even when he retired, he didn't go and make money. He's on the board of the LKY School for free. In Indonesia he was on the advisory council, chairman, with me, for free. Now he does this job for Obama, probably also for a small honorarium. He's a most unusual man but he thinks he's got enough. The only position where he would have made some money was when he joined James Wolfensohn[10] in a boutique investment firm. But that's him and you're not going to find many Paul Volckers in America. They are all aware of what they can do, the speech-making, the networking, and so on.

Q: *If this salary policy is crucial to Singapore's success, as you maintain, why do so many Singaporeans object to it?*

A: You need to be in a different country, then you come to understand how unusual it is. We're in this part of the world where "money politics" is the culture, we're not in Europe, nor Australasia or some region where different political cultures prevail, different standards of living and different population to resource ratio. Are we able to maintain this system? You can see your counterparts, their wives are bedecked with jewels. And yours? You are not in the competition. My wife wears no jewellery, probably just one gold watch, a pearl necklace. And it goes for all ministers. Can we maintain that system? Yes, if we have men of high purpose and integrity.

Can we maintain the system if you just change governments every few years? No. You will go down the same route inevitably: If I do you this favour and give you this licence in Singapore, you will give me this licence in your country, or some forest concession. How do you prove bribery? You do me a favour, I do you a favour, that's that.

We're in this regional environment but have to stay clean, like keeping healthy in a virus-endemic region. It's not easy. You need people who are inoculated against corruption. Once we lose that standard of leaders, our standing goes down and the PAP is out.

Q: *Looking back on the 14 years since the government reworked the system to peg ministerial salaries to top private-sector incomes, are you satisfied with the outcome?*

A: There have been three elections since then. At every election, the high salaries issue crops up. If it was that big an issue, and we were not delivering, the elections would have gone the other way. The PAP would be out. But we are delivering. The system is working. Will it continue to work? I hope so. But will it need adjustments? Yes. I don't know how the economy and the private sector will go. Certain sectors may grow faster than others, and we adjust the formula.

You can take the communist approach, you are worth this much, I decide you're cadre class 1, class 2, class 3, class 4. As Class 1, you are entitled to go to this top shop, this top hospital and so on. That system collapsed when all shops were flooded with goods but you need money to buy. Money was the determining factor whether you had or you did not have the things you wanted. Immediately the officials said, "I give you this licence, you can make millions. You give me some of that." So corruption set in. That's how the Russian officials became corrupt, so too Chinese and Vietnamese officials.

We have not become corrupt. Once we are corrupt, we are finished. Our investments come in whether or not there's a recession because during a recession, they say, "OK, I'll come to Singapore when it's cheap, by the time I finish building, the recovery has taken place, and I'll do business in the region again." Why? Because we are efficient, honest and reliable. We don't chop and change our policies.

Q: *One concern is that with such high pay, ministers will become beholden to the PM and afraid to go against the PM's wishes because there's too much to lose.*

A: Shanmugam, is he afraid to go back to law? He can go back at any time. He has built up his reputation. Ng Eng Hen may be out of practice with his hands but he's still a top-class surgical oncologist. They are not beholden. It's ridiculous, absurd. If you don't measure up, you're dropped. If you measure up, then it's difficult to find a substitute. It's that simple. If a prime minister uses his patronage to keep a minister obedient, he will end up with a dud Cabinet.

Q: *You're saying that there are no yes-men in Cabinet because they have options, they can leave. You've mentioned people like Shanmugam, Ng Eng Hen. Most people would agree someone like Shanmugam has options. But isn't it less true of some other members of Cabinet, especially those who have crossed over from, say, the army or from the civil service and who were scholars from the start?*

A: If they're quality people, they have no trouble going out. If you're successful as a minister, you have no trouble going out. This is a small community. At the very top, you have no more than, say, if you get a Who's Who list of CEOs, COOs, CFOs, chairmen, deputy chairmen, maybe about 3,000 people. You just pick up your phone and ask, "You know this chap? What's he like?" There are headhunters who know the quality of every outstanding person.

The high pay issue will never be fully settled. Some Singaporeans believe ministers ought to do it for honour and glory. But how many will do it for more than one term? My generation did it because we had prepared ourselves to give up everything. We staked our lives to do what we believed in.

Can a successor generation do that? No. They now have many options. If I'm now 30 years old, will I inevitably go into politics? No. Why should I? I lose my privacy. What do I get out of it? Brickbats. I can go into a profession. My brother, as a lawyer, made over $100 million; from the law, he went into properties and shipping. Why should I be doing this? There's no glory. It's a sweat. You've this load, all the worries over water supply, next year's economy, pollutive industries like steel mills being planned in our neighbourhood, and then monsoons will blow the smog over us. You have to worry about all these potential problems.

So a younger generation thinks, "If I stay out of politics, and things go bad, I just pack up and go. I have a US green card." These are now the alternatives open to well-educated Singaporeans.

You need another revolution to produce my generation. When I went into politics, I put my life on the line, not just my fortune. If I had lost, the communists would have fixed me and brainwashed me. My generation is not reproducible.

Q: *In two speeches in 1994, you said that settling the ministerial pay policy would address the problem of a lack of ministers with private sector experience, a Lim Kim San deficit, as it were. Are you happy with the mix of ministers that you have in Cabinet now?*

A: Today's Lim Kim San may not want to come in. Lim Kim San came in because he knew I was in a bind. He was good friends with Goh Keng Swee, he knew me. He realised that if capable men like him didn't come in, Singapore could collapse. Then what would happen to his business? But in today's environment, a Lim

Kim San will say, "No, no, leave me out of this. I'm not the speech-making type, I don't like to go around kissing babies." That's that. The situation has changed. Our society has changed, the political scenario in going forward has altered. They see no reason why they should make this sacrifice.

I had Eddie Barker give up the law because I told him, "Eddie, do you think you're going to practise law if I collapse? When the communists take over, what is the law?"

He thought it over. I was right, so he came in. But once Singapore got going and things looked stable, he said, "Look, I've not paid off my mortgage on my house." That was when I started changing the salary scales. By the time he retired several terms later he had lost the energy to go back to the law.

We cannot assume that the situation which exists now will exist in the future. Take *The Straits Times*; you give SPH scholarships. How many have stayed? You face the same problem, right? Why should I be a journalist working at these odd hours when I can be the communications director for a corporation?

Even my second son did not want to stay in the SAF as a permanent career. They told him that if he stayed, he would be Chief of Defence Force because he was of that calibre. "No," he said, "I will join SingTel." After SingTel, he's off to Fraser & Neave, and now he looks after his own portfolio.[11]

It is a different generation. He was too young to have been caught up and understand what the riots were about and the sudden curfew in 1964.

My elder son was caught up in that. He was old enough to follow me around canvassing and on my constituency tours and the election campaigns. He knew the fight I was in. He decided, "I'll come in." You cannot reproduce in the next generation the same motivations because the conditions that existed have changed. Every generation is different.

Performance, not pedigree

Academic intelligence is not the only attribute the PAP looks for in its ministers.The rise of non-scholars such as Wong Kan Seng, Tharman Shanmugaratnam and Deputy Prime Minister S. Jayakumar in Cabinet is evidence that it is performance that counts. Scholar stars have also been booted out early for failing to perform.

It was through trial and error that the PAP came to recognise that it is an amalgam of abilities – not academic scores – that makes for a successful minister, said Lee Kuan Yew. The conclusion dovetails with recent theories in human intelligence and leadership put forth by several well-known scholars.

One such theory is that offered by Professor Joseph S. Nye in his 2008 book, *The Powers to Lead*. It argues that what leaders need is contextual intelligence – a combination of IQ, EQ and tacit knowledge accumulated through years of experience on the job.

Lee quoted several times from his copy of the book, a personal gift from Prof Nye and inscribed with the words "With friendship and admiration for a great leader", Lee told us as he offered to lend us his copy. Both are members of the advisory board of French petrochemical giant, Total.

Q: *What do you say to the critique that only scholars make it to the higher ranks of government?*

A: We started self-renewal by '68, we had Chiang Hai Ding, Wong Lin Ken, PhDs and so on. Didn't work. Tan Eng Liang, Rhodes scholar.[12] And we began to go deeper: What makes for a successful leader? What makes for a minister? Then over the years we refined the system and we learnt from other organisations how they choose leaders. And it's not just political leaders. In any field you need leaders whether it's academia, whether it's a corporation or whatever.

Over the years, if you look at the ministers, for instance, how many president's scholars have there been but how many have succeeded? How many SAF scholars have succeeded? How many local merit scholars, overseas merit scholars have succeeded?

I was not a scholar. Jayakumar was not a scholar. Wong Kan Seng was on local merit bursary. Tharman Shanmugaratnam, none. Why did we pick him? He didn't get a first in LSE, he got only an upper second. But we saw his performance in MAS and although he leaked information, I decided we should not sack him but warn him.[13] Finally, we decided he's so good we bring him into politics and he's shaping up as a very thorough Finance Minister and an Education Minister. But he's not a scholar.

Now, how did we come to this conclusion? By trial and experience. We started just about academic qualifications and the attrition rate was very high. They didn't have the other qualities. Slowly, we decided: How do we reduce this attrition rate?

Over the years we found that whatever the field, whether it's General Electric, IBM, Microsoft, the leader is somebody who's got these basic qualities.

High IQ, yes, necessary, but that's only one fragment. EQ, leadership, stamina, determination, resourcefulness, a whole host of other things, which eventually manifest themselves either in your success in your profession or your business.

When we came in, my Cabinet had about five star players, and the rest were mediocre. So I gave the heavy loads to the five star players. You can take a look: Goh Keng Swee, Hon Sui Sen, Lim Kim San, S. Rajaratnam, one or two others. The others are average. Toh Chin Chye took a PhD, he's good at research. But has he got the helicopter quality? So I had to move him out from Deputy Prime Minister, although he was a founder of the party, because he lacked that balance and in a crisis, he does hasty things. When I was away and the second riot took place in September '64,[14] Eddie Barker told me, "If he's in charge I'm leaving the government." So quietly, without making him lose face, I moved Goh Keng Swee there because Goh Keng Swee had the gravitas to face a crisis. Do I publicise that? No. But do I take note over the years that he lacks that? Yes, because otherwise we are in trouble. So you can see from the responsibilities I give him that they are finite. I don't want to diminish his contribution but he has his limitations.

Wong Kan Seng is not a scholar. Jayakumar is not a scholar. But they've got judgment, they can handle people. Why did we choose Wong Kan Seng? Because when the boat people came here from Vietnam, in Mindef, Goh Keng Swee says, "Send them all away." So he worked like mad, repaired their motors, gave them water and food, pushed them on or they will just flood us.[15] He is a doer. He's got that quality. What did he take? I don't know, a two-one, a two-two? Doesn't matter. But he has got enough intelligence, high sense of reality and imagination, gets things done.

Q: *How do you persuade the average young Singaporean who wants to know, how do you know that you've scoured the country and found all the able men who can lead the country politically?*

A: I'm not saying that we have found all the able men who can lead the country. All I am saying is, we're looking for the men who show the qualities that could make a leader and we have to try them out. Chiang Hai Ding is a good historian. In the end we had to make him an ambassador. He couldn't make the cut. Wong Lin Ken, we appointed him minister but he couldn't make the cut. Tan Eng Liang, we had to drop him. Finally it is your performance. So Jayakumar, Wong Kan Seng or Tharman Shanmugaratnam. Nothing to do with your academic qualifications. Have you got it in you? But the chances are, in more than 50 per cent of the cases, those who're going to make the cut usually show throughout their career that they are amongst the top 5 per cent. Because it's not just IQ that got you there; it's the capacity to apply yourself.

THE SCHOLARSHIP
SCRUTINY

The prospective Public Service Commission scholar is one of the most carefully scrutinised 18-year-olds in the world. Outstanding academic results get an applicant to the starting line in the race for the country's most prestigious scholarship awards. But every candidate then has to navigate his way through a multitude of tests to map and measure him. The ultimate aim is to assess his potential as a future public service leader.

The rigour of the process has a bearing on the quality of Singapore's political leadership as scholarship winners tend to dominate the front bench, accounting for 12 of the 20 ministers in the 2010 Cabinet.

Every candidate has to navigate through a multitude of tests to map and measure him. The ultimate aim is to assess his potential as a future public service leader.

The scrutiny begins in junior college, when principals and tutors observe and prepare reports on top-performing students. These are sent to the PSC even before the 'A' level results are announced. These reports measure on a 12-point scale a range of personality traits: integrity, emotional maturity, leadership, interpersonal skills, creativity and helpfulness. The principals also rank the students. A tutor writes an evaluation, taking into account his co-curricular activities (CCAs), behaviour and weaknesses. Another report contains his achievements in CCAs and community work.

The applicant then sits for a battery of multiple-choice tests that measure his ability to reason verbally, mathematically and spatially. He has to write an essay on his core beliefs and values: one wrote about "responsibility" and his struggle to keep his sports team together, another on his work with refugees and the disabled. He also has to take a personality test comprising nearly 200 multiple-choice questions which map his warmth, emotional stability, sensitivity, perfectionism and dominance, among other traits. A second test requires him to reflect on a stressful episode in his life. Next is an interview with a PSC psychologist on his goals, family, relationships and attitudes. The psychologist submits a lengthy report, citing even observations such as eye contact. Male applicants also get a report on their national service performance.

By the time an applicant appears before the PSC panel that awards the scholarships, a thick dossier on him would have been compiled. But still the questions keep coming during this final interview. The assessment continues after the scholarship winners graduate and return to serve in government. As Lee said, "You cannot, at 18 or 19, say what the man will be at 25, 30."

Endnotes

1   Dr Balaji Sadasivan worked as a neurosurgeon until 2001, when he was first inducted into politics. He then became an MP in the Ang Mo Kio group representation constituency and Minister of State at the Ministry of Health and the Ministry of the Environment. He decided to remain in politics. He was Senior Minister of State for Foreign Affairs, which is one rank below that of full minister, when he died in office on September 27, 2010 after a two-year battle with colon cancer.

2   Ong Ah Heng is an MP for Nee Soon Central, a single-member constituency.

3   Ang Mong Seng is an MP for Hong Kah group representation constituency.

4   Ng Ser Miang is the chairman of the organising committee for the inaugural Youth Olympic Games held in Singapore in 2010. He is also vice-president of the International Olympic Committee.

5   A group of elite educational institutions in France which have traditionally produced many of its top civil servants and scientists.

6   Koh Boon Hwee is the former chairman of the Development Bank of Singapore (DBS). Before that, he was chairman of SingTel and its predecessor organisations from 1986 to 2001, and chairman of Singapore Airlines from 2001 to 2005. He left DBS in April 2010 and is board chairman of beverage company Yeo Hiap Seng.

7   Treated and purified wastewater. The first NEWater plant came online in 2002.

8   Clement Attlee was Prime Minister of Britain from 1945 to 1951. Hugh Gaitskell was Chancellor of the Exchequer from 1950 to 1951 and leader of the opposition from 1955 to 1963.

9   American economist Larry Summers was US secretary of the Treasury from 1999 to 2001 and is now director of the National Economic Council. Tim Geithner was president of the Federal Reserve Bank of New York from 2003 to 2009 and is now secretary of the Treasury.

10 James Wolfensohn was president of the World Bank from 1995 to 2005.

11 Lee's second son, Lee Hsien Yang, is a president's scholar and Singapore Armed Forces overseas merit scholar. After serving in the army and

attaining the rank of brigadier general, he became chief executive officer of SingTel from 1995 to 2007 and chairman of Fraser and Neave in 2007. He is also chairman of the Civil Aviation Authority of Singapore.

12 Dr Chiang Hai Ding entered politics as an MP in 1970. He was a career diplomat and stepped down as an MP in 1984. After quitting politics, he served as Singapore's ambassador to more than 10 countries for over 10 years.

Dr Wong Lin Ken became an MP in 1968 and was Minister for Home Affairs from 1970 to 1972. He was also a career diplomat and passed away in 1983.

Dr Tan Eng Liang was an MP from 1972 to 1980 and served as Senior Minister of State for National Development from 1975 to 1978. He resigned as Senior Minister of State for Finance in 1979. He was also chairman of the Singapore Sports Council for 16 years until 1991 and then became vice-president of the Singapore National Olympics Council.

A more recent "fallen star" is David Lim, who resigned as Acting Minister for Information, Communications and the Arts in 2003 after a political career that lasted only six years.

13 Tharman Shanmugaratnam was convicted in 1994 for breaching the Official Secrets Act. Then director of the economics department at the Monetary Authority of Singapore (MAS), he unintentionally leaked a flash estimate of economic growth. He was charged, found guilty and fined $1,500.

14 A first round of Malay-Chinese clashes in July 1964 killed 23 people and injured 454. A second riot broke out in September, leaving 12 dead and 109 wounded. Lee was overseas during the second riot and had left Dr Toh in charge as Acting Prime Minister.

15 Wong Kan Seng joined the administrative service in 1970, holding positions in the Ministry of Labour and the Ministry of Defence.

It was as head of the navy personnel department that Wong had to deal with refugees from the Vietnam War in 1975; Goh Keng Swee was then Minister for Defence.

Wong left for the private sector in 1981, but entered politics again in 1984 as an MP. From 1985, he was Minister of State for Home Affairs,

Community Development, and Communications and Information. He was Minister for Community Development from 1987 to 1991, Minister for Foreign Affairs in 1988 and Minister for Home Affairs from 1994. He became Deputy Prime Minister in 2005.

4 KEEPING THE ECONOMIC MIRACLE ALIVE

WARFARIN IS A drug that thins the blood, helping people with heart trouble. Lee Kuan Yew started taking it when he had a pacemaker installed in December 2008 to correct his atrial heart flutter. He brought it up when asked about Singapore's role in the world economic order. "I heard the argument between my cardiologists and the Americans when they were discussing my pacemaker. They said, give him Warfarin, the full dose. A whole team of my cardiologists just put their hands up in horror and said, 'He will bleed to death.' You give that to the Indians or to the Caucasians, yes. You give to the Chinese, no!" he recounted.[1]

When prescribing Warfarin, doctors decide how strong the anti-coagulant therapy needs to be. This depends on something called the international normalised ratio (INR), which is the ratio of the time taken for a patient's blood to clot compared with a normal person not taking Warfarin. It turns out that if you give a Chinese person the same dose that you give an Indian, he will bleed to death because his DNA is a different DNA and the INR numbers are different.

In less than 50 years, Singapore has gone from a port hub in the Straits of Malacca to an international business and financial centre, as well as a cutting-edge manufacturing destination. Can it produce a pharmaceutical giant that can invent Warfarin? Probably not, said Lee. But it can adapt the drug for use in Asia, one of the fastest-growing markets in the world for pharmaceutical products. These are fields where Singapore can contribute, he concluded. It should know the practical limitations of its economy's small size and limited resources.

Indeed, pragmatism was a theme he returned to often as he discussed new imperatives that a new generation of economists and analysts is proposing, as Singapore enters the new globalised millennium. But in the new globalised millennium, economists are asking: Should the country develop a more balanced economic model that relies less on Western economies and multinational companies (MNCs) for growth? Can Singapore afford to continue to grow its economy as fast as it can, in the face of a widening income gap? And why shouldn't Singapore's government-linked corporations, such as Singapore Airlines (SIA), for example, be completely privatised?

Lee's curt answer was to get real. "The economists who say that have not sat down as we have, for the last 40 years, working out the different variables, the size of our market, the level of our technology, the entrepreneurial skills available, and what is the alternative," he said, cutting you off before you could even finish framing the question.

Hours later, you come away from the interview feeling disheartened, even though your initial instinct might have been to be inspired by the story of the little island economy that could.

For smallness is a big problem, at least according to Lee. There is a limit to what Singapore and other small nations can achieve, and they must know their place in the economic world order. With a small population, Singapore is not likely to produce a global manufacturing champion or have enough talented private sector CEOs.

Forget wanting to grow a Microsoft or a Sony from within, because the success of a place like Singapore must depend on the outside world. You told Lee that this sounded depressing but he declared, "I am not depressed by this. I am realistic. I say these are our capabilities, this is the competition that we face and given what we have, we can still make a good living provided we are realistic."

These are not new issues, but they have returned with a vengeance because the past economic downturn hit Singapore harder than many other Asian countries. The pivotal role that developed economies like the United States and Europe play in Singapore's economic success has always been cited as one of the country's main weaknesses.

Critics ask whether Singapore, along with much of Asia, should continue to rely so much on these Western superpowers to generate demand for its goods and services. New government data shows that Singapore's reliance on external demand for its exports has grown from 70 to 76 per cent in the last 10 years, and more than half of its exports still go to the United States and Europe. If both these regions had experienced deep and long recessions in the aftermath of the 2008 financial crisis, Singapore – along with more open Asian economies like Taiwan and Korea – would have been hit hard. The recession has turned out to be short-lived, but the lesson it has again taught on the vulnerabilities of these economies lingers.

Could Singapore have moved earlier to develop a more thriving domestic market? Should it now, with the rest of Asia, start developing intra-Asian trade as a new source of export growth, especially with emerging powerhouses like China and India?

Another perennial bugbear: Why can't the economy be less reliant on Western MNCs like Philips and Motorola? In the early years of independence, MNCs were crucial to the economic success of a small island nation with no natural resources that had abruptly been cut off from its large Malaysian hinterland. The MNCs created jobs by the thousands and drove much of the country's economic growth. Today, the manufacturing sector is no less important, contributing a quarter of

Singapore's GDP and employing more than a fifth of its workforce.

But the Western MNCs that make up the bulk of the sector are no more rooted in Singapore than they were before, constantly moving manufacturing operations to more cost-efficient destinations. In a recessionary environment, MNCs are also quick to downsize operations. Singapore therefore runs the added risk of production pullbacks and job losses it has no control over, because they are ordered by head offices in the United States, Europe or Japan.

In 1980, Professor Lim Chong Yah – one of Singapore's most respected economists and academics – said that Singapore's problem was that it had only gone through a "quasi-industrialisation", building an economy based on servicing MNC masters. Today, some economists reprise that point, and talk of a "brittle" Singapore economy that could be "here today, gone tomorrow".

Ultimately, it is a question of balance, economists argue. Some point to the comparative success of South Korea, which has nurtured its own global MNCs like Samsung and LG out of a clutch of nascent local enterprises in the 1970s. Similarly, government funding in Taiwan helped build up semiconductor giants like TSMC and UMC, as well as leading computer brands like Acer.

Could Singapore have allocated more money and resources to growing a local manufacturing elite that would have been more rooted here? And even if its reliance on MNCs was born out of necessity, why hasn't Singapore tried to change course now?

In early 2010, amid a tenuous recovery from the global recession, Singapore's high-powered Economic Strategies Committee revealed a new, bold strategy to take the Singapore economy on a route of more sustainable growth. One of its core recommendations adopted by the government, was to nurture 1,000 small and medium enterprises (SMEs) with an annual turnover of more than $100 million over the next decade. There were 530 such companies in 2007. So while MNCs will continue to form the critical mass in Singapore, the government has at least now shown some intent in developing a strong and sizeable SME base as part of Singapore's economy.

Commenting on this later in the year, Lee said in an emailed reply that his comments did not preclude nurturing the SME sector. "Eventually, some of them must be able to compete worldwide and be a Singapore MNC. But he added, "the MNCs will always drive the Singapore economy because it is highly unlikely that 1,000 SMEs will become 1,000 MNCs."

When size matters

Asked to respond to these unfavorable comparisons with other "Asian tigers" that Singapore is often grouped with, Lee produced a recent *Wall Street Journal* editorial critical of what was happening in Taiwan, where the government had to bail out its chip companies. He handed it over to you with an air of finality, and it was with the same confidence that he predicted the inevitable death of companies like Malaysia's car maker Proton.

In his almost Darwinist take on the issue, he argued that the forces of globalisation would see larger and more powerful MNCs eliminate their smaller rivals over time. Key ingredients in the success of these super-sized behemoths are innovation and talent, both of which are functions of a country's population size.

This is why countries like Singapore lack the critical mass to produce global manufacturing champions, and should not even try, he said. Going through a list of small and medium-sized nations that have homegrown companies on the Fortune 500 list of global corporations, Lee muttered their population figures under his breath before proffering explanations as to why they might be the exceptions to the rule.

You pointed out that Norway (population: 5 million), Sweden (9 million) and Finland (5 million) all have companies on the list. Ah, but these Scandinavian countries are really one larger integrated region, he replied.

On the other hand, the potential of some of the world's largest economies seems limitless to Lee. Japan (127 million) and South Korea

(49 million) have the sort of numbers to compete in the big league, and he was convinced that the United States (310 million) would recover from its current economic troubles because it had shown throughout history that it has the societal culture and talent to innovate, create breakthroughs and bounce back. Similarly, China (1.3 billion) has opened its doors to MNCs from America, Europe and Japan, and is just "20 years" away from producing luxury cars similar to the likes of Lexus and Mercedes-Benz.

So the reality is that Singapore's manufacturing sector will therefore always be dominated by foreign MNCs, said Lee. The idea is to try and pick the eventual winners in their respective fields and to keep them in Singapore for as long as possible. Singapore has been, and will always be, an interlocutor, he said. "We provide superior environment and superior services. Without that, we are finished."

For that reason, Singapore has chosen to assiduously invest instead in key elements of its supporting services sector, such as growing an international financial centre and ensuring excellent air and sea links and telecommunications facilities.

It is the same sort of logic regarding the limitations of Singapore's size that led Lee to conclude that the government still needs to control some of Singapore's largest corporations through investment vehicle Temasek Holdings.

Lee knows the theoretical arguments well. He nodded sagely as you rattled them off – that corporations which are privately-owned and run are generally more efficient and innovative, that the market power of government-backed corporations crowds out an already weak private sector, that there is a risk of "groupthink" developing among a small group of individuals entrusted by the Singapore government to run the companies that it owns.

But is there really an alternative, he asked. "We want to privatise, but at the moment, who do you privatise to?" The answer lies again within the problem of Singapore's small size, argued Lee. What little talent the country can produce either goes to the public sector, where the best brains are needed, or to high-paying professions such as medicine, investment banking and law. The result is that Singapore's small and medium-sized companies are recruiting mostly at the "second or third tier" of talent, he said.

Lee gave another example of what he meant. "You look at small countries and ask what is it they're capable of doing? The nearest to us is Hong Kong and they have double our population and very bright entrepreneurs from the mainland, which we didn't have. But what are their children doing?" he asked. "Real estate, and now they've gone back to China."

But occasionally, in the search for private sector talent in a small local pool, you stumble upon "a gem", Lee said. And when you do, you hold on to it and fully utilise it, he added, citing as examples men like Koh Boon Hwee (who has been chairman of Singapore Telecom, Singapore Airlines and banking giant DBS Group Holdings) and Stephen Lee (who has helmed port operator PSA International and Singapore Airlines).

New growth models

We eventually turned to a new issue that is emerging: the "unevenness" of Singapore's economic growth. The worry is that the pursuit of high growth inevitably leads to a widening income disparity.

Singapore's Gini coefficient score – an internationally-recognised measure of income inequality – is currently one of the highest in the world. In 2008, it was 0.425. The Gini coefficient measures the income gap, with perfect equality at 0 and total inequality at 1. In comparison, for the Scandinavian countries of Denmark, Sweden, Finland and Norway, the Gini coefficient in 2009 ranged from 0.247 to 0.269. In 2006, Citigroup economist Chua Hak Bin noted that this was perhaps the result of Singapore having developed into a sort of "dual-speed" economy, with higher-earners enjoying double-digit growth far distinct from a lower-income strata, for real wages have remained largely stagnant.

Many agreed with this assessment, noting that although Singapore was growing 6 to 8 per cent in the last four years before the recession, ordinary people did not seem to "feel the growth on the ground".

Should the government be concerned about the widening rich-poor gap and take measures to contain it?

One route that other developed nations have taken is to sacrifice some economic growth to level up society. For example, in Scandinavian countries and Japan, society seems to have accepted the economic "GDP cost" of hiring and training more expensive local labour as opposed to the easier option of importing cheap labour from overseas. And yet some Scandinavian countries, for example, remain competitive economically. Denmark ranked third in the World Economic Forum's influential Competitiveness Ranking in 2008, ahead of Singapore which was fifth. Sweden was fourth, Finland sixth, and Norway 15th. Singapore, however, has always said that in a globalised, dynamic world, a small and open country like itself must aim to grow "as fast as possible". In that regard, low-cost foreign labour is essential to the growth of sectors like manufacturing and construction, especially to take on jobs which Singaporeans are unwilling to do.

The government's strategy is therefore to "make hay while the sun shines" because as long as the country experiences growth, it will have adequate resources to take care of underlying social problems. This approach has led to many years of impressive economic growth in a country bereft of natural resources and a large domestic market.

In a way, this reflects the social compact that is implicit between the Singapore government and its people, say political economists. As long as the government delivers the economic growth, its people will tolerate the accompanying social problems and trust the government to neutralise these "side effects" by redistributing some of the gains. Still, critics suggest that this sort of social compact that was made between the government and the people of Singapore could be breaking down. That is because growth is necessarily slowing down as Singapore enters a more mature phase of economic development.

A second aspect is to do with the fact that new generations of

Singaporeans are being born into relatively affluent surroundings. Better educated and more socially aware, they may be more willing to trade off a marginal increase in their per capita incomes for the security of a more equal distribution of wealth within society.

Economist Linda Lim sums up these sentiments when she says that economic growth should be "growth for people", not "people for growth". She suggests that "in the long run, a lower rate of growth which delivers a higher ratio of benefits to Singaporeans may be more desirable than a higher rate of growth which is unstable and inequitable".

Tackling these questions, Lee again drew the distinction between economic theory and the reality on the ground. He questioned whether the "haves" in Singapore, who, in many cases, may have done well because of their abilities and effort, were really willing to accept slower growth or higher taxes, so that the government could give more help to the "have-nots".

The real grumble about Singapore going for maximum growth, said Lee, is not so much with widening income disparities as with the arrival of foreigners to meet the labour needs of the companies that drive economic growth. Singaporeans are uncomfortable with the changes in the social fabric that these foreigners bring.

Still, the ever-pragmatic Lee went on to wrap up the discussion over two lengthy interviews by saying, "Look, we are realists. There are few things that economists can tell me which we haven't investigated. Our job is to preserve and advance the well-being of the people we are in charge of. If there is a way that we can improve, we will."

"I decided we had to be
different … or we are finished."

Q: *Should Singapore have tried to build a credible local manufacturing elite?*

A: In this globalised world, unless you're big enough to be on top of the pile in that particular industry, you'll play a secondary role. When I joined the board of (German car manufacturer) Daimler-Benz in 1992, then chairman and CEO Jürgen Schrempp told me that the many brands across the world will reduce in number and consolidate to probably 10 or 12. He was determined that Mercedes Benz will be one of them. So he felt he had to go global. He acquired (American car manufacturer) Chrysler but it failed because the cultures could not merge. He went to Japan and Korea, but he also failed.

Look, unless you are big enough, the champions in any particular industry will be the ones who are the best in their field. Take Taiwan. It thought it had the size – 20-plus million population. So it blocked out imports and tried import substitution. In the initial stages it succeeded with laptops, semiconductors and computer chips.

But now this recent *Wall Street Journal* article says they've been outpaced. They cannot compete with the Japanese and the Koreans because these countries have a bigger population base and more talented people. I think Taiwan's (President) Ma Ying-jeou is trying to keep the big Taiwanese companies going by pumping in money. But that's a short-term measure. The question is, have you got the R&D to keep pace?

Hong Kong is seven million and also hasn't got the numbers to compete. What has Hong Kong got? Property developers and market players. Is Li Ka Shing making a product that is selling worldwide? No, he's just acquiring real estate, ports, retail stores and telecoms companies. He's working the market. What is the most successful company in Hong Kong? Li and Fung. Two bright brothers, but they are in logistics chains for every company.

They're not in manufacturing because they can't compete. China is into manufacturing. Even then, Hong Kong started with more entrepreneurs ready-made from the mainland. We didn't even have that. We started with descendants of farmers, some of whom became traders. And it took some time for many to eventually become professionals and entrepreneurs.

Q: *But couldn't a Singapore company like Creative (Creative Technology, a maker of digital entertainment products) become a global player? It was once a global leader in sound cards.*

A: Yes, in Singapore, Creative was one of the few companies that were trailblazers. But look at the trials and tribulations they had to go through. They've had to recruit people from Silicon Valley to keep up with the competition because Singapore doesn't have the critical mass of talent. And in the end all that Creative has got now is MP3 players. Their Soundblasters and so on ... other companies have caught up.

In food and beverage, Tee Yih Jia is doing well. But once it begins to succeed in America, it will be taken over by conglomerates like PepsiCo. How do I know? Because I've attended PepsiCo meetings. They collect foodstuffs from around the world and sell them in their outlets in Latin America and in all the cinemas across the world. They will buy up Tee Yih Jia, and Tee Yih Jia can't compete with them because where are its outlets?

So I find that the usual stereotype economists haven't sat down to think. In a globalised world where your markets are open – and it's a kind of world which is going to come whether you like it or not – what is our future? Try and compete? Where? Make what? Widgets? What widgets? Anything we make, the Chinese and Indians and Vietnamese will eventually do the same.

Q: *Yet we are still trying to make a name for ourselves as a* *manufacturing hub, and we keep going into new areas like life sciences...*

A: True, we latch on to a growth area like life sciences, but are we going to be leaders in life sciences discoveries? No. What we provide companies is the security for the discoveries, copyright protection, an attractive living environment for their researchers and scientists, and the facilities for research and to trial new products on our population, because our hospitals maintain good records and we have different races and genetic pools.

But even here, we're not going in blind. We've argued, okay, so the Chinese will eventually get their hospitals right. And for testing of drugs on Chinese patients, companies will go to China because there is a bigger Chinese pool. But they have not got intellectual property protection, and because they also haven't got the Indians and the Malays and the Caucasians and others we have, so we're able to stay in this 20, 30 or maybe more years. I don't see the Indians getting their hospitals to world standards, or protecting intellectual property within that timeframe.

The free market in a technologically globalised world is what you have to face. Every country has to face that. Taiwan can't do it and Hong Kong can't do it. But Shenzhen can – not because they have seven million but that seven million draws from 1,300 million. What do we draw on? 3.2 million Singaporeans. Without the foreign employment pass holders bringing in the expertise, we won't be able to do this. So in the long run we must continue to draw more talent in. If we're inhospitable to talent, we're not in the running. That's life.

Q: *So what you are saying is that a small country with a small population and limited resources necessarily lacks the critical mass to produce a world champion in manufacturing, so don't even try?*

A: Yes, you will be taken over if you're successful. Get to world class and there will be a company that's already eyeing all these possible takeovers.

Q: *But Finland has produced Nokia, and Sweden has companies like Ikea. These are companies that seem to punch way above what the country's physical size seems to suggest.*

A: All right ... Sweden, Ikea. Do we want to go into that? Have we got the wood and the designers? The Swedes are good designers, right? Nokia's roots in history were from a controlled society overshadowed by the Soviet Union. Finland is about five to six million people. Can they keep up with the competition from Korea and Japan in the long term? How many bright fellows have they got with inventive, creative minds?

Compare that to Japan and the United States. The Japanese work on any product and improve it all the time. I use an electric shaver and every six months they come up with a new model. Sometimes it's not much better and the improvements are gimmicks, so I say no, we're not going to buy. But they're working on it all the time. Take the abacus – the Chinese have two and five (two beads on each rod in the upper deck and five beads each in the bottom), but the Japanese have one and four and they sharpen it so that it's soundless. They've refined everything from chopsticks to cars.

The American culture, on the other hand, is that we start from scratch and beat you. That's why I have confidence that the American economy will recover. They were going down against Japan and Germany in manufacturing. But they came up with the Internet, Microsoft and Bill Gates, Dell and so on. Suddenly they've flooded the market and cut costs, so the Europeans and the Japanese have to catch up.

The Japanese were the first to have just-in-time inventory. They save on the margins but the Americans break through with something new altogether. What kind of mindset do you need for that? It's part of their history. They went into an empty continent and made the best of it – killed the Red Indians and took over the land and the buffaloes. So this is how they ended up – you build a town here, you be sheriff, I'm the judge, you're the policeman and you're the banker, let's start. And this culture has carried on till today. There is the belief that you can make it happen.

Q: *There are quite a number of small European countries in the Fortune 500 list of companies. There is no Singapore company but Finland has two and Sweden has six. Switzerland has 14.*

A: First, let me tell you their advantage. They have the European market, right? The European Union entitles them to use that market. So they've got a bigger base. European Union citizens can move across borders and they don't need passports or anything for that. So if you say Sweden, it does not mean the Swede is the entrepreneur. Anybody can go into this. Any of the Nordic countries are interchangeable with them and they just go and use the Swedish base and build from there. The Danes, Swedes, Norwegians ... they're the same people. Ireland, with the number of immigrants there, is more cosmopolitan than Singapore. It also has a large pool of Irish diaspora. So you're drawing talent from a bigger manpower base, and that is a great advantage. In Singapore you face restrictions in Indonesia, Malaysia, Thailand and Philippines. Where is your market?

So being in Singapore and faced with these problems, we've to go back and think them through. Economists and other observers come in and go by what's happened elsewhere. They say we're not producing entrepreneurs. The question is: Can we produce enough entrepreneurs to keep our economy going? Hong Kong and Taiwan cannot. Can we compete with the large economies in R&D without having the same critical mass?

If we are all Jews, then maybe we can do it. The Jews have more brainpower per one thousand of population than any other race in the world. I was reading in *The Economist* that when the Russian Jews went to Israel, people said to look out for them when the plane lands. If a person carries a big luggage, he must have a double bass, if it's a small one it's a violin, and if it's an even smaller one it's a trumpet. If he carries nothing, he must be a pianist or a scientist because he is carrying documents. That is the quality of the people whom the Russians were stupid to chase out. They could have served Russia.

Fortunately, our strategy was okay. We said let's open up and get the best. Now, China had the choice, when it started industrialising, to do it the Japanese and the Korean way. China is not stupid. They know they've got the critical mass and the brainpower. They're training their chaps all up the ladder – top schools, top universities, R&D everywhere. What do they do? Try to make their own champion car? No. They tell the MNCs to come in, all of you. Yes, you bring your older models, never mind, but you are employing my engineers, my designers and my workers across the board. China cannot catch up with Hyundai or Toyota on their own. But with such a plethora of top ranks and top brains working for the multinationals, they are going to synthesise and produce their Lexus. Today they got the little Chery. I give them 20 years and they'll produce a Lexus and Mercedes Benz. Eventually, they're going to go in for jumbo aircraft.

Q: *So in the case of Singapore, for manufacturing we will always be dependent on multinational companies?*

A: Of course.

Q: *And we'll always be an economy that services the large MNC manufacturers?*

A: I say look at your neighbourhood and you will come to your conclusion. Are you in Europe? Are you in the Pacific? If you're in the Pacific, you're a dead duck. Supposing we're in Fiji ... who flies to Fiji? In the old days you fly to Fiji to go to Australia. Now with long-range aircraft you only go to Fiji if you want a cheap holiday. If you're in Fiji, how are you going to succeed? So it becomes a holiday destination for Americans. White shorelines, easygoing people, coconuts. Nice hotels built by American chains and you service tourists.

We're in Singapore, which gives us six hours range, a market of about two plus billion people reached by air. We climbed up the ladder within one generation. How did we do it? Because we looked at the outside world and said, look, this is the way we go, maximise our strengths and we got here. How do we go further up? By not competing with Chinese and Indians where we know they're going to enter in a big way. We succeed by staying in little niches, securing qualities which they cannot match, like credibility, reliability, intellectual property and the rule of law. They cannot match that for a long time.

If I had Shenzhen in Johor Bahru, I think we will sit down and say, okay, shall we join them? No laughing matter. I mean not all the best go to Shenzhen but many of the best are there. And Shenzhen speaks Mandarin, not Cantonese. It's transformed in a short time since Deng Xiaoping opened it up in 1980. (Shenzhen became a Special Economic Zone on 1 May 1980.) That's 20-plus years from a little village, now to a metropolis of seven million. Hongkongers go there for haircuts, manicures and to make cheongsams. Hong Kong tailors can't compete. If we get that kind of JB, we got to sit back and say, okay, where do we go?

Q: *Your views on the limitations of home-grown manufacturing in Singapore ... is that the reason why people are saying that the Singapore government doesn't give enough support to local* *industry as they do to MNCs?*

A: No, no, no. Look, the American SMEs don't go to the government for support. In Silicon Valley, they go into the garage and tinker around and they build up fortunes. By the time they're looking for the government support and have to be taught management and given loans, they are not going to be any good.

Remember this: don't believe that the chaps on top are just entrepreneurs. They are all powerful minds. Bill Gates, Michael Dell, John Chambers of Cisco ... I've met them and they are very able people. Where are our able people? In the SMEs? No, the SMEs are collecting talent at the second, third tier. The first tier will not work for them. That's our luck, right?

How does Malaysia do it? By blocking out imports and saying, well, okay, you run (oil and gas company) Petronas, and you run Proton. But when they started Proton I remember what Jürgen Schrempp told me. He said, "It's doomed." Yes of course it's doomed, no chance. The world is consolidating and you want to start a little manufacturing outfit of your own when trade ties have opened up? Thailand has become like a Detroit in Southeast Asia, with all the spare parts being made there and the cars assembled there. How can you compete? So to protect Proton, the Malaysians say "block imports" and the free trade agreement is postponed. It's national pride, but can Proton be saved? Volkswagen wants to take over but they say no, Malaysians must remain in charge. Now it's still a loss maker. We would have said, "Cut this one out because it's stuck at the low end of the auto industry and doomed to fail."

Q: *What SME-type critics like to say is that it's a question of balance. The government seems to have favoured MNCs for a long time and they say if you have given us some of that attention and let us ferret out where we can compete, we might have become stronger. We may not want to compete along with the Coca-Colas* *and the Samsungs but we can do something good on a smaller scale in Asia.*

A: The SMEs have thrived by basically becoming suppliers to the MNCs. So if the MNCs go abroad, they follow them. They produce intermediate items the MNCs do not want to produce. That's how they learn, and from there they grow. The MNCs triggered off the manufacturing capabilities of our SMEs.

Look, we started with no manufacturing. No merchant wanted to go into manufacturing. That's why we had the Development Bank of Singapore (DBS). The banks did not want to lend money to the traders here because what do traders know about manufacturing? Did it succeed? All right, so we had NatSteel. What can we do? Buy the raw material and grow the business. But for what? For construction ... what else? Can you compare with the iron and steel business of Korea or China? China is the biggest producer of iron and steel now. In Japan, they have high-tech steel mills. Anyway, the pollution would have been enormous. I went to Perth and nearby there's a big iron mine. So I went to see it. There's an Australian developer, a miner who wanted to have a station in Ubin or Tekong to store it and save on transportation. I had one look at it and said the whole of Changi will be shrouded with this dust. So I said, "No. Out."

We have explored everything. You want to go into motorcars? We assembled motorcars. We assembled refrigerators and air conditioners. You want to make air conditioners and invent like the Japanese do? You take this remote control ... control speed, click, click, click, fans go up and down. Can you do that? No chance. Look at the trouble Creative has had. (Singapore drinks manufacturer) Yeo Hiap Seng goes to China and has a tough time because they're meeting competition. They say, "Oh, is that what your chrysanthemum tea is about? I will improve on it." So when Yeo's makes a chrysanthemum tea and exports it there, it costs more. Can they compete? Where is their R&D? It cannot be done, let's be realistic.

Q: *You've made all of us very depressed...*

A: No, I am not depressed! I am realistic. I say these are our capabilities, and this is the competition that we face. Given what we have, our assets and our capabilities, we can still make a good living provided we are realistic.

Q: *Okay, so we don't have the critical mass to be manufacturers of the best things in the world or to be top innovators. What then is our competitive advantage? It seems to be our ability to gather the right infrastructure, the rule of law, the system of governance. But are these attributes enough to keep us going?*

A: Supposing we don't have those attributes, what would happen to us?

Q: *Yes, but now that we have these attributes, are they enough to keep us going?*

A: These are the basics that differentiate us from our neighbours. When I started, the question was how Singapore can make a living against neighbours who have more natural resources, human resources and bigger space. And we were dependent on them for our trade because we were entrepot. So thinking it over and discussing it with my colleagues, I decided we had to be different. We had to differentiate ourselves from them or we are finished.

How did we differentiate ourselves from them? They are not clean systems, we run clean systems. Their rule of law is wonky, we stick to the law. Once we come to an agreement or make a decision, we stick to it. We become reliable and credible to investors. World-class infrastructure, world-class supporting staff, all educated in English. Good communications by air, by sea, by cable, by satellite and now, over the Internet. So it is a location which is different from any other in this region. You want to work in Bangkok? Are you assured the airport will be open? You want to go to KL? Jakarta? Manila? You've got this valuable equipment, where do you want to place it?

Look at (petrochemical hub) Jurong Island. We are land-scarce so we joined up the land there. We just fill up, now we're going to dig (oil storage) caves in the ground. Why? Because we are a reliable, dependable location. There is rule of law, we never break our word. We maintain stability, industrial peace and we are completely to be trusted. So you want to put that money into China. Yes, but only if the Chinese put half and you are in control. But here, it's totally theirs. ExxonMobil is putting in an additional US$4 billion worth of investments to build downstream products.[2] Its CEO Rex Tillerson is bringing his whole board here to look at the place. He will ask me to meet the board. What for? So that the board will know that his judgment is right. It's not easy to reproduce Singapore and if you destroy it, you may never rebuild it.

Q: *You've suggested that innovation and R&D are quite critical to how a country develops.*

A: Yes, absolutely.

Q: *And you appear to have ruled it out as a viable option for Singapore...*

A: In manufacturing.

Q: *But that scenario doesn't quite gel with what the government itself is trying to do, which is to emphasise R&D and innovation.*

There were a couple of recent surveys which Singapore topped in innovation. I would have thought that if we want to emphasise R&D and innovation, one way would be to empower SMEs, our own companies...

A: But where are the researching minds? I once talked to the head of R&D for (Dutch electronics giant) Philips. He came here 15 or 20 years ago and I'll never forget what he told me. He spoke very frankly and said that when you do research, you must have a mind that is focused and determined to break through until you see light at the end of the tunnel. You burrow away, you burrow away and you never give up.

Have you met a Singaporean who does that? His mother, father, brothers, sisters, uncles are in the financial business, does he make a lot of money compared to them? Some are doctors and lawyers. They will say, "So you do R&D ... what's that?" You're going to discover drugs against Pfizer, Merck, GlaxoSmithKline? Can you beat them with their tens of thousands of researchers all over the world?

I met the chief of (pharmaceutical company) Novartis,[3] who is Swiss and has great confidence in Singapore. So I said, "You know, we are trying to go into R&D." He says, "Very difficult. You need a big talent pool. From Switzerland we have put R&D in Boston. There are seven or eight universities there we collaborate with at any one time." The talent pool is not just in Novartis but in the community around Boston where all the bright minds are teaching and researching.

So I had my very serious doubts when they put up this proposal to go into the life sciences. It was Philip Yeo's plan.[4] I said, "Look, where is the brainpower? Whatever we do, the Chinese and Indians will do, the Vietnamese will do. How can we compete?"

So Philip Yeo says that we can bring all these bright chaps from overseas here and give scholarships. Will they stay? Ah, let's give it a try. It's not the "whales" or the prominent scientists coming here that will stay or not stay because they will stay as long as we fund the research. But the scholarship holders that we send for PhDs who come from all over the world and mostly Asia – if they go back to their own countries, then we are in trouble.

So we are hoping that they will be rooted here, marry locals or marry their own kind and start a family here because it's better than China or Vietnam or India. We need them. And they will do it because what is the alternative for them? Now, the Singaporean has that alternative. He can be a lawyer, he can be a doctor, he can be an accountant, a banker, a broker, he can be in real estate. He will say, "You want me to go and find a cure for this disease? I could spend my lifetime doing this and not find anything!"

Q: *But apart from hoping that this group will stay and sink roots here, could more be done to support our companies so that some of the spillover effects, in terms of knowledge transfer or whatever, also come over to the companies sector and not just the manpower?*

A: To spill over, you must have people with brains to absorb the spillover! Philip Yeo has been sent to (enterprise development agency) Spring Singapore to build up the SME sector. And the first thing he has to do is to tackle just the basics of administration and how to run a business properly. What is it Singaporeans do when they go into business? They set up a shop, because that's what they think business is. Set up a shop or a restaurant and buy and sell. What else do they do? You look at our history, what have we done?

The Taiwanese tried but they gave up, cannot compete. But the Koreans are trying, there's 50-odd million of them and they are not stupid. They hire Japanese experts who have been retrenched or whom they met at college and now they have some breakthroughs. So they try cars, flat screen televisions and cell phones. I have met the *chaebol* chiefs, asked them how they did it and they explained to me. They went to universities in Japan, their contemporaries working there. So they pay these Japanese more and bring them to Korea to pass on their knowledge.

Can we do that? Can our SMEs have that? When you say transfer, I mean you just look, transfer to whom? You must transfer to another capable vessel, right? (Minister for Transport) Raymond Lim says "Privatise SIA." I said, "I agree." But sell to whom? What corporation will be able to maintain and ensure that the leadership in SIA will be always good and it will not lose money? Far East Holdings? No experience. Hotel Properties' Ong Beng Seng? No. The banks? No. So who can you hand it over to?

We try, but unless we have enough people with the brainpower to run these companies, it can't be done. You look at all the successful companies, what is the key? Their brainpower. The thinker, good management, good innovators.

Q: *One final question on this MNC-reliant model that we have today ... we've talked about the validity of it going forward but are there weaknesses to the model that you worry about?*

A: Well, the weakness is that the top MNCs may not come and we get the second tier who will be defeated by the top MNCs, which have gone to countries like Vietnam because it's cheaper and smarter, and then the production in Vietnam will beat the production in Singapore.

What have we got to offer? Not cheaper labour or land, but higher quality infrastructure to justify the higher cost. The Vietnamese are very smart. We can see it from the students that we give scholarships to. They catch up and they are one-third of our salaries, one quarter the price of our land. So we got to offer what we have that they cannot offer: stability, security, connectivity, good healthcare, schooling for children because the top people want their children with them and they want good schools. We have already made progress in these areas and the Singapore American School (SAS) here is the best American school in the region.

Q: *How do we address that weakness?*

A: We just have to stay ahead to become attractive to the best MNCs. There are now about 4,000 Indian firms and about 4,500 Chinese firms that come to Singapore. From here, they will spread into the region. They use Singapore as a base and take our people when they go into the region because they don't know the region as well as us. Our people know the region, speak the languages and can help them break through. This is our role. We are interlocutors.

In the longer term, we are better off than Hong Kong because we have neighbours who are not likely to overtake us in the quality of their education, their workforce and the infrastructure. Shanghai is already equal to Hong Kong in its infrastructure. What they lack is the English-speaking skills and the supporting staff. You give them another 15–20 years and they have that. The same is happening in Shenzhen. A Hong Kong secretary for labour I had met asked me, "Why do you keep your manufacturing?" I told him that's because the manufacturing sector provides jobs. I said, in the case of Hong Kong, you have neighbours who will always improve on your manufacturing and do better than you. We have neighbours who will find it difficult to catch up with the skills and education of our workforce.

Q: *Another criticism of the Asian growth model – not just Singapore's – is that we are too reliant on the West as consumers for our products. How does the current economic crisis affect the sustainability of Singapore's economic model given that America cannot be the customer of the world that it has been?*

A: Let me go back to fundamentals. Is the world going to

become an ugly, depressed place with protectionism and depressed economies all over the world? If it is, we are all finished. Are the Americans going to do that? No, because their big companies depend on external markets for more than 50 per cent of their revenue.

I am not at all pessimistic. I don't know how long this recession will take. Maybe if US Federal Reserve chief Ben Bernanke is right and they clean up the banks, by 2010 America could recover and have a small growth. If Bernanke is wrong, it may drag on to 2012 or 2013, but America will recover. So they talk about protecting jobs. You protect your jobs, the Americans protect their jobs, Japanese and so on. Are the Americans really going to go into a different model and just rely on their local suppliers and domestic market? No. The technology is already discovered and spread. If you don't exploit the benefits of that technology and free trade, your competitors will and you will lose out.

Q: *With America and Europe subdued over the next few years, a lot of people are talking about the potential for intra-Asian trade, of products made in Asia for Asia. What is your assessment of the potential of intra-Asia trade? Do you think it's something that we can aspire towards?*

A: Well, it is an extra string to our bow, but remember, the average consumer in Asia is not yet a wealthy or lavish consumer. The Chinese are even more savings-prone than us. We have been saving almost 50 per cent of our earnings for decades, that's how we got these resources today. The Chinese save more because they have to depend on their own resources to deal with floods, accidents, earthquakes, devastation, wars.

I give this anecdote and you will understand their mentality. I had a frozen left shoulder from golf and I was going around the region in China with a minister for space. I said, "I've stopped playing golf." He said, "I will send you a chap, he will cure your shoulder." I said, "No, no, don't worry. My orthopaedic surgeon says it cannot be cured." But he followed up, he sent this chap. (He's dead now.) So I had to sit down on my couch in my office, 45 minutes every day for about six weeks, and he cured me. So what do I do? I talk to him.

At that time there was a flood near Shanghai. I said, "Oh, big trouble. You get help from outside." He said, "Help from outside? When will it arrive? It can arrive in Shanghai but how do you get it to the villages upstream?" He said in China, every town, every village, there's a little hillock where they keep all the essential foods: salt, rice, blankets, whatever, so they can survive a disaster. He said, "When we get these disasters, the government can't reach us, we got to help ourselves. We learnt to look after our survival in the case of calamity."

What do the Chinese do when they have money? They save. If they are affluent for say two or three generations, then they might breed a new generation more willing to spend. But I do not believe for the next 30 or 40 years, they're going to spend like the Americans. They're going to save, they're going to build houses and they're going to buy goods which will increase in value over time. Yes, they will consume, but mostly on essentials. So there's a limit that China and India can do for us. In Asean, you have the non-Chinese spending a bit more. But you watch the Chinese in Malaysia and Indonesia – they've been saving up because of the history of sudden disasters and no help from the government.

Postscript

After our interviews had concluded, Singapore experienced a dramatic rebound from the global recession, posting an eye-popping 15 per cent growth rate in 2010, possibly the highest growth rate in the world. The recovery was boosted by robust growth in Asia and other developing markets, as well as domestic factors such as the opening of two new integrated resorts. However, growth continues to be weak in the Western world. The United States has blamed its woes on China, which it argues has persistently undervalued its currency to boost its export competitiveness. China and other emerging economies, meanwhile, accuse the United States of trying to boost growth by flooding the market with cheap money, weakening its currency and giving rise to large capital flows that could destabilise Asia and other developing markets. Against this backdrop we posed more questions to Lee.

Q: *People now speak of the dangers and imbalances of a "multi-speed" economy, with the West's pace of growth slowing almost to zero and emerging economies rebounding at a record pace. What is your take on this? Will there be an economic fallout? And does this multi-speed world economy pose serious risks to the geopolitical world order?*

A: I am not sure the West is slowing down almost to zero. Germany is still growing at a steady pace of 3–4 per cent. On September 30, 2010, the National Institute of Statistics and Economic Studies in France estimated that the French economy would grow by 1.6 per cent in 2010. The emerging economies are going at a record pace because they are starting from a lower base, huge populations, and therefore a hungry local market. A "multi-speed" world has been thus for decades if not centuries. Why should it pose serious risks to the geopolitical world order?

Q: *What do you make of the "currency wars" that are going on in the form of competitive undervaluation?*

A: The "currency wars" have been overblown in the US media.

The crux of the problem is that the Chinese renminbi has been kept at the old rate of exchange and the American dollar has been losing value. And unless the Chinese currency further appreciates, there will be a serious problem between the American and Chinese governments.

Q: *How do you see the US and China working out this and other economic imbalances in their relationship?*

A: China will always have a difficult relationship with America. America sees China as a power that is likely to eventually overtake them in gross domestic product in 20 years, and will have a stronger voice in international fora, especially on issues between the US and China.

Q: *The aftermath of the 2008 global recession has seen a new wave of protectionism, with some trade tariffs up, and certain countries imposing capital controls against what they see is "hot money" from the West. What is your assessment of the current state of affairs compared to past crises which also sparked such protectionist instincts?*

A: Protectionism always becomes pronounced when there is imbalance in trade between countries, in this particular case between America and China. I do not think it is correct to say that 2008 saw a new wave of protectionism.

Q: *Did the pace of the economic recovery in Singapore surprise you? What do you think Singapore did right? How much can be attributed to policymakers here and how much to the rising tide of the global recovery that appears to have lifted all boats in Asia?*

A: The pace of the economy in Singapore was only slightly better than I expected. Singapore's banks, and the fundamentals of its economy, are sound. I am not that sure the rise in tide of the global recovery has lifted all boats in Asia. China and India have lifted some of their neighbours, but not all their neighbours.

Q: *The Economic Strategies Committee made some broad recommendations. One of them is to grow 1,000 SMEs with an annual turnover of more than $100 million over the next decade. Do you think this is something worth pursuing given your view that it is MNCs that drive the Singapore economy?*

A: We should still try to get our SMEs to grow. Eventually, some of them must be able to become competitive worldwide and be a Singapore MNC. The MNCs will always drive the Singapore economy because it is highly unlikely that 1,000 SMEs will become 1,000 MNCs.

Q: *People always say that when the economy recovers from a crisis, lessons are very soon forgotten. What is the one lesson that Singapore must learn from this recent crisis, and arising from that, what changes would you consider a must?*

A: There is no one single lesson that Singapore must derive from this crisis. Each crisis has different origins. The next crisis is unlikely to be exactly the same.

Q: *Have the integrated resorts made a bigger impact than you expected? Do you worry about their ill-effects? And is there a next big thing for the economy?*

A: I expected the integrated resorts to increase tourism and increase revenue from the casinos. We have done our best to anticipate the ill-effects by imposing a $100 entrance fee for

Singaporeans and permanent residents, and allowing members of the family to bar another member who has got caught up with the casino habits of gambling. However, there will always be casualties.

There will always be another big thing coming for the economy. It is only a matter of time.

Is Singapore growing too fast?

Q: *Ten years ago, I don't think I heard the criticism that Singapore is growing too fast, but increasingly the argument is that there is a price to pay, having to import lots of foreign workers and foreign talent, with all the social costs associated with it. Is it sustainable to want to grow "as fast as possible" which appears to be the government policy?*

A: We should grow as fast as we can sustain that growth. If we can make that growth and we choose not to, then we are stupid. Some Singaporeans do not understand what slow growth means. We get slow growth and we will have fewer jobs and lower pay, less this, less that, less everything. Will you have a pay cut deliberately imposed on yourself? That's stupid, isn't it? If you can make the growth and you don't make it, there's something wrong with you.

Q: *But some people are so unhappy with the social problems they associate with high growth that it's conceivable they may not mind slower wage growth.*

A: All right, so why this grumble? Because the MRT and buses are getting more crowded, so our people feel that the foreigners are squeezing them for space. And when they go to the shops and *kopitiam*, they don't like it when the workers can't speak English. Supposing these foreign workers were not here to prepare the food and clean the tables, can the *kopitiam* continue to operate?

The real truth is Singaporeans have watched the new immigrants and say, "Wow, their children are going to compete with mine for school places, scholarships and jobs". Their children work hard and do well in school. They came to Singapore without much English and after four or five years, many top the class in English. Furthermore, the vast majority of foreigners are work permit holders doing the heavy jobs, those who do not have the qualifications to become PRs or citizens. The concerns with the work permit workers have to do with security and social disturbances. Singaporeans know that these workers are here temporarily. They can't bring their dependants with them. The unhappiness about competition is with the new citizens and their children.

Q: *Putting aside those worries about foreigners usurping jobs and school places, the problem is that an influx of low-cost labour depresses wages for the low-income, and this increases the gap between rich and poor in Singapore.*

A: This is a worldwide phenomenon. In the first stage of globalisation, you will have access to a labour market filled with hundreds of millions of cheap workers. But will this go on forever? In 30 years, the people in the developing countries will become better educated and better paid. Every year, the education system in China is reducing the country's illiteracy rate. They're raising standards. So it will find its own level. I mean, you take China today and 20 years ago. Look at the output of engineers and scientists. Look at the numbers who go into universities. So the income disparity will not widen forever.

We have kept the differences between lower and higher incomes as bearable as we can make it. If you take too much from the high income earners, they will leave. Why should they stay? The foreigners will definitely leave. You raise income tax and they go off to Hong Kong or some other place and put up with the pollution there. And some of our own people may also say I'm going off to another place where I don't have to pay this level of income tax. So you got to balance all that and in the end, in order for there to be any motivation to succeed, you must give them the opportunity to accumulate or keep a major part of their earnings.

Then you find a way through the overall Budget to support and redistribute – through subsidies for water and power bills, S&C (service and conservancy) charges, education, housing, healthcare and, more important, ensure that the next generation has the opportunities to start on a more even playing field. Nobody in Singapore and no child is being disadvantaged, whether your family is dysfunctional or otherwise. You've got some group that will look after you and make sure that you get all the opportunities to receive a proper education. If you choose to drop out, that's your decision. Fewer are doing so, as parents can see how their neighbours' children who did well in education have moved up and out to better flats.

You also give them a substantial amount to buy a home which we know is going to increase in value. It is the most substantial stake they will have when they retire. It may cost $200,000 when they buy it and by the time they retire, it's worth a lot more. The properties must go up in value because our economy is growing and the government regularly improves the infrastructure and living environment. We have more and more underground and above-ground trains, beautiful parks and waterways, it's a deliberate policy to give everybody a stake in sharing the country's growth.

Q: *Still, the disparity in Singapore is more severe than in other countries, as measured by the Gini coefficient. It's more severe than say, Japan, where they do not have an open door policy that brings in large numbers of foreign workers.*

A: No, no, no. Japan is not the model for us. Japan is going to go through a very tough period – a shrinking and fast-ageing population. They do not want migrants and there's a xenophobic streak in them. But I think they are in deep trouble. No, you've got to compare Singapore with Hong Kong, KL, Bangkok, Manila and Jakarta. That's our environment. How can you compare yourself with Japan? Japan is a totally different country with a very different society and culture.

Q: *The point is that we might want to bring about a more equal society that's closer to their model...*

A: If you want an equal society with equal rewards, then you go back to the iron rice bowl. No, we have created a system which is fair in that what you earn depends on your performance. And your performance depends on your education, skills and abilities. That's that. If we pretend that everybody is equal when they are not, the system will malfunction. That's a fact of life.

My major objective in the early days was to make sure that nobody derails the idea of having individual accounts for CPF and Medisave. Whatever you earn, it's yours. Because once you have that individual account, any suggestion that you put it into a common pool and everybody takes out from it (as with other welfare systems) is bound to lose you votes. Before these accounts became substantial, the idea might have sold. So if Low Thia Khiang says now, let's set up a common pool, I think he'll lose votes in the next election. Are you prepared to put your money into a common pool, having slogged and built up your CPF nest egg? It's yours. If you don't use it, you can leave it to your children or your relatives or whoever you like. Why should you put it into a common pool and everybody draws out at your expense, which is what's happening in some Western countries? The system has collapsed. Tony Blair tried to create individual accounts in Britain, he came here and studied us, but there was huge opposition from the people, so he was stuck.

Q: *So you are saying that we shouldn't change our policy on foreign workers in the name of narrowing income disparities?*

A: It's far more economic and effective to import foreign labour and get the work done, and give the low-income something on the side to close the gap with the higher earners. Here is an opportunity to use labour, which is hungry, at a fraction of your cost and you don't want that? You look at the British. How have they kept their economy going? Because they invite foreign workers in. The net result is they got a very polyglot community now. Eastern Europeans, South Asians, North Africans, Africans south of the Sahara, Caribbeans ... are all there because the British don't want to do the jobs they are willing to do.

We have had free flow of talent. It has helped our economy and helped our growth. We are not ignorant or silly. We are doing this with the interests of the population of Singapore at heart. If going the other way is better, are we that stupid not to adopt it? Would we be here today if we had stopped these work permit holders from coming in? In construction we tried pre-fabrication for HDB. We can look for other ways to reduce our reliance on foreign workers but there's a limit to what can be done.[5]

Q: *One benefit of doing it differently is that the productivity of the local workers must go up, whether it's in construction industry or elsewhere. I know what you are saying about the difference between Japan and Singapore. We're obviously not Japan but one consequence of their way of organising society is that the wages at lower levels have gone up.*

A: But what has happened to the economy as a whole? I mean, look at the end result. Is Japan better off? Are the Japanese people better off? Electorally, the politicians will say, well, I'm winning the votes this way. But is this the future for Japan? Rather bleak and dismal, isn't it? They've got to change.

You just envisage what Singapore will be if we had adopted the Japanese model and closed our doors to immigrants and foreign workers. Will we have today's Singapore? Let me give you a few personal encounters to understand the Singaporean outlook on life. I have a shoemaker who's a Hakka. He is now 40 plus, took over the job from his father who used to be my shoemaker. But it's a dying trade. It's not that he is not making money. I have to pay him $300 for a pair of shoes. He has to take my footprint, measure it and let me try the shoes. I often say no, have soft leather and so on. So he charges me $350 or $400, it can't be helped. But does his son want to do that? No, the son wants to go to university and work in an air-conditioned office.

The trade is dying. Who's going to climb up your scaffoldings at the construction sites? Who's going to go to the dockyards and take up a blowtorch? Are Singaporeans willing to do these jobs? You can pay them twice the salary, they will still say no.

You watch the buildings being constructed. When they are already up, then Singaporeans come in and put the electric cabling and other things in, in covered conditions. When it is open to the elements, you find Indians, Bangladeshis, Chinese from China and others. We can pay Singaporeans more, but will they do it? No, because there are other job opportunities which they consider more attractive. It is the mindset, what they think should be their status in life.

The Australian building industry forced it, because they did not want to bring in Asian workers. So they said, all right, we pay a much higher cost for our construction. But now Asians are coming in and their system will break down. It's happening even in China. We used to get these black-and-white *amahs* (housekeepers who wore black trousers and white tunics at work). Now they are educated, they're not going to come here and be your *amah*. They're going to work in a factory or a hotel.

So the world is going through social changes. If you are an Indonesian or a Filipino or an Indian or a Bangladeshi, you have no choice. So just be grateful that your sisters and cousins and so on do not have to work as maids. But if you mismanage this place, the bright fellows will leave. The not-so-bright, not-so-educated cannot leave and then they are in the position the Filipinos and Indonesians and Bangladeshis are in, that's that.

Q: *But that doesn't change the fact that there is a political cost. People at the lower end feel that to some extent the system is stacked against them. A large part of the growth benefits those at the top. It's made for a more cynical society as well, at the lower end. Do you accept that there is a cost to that system?*

A: The pressure of envy is inevitable. But consider the alternative, which is slow growth. The disparity will still be there between the high end and the low end because of globalisation, but we are all poorer, right? We are all poorer because if you do away with the foreign talent and the foreign workers, our GDP will go down by at least 2 or 2.5 percentage points. You can calculate based on the workers and their inputs.

A Singapore company succeeds and it goes to Qatar. The people who are going to be taken there by our companies are going to have to be paid more to put up with the heat and the strangeness of the environment. He is going to be paid at least 150 per cent of his salary here – house, cost of living, children's education if necessary. Similarly, if he goes to China or Vietnam or India.

I'm a worker, I see my supervisor going abroad because they need someone to supervise the workmen there. But I'm not taken because they've already got unskilled and semi-skilled workers there. I feel some angst. I say this is unfair. But the world is unfair.

So I see no benefit in stopping growth because the envy will still be there. Instead, we cream off the growth and redistribute it to support the lower end. And you got to support them in ways that don't remove motivation.

Q: *As the income disparity widens, wouldn't the political pressure on the Singapore government build to redistribute more and more to the lower income?*

A: So you say to me, the chaps at the bottom will become anti-government. Do we change because of that or do we say, "Right, we are likely going to lose that number of votes each time and so we've got to win from the median upwards"? I mean, that's politics. If the median upwards is less than the median downwards, then we have to lower the median. We're watching that very carefully. How many are in private homes, how many in executives, five-rooms and now four-rooms? Four-roomers used to be above the median but because everybody believes that they can have bigger capital gains, they buy a four-room when they can really only afford a three-room.

But I don't think we should redistribute more and more in a way that will remove motivation. Our biggest redistribution is through public housing. Every Singaporean gets a home. Your home is sold to you and with generous subsidies. So in other words, immediately you start with chips on the table. And 30 years later, when you retire, the value of that home will increase manyfold.

Then next, CPF. The government keeps on topping up the accounts, not for people to spend the money but for their retirement, healthcare needs and children's education. We also issue New Singapore Shares and Economic Restructuring Shares to Singaporeans when there are surpluses.

Q: *Listening to you, is it possible to do both – be open to foreign talent and let the upper end earn high wages, but also do more for the lower end in terms of the salaries that they can command? Assets in the home and CPF, that's good, but can we go further?*

A: So we have Workfare (an income supplement scheme for low wage workers). Workfare is just beginning and we'll have to refine it. But the principle is that you must work. We are not going to pay you for lying around. The Workfare will have to go up, not too fast I hope, because it's bound to balloon.

Q: *Actually one view of Workfare is that it's the beginning of this entitlement mentality that you warn against.*

A: Not quite. A person must work before he can receive Workfare.

Q: *Yes, but the way they structure it now, if you are above 35 years old, you can work just two or three days a week so that you fall under the income criteria...*

A: No, Singapore is in a recession at the moment so we got to help them out. But the point remains that they need to work before they can receive Workfare.

Q: *But Workfare was created in the boom years. It started in 2007, so there is a point of view that actually Singapore is already beginning the slippery slope down to welfarism.*

A: Well, every time we do something like that, we are taking a little step into the unknown. But as long as people know they need to work, it is okay.

Q: *Could it become an incentive to under-work?*

A: No, I don't think so. If we give too much, then it becomes an incentive and people don't want to work. But you give just enough to tide him over and he knows if he learns a new skill, he'll earn more.

That's why we are putting so much effort into SPUR (Skills Programme for Upgrading and Resilience) and other job training and upgrading programmes. We encourage the workers to retrain so that when the economy picks up, they are into a higher category and their earnings would go up. In today's world, your worth is determined by your skills and knowledge. You may be a genius but if you got nothing to sell in the market, how much are you worth?

Q: *Given the angst that people feel about the widening income disparity, do you think politically it would be good for the government to take on, let's say, controlling the Gini coefficient or the size of the disparity as a defined policy objective? Right now civil servants have their bonuses tied to GDP and some have suggested we should tie it to some extent to some measure of income inequality or to the lowest income levels.*

A: We need to pay competitive salaries in the public sector because we are competing for talent against the private sector. And already today as we study the number of president scholarships, overseas merit, SAF, police, the numbers do not tally with the bright kids coming out from junior colleges. Why? Because they are either self-funded or going on private scholarships. The bottom line is that we are in competition with the private sector, not just companies in Singapore but from around the world. You got to face that reality.

Q: *I guess if the civil servant successfully narrows the income gap, he will get a bonus.*

A: (Laughing) To narrow the income gap, you need the whole machinery of government and you may not succeed. Look, the Japanese were one of the most egalitarian of all the developed countries, right? Modest take-home pay for their corporate leaders and lifetime employment. Under international pressure of globalisation, they're changing. Sony and Nissan are both taking Westerners, right? They're competing for top talent. They've got to break out of their own system to compete globally. So more and more foreigners are entering their corporate system and changing the system.

It is not a static situation in Japan. Now you see pictures of people sleeping under bridges in winter. That never happened in the old days. They went through a war in which the poorest of the farmers bore a grudge because they lost their sons and they lost their homes. So there was a tremendous feeling that they owed something to these people.

Similarly, the British. It came from a guilt complex. The people who lost their lives and their homes were not the officers who went to Oxbridge but the rank and file, the conscripts. So the rich came out with a system supported by the Labour Party and adopted by the Conservative Party. From cradle to grave, the upper class owes it to them.

They didn't think of the consequences and the impact on motivation until the system malfunctioned. Then Margaret Thatcher began to reverse the process. Tony Blair carried on with the process. Now Gordon Brown is tempted to reverse it back to win votes from the lower income group.

You've got to understand we're not going to be in this income inequality position indefinitely. How long will this position last? 10, 20 or 30 years. And then what? Then new technology, new competitors, new patterns of work and lifestyles will begin to impact us.

Why control so much of the economy?

Q: *What is your response to the view that the government controls too much of the economy? I think the criticism is not so much in the early years where people understand that the government needed to take control. But the dominance of the state is still fairly prevalent and widespread. Do you see that as an issue or a problem, going forward?*

A: As more and more of the talented don't join the government and join the private sector – provided they're not leaking abroad, if they come back – then the private sector will in time have the intellectual capacity to take over these big corporations from us. As I said, we want to privatise, but at the moment, who do you privatise to?

You look at DBS and OCBC (banks). They've got to go for foreign talent. UOB depends on (its chairman) Wee Cho Yaw, but who's taking over from him? Where's the talent pool in UOB to select a strong CEO? The chap that used to be in line, Ernest Wong, left because he knew he wasn't going to get the job. Wee Cho Yaw was grooming his son.

If these bright students who are now going abroad and not taking scholarships don't permanently stay abroad, then I can see in 10 or 15 years you can have a private sector that can match the public sector talent. We can already see the public sector talent pool has shrunk compared to what we were gathering 10 or 15 years ago. I mean how many ministers' sons have taken scholarships? Lim Hng Kiang's sons have not taken scholarships. Teo Chee Hean's has.

Q: *But in the meantime, what's the solution? Is the private sector destined to be weak?*

A: No, as I told you, will the talent go there? Look, we've got to run (shipping line) NOL, so who do we get? Cheng Wai Keung. For SIA, who do we have? Stephen Lee. For DBS, Koh Boon Hwee.[6] Who else, you tell me? Who else we can entrust the big corporations to?

Q: *You mentioned SIA earlier. How did you come to that conclusion that Ong Beng Seng can't handle SIA as opposed to Stephen Lee?*

A: Because I know Ong Beng Seng and I know how he operates. He's not an organisation man. He's an entrepreneur and an oil dealer. He goes out and captures this deal and that, then he hands it over to somebody to run it.

Q: *Can Ong Beng Seng hire an organisation man to take care of the organisational parts?*

A: Yes, he can. But does he want to run an organisation? I go abroad and bring him along. He strikes friendships and does deals. His target, he is off on his own. That's his forte. He started life as an oil dealer for his father-in-law. In the end, he did better than his father-in-law. Then he did hotels, his wife did boutiques. He's in London with Nobu Japanese restaurant. He took a partial share in a hotel at Canary Wharf. So he goes into many little ventures, then sells out for a profit.

But Stephen Lee ran his father's textile company and carried it forward, and moved into other sectors. He speaks Mandarin, which Ong Beng Seng doesn't. So he can operate in China and talk to their corporate and government leaders. He also has great experience dealing with the unions.

These are gems, but where do we find more of them? We use them, and overuse them, overload them because there are so few of them. In China, they have so many talented people but then, at the top, they only have a few they entrust with heavy responsibilities.

Q: *So these are people you trust. Do you trust Stephen Lee?*

A: I trust them and their judgment. Over repeated meetings, I found him upright. A few ministers who have worked with him also hold the same views.

Q: *Is there a danger that you are in fact overusing them? Is there a danger, because the government is so dominant in the economy, of "groupthink"? That there is one particular thinking about how the economy operates and what needs to be done. We don't have the same diversity that you would have had if it were all completely private sector and different CEOs and different entrepreneurs running different sectors of the economy.*

A: You tell me what the different sectors of the economy in Singapore are. The manufacturing is done largely by MNCs. In logistics, we are in open competition – PSA against Maersk in Tanjong Pelepas and so on. SIA is in competition against other major airlines. Changi Airport is in competition with KL, Bangkok, Incheon and Hong Kong. Everywhere you face the competition. Now Dubai. You name me the sectors where you feel we have "groupthink". Each sector is facing a completely different set of circumstances.

Q: *Were Singapore's attempts to hire top foreign talent for our companies failures?*

A: They say John Olds was a failure and who else? Philippe Paillart, Flemming Jacobs? Are they failures?[7] No, I don't think so. John Olds sent me papers about what the weaknesses in DBS were and they were insightful. I made DBS look into them and to change. Why did he leave? We didn't kick him out. He left because he did not see DBS as a big regional bank. He went back to San Francisco because he did not want to run a medium-size Singapore bank.

In the case of Flemming Jacobs, NOL was in trouble anyway. Look at Maersk in Denmark. The CEO was sacked because he took over P&O and caused a big loss. In the end, we put the APL CEO, an American, in charge of NOL, when we merged with APL. We faced the company's problem of the two merging company cultures. We could not Singaporeanise APL because Americans ran the whole system. So we say, "All right, get the Americans to look at NOL, the non-APL side, and see what he can do." This was Cheng Wai Keung's recommendation to us. He is a shrewd private sector executive.

Successful CEOs are like gems you find on a beach. There are many pebbles, many beautifully coloured ones, but they are all stones. Now and again, you will come across a real precious gem, a real emerald, pick it up, polish it. He must have a set of qualities that fits with the job, has energy, drive, ability to interact with people, ability to get people to work with him in a team.

Q: *Since we have Temasek and GIC, and these are huge investment vehicles, why can't we get them to put more money into, let's say, our 10 of the biggest up and coming private companies here in Singapore and help them to grow globally and then they can compete?*

A: That depends on whether these investments can yield good returns. You tell me which 10 companies.

Q: *Maybe we are not looking hard enough. We have done it before with promising companies. Temasek did invest in Hyflux and helped it to grow.*

A: First, GIC does not invest in Singapore at all. This is a deliberate decision to safeguard our reserves. If our assets are abroad and the Singapore economy turns down, not all our assets will be down.

Temasek is different, they take over and run a company and sell it off again for a profit. They took over Indosat in Indonesia. The Russians came in and wanted to buy us out. We refused, so they bribed Indonesian officials who put pressure on us. We sold out to Qatar, and Qatar settled with them. Qatar remains the owner, and we did not lose money.

A Singapore company that can go global and succeed as an MNC will have no problems raising capital from the banks and financial markets. It does not need to wait for Temasek to invest in it.

Q: *Finally, how do you see the Singapore economy developing long after you have gone?*

A: In the next 10 years, I think, we are going to forge ahead. You look at the URA plans which are coming to fruition: Marina Bay, Singapore River, Collyer Quay, Boat Quay, Orchard Road, Formula One, two integrated resorts, and the strong confidence of investors in us. ExxonMobil brought their whole board to meet the Prime Minister and me. In this recession, they had decided to proceed with a new cracker plant in Singapore that's worth more than US$4 billion. Why? It's because Singapore is steady and reliable. The government is stable, the labour-employer situation is good. We have connections with major cities across the world. We are no longer going for low-end factories and low-tech industries. We can't compete in these sectors.

Our challenge now is how to retrain and upgrade the older workers, those above 40 and who missed their education because we did not have the ITEs and the polys then. That's a big challenge.

The young workers are better educated: 25 to 30 per cent in universities, 40 per cent in polytechnics, 20 plus per cent in ITEs. But not the older workers. And that's why the Ministry of Manpower and NTUC place a lot of emphasis on skills retraining and job upgrading.

The next 10 years, maybe even the next 20 years, can be a quantum leap for Singapore's economy.

Endnotes

1   Lee has switched from Warfarin to another blood-thinner called Plavix. See chapter 11.

2   ExxonMobil is building its second petrochemical complex on Jurong Island, a US$5 billion investment. It is expected to be in operation in 2011.

3   Dr Daniel Vasella, Novartis chairman and chief executive.

4   Philip Yeo is currently chairman of Spring Singapore and the Special Advisor for Economic Development in the Prime Minister's Office. During his tenure as chairman of the government's Agency for Science, Technology and Research (A*Star), Yeo played an integral role in developing the biomedical industry of Singapore.

5   The Economic Strategies Committee noted that continuing to increase the number of foreign workers as liberally as was done in the past would lead to real physical and social limitations. Companies would also have little incentive to invest in productivity improvements, which would keep wages of lower-income workers depressed. So while foreign workers will remain important to Singapore's labour force, in a shift from previous thinking, the government will raise the foreign worker levy progressively in a bid to control the inflow of labour from abroad.

6   The foreign versus local talent debate shows little sign of abating. Peter Seah took over from Koh Boon Hwee in 2010 as DBS Group's chairman. In his first interview (June 2010), Seah reignited the debate. He said that in a choice between a Singaporean and a foreigner for the post of chief executive, where both have the same qualifications, the job should go to the local. This has nothing to do with nationality, he said, as there are "natural advantages for Singaporeans in terms of relationships with the business community, people, and with the government". DBS has not had a home-grown CEO since 1998. Current CEO Piyush Gupta, while now a Singapore citizen, was born in India.

7   John Olds, an American, was chief executive of DBS from 1998 to 2001. Frenchman Philippe Paillart succeeded him, holding the post until 2002. Flemming Jacobs, a Dane, was chief executive of Neptune Orient Lines and stepped down in 2003 after helming the company for just over three years.

5 TOUGH LOVE

I N THE QUIET of the West Drawing Room at the Istana, framed, autographed pictures of the world's dignitaries and their beautiful, accomplished wives are displayed on credenzas, parting gifts from courtesy calls. They are fitting witnesses to what Lee will speak on over the course of two conversations in April 2009 on the subject of social policy, welfarism and his pet topic – the inheritability of intelligence.

If Lee notices the interviewers' discomfiture at hearing him talk about intelligence deterministically as if it were a physical feature that is passed on – like curly hair or brown eyes – he does not let on. Nor is he apologetic about his most politically incorrect assertions. Indeed, he goes on to draw from a wealth of anecdote to back this firmly-held view on the link between genes and intelligence.

In a nutshell, his beliefs are these: Human beings are created unequal, and no amount of social engineering or government intervention can significantly alter one's lot in life. At most, government policies can help equalise opportunity at the starting point, but they cannot ensure equal outcomes. Society is bound to end up with unequal outcomes, where the more able end up better off financially and socially than the less able. For Lee, this is no reason to hold back the able. Instead, the solution is to create the conditions for the ablest to go far so they can bring in jobs for the masses – and then redistribute the surpluses to help the less able. It's a controversial topic for any country's leader to discuss: The distribution of wealth in a society, and how much help to extend to the have-nots.

In the case of Lee, it is even more so, given the strong views he holds.

To argue his points, Lee goes back to his formative years as a young political leader. It was the early 1960s. The problems in Singapore's Southern Islands worried Lee. They were strongholds of the Malay-based UMNO party which was dominant in peninsular Malaysia and was trying to make inroads into Singapore. The People's Action Party was trying to exert its influence in the Southern Islands with Parliamentary Secretary Yaacob Mohamed as its representative. Yaacob would later be elected assemblyman for Southern Islands from 1963 to 1968.

Social conditions in the islands were poor. Even nutrition was an issue. The PAP government wanted to introduce goat farming on the islands to create a more sustainable livelihood for the people. It got Works Brigade volunteers and officials to help clear land and introduced grasses specially chosen to be good feed for goats. Two hundred goats from Kelantan were bought and given to 76 families in 1961.[1] But the goats soon disappeared – presumably slaughtered for their meat.

When Lee recounted the incident to a doctor who was attending to him, the orthopaedic surgeon said the islanders faced bigger problems. Intermarriage had shrunk their gene pool and they had all sorts of orthopaedic problems – and the doctor suspected the problems extended to their brain structure.

Later, Lee mulled over the doctor's words. If intermarriage within a closed community resulted in problems with the bone and skeletal structure, could it indeed affect the development of the brain? If that were so, mused Lee, would the community be better off being integrated into the larger mainland and marrying among a more diverse gene pool? From the doctor's observation about the orthopaedic problems of a closed society whose members intermarried one another, Lee drew two conclusions. One: that diversity enriches the genetic pool. Two: that traits like intelligence – or bone structure – were influenced greatly by genetic heritage.

Lee's belief that intelligence is genetically determined is well-known and has been commented upon. What is remarkable is that at age 86, he shows no sign of having softened his views.

He did not start off with that intuition though. Instead, like other idealistic young people of his generation who grew up in the 1930s and 1940s, he bought into the prevailing socialist theories that people were innately equal, and that it was only unequal opportunities that resulted in some doing better than others.

In England, he attended a few lectures by prominent English political theorist and Labour Party leader Harold Laski and found his ideas attractive. As he wrote in his memoirs *The Singapore Story*, "It struck me as manifestly fair that everybody in this world should be given an equal chance in life, that in a just and well-ordered society there should not be a great disparity of wealth between persons because of their position or status, or that of their parents."

Lee was attracted to the ideal of an equal, just and fair society. He did not subscribe to the Leninist revolutionary methods of overthrowing the capital-owning class to create a classless society. He found the more reformist Fabian socialist ideas attractive for their step-by-step, evolutionary approach to creating a just society, for example by providing nationalised healthcare and education for all. He subscribed to the Fabian magazines and pamphlets for many years.

In an interview for the book *The Man and His Ideas*, he said, "We believed, all of us ... when we started off in the 1940s, that differences between individuals and individual performance and results were mainly because of opportunities. Given better opportunities of nutrition, food, clothing, training, housing and health, differences would be narrowed. It was much later, when we pursued these policies in the '60s, in the '70s, that the reality dawned on us."

There is a tinge of regret at having to give up an emotionally-appealing ideal in the face of reality. "It was only after I had been in office for some years that I recognised that performance varied substantially between the different races in Singapore, and among different categories in the same race. After trying out a number of ways to reduce inequalities and failing, I was gradually forced to conclude that the decisive factors were the people, their natural abilities, education and training," he wrote in *The Singapore Story*.

Listening to Lee during the April 2009 interviews, one can discern several incidents and influences that led him to conclude that people were not created equal, and to abandon the ideal of creating a society that had equal rewards for all.

First was the sheer pressure of actually running a country, once he became Prime Minister in 1959. With the pressing problems of creating jobs, building homes and schools, Lee learnt fast that talk about an equal society and equitable income distribution rang hollow unless there was income to distribute. He realised it was more important to create wealth first – and worry later how to distribute it.

Exposure to the problems faced by different communities in Singapore also led him to conclude that abilities varied across different social groups, determined by the genetic heritage of each race or socioeconomic group. Two incidents stood out in his recollections. One was an exchange with a constituent of his ward in Tanjong Pagar, a Chinese teacher who taught English at Pasir Panjang School. Among the students were Tamil children, offspring of the Tamil cleaners brought in by the British to work at power stations.

"One day after a meeting, I said, 'How's your school?' He said, 'Well, not too bad.' But he added, 'The Indian children, the Tamil children from that Pasir Panjang power station, they can't add, they can't multiply.' I said, 'Why is that?' He said, 'I don't know.' So I asked a neurologist, 'Why is that?' He said, 'Well, some people are innumerate.' There's a word which says that you can't handle numbers: dyscalculia."

Lee prides himself on his interest in theories of human society, and tests his theories against observations of reality.

"I began to watch the Indians and they have a caste system. If you marry below your caste, your children will belong to the lower caste, so they never marry below their caste."

He recalls that he had a secretary who was from the Brahmin class, son of the chief priest of the Tank Road Temple. "He was as bright as any administrative officer, but in his time no scholarship, he didn't go to university, so he became a PA (personal assistant) but a very able man. And of course he married another Brahmin.

"So I made enquiries. I said, 'Why are Brahmins so bright?' And I asked the Indians. They said, 'Well, because the priests must be Brahmins and they must know whatever language they're living in and also know Sanskrit, to read the sacred texts.' So their literary capabilities are very high, and mathematics capabilities too. And all the rich Brahmins want their children to marry the priests' daughters or sons because they're sure that the genes will be good."

As he absorbed these explanations on why Indians of the Brahmin caste tended to marry each other, resulting in a closed gene pool not accessible to other castes, Lee thought, "No wonder. The chaps at the bottom of the heap never got the advantage of those genes."

This was different from, say, China, where generations of able scholar officials selected by a merit-based imperial examination system married into the Emperor's household and had multiple wives or concubines. "When they retire they go to Suzhou ... and have umpteen wives. So a large progeny. So the genes pass down ... This is not by accident."

The way Lee sees it, the best way to nurture intelligence is through selective crossbreeding over the generations, to get the best possible genes to make smart babies. But even Lee accepts that this is not possible in today's society. It did not, however, prevent him from trying to introduce some element of eugenics into government policies in the past.

Lee's views on the heritability of IQ are contentious, with scientists divided on the issue. The idea that the differences in IQ scores among the races can be attributed to genes was popularised by psychologist Richard J. Herrnstein and political scientist Charles Murray in their book *The Bell Curve*. Lee rated the book highly when it was first published in 1994. Herrnstein and Murray argued that performance varied by race and that some racial groups have better cognitive capabilities than others. Further studies by psychologist Richard Lynn found that East Asians had the highest average IQ score of 105. East and West Africans, Australian Aborigines and Bushmen had the lowest scores. Herrnstein and Murray's results were hotly contested by evolutionary biologist Stephen J. Gould, who wrote *The Mismeasure of Man* to criticise the use of standardised psychometric tests as an indicator of intelligence.

Other economists, biologists and statisticians have questioned Herrnstein's and Murray's methodology and findings. Even if IQ showed strong signs of heritability, critics say it is simplistic to conclude that smart parents breed smart children. IQ is not fixed over an individual's entire lifetime. Neither does high IQ consistently predict professional success. Traits such as intelligence are also highly dependent on learning and the environment. For example, an impoverished environment could suppress otherwise bright individuals. Evolutionary geneticist Richard Lewontin, neurobiologist Steven Rose and psychologist Leon J. Kamin have found that the heritability of intelligence increases with education and social class. A French study of adopted children from poor backgrounds found that those adopted by farmers and labourers saw a smaller increase in IQ after nine years than those adopted by middle class parents.

Lee's views on the intransigence of genes are so strongly held as to be dogmatic and indeed repellent to some. Not that he cares, so convinced is he that he is right.

Having observed goats and dogs, and Indian students, he went on to observe American professors. In 1968, in his ninth year as Prime Minister, he took a sabbatical at Harvard University in Cambridge, Massachusetts to recharge and get fresh ideas. He noticed that Harvard professors whose wives were also professors had very smart children who went to the Ivy League universities. Those who married their graduate students had children who were bright and some not so bright. Hence Lee inferred that a smart man who married a smart woman would more likely sire smart children.

Lee's PAP colleague Toh Chin Chye did not believe theories about how IQ is inherited, and was wont to say, "Five washerwomen will produce a genius." But to Lee, this was "rubbish", given that the law of probability would stack the odds against such an occurrence happening. (At least one Cabinet Minister, Mah Bow Tan, is the son of a washerwoman. Lee's counter to this would be that societies get assorted with rising levels of education.)

When Lee's children were growing up, he used to tell them about the statement philosopher George Bernard Shaw is reputed to have made when a beautiful woman proposed to have children with him: "If you marry a girl and you think your daughter will be as pretty as her and your son will be as bright as you, you're dead wrong. When you marry a girl, if the son is as bright as the mother, you must be happy that that is so."

The message hit home for the young Lees, recalled the proud father. Both his sons, Hsien Loong and Hsien Yang, married successful women and all seven of his grandchildren have a high IQ, he said.

Eldest grandson and son of Lee Hsien Loong, Yipeng, suffers from Asperger's syndrome, a mild form of autism that impairs his social skills. He is also an albino, with weakened vision. "But he has got high IQ and he graduated from NUS (National University of Singapore). He's slower because he had to have binoculars to read the blackboards and bus numbers. All the other six, no trouble in their studies," said Lee.

"So when the graduate man does not want to marry a graduate woman, I tell him he's a fool, stupid. You marry your clerk or your secretary, you're going to have problems, some children bright, some not bright. You'll be tearing your hair out."

He subjects himself to the same genetic scrutiny. He compares himself to former Vice-Premier of China, Li Lanqing, whom he has met several times. Lee thought the Chinese leader was like Singapore ministers – intelligent, good at debate and persuasion. He only found out later, when Li launched a series of books in 2006 in Singapore on music, education and art, and exhibited his seal carving art, just how accomplished a pianist and artist the Chinese leader was.

Li is from Zhenjiang near the Suzhou area, famed for its intelligent and cultivated people. Suzhou is also where court officials once retired to.

"You want to equal him? Can I do that? I can do mathematics, I can do the arguments. You ask me, 'Can you play piano?' I can't, he can. He knows Mozart, Beethoven. He writes about them. I read his book. I was dumbfounded. When I met him, I thought he was just a minister like the way we are. But no, he's a cultivated man of many parts.

"Why? Generations of talent. In China you breed them for culture, for calligraphy. He does calligraphy. He carves seals. He plays music on the piano. And he's also got brains. Just consider that. That's selective breeding over the centuries."

Lee says he himself came from humbler stock. Chinese scholars worked out his genealogy. "They gave me my genetic table of my family in Dapu. The only outstanding ancestor was six steps up. He was the military governor of Guangxi. They underlined him, only one."

Doesn't this disprove his theory about the genetic basis of intelligence?

"Ya, but the Chinese go by only the male line. Somewhere along the line, some female passed it on to me. My mother? I don't know. The Chinese fixation with the male is mistaken, completely mistaken. It's gone on for so many years, so many millennia, they can't change. It's a mindset. But in actual practice they know. Watch the leaders, watch their leaders' children, who they marry. These are people who have risen from the ranks. They are producing a new elite."

To Lee, environment and nurturing plays a much smaller role in shaping one's final abilities. "When I grew up, my father had no books at home. He's not a reader. He was a rich man's son who had accounts in John Little and Robinsons.[2] His father paid for it. He had no books, no dictionaries.

"My mother was educated to standard two or standard three. But she's a capable woman. She encouraged me to forge ahead. And so did my brothers and my sister. In her generation, girls don't matter, just get them married. That's then.

"Would I have been a greater, more knowledgeable person if I had a home with books and classical music and so on? Not too much. I have achieved my maximum. What I missed in the early years, I've made up in subsequent years. That's life."

"The problem for the
government is: how do you keep
a society united when that lower
layer can never catch up?"

Q: *How did you form your views about the correct social policy for Singapore, and how have those views changed or not changed over the years?*

A: What I know now I did not know when I started. I had certain basic beliefs which were gathered from books, from teachers, from friends, namely that all men are equal and all men should have the same rewards in a just world. That was why socialism was supported by so many people all over the world. And you must remember that was in the 1950s when the Soviet Union sent Sputnik up. So it was even prevalent in Cambridge (University). Although the main trend was against such beliefs, many students believed that this was one way of moving forward quickly for newly-independent countries.

It doesn't work. In the end, Deng Xiaoping knew the iron rice bowl doesn't work. Human motivation and human nature being what it is, the driving force in a human being is to stay alive, then to sacrifice his life for his wife, his children, his mother and father in the family and the clan, in that order. I came to that conclusion watching how Britain's socialism policy of cradle to grave, womb to tomb had failed.

Q: *You mentioned in the past that not all of your Cabinet supported this view – that people are innately unequal. How did you get your views to prevail?*

A: Logic. The people who were solidly in my support were Goh Keng Swee, S. Rajaratnam, Hon Sui Sen, Lim Kim San, all the practical people who got to handle the finances. And it's the socialist types, you know, influenced by the ideal of an equal society who wanted an egalitarian society. And I didn't believe it was possible.

As I watched first the Soviet Union, then China, now Vietnam, the first generation – they came from all ranks. They were the freedom fighters. They believed in Marxism and an equal society. Second, third generation, they become assorted. You marry your equal, you go to universities, you don't marry somebody with primary school qualifications. So if you observe as I did, Jiang Zemin's son, Li Peng's sons, Zhu Rongji's son whom I met recently – all top class.[3]

So in every society in the end, it's a natural process. As the society stabilises and educational levels are set according to your ability, your performance, people begin to marry within similar social classes. So if you watch doctors now, you find that in the old days the doctors used to marry the nurses, then the children – some become doctors, some don't.

Today, where doctors marry doctors and the children all become doctors if they want to – some get very angry when they don't get to NUS (National University of Singapore) and they have to pay to go abroad. Why? Because double helix, both sides have got that high energy level, high IQ.

Once, the British gave us some beautiful dogs. These labrador retrievers are supposed to be hunting dogs and fishing dogs.[4] But these were show dogs they gave me, or they gave Mindef (the Ministry of Defence). So (Minister) Goh Keng Swee found no use for them, sent them to the police training school. They were show dogs to win championships. They were beautiful dogs, they made good pets. But I had been reading that these black labradors from Scotland will catch you the fish, the trout, collect the fowls, you shoot birds, pheasants, and they bring it back to you with a very gentle touch, they will not bite the flesh.

In 1970, Alec Douglas-Home was then in the (British) opposition. I'd known him when he was a minister. He flew in from Australia on his way back. So I put him up. I said, "I read that your dogs could catch salmon, trout, and bring these birds back." He said, "Oh no, they're specially trained and each has a pedigree

– so-and-so field champion, so-and-so field champion, mother, father sire field champions." I said, "My dog was bred for beauty, so I gave it away."

He said, "Oh, you're interested in a dog?" By 1971 he had become a minister and we had a Commonwealth conference here. He brought a labrador pup for my daughter. It was the most intelligent dog I've ever had. We sent her to the police training school, learnt all the tricks just like that. After a while you ask her to do it, she gets so bored she performs all the tricks for you – sit down, lie down, creep, so on. And instinct tells her: water, you go in. So she goes into the Istana pond, and we got to wash her.

So I decided that if dogs are like that, the human being – since I believe in Darwinism and I'm not an American fundamentalist who believes in creation and the Bible – I think there must be an affinity between these animals and us, and especially the apes and the chimpanzee.

Q: *Given the way society has developed, and the inevitability of the assortment process as you see it, what is the role of government in this?*

A: The problem for the government is: How do you keep a society united when that lower layer can never catch up? So we have offered those at the lower end: If you sterilise after two children, we'll give you a free flat.

No takers. Why? Because once they sterilise and the husband leaves them, they look for another husband, but without having children with the new husband, they are not anchored. So they produce more children. If this continues, we will have more and more duds and the whole society has to carry them. Nobody wants to talk about these hard truths.

Q: *That sounds very deterministic and depressing. Isn't it* *possible that some of those in the bottom 20 per cent are there because they have not had the same opportunity as some of those born to better homes?*

A: Lim Chee Onn's[5] father started as a taxi driver. He didn't have the opportunity. But his son got the opportunity – went to university – and rose.

Q: *Among those at the bottom today, despite the assortment process, could it be that some of them would benefit from extra effort to help them level up?*

A: I tell people frankly God has made you that way. I'm not God, I cannot remake you. I can give you extra tuition, better environment, but the incremental benefits are not that much. And their peers with bigger engines will also make progress. So the gap will never be closed.

Still, we are trying, we are always trying: give them extra tuition, give them extra attention, encourage them. So when I receive an honorarium for my speaking engagements, I donate the money to give out scholarships and prizes to the lower end to encourage them to do well and upgrade from ITE (Institute of Technical Education) to polytechnics and so on. Occasionally, some do make it.

So we will continue to provide the additional resources and support to help them succeed. But who is going to identify the pebbles on the beach that can be polished and become better than a pebble? Parents will not accept that their child is not as good as the neighbour's child.

I've watched Tanjong Pagar and Kreta Ayer. They're old constituencies. I look at the activists in my community centres. Some have children who have done well. One is now an eye specialist in Mount Elizabeth Hospital. Some are professionals living in private condos or landed property.

And those with children who didn't do well, their children have got an HDB (Housing and Development Board) flat, four-room, five-room and they feel disgruntled because they say, "How is it that my neighbour's children can do better?"

Because their children cannot make it. That's all. Nobody hindered their children.

Q: *Would a bright child of a taxi driver today – not in the past but today – be able to have the same opportunity as Lim Chee Onn did to rise to the top?*

A: If that child is bright, he will be in school, he will make it. He's not denied opportunities to develop his capabilities. We are putting in as much resources in the neighbourhood schools as in the branded schools.

You can see that the school facilities are the same, computers, everything there, and the principals and the teachers.

Q: *But what about the role of family background? The taxi driver's son may not have access to tuition, all the extras. Doesn't that play a part in hindering his opportunities versus the son of a doctor, say?*

A: There are many sons of doctors who have married doctors. Those who have married spouses who are not as bright are tearing their hair out because their children can't make it. I have lived long enough to see all this play out.

And let me tell you what I told my children as they were growing up. I said, "When you choose a spouse, remember what George Bernard Shaw said: 'If you marry a girl and you think your daughter will be as pretty as her and your son will be as bright as you, you're dead wrong. When you marry a girl, if the son is as bright as the mother, you must be happy that that is so.' Think carefully about that."

So the message sank in.

My second-youngest grandson – Loong's youngest son – is now doing his NS (full-time national service army training), could easily get a scholarship, but doesn't want a scholarship, decided he wants to do IT. And after getting his first degree he's going to stay there and learn as much as possible and maybe get experience, work there and then come back or maybe get a second degree.

I said, "But you can do that even with a scholarship." He says, "No, no, I will go on my own."

Did the father chase him to work? No. The father and mother just left them alone and they just work. He reads voraciously. He's interested in reptiles, dinosaurs and he has stacks of books. Finally decided he's interested in IT. That's all.

And my daughter who is a neurologist has tested them all. Their IQ is 140 and above. So the parents don't have to worry. That's a fact of life.

So when the graduate man does not want to marry a graduate woman, I tell him he's a fool, stupid. You marry a non-graduate, you're going to have problems, some children bright, some not bright. You'll be tearing your hair out. You can't miss. It's like two dice. One is a Jack, Queen, King, Ace, other also Jack, Queen, King, Ace. You throw a Jack, Queen, King, Ace against dice two, three, four, five, six, what do you get? You can't get high pairs, let alone a full flush.

Q: *What is not so clear to me is what can we do about it? What is the role of government in all this?*

A: The role of government is how to keep the society united so that you don't have an underclass that feels disaffected, discontented and rebellious as in America. And the answer in Britain and in

Europe is welfare ... We cannot go that way or we will not perform.

So what we are doing is not give welfare, but we give a good education and capital gain. You decide whether you'll spend it or you build on it. You spend it, that's your business. You build on it, you've got a nest egg. What do we give them? A house. You haven't got enough money? Give you a subsidy of up to $80,000 to buy a house. Top up your CPF (Central Provident Fund). Give you bonus shares when we have surpluses to distribute. You want free bus fares? No. You have trouble? Here, I give you this cash or assets. You decide what you will do. You can work or you can spend it. The less bright will sell their shares and use up the cash. Most of them hoard it and they become minor capitalists. So we have a property-owning democracy. The amount you own depends on your capabilities.

We have created a property-owning democracy, that's why we have stability in Singapore. You want people to defend this country, you must give them a stake. They are not going to defend this country for Far East Properties or Hong Leong or whoever. You own this home. You will fight for your family and yourself.

That's worked. Why? Because we accorded with human nature. Can you make all Singaporeans into Jesuit priests? Jesuit priests sacrifice themselves. There are such people, but how many? Today, how many Jesuit priests have the Church? We accept human nature as it is, then we base our system on it. Your system must accept that human nature is like that. You get the best out of people for society by incentives and disincentives. If you remove too much of their rewards from the top tier, they will migrate.

Q: *The government will face fiscal pressure in the years ahead as those left behind and the aged need and demand more social services. At the same time, tax rates are falling. How will it cope?*

A: I cannot predict how our revenue and our expenditures will grow. With ageing, our health services will become a very big budget item. (Health Minister) Khaw Boon Wan spends a lot of his time anticipating these problems. He tries to moderate the high cost of ageing, better treatment for long-term illnesses, diabetes, cholesterol, whatever. More medical discoveries will prolong life, more expensive patented medicines, and more medical, surgical procedures. Singaporeans will want the best. Because we've got the best medical services in Asia.

Why not we start private hospitals where you pay and you can get the best? I would build a separate hospital. Nobody will spend the money to build a hospital because it's an enormous investment. I would use state money, build a hospital, equip it, and say, "Right, we staff it, you run it and we'll charge you a rent for your use of the place. Gradually you pay for your paramedics and everything. You can treat anybody, foreign patients, local patients, charge what you like. Then we can have liver transplants, any transplants people want."

If you start these in SGH (Singapore General Hospital), some people will say, "they went there and got this ... and I didn't get this". That's trouble.

Q: *Why won't the younger ministers do it?*

A: Because there will be a big row. In England, the Tory Party tried to start a few private hospitals. The public immediately sensed that this will end up in a two-tier system. Now the Tory Party, wanting to win an election, promises, "When we get into government, we'll keep the National Health Service." They're stuck.

Q: *You have mentioned in this interview a couple of things that you would have done if you were in charge which the younger ministers are not doing. Is that of concern to you?*

A: If I were in charge in the conditions that I had at that time, yes. I'm not sure conditions now would allow me to do it.

Q: *Do I detect in you a feeling that maybe the younger ministers could be tougher or they are not willing to take the difficult positions?*

A: No, no, I don't think so. They have to take into account the prevailing attitudes, people's expectations. You cannot suddenly lower those expectations. Look at (French President Nicolas) Sarkozy. Frenchmen have got a certain way of life: I want my job guaranteed, I don't care whether it's globalisation or whether banks have collapsed. Never mind, Sarkozy, you got to fix this. If you don't fix it we will have a big demonstration, block the traffic, close down the railways for one day to demonstrate the workers' power.

Sarkozy has to take that into account. He knows what he can do to change things but he also knows that there will be rebellion. That's the situation in France. If I have that French situation what can I do?

No society remains static. The world is not static. You must go with the flow of world events. Singapore is a microcosm of what is happening around the world.

Q: *Can the government create other paths to success?*

A: We have tried, we are trying like mad: music school, art school, sports school. There are many ways in which you can earn a living and excel, right? Not just academically.

I went to Nanyang Polytechnic and spent a day there. There was this Malay girl and her graphics were the most colourful. She was superior to the other students there, because she had that capability: colours, combinations, shapes, forms. You go to Malay houses, you see them – nicely furnished. You go to Chinese houses, they are spartan. They don't spend money on curtains and carpets and so on.

Look, I have three children. Their talent profile from primary school to university is exactly the same, slight variations. They're good at maths, science, writing essays, languages. For drawing, music – at the bottom of the class.

Yes, the boys learnt how to play the euphonium, the recorder and the clarinet – they're bright, they read the notes and produce the sounds but in a mechanical way. Whereas you get a natural musician, a Filipino, he listens to it, he can, without looking at the notes, reproduce for you the sounds. He's got the mental and the musical capabilities.

I don't know which part of the brain that is. But I read that even when you get Alzheimer's and a fellow is completely blank, if he's a pianist and you play Brahms or Beethoven, he'll go to the piano and play it. It's one of the amazing things. The musical part of the brain is different from the verbal, mathematical side – it's more like the original in the reptilian mind. That is missing in me and also in my wife. So that attribute never came through. I just accept it. But my son, Loong, married a girl who's musical. And the daughter and the son are both musical. She plays the piano and the guzheng.[6]

I give you another example, and this was a very unforgettable lesson for me. I wanted these roundabouts to have nice trees, bushes like the Japanese garden. So we had two Japanese landscape gardeners come here. I think it was partly through a Japanese aid programme. So they were here about nine months or so and they taught our chaps and then you could see roundabouts and corners looking very nice. Then they went back.

But after some time, the gardens reverted to their original state. So I said, "God, I thought our chaps could do it." So we persuaded the Japanese government to bring them back. The two told me, they said, "In Japan, from an early age, they find out whether you have this artistic talent: shapes, forms, beauty, proportions. If you are very good you become a painter or a sculptor. If you're not so good, you become a window dresser or a fashion designer, and some become landscape gardeners. But you must have that."

They said, "You are hiring them based on their 'A' level results."

I said, "Wow, I'm a stupid man."

So we immediately changed, and you look at the Istana now, the trees and the shapes have all improved because we are choosing our people on the basis of their capacity to imagine what it would be like if you have these bushes put together, which the chap with an 'A' level in maths or science cannot do. So you look at the old HDB flats, all stereotype. That was another lesson.

Q: *While genetic influence definitely may play a big part, there's surely also a role for education as a social leveller?*

A: You don't have to tell me all that. I read all the literature on that.

Q: *When we were doing the research for this, we were a bit surprised that on some indicators, Singapore's spending on education appears low even compared to South Korea, Taiwan and so on.*

A: Are they doing better than us? Is Taiwan doing better than us?

Q: *Can more be done in terms of investing in our next generation?*

A: The Ministry of Education's budget has been increasing over the years and we're doing as much as we can to get maximum value. So in this downturn we've got all the physical equipment, labs, everything there. What is missing? Quality teachers. So we're hoping to hire more quality teachers not just from primary school upwards, and for kindergarten, too.

We're sending all the kindergarten teachers for retraining. But that's just polishing. And you can only polish a stone if it's worth polishing. (Laughs) You go on the beach. My wife used to pick pebbles. There's a nice stone, she'll pick it up. Rounded little pieces and she'll put them in a little wooden box or little wooden tray and admire them. Harmless, very economic way of appreciating nature. But not all stones are like that. That's life.

Q: *How confident are you that today's system would be able to pick up those pebbles that are capable of being polished?*

A: We're trying our best. If you have a better idea, you tell the Ministry of Education or MCYS (Ministry of Community Development, Youth and Sports). They will discuss it. If practical, they will implement it. We're trying our best. It's not that we don't want to do it. But there's a limit you have to accept.

Q: *But even incrementally it may be worth doing?*

A: We're trying. Look, Mendaki (Malay Muslim self-help group) and Muis (Islamic Religious Council of Singapore) have been putting in a lot of effort and there's been incremental improved performance in mathematics and science.

But I told the Malay leaders they will never close the gap with the Indians and the Chinese, because as they improve, the others also improve. So the gap remains. They are improving but they are not closing that gap. That's a fact of life. Sidek (Saniff) finally accepted that.[7] He never believed it. When he came in he was president of the Malay Teachers Union. So we brought him in. I said I'd put you in education, you just see it. We go back to British days, see the examination results. Where's the bias? Dyscalculia existed from colonial days.

Do you think you can create an equal society, as the communists believed? After a while they stop believing in it. They pretend that it's an equal society. But the whole society malfunctions. So Deng Xiaoping said: Some will get rich faster than others. Maybe the rest will get rich later. Proceed and open up. And he overrode all his old guard colleagues who were so deeply committed to an equal society.

Q: *To what extent are some of your views on genetics, heritage, and society not being equal, shared by the current Cabinet?*

A: That's a reality that they're all slowly coming to accept. I don't have to convince them. This is my position. You just watch. They read and watch. There's a lot of hypocrisy. Larry Summers (American economist and president of Harvard University, 2001–2006) got sacked from Harvard because he said girls don't make as good mathematicians and scientists. It is true. Some do. But as a rule, they don't.

And if you study the brain with an MRI, women use both sides of the brain most of the time. The intuitive part of them is dominant. So they're good at interpreting a person's real intentions. The man uses the left side of the brain, very analytical. You may or may not believe it. But why is it that there are few Darwins or John Maynard Keynes[8] who are women, or women Nobel Prize winners in mathematics and science?

Q: *Hundreds of years of unequal education...*

A: There is a biological difference.

You look at the DNA. Two X helixes will produce a girl. The X helix is bigger than the Y helix, and an X and a Y will produce a boy. The Y helix is smaller. Empirically, girls resemble more their fathers, more than boys. Boys resemble more their mothers. I look at my sons. Both of them look more like their mother than me. I didn't say that. People say that. My daughter is as combative as me.

I read theories. I'm quite interested in theories, because I like to theorise myself. But I like to see theories proven in real life. I've not found a theory that all men are equal in real life.

Q: *What degree of inequality do you think is tolerable in a society? Do you worry about the emergence of class wars?*

A: Put yourself in the position of running the government. And for 50 years I've tried to plough my way through. Didn't succeed. You won't convince me. Whether I convince you or not is irrelevant to me because I know these are the real facts. You're not going to shift me. And if the ministers believe like you would, that all men are born equal, then they are going to waste a lot of time and money. Slowly they are coming round to my point of view.

Raising a special child

For Lee, the issue of special needs children and special education is one his family has lived with. His eldest grandson, the son of Prime Minister Lee Hsien Loong from his first marriage, is Li Yipeng, who lost his mother at a young age. Lee Hsien Loong later married Ho Ching. Yipeng has Asperger's syndrome and is albino.

Q: *You mentioned changing expectations from society. Parents with special needs children say there are state resources but these are in limited supply and some of them have to end up going to the private sector. Is this an area that you feel for?*

A: We have set up dyslexia schools, schools for autism and schools for the visually handicapped. We get the basics right first.

Without the basics right, we could not afford this.

Q: *People argue that we already have got the basics right and so it's time to sort of look into some of the marginal areas.*

A: It's not money, it's the trained manpower to run the schools. You need special training for these jobs. You just don't build the schools for autism or whatever and then it runs, no. Needs years of training, not of one person, but a whole group of persons. Who do you learn from? America, Britain, Australia.

MP Denise Phua has been pushing me and the ministers. How many years are needed to train personnel and get the facilities going? I have told her, even if we were to take over the schools, we should have people like her who are highly motivated and involved in running these institutions for disadvantaged children. They have to be in charge of officials who take the task as a job. It is impersonal for them.

Because she feels passionately – her son is autistic – she pushes. I've told my colleagues, all these special schools for the disadvantaged, we must get the parents to be on the board to monitor and push the staff. They have the real interests. They feel passionately for their children.

I've got one grandson who has Asperger's and is albino. It was difficult to get him back into the normal school system.

Q: *Do you think he would have made it as a university graduate if your family did not have additional resources?*

A: No, he would not.

Q: *He would not?*

A: He would not. He was sent to Dover Court Preparatory School, run by the British. In the early days only they had the expertise to overcome his shyness and his half-blindness. They put him in the front row and made him feel welcome and confident. So he made the grade. For secondary school, the mother, Ho Ching, carefully looked for a principal who would look after him, accept him as a strange boy in the class. Many schools just said no, we don't have the resources.

He went to Zhonghua, not a popular school. The principal was compassionate. He'll take him. And Yipeng flourished. Passed his 'A' levels eventually, took more time, more years because he's disadvantaged, can't see well. He has a sensitive ear for music. He rattles off the names of all the conductors and the composers. He can be a classical music disc jockey. I said to him, why not you do that? He said, no, no, I don't want to do that.

Q: *So he was fortunate enough to benefit from the family's resources?*

A: Not just resources, attention. Personal attention.

This is not just resources. It is the personal attention of Ho Ching and the father. Ho Ching scouted around for a secondary school that will look after him and accept him with his disadvantages. He was turned down in so many schools. They said, no, we haven't got the teachers to look after him.

This school principal said he would try. And it was a success.

All right. So we have such a school. Can we solve it? No, we can't. We can only solve it if the parents drive the direction in which the child can go and get the officials to put in the effort. Otherwise the officials will do it as a job: 9 to 8 or 9 to 5, and off they go. Such systems in Britain do not truly nurture the disadvantaged children in their care.

Q: *So in other words, if a child is not able to maximise his* *potential in this case, you would see it as the failure of the family rather than of the state?*

A: Both. The state for not providing the facilities, the family for not driving it. The motivation must come from the family.

Q: *So you acknowledge that there was a failure of the state as well, in the past.*

A: In the provision of the schools and the personnel who can do the job. I don't acknowledge it's a failure. We had to do first things first.

Just getting four language streams into one national stream was an enormous problem. Finally to convert Nantah (Chinese-language Nanyang University) into English, and then to change all secondary schools and primary schools into national-type schools, English and mother tongue, second language – that had to wait till the 1980s.

I knew that was the way we must go but how to do it?

They take a long time in the gestation. You cannot do it overnight. You can produce a school but so what? It's just buildings. It's not the school buildings, it's the people who run those schools, the expertise, the care, the passion to help these children, which must come from the parents. You are a specialist but your children are not in these classes. You just do it as a job. If your child is one of them, it's different.

GROW
NOT EQUALISE

The last few years have seen soul-searching in Singapore on the merits of a "grow-at-all-costs" model. Economists and social commentators question the policy of open capital and labour markets that fuel GDP growth, but drive up prices of housing and transport, and result in incomes of the bottom 20 per cent stagnating.

So should Singapore aim for a more sustainable rate of growth?

Lee's retort: "You want an equal society with low growth? Or an unequal society with high growth then you take part of the growth and support the lower strata? With no growth, everything goes wrong ... We work towards equal opportunities. Not equal results but equal opportunities in life."

"You want an equal society with low growth? Or an unequal society with high growth then you take part of the growth and support the lower strata?"

Can Singapore learn from other societies on how to balance the demands of growth and equality? The Nordic countries, for example, are both competitive economically, and have strong social cohesion. But Lee dismisses the idea that Singapore can become like them. These Nordic societies are bound by a long common history and strong ties of ethnicity. They are prepared to make sacrifices for each other, and pay high taxes so every family can maintain a high standard of living.

"They are a homogeneous people, the Nordic peoples, they invaded Eastern Europe as far south as the Caucasus. They captured Russia, but the Russians pushed them back. In the end they were defeated. Now they've broken up into three countries: Norway, Sweden, Denmark. But they are one people, one language, one culture, each slightly different from the others. But there's a sense of affinity.

"If you read Edward Wilson, he used to teach in Harvard. He taught etymology but he ventured into this field. He said the strongest human drive is to identify yourself with a person who shares your DNA. When two Maori tribes are fighting each other in New Zealand, a third tribe will come in and calculate which tribe is closer to them. Then they back that side."

Edward O. Wilson, whose work Lee cites in arguing this genetic basis for social solidarity, is a scientist who became a leading proponent of sociobiology – the idea that there is a biological basis behind social behaviours. The field today has morphed into evolutionary biology. The central idea is that genes influence behaviour – of animals and people, both individually and as a group.

So, for example, an individual selects a mate likely to produce healthy, capable offspring to carry forward his genetic line. At a group level, an individual is more willing to make sacrifices for others they are most closely genetically related to, a theory called kin selection. In some rare cases, an individual may even be prepared to give up his own chance to pass on his genes by remaining celibate and devoting himself to the cause of the group – as religious priests may do, and as worker ants may do in what are called "eusocial" insect colonies.

So Lee believes that societies like America and Singapore, which draw their populations from diverse ethnic peoples, have a tough job making one nation out of disparate peoples with a different genetic heritage.

"So he (Wilson) said America is so diverse, how are we going to make it? But he said they have sublimated their instincts to rise above this, and a concept that we're all Americans. We must also aspire to do this because we don't share the same genetic pool.

"Can America succeed? So far it has. The idea of being an American people – sharing the same language and culture, above all things."

Lee thinks it would be difficult to gel people from different races into one nation, but that it is important to try. He believes people work hard for their families and themselves, not for their lazy neighbour. Hence, the role of the state is to facilitate workers' intrinsic drives and motivations to compete and do well for themselves and their kin. Those who cannot compete will get help to survive. But the amount of social benefits on offer should never be so attractive that people prefer not to work.

In sociologist Gøsta Esping-Andersen's book *The Three Worlds of Welfare Capitalism*, a society like Singapore is described as a "liberal welfare state", where welfare benefits are means-tested, and social insurance and income transfers are modest. Such states end up with high levels of income inequality because the government only guarantees a minimum level of subsistence and leaves it up to individual effort to make up the rest.

Unlike Singapore, countries such as Austria, Italy and France have a conservative welfare regime, where social benefits preserve class and social status. Scandinavian states such as Norway, Sweden and Denmark have expensive social democratic welfare regimes, which seek to equalise standards of living to a high level for all.

Given Singapore's open economy and minimalist welfare policy, income inequality would appear to be an inevitable feature of its society. The government will face pressure to increase social spending and dip into state resources to subsidise the long-term unemployed, the low-income and the needy.

With society ageing and expectations rising, the cost of financing the social safety net will rise sharply. Will Singapore end up with deficit financing, having to draw down on its reserves to finance social spending programmes? Answer: "I do not want to anticipate these problems which will not be in my lifetime."

But what would be his advice to younger ministers grappling with this problem?

"They have to decide what our economy then will be, what are our future prospects, what we can afford and sustain for the long term. I cannot foretell that. I could not have said in 1960 that we'll be here in this Singapore in 2009.

"We seized every opportunity and got here. A little bit too fast, the transformation too rapid. So disorientation. Everybody thinks oh, it's easy, we'll always go up, like going up the escalator, automatically we'll get there. It's not true. We had an unusual set of circumstances; the world was expanding rapidly; seized the moment, went ahead of the other countries, and we got ahead."

Given the challenges, what are some fundamental values on social policy which should not change?

Lee was quick with his response: "The fundamental issue is, we must not demotivate people. Once we demotivate them and they feel that it is an entitlement – 'Society should look after me. I am born, you are the government, you have to look after me' – then we are in trouble.

"You are born, the government has to provide conditions for good healthcare, good housing, good education. You must strive. What you make of yourself depends on you. We can't equalise everybody's results."

Endnotes

1   *The Straits Times*, 27 October 1961, p. 5. "A farm to help give island folk a better life".

2   Department stores with a long history in Singapore, extending to the 19th century.

3   Former Chinese President Jiang Zemin's son, Jiang Mianheng, was chairman of China Netcom and co-founded Semiconductor Manufacturing International Corporation. Erstwhile Premier Li Peng's children control China's energy sector: daughter Li Xiaolin is chairman of China Power International Development, an electricity monopoly, and son Li Xiaopeng was president of the China Huaneng Group. Levin Zhu, son of another ex-Premier, Zhu Rongji, is the chief executive of China International Capital Corp.

4   Labrador retrievers are divided into two main types: those bred for work in the field or for hunting, and those bred as show dogs to conform to standards of canine beauty. Centuries ago, they were fishing dogs, trained to drag fish from nets. They have a water-repellent coat and love water. They are also used for hunting as their keen sense of smell and their gentle demeanour allow them to carry eggs or wounded prey in their mouths without damaging them.

5   Lim Chee Onn has a First in Naval Architecture from the University of Glasgow. He entered politics in 1977. He was head of the labour movement and Minister Without Portfolio in Cabinet. Lee Kuan Yew once described him as a man capable enough to be prime minister. Lim left politics in 1992 and has been with Keppel Corp, leading it from being a shipyard operator to become the world's largest offshore oil rig builder. He is currently chairman of Temasek Holdings-owned SingBridge International Singapore.

6   Lee Hsien Loong's first wife was Wong Ming Yang, a doctor, with whom he had two children, daughter Xiuqi and son Yipeng. She died in 1982. Lee married Ho Ching, an engineer, in 1985. They have two sons, Hongyi and Haoyi.

7   Sidek was also an official in the Education Ministry, which he joined in 1988. He spent nearly 10 years there, first as Senior Parliamentary Secretary before rising to Senior Minister of State.

8   Influential British economist.

6
REGARDING RACE, LANGUAGE AND RELIGION

A S A YOUNG boy, Lee Kuan Yew trekked up to Bukit Brown every Qing Ming festival with his father to pay his respects at the grave of his paternal grandfather. At their house, the family's two Cantonese maids put up an altar on every anniversary of the grandfather's death. Lee's father would pray before it. But the elder Lee never insisted that his sons give offerings. By the time he became a man, Lee had abandoned the religion of his ancestors. His three children grew up without a faith. "To get my children or me to believe that if you go and pray at his grave, you will get an inspiration, the world will be kinder to you, I don't believe that at all," he said one evening about visiting his grandfather's tomb.

To this day, God or spirituality holds little appeal for Lee. But at 86, he has contemplated his own passing and that of his loved ones. Neither he nor his wife believed in the after-life, he said. "Now I am faced with what to do with my wife because she's not a Christian. I have to give her a final eulogy, so will my sons, so will my grandchildren," he said, as he revealed thoughts, unbidden, on the matter of his wife's frail health. In 2009, Kwa Geok Choo, his wife of 62 years, lay bedridden after being weakened by a series of strokes. She died on October 2, 2010.[1]

Lee betrayed little emotion. A quiet sadness though made its presence felt even as he said matter-of-factly, "I'm not likely to meet my father again in heaven or my wife. I mean, yes, for sentimental reasons we'd like our ashes to be near each other but that's about it."

But he conceded the power of religious conviction. He recounted how he had seen his close friend and old guard minister, Hon Sui Sen, and his family drawing strength from their Catholic faith as he lay dying in 1983. "He was fearless. I was at his bedside. The priest gave him the last sacrament. His profound belief was from childhood. Because he had that belief, he had an equanimity of mind and spirit."

What was his own spiritual sustenance? Pausing before he replied, Lee said he had developed other "defensive mechanisms" to cope with the vicissitudes of life. "I've survived all kinds of crises. There must be something in me which helps me bounce back. I don't need to believe in the supernatural to bounce back," he said.

Lee is in the minority among Singaporeans, 85 per cent of whom profess a religion. For Lee, religion has been less a moral anchor than a delicate yet potentially debilitating sociopolitical reality to be managed and, where possible, harnessed for the national good. His lack of religious beliefs was a blessing as it freed him at the outset from any suspicion that he favoured one religious group over another. Indeed, he viewed religious beliefs and practices through the same pragmatic lens with which he surveyed other aspects of governing Singapore's heterogeneous society.

Such management had always required a skilful balancing act, given the island state's racial makeup of 74 per cent Chinese, 13 per cent Malay and 9 per cent Indian – ratios that had remained largely unchanged in over 40 years except for a slight increase in the Indian population.

Religious affiliation was to prove more fluid, with Buddhism and Christianity making gains at the expense of Taoism. In 2000, some 42.5 per cent of the population was Buddhist, up from 27 per cent in 1980. The percentage of Christians also rose from 10 per cent to 14.6 per cent over that same period, even as Taoism saw its share fall from 30 per cent to 8.5 per cent. The percentage of Muslims, most of whom are Malay, remained largely unchanged at 15 per cent, with Hindus making up another 4 per cent. This set of numbers was taken from the 2000 population census and though anecdotal evidence suggests growing religiosity, there has been scant official data confirming it. Analysts expect the shifts to be clear by the time the 2010 census is completed.

From the start, Lee's vision for Singapore was of a multiracial meritocracy, "not a Malay nation, not a Chinese nation, not an Indian nation" but a place where "everybody will have his place: equal; language, culture, religion". That was the pledge he gave citizens on 9 August 1965, the day Singapore became independent. Yet he also regarded race, language and religion as deep fault lines that would continue to divide for decades. His approach was for the government to manage those divisions as best it could, and he faced down strong opposition to enforce tough policies aimed at containing those differences.

At independence, interaction among the races was limited as many chose to live in their own enclaves, went to their own vernacular schools and even controlled certain jobs. The PAP government made English the main language of instruction in schools, for business and administration to spur economic development, as well as ensure that "no race would have an advantage". Later, it introduced racial quotas for public housing estates, where more than 80 per cent of Singaporeans live, to prevent the formation of racial enclaves. It went on to change the electoral system to safeguard multiracial representation in Parliament. These policies reshaped the lives of Singaporeans on a day-to-day basis. Over time, they grew accustomed to living next door to neighbours of a different race. Indians, Chinese, Malays and Eurasians worked alongside each other. Their children attended school with one another. As the use of

English became more widespread, they could also converse easily with one another.

While he drew satisfaction from increased integration among the races, Lee always maintained that the true test of whether people were race blind would come in a crisis, when one's life and the survival of one's own family were at stake.

Indeed, in 2009, he observed in a magazine interview that Singapore was not yet a nation, but a society in transition. Echoing a comment he made in 1996, he again wondered if, in a famine, a Malay neighbour would share her last few grains of rice with another neighbour or her own family or fellow Muslims. The comment triggered strong reactions on the Internet, a sign of a more engaged population keen to debate the ideas of race and nation-building.

In our meetings, Lee also identified religious revivalism, which began sweeping through societies all over the world from the 1970s onwards, as a source of uncertainty for the future of interracial ties.

"I don't know how far religious revivalism will move the Malays into a separate stream," Lee told Malay-language newspaper *Berita Harian* in a 2001 interview to mark the Malay translation of his memoirs.

In two interviews with the authors in April 2009, he was far more blunt. He lamented the way some Muslims were moving towards a stricter observance of Islam. The change would inhibit social interaction between Muslims and non-Muslims, he warned, and result in Muslims remaining distinct and separate from Singaporeans of other religions.

A veil between Muslims and non-Muslims?

As a child in 1920s Singapore, Lee counted among his playmates the Malay children who lived in a kampong near his grandfather's bungalow in Telok Kurau. At school, he mixed with Malay boys in class and on the playing fields. As a young politician in the 1950s and '60s, he drew into the PAP ranks able Malay men who shared his vision of a multiracial meritocracy – Ahmad Ibrahim, Rahim Ishak, Othman Wok.[2] They spent weeks on the campaign trail together and shared many a meal.

As a result, the Islam that Lee became most at ease with was the relaxed, easygoing version practised by his childhood friends and old guard colleagues. It was not strict about what Muslims could eat or drink or how they should dress in public. It was tolerant of pre-Islamic rituals – like "put a chilli up and we get the bomoh to pray so there will be no rain", Lee said, revealing an intimate knowledge of these by now forsaken practices of the Malays.

To him, this version of Islam melded best in the multiracial milieu of Southeast Asia – an Islam that was brought to this region by traders in sailing ships from places such as Arabia, Iran and India centuries ago, and which was then absorbed by and adapted to the needs of the local Malay population.

But that form of Islam was to undergo cataclysmic change in the last three decades of the 20th century. The transformation had multifaceted roots, including the Iranian revolution of 1979, which energised young Muslim populations, and a boom in oil prices that underwrote a wave of Saudi-funded missionary activity. This missionary zeal was evident in the building of mosques and madrasahs or religious schools among Muslim communities worldwide, and the dispatching of ulama or preachers who exhorted Muslims to adhere more strictly to religious codes of practice.

A deeper concern was whether this rising tide of Muslim consciousness might lead to one's national or ethnic identity giving way to a new and broader sense of religious identity. Prime Minister Lee Hsien Loong cited as an indication of this trend, the "greater engagement with issues that affect Muslims everywhere, notably the Israeli-Palestinian conflict".

For Singapore Muslims, the issue of religious identity versus national identity was one they had been forced to grapple with ever since Singapore gained independence as a Chinese-majority nation flanked by two far larger Muslim-majority states. Official concern that they would feel conflicting loyalties should Singapore have to fight a war against either of its neighbours, led to young men of Malay-Muslim descent being excluded from the ranks of the armed forces in the early years of independence. Unlike their peers of other races who served their national service in the armed forces, Malay males tended to do so in the police force. That policy changed gradually. Over time, an increasing number of Malays were appointed to sensitive posts in the armed forces. But even as late as 1999, at a Singapore 21 Forum to discuss the country's future, Lee made clear that such appointments continued to be selective and made with great care. He broached the highly-sensitive issue at a public forum, in response to a question from a polytechnic student: "If, for instance, you put in a Malay officer who's very religious and who has family ties in Malaysia in charge of a machine-gun unit, that's a very tricky business. We've got to know his background. I'm saying these things because they are real, and if I didn't think that, and I think even if today the Prime Minister doesn't think carefully about this, we could have a tragedy."

The policy continues to be a source of disquiet in the Malay-Muslim community. At the time of this book's publication, the highest-ranking Malay-Muslim officer in the Singapore Armed Forces held the rank of brigadier general, in a national defence force commanded by a major general. A major general is one rank above a brigadier general.

The turn of the century was also when the spectre of terrorism pursued by fanatical Muslims reared its ugly head in Singapore for the first time. In 2001, the authorities swooped down on Singaporean members of a regional terrorist group, Jemaah Islamiah. The government later revealed that members of the Singapore cell had planned to bomb several targets in the country, including the American school, US Navy vessels and American firms. The government took great pains to draw a distinction between this small band of violent extremists and the vast majority of Muslims in Singapore who were moderate, peaceful and loyal to the nation. But with terrorism shining a harsh spotlight on the community, Muslims came under pressure to demonstrate that they belonged firmly to the moderate, rather than extremist, brand of Islam.

After the September 11 attacks, Muslims also found their practices subjected to greater scrutiny. The issue of dressing, halal food or shaking hands with members of the opposite sex were openly debated. Against that backdrop, two bloggers were convicted of sedition for insulting Muslims and jailed and fined. Members of the Malay-Muslim community did not shy away from standing up for their beliefs. In 2003, the Singapore Islamic Scholars and Religious Teachers Association or Pergas articulated the community's stand in a series of papers addressing the issue of moderation in Islam in the context of the Muslim community in Singapore.

They stressed that many Singapore Muslims had no wish to revert to pre-Islamic rituals from decades past. They explained that some of the old ways of doing things contradicted the teachings of Islam but were once practised out of ignorance. Muslims themselves were in the best position to judge what was acceptable according to the teachings of Islam, they said, and they asked non-Muslims to accept their choice in the practice of religion.

"Some religious practices are said to be obstacles in the interaction between Muslims and non-Muslims. However, we cannot accept that wearing the headscarf, not shaking hands, or not participating in celebrating certain festivals alone, result in being rigid, radical, narrow-minded and not pro-integration. Differences may be discomforting but they are a reality of our pluralistic world," they said.

Lee disagrees, clearly, as he does not see the difference between greater piety and a desire for exclusivity. The injunctions on food, drink and dressing that an increasing number of Singapore Muslims want to adhere to strike him as evidence of Islam's exclusive nature. If the others in Cabinet share such sentiments, they are unlikely to say it publicly. Lee is probably the only one who could say it without incurring a huge backlash, partly due to deference to his standing and also because he has been consistent and immovable on this subject in the past decade, varying only in his nuance. One Cabinet colleague, however, who disagrees with his views on Islam, is Yaacob Ibrahim, the Minister-in-charge of Muslim Affairs. Lee revealed as much to us. But this was how Lee put it: "He disagrees, he has to."

Of course, Yaacob is a Muslim. Lee is not. But they are also men of different generations. Lee grew up among peers who had an easygoing approach to religious practice. By contrast, Yaacob and the other younger ministers reached adulthood in an era when rising religiosity was a reality, not only among Muslims but also Christians and even Buddhists. There were two factors at work: the influence of global trends and rising education levels among Singaporeans, which inspired in some a desire for a deeper understanding and more devout practice of the religions they professed. The shift has altered the tenor of society. Pious members of various religions have begun spending more time at their places of worship, around which many of their activities revolve.

Evangelisation has become more prevalent, and the result has been a rise in the number of conversions outside of the religion people were born into. Religiously-informed views have emerged as a factor in certain public policy debates, with Christians making their voice heard more clearly than before.

A rising Christian tide?

Singapore's Christian minority, who according to the 2000 census made up just 14.6 per cent of the resident population here, seem to have a larger impact on society than their numbers would warrant. That is likely linked to their higher educational qualifications, as one in three university graduates is a Christian.

Tang Liang Hong, an opposition politician, tried to make an issue of the trend in the 1990s when he warned of growing numbers of Christians in senior positions in government and Cabinet. The government dismissed his views as coming from a Chinese chauvinist and countered that it had never allowed religion to influence decision-making.[3]

In more recent years, Christians have begun to make their voice heard in public policy debates over issues ranging from casinos to homosexuality. In the debate over whether Singapore should have casinos, Christian groups organised online petitions. Similarly, during the debate on whether the ban against homosexuality should remain in the law books, Christian groups made their disapproval of any lifting of the ban clear. The authors' two interviews with Lee on race and religion took place in the midst of public concern that a group of Christian women had taken over women's group Aware, a well-established secular non-government organisation. The group of Christian women at the centre of the controversy denied they had deliberately moved in to take over a secular organisation. They said their involvement was due to concern over Aware's promotion of a homosexual agenda in its sex education programme for schools.

National concern grew that religious leaders were mixing religion with politics. That happened after a pastor at the church which many of these women belonged to, said in a Sunday sermon that the homosexual issue was a "line that God has drawn for us, and we don't want our nation crossing the line". At that point, the national leaders of Singapore's largest religious groups stepped in to warn against the use of the pulpit in such matters, a move welcomed by the government. Deputy Prime Minister Wong Kan Seng also underlined the secular nature of Singapore's political arena, on behalf of a government that keeps a close eye on such potentially discomfiting developments.

"Our laws and policies do not derive from religious authority, but reflect the judgments and decisions of the secular government and Parliament to serve the national interest and collective good. These laws and public policies apply equally to all, regardless of one's race, religion or social status. This gives confidence that the system will give equal treatment and protection for all, regardless of which group one happens to belong to," he said.

Nevertheless, Lee was more sanguine when asked if he shared the non-Christians' concern that Christians were seeking greater influence in society and within government. The ability of any religious group, including Christians, to influence public policy would remain limited, he said, as long as the government remains secular and Singapore continues to be a multireligious society where no single religion is dominant.

Still, those unmoved by the wave of rising religiosity wonder whether religious groups will seek to influence, or worse, pressure government into taking their side in policy-making. Will there be forces that ride on religious sentiment to get into Parliament? Can the government continue to be the dispassionate arbiter? These are questions they – and others – must surely ponder over, whatever their religious persuasion.

"I just felt the world had
changed, my friend had
changed ... that being a Muslim,
the pressure is on him to act
like one publicly."

Q: *Your views on multiracialism have been a cornerstone of Singapore's development over the last 45 years. The day Singapore became independent on 9 August 1965, you pledged on TV that Singapore would not be a Malay nation or a Chinese nation or an Indian nation. Looking back now, what is your assessment of how Singapore has progressed on this road to multiracialism?*

A: I have to speak candidly to be of value but I do not want to offend the Muslim community. I think we were progressing very nicely until the surge of Islam came and if you asked me for my observations, the other communities have easier integration – friends, intermarriages and so on, Indians with Chinese, Chinese with Indians – than Muslims. That's the result of the surge from the Arab states.

So if you want to marry a Muslim, you become a Muslim, which is a very big step for any non-Muslim to take. I mean, a way of life is changed. You go to the mosque, you learn Arabic, even your prayers and your diet and everything. And I think this is a kind of barrier which would be very difficult to overcome.

I adopted Rajaratnam's idealistic pledge at a time when I knew full well it was not likely to be achieved for many decades, and it was slowly gathering steam until this resurgence came. I would say today, we can integrate all religions and races except Islam.

Q: *Are you saying that the existence of Muslims in Singapore is the main impediment to multiracial harmony in Singapore?*

A: No, I'm not saying that. I think the Muslims socially do not cause any trouble, but they are distinct and separate.

The generation that worked with me – Othman Wok, Rahim Ishak – that was before the wave came sweeping back, sweeping them; that generation integrated well. We drank beer, we went canvassing, we went electioneering, we ate together.

Now they say, "Are the plates clean?" I said, "You know, same washing machine." Halal, non-halal and so on, I mean, they are all divisive. They are distinguishing me from you: "I'm a believer, you are not." That's that. Nobody doubts the hygiene. It's got nothing to do with hygiene, it's got to do with the religious conviction that this is not something you do.

Q: *So what do Muslims need to do to integrate?*

A: Be less strict on Islamic observances and say, "Okay, I'll eat with you."

Q: *But there are other ways to integrate without sharing a meal, surely?*

A: I'm telling you the reaction of a non-Malay, a non-Muslim.

The Prime Minister was giving a farewell dinner to all the retiring Members of Parliament. So Othman Wok, a retired MP, was invited. He was at my table. So I found he was given special food. I said, "Othman, did you ask for special food?" He said, "No." So I called the butler. I said, "Why did you give him different food? Why can't he eat the same food as I do? There's no pork." He said, "Sir, the rules are all Muslims get Muslim food now because otherwise there could be a lot of unhappiness."

Q: *Were you offended by the fact that he had his own food?*

A: No, I just felt the world had changed, that my friend had changed. He's the same old friend of so many decades, and the Othman Wok who went campaigning with me in the 1950s and '60s and '70s has now changed. That's a fact of life. I'm not saying it's right or wrong, I'm just saying that being a Muslim, the pressure is on him to act like one publicly.

I went to Telok Kurau English School and I had many Malay friends, and at Raffles Institution. Some of my Malay friends from Telok Kurau also went to Raffles and we were friends throughout our school career. We ate together nasi lemak or nasi goreng, bought from the women who made these things and stood outside the schools.

In those days, you didn't have a school tuckshop, so you bought two cents of nasi lemak and you ate it. And there was a kway teow man and so on. But now, you go to schools with Malay and Chinese, there's a halal and non-halal segment and so too, the universities. And they tend to sit separately, not to be contaminated. All that becomes a social divide. Now I'm not saying right or wrong, I'm saying that's the demands of the religion but the consequences are a veil across and I think it was designed to be so. Islam is exclusive.

Q: *But is it necessarily an impediment to nation-building?*

A: The SAF has got to run two diets. You go to battle, you have segregation during meal times when bullets are flying around you. But we manage. Look, you are putting to me questions, theoretical questions. I have been running the system and I'm now seeing how the younger generations have to handle ever more differences, habits. So two caterers, two this, two that. That's life.

Look at the immigrants. We can't get Malays or Indonesians to come, or very few of them, because they look at us as an un-Islamic nation. Also, they don't get special privileges. So we're trying to get Arabs but the Arabs are prosperous. A few marry Malay wives who are brought up here and come here, but they are so very few.

So as a result the Indian population is creeping up to the Malay level, from 7 per cent they are now 9 per cent. The Malays are 14 to 15 per cent.

Q: *Even with the higher birth rate of the Malays in Singapore?*

A: The migration will overcome that higher birth rate because we are now getting high-quality Indians. They are not the old Indians from the south who were labourers, these are highly-educated products of their best universities and institutes. And it will be something sensitive which we have to look at and manage. And we have managed it fairly well.

We haven't interfered with Muslims' religion, with their diet, with their mosque activities, and they're having more and more activities in the mosque including tuition classes.

Q: *The fact that Singapore is surrounded by Muslim neighbours, has that also been a big factor?*

A: The relationship of the Muslims in the region and our Muslims is a reality. They meet, they watch television. The headscarf becomes an issue in the schools because they see the Malaysian police also having headscarves and the Indonesians are slowly also covering their heads. Not all. I think some of the leaders refuse to do so.

And so we had to stand firm. I said, "This is not the school uniform, no, and if you want to be on the front end of the desk, you do not wear a headscarf, you wear this uniform. If you want to wear a scarf, you go to the back end." We accommodate as best as we can but we must remain uniform in our presentations to the public and to visitors from around the world.

We say no, you want to do that job, you wear exactly what the others wear. You want to wear this, you go down to the back room and work the computer. No, there are enormous problems which never existed. Why? Oh, they said because now we know better. For hundreds of years, Islam was the Islam brought by the Arab traders who came here by sailing boat. It probably took them three or four months. They also left their habits behind and joined the locals.

Q: *Some of the administrative measures that the government has introduced such as the HDB racial quotas, group representation constituencies, do you foresee a day when they can be dismantled?*

A: When the oil age is over. I cannot tell you what's going to happen in 10 or 20 years. But I do not think so.

Q: *With the influx of foreigners, who are mainly Chinese and Indians, in the last few years and with the racial composition changing, have you thought about how that will impact us as a society?*

A: Yes, I'm quite concerned about that going forward. I'm not concerned about the Chinese because our local population is diminishing rapidly. So the immigrants are just barely making up. The influx is more of large numbers of highly-qualified Indians, which we can't reject. It's stupid to reject them – IT specialists, banking specialists. And they're going to have bright kids.

They might be 9 per cent. They used to be 7 per cent. I cannot say how long this trend will last. My feeling is the trend will last many years because the Indian cities will not catch up with Singapore for a long time.

The Chinese cities will catch up. In 20, 30 years, the coastal cities will be as good as Singapore and you may see the numbers may drop considerably because why come to Singapore when I've got the same opportunities, same quality of life? Not immediately but already we can see a difference. We're getting them more from Sichuan, Hunan, Hubei, Liaoning and the poorer provinces. Not from the coastal cities because once you come from the coastal cities, you've mothers and fathers who've got more money. And the moment they have got their higher school certificate or their international baccalaureate, they go off to America.

So my worry is that the Chinese inflow may not keep up as

China progresses. The Indian inflow will keep up because the Indian cities, the opportunities will be there but they want to stay in Singapore, go back to exploit the opportunities and have their families in Singapore. So we may have a situation where they would reach 12 per cent but we make the Malays uncomfortable. But we're trying our best to get Muslims from the Gulf – some but not many, because they're wealthy. Very few will come from Malaysia and Indonesia. There are a few, cross Singapore-Malaysian marriages, a few Singapore-Indonesian marriages. But as a percentage, it's minuscule.

Q: *When you look at it geopolitically, is it better to have a much smaller Malay population or keep the ratio as it is?*

A: No, geopolitically I think we want to keep a significant Malay population to remind ourselves that this is an important component of our lives and it is an important component of the region. Supposing the Malay population drops to 5 per cent, then the Singaporeans may say, well, okay, we can give this 5 per cent what they want and don't bother about them – that will be very wrong.

The problem now is, if we want to attract low-level labourers, you can fill it up any time, then we're carrying them forever. So we want PMET (professionals, managers, executives and technicians), people of higher education, but the good ones, even the fair ones, are given scholarships or benefits in Malaysia. They don't want to come, unless they marry a Singaporean Malay. We might be able to get more Indonesians because the Indonesian professionals may not be progressing as fast. The country is bigger, the growth is slower, so they have fewer opportunities to realise their potential. Besides Jakarta, their cities are not sparkling. Even Jakarta has floods, many problems, traffic congestion. We welcome immigrants from the region who can contribute to Singapore, but we don't want those who will add to our problems.

Q: *You hold very strong views about Islam and Muslims, and said that in your view, we can absorb all other religions and races except Islam.*

A: Because you're unable to socially interact without inhibitions. You can't borrow your neighbour's food, it's become like that. And definitely, intermarriage becomes very limited because you have to convert and so on.

Q: *Was there a turning point that shaped your view on Islam? Was it the September 11 attack on America?*

A: No, no, no. I've seen this develop with the rise of the oil states and the exporting of their form of Islam, especially the Saudi Islam, Wahhabi Islam,[4] because they have the money and they build mosques all over the world.

So when the Prime Minister of Mauritius came and met Goh Chok Tong, then Prime Minister, he asked, "Have you had any change amongst your Muslims?" Chok Tong said, "Why do you ask?" He replied, because now my Muslims don't mix so easily. They all go to their mosques, they have a separate social and cultural activity and they are becoming different from other Mauritians, Chinese, French, Creole, Africans and so on.

Then Chok Tong explained that was happening with us too. At that time, the veil for students was an issue and we said no, everyone has to wear the uniform of the government or the school. All counter people must be in uniform. If you want to put on your headscarf, you take a back-room operation. We were already alerted as to this worldwide phenomenon. It has nothing to do with 9/11. It's the surge of Wahhabism and the oil money that funds it.

The Saudis have been building mosques all over the Muslim world and to the mosque, they send their preachers. Here, we build our mosques and we don't need their preachers. Our situation is less severe. If they send preachers, then they will preach Wahhabism, which sets out to be very exclusive and looks back to the past, to the 7th century.

We got Muis (the Islamic Religious Council of Singapore) to agree: no foreign preachers. That is always a worry, but they can go to Batam or Johor Bahru and hear all the rousing speeches from fiery mullahs. Some are still going to Medina to study. If they go to Jordan, it's not too bad because that's more in consonance with the modern world. The Jordanians want their Muslims to be part of the modern world.[5]

The Saudis want their Muslims to be part of original Islam. That way the royal family stays on top. There was a pact between King Saud and the Wahhabi leaders that he will support them and their activities, and they will support the royalty. To this day, that's the power-sharing arrangement. The Saudi family controls the wealth. Now we hear of democracy and of women driving cars, modernisation, money and travel will be spread across the population. It will happen in the long run because they want to educate their people.

So they have King Abdullah University of Science and Technology, where all rules are suspended for the university area. That is consonant in the long term with preserving the old state of affairs. But over time, with the Saudi students abroad for studies, even in Singapore, when they return, while they have to conform or won't get jobs, they know how other societies behave without being un-Islamic. It may take one or two generations, or until the oil wealth runs out, whenever that may be. Meanwhile, the funding of all these mosques and spreading of preachers will continue.

After the oil crisis that raised oil prices, 1973, or slightly before that, Libya had been sending people to the Philippines to resolve the Southern Philippines struggle between the Moros and the Filipinos. With oil money, it was interfering in other countries and spreading its version of Islam. But when Saudi pushed Wahhabism, we have prevented that from overwhelming us, fortunately, by building our own mosques. We don't need their money or preachers. Our form of Islam does not look to the past, as Malaysia.

Q: *Do you worry about what is happening in Malaysia and Indonesia?*

A: Yes of course, because it's bound to affect us. Apart from just the people to-ing and fro-ing, Singaporeans can watch their TV programmes, they can watch ours. Apart from relatives across the Causeway, going backwards and forwards, our retirees who build houses or buy houses around Johor Bahru come back to Singapore for their hospital and medical needs. So there is constant contact which will not stop. Since our Malays are outnumbered, the Malaysian influence will be strong. We have to accept this as a fact of life and manage it until such time as the tide turns, as I'm sure it will, because if you prevent modernisation, you're going to stay a backward community. That's inevitable.

The Iranians are trying to be both Muslim and modern because they want to acquire science and technology. But then, they have problems now with their political structure because of the desire for more freedom, more liberties, rights for women. The women in Iran, I haven't been there, but Chok Tong, who's been there, said they wear a little veil which is more for fashion, thin gauzy scarves. They're just paying lip service to Islamic dress codes. They put on their chador, but when they go home, they take off the chador and show the beautiful Paris dresses and shoes to match. It's a double lifestyle, one in public, another in private. It shows that if you are educating the women, which they are not doing in Saudi Arabia, you cannot prevent them wanting the country to be modern. You can say Islamic and modern but you can't be modern and accept 7th century governance. That's what the ayatollahs are doing. How long can they maintain it?

Q: *But coming back to Singapore.*

A: You want to know why I've developed this thinking. Nothing to do with 9/11. This goes back to the oil crisis and the growing international conferences which the oil states pay for. All our Muslim leaders have been to Saudi Arabia and Iran, paid for to attend conferences. They say, ours is the genuine Islam. Yours has been diluted. Islam came here to Southeast Asia in sailing ships. It took months, according to the monsoons. So Islam evolved in a totally different fashion.

Q: *Singapore Muslims may not intermarry Singaporeans of other religions but are you saying they can't live harmoniously with the other races and be as Singaporean as other races?*

A: No, I'm not saying that. I'm not saying that they cannot be peaceful, good citizens. What I'm saying is, they are going to be a distinct part of our community.

We may have new Indians and new Chinese who are not a part of our community yet but their children will definitely become part of us. You will not be able to distinguish this swimmer Tao Li[6] from Singaporeans born here. She came here, aged four or five. She speaks Singapore Mandarin, Singapore English. She's a part of Singapore.

To me, one of the most telling incidents was when our Pakistani-descent Muslim, after 9/11, went to Karachi and joined the Taleban to fight the Americans. He was captured by the Northern Alliance and the Americans asked if he is our citizen.[7] At the same time, a Pakistani of the same age, born and bred in Birmingham, also went to fight for the Taleban.

That's why Indians have endless troubles from Pakistani terrorists. President Musharraf wanted to settle Kashmir. He could not because of the extremist Muslims. They have 50,000 madrasahs churning out suicidal jihadists, enough to keep an endless supply going to Kashmir ready to die. It is an unequal fight for Indian special troops who want to live to return to their families.

India sent special troops, highly trained, highly skilled, with families back home depending on the father. So when you lose a commander, a whole family suffers. But on the Pakistani side, if he goes, he believes he's going to heaven, where he's got 72 virgins waiting for him.

Q: *But that's a small minority.*

A: One bomb in an MRT station can cause havoc; not just the deaths there but the suspicion and the unease that will develop between our Muslim and non-Muslim community, as in London. Even in the buses, when Londoners see a Muslim, they move away. They worry that the man may be carrying a bomb. If he explodes it, you'll be dead. Human beings react that way.

Q: *This veil between Muslims and non-Muslims that you speak of, I think most Muslims I know have lived with the conviction that they can be fully Singaporean and fully Muslim and they somehow believe in the Singapore that you have imagined for your citizens. And now to hear you say that there's a veil between Muslims and non-Muslims, my question to you is, have the Muslims been deluding themselves, that they will be accepted?*

A: No, there are different kinds of Muslims. When the Association of Muslim Professionals started, they were opposed to Muis, opposed to our PAP Malay leadership. They came out in opposition to it. They believed they could do better for the Malays. So we gave them the financial support. Then they found that they couldn't do more than Mendaki or Muis. They slowly came around because Mendaki and Muis were rendering good service.

We are not saying the position is hopeless. There is that small few who're under the influence of the Arab jihadists. One or two can spoil the whole relationship. One big bomb, and we cannot stop the reactions. I mean the day after a big bomb, say in Ang Mo Kio or Tanjong Pagar, where there are very few Muslims, or even if there are Muslims, say in Raffles City, Muslim and non-Muslim relationships will change fundamentally, as they did in Britain.

The British had confidence building councils. But British intelligence announced that there were 2,000 would-be jihadists they are monitoring. 2,000. Where do they find so many security officers to monitor 2,000? They do it by Internet and technical surveillance.

We haven't got to that stage. But a lone jihadist can cross over from Batam, with a bomb belt. We have to be careful. We cannot guarantee that somebody will not slip through, go into the underground station and blow himself up, or worse, go into the tunnel and blow himself up. Then, you have a tremendously difficult rescue operation, with fire in the tunnel, not just at a station where there are fire hoses. So our Home Team is learning how to deal with such situations. It is a contingency but if it happens and in a train with 1,000 passengers, we can't just leave them there to be incinerated. Even if you can rescue only a part of them, you have to try your best.

It's not a joke. We are faced with a new situation, never faced before in the history of civilisation. We have a group of people willing to destroy themselves to inflict damage on others. The only ones before them were the Tamil Tigers. But they were fighting for a tangible cause, for a homeland for Tamils in Sri Lanka. This is fighting for Islam, different cause springing from a religious conviction.

From their skewed point of view, any good Muslim cooperating with an infidel government is a bad Muslim, full stop. If we do not make this distinction, we'll have no Malays in the government or in the civil service or in all the security branches. You must make that distinction because we have completely different groups. But one poisonous group can destroy interracial, interreligious harmony.

We sent a team to study what they did in London. They have different kinds of Muslims who cannot unite. Because of their free speech laws, they've allowed all kinds of rabid preachers to purvey highly inflammatory sermons in Britain's mosques. Now, they're banning the rabid ones. They get Muslim counsel, go to the High Court and on appeal over their human rights and liberty of speech. In the end the judges have allowed the government to push them out. If we had accepted Saudi money for mosques, we will get Saudi preachers. Luckily we have preempted that by having the Mosque Building Fund so we don't need their money.

Q: *But do you fear that your views may be misinterpreted by a younger generation of leaders, who may not have gone through what you have gone through? You are familiar with the Muslims and the Malays and you may know how to handle or manage them, whereas out of fear, might there be an overreaction among the younger leaders?*

A: No, I don't think so. I mean, they've worked with me. Goh Chok Tong worked with me for 15 years before he took over and he sat in all my meetings with the Malay leaders and so on. Hsien Loong has mixed with many Malay friends, learnt Malay, he understands them. He's gone around constituencies with me as a growing boy. He understands their sensibilities. Whoever takes over from him, sitting in Parliament, intermingling with the constituents, will understand, and will adapt.

I do not see intolerance. Every Singaporean knows the first ingredient, the first attribute we must have to be a successful multiracial, cosmopolitan society, is a high degree of tolerance. It's our way of life – Jews, Christians, Muslims, Zoroastrians, Buddhists, Taoists, whatever. See our prayer blessings for the SAF. Every religion is included. It's your faith and gives you comfort in battle. If you die, well it's for a good cause.

Q: *How would you describe the level of trust that you have towards Singapore Muslims?*

A: I would say those who are more English-speaking, this is a rough rule of thumb, the more English-speaking they are, the less they are prone to this. Their first language now is English. So when they go on the Internet, they're reading English. We do these surveys in primary 1 admissions. More Malay children are beginning to speak English at home. Once the children speak English at that age, we know that the parents are well-educated, want their children to succeed in our society. It's moving that way. We have switched to English and opened up a wider world for them.

Q: *So looking at the developments in the Muslim community in Singapore, the pervasiveness of English within the community, the motivation in the community towards these things, surely there must be some sense of satisfaction, from your point of view?*

A: That group will grow over time, but the minority of jihadists, we cannot make them disappear. However small that minority, they can damage our whole interracial harmony.

Q: *Can we turn to the other religions? Some have said that the trend of increasing religiosity in Singapore extends to certain fundamentalist Christian groups. How do you view the Christians becoming more vocal on issues?*

A: The Christian missionary movement started in the 1970s and it started in the schools. My granddaughter has been converted. My grandsons have not. I don't know how they converted her. She was in Raffles Girls' School before she went to Hwa Chong. She's now a deeply religious person, she wears a cross. She goes to church every Sunday. She reads the Bible.

Q: *The Christians are getting organised and speaking up against issues such as the decision to allow casinos here.*

A: But they do not go out with bombs on their bodies to blow people up. If they do that, we got a real problem, and we'll stop them. And we'll stop the missionaries too. They are law-abiding.

Q: *Among some non-Christians, there's even concern that quite a number of Cabinet ministers are Christian and that seems to be tied to education as well. A growing number of well-educated Singaporeans are becoming Christian.*

A: The broader explanation for this conversion into Christianity is because Buddhism and Taoism and ancestor worship, to the Western-educated, are not convincing religions. You see this phenomenon in Korea. For some reason, the educated Koreans have abandoned Buddhism, Taoism and ancestor worship. They say this is superstition. They believe there's a superior being somewhere that created this world, this universe.

In Taiwan, with development, people also get religious. It's what they call anomie as a result of rapid economic and social change. So we sent a team to study what's happened to the religious movements in the fast-developing countries: Korea, Taiwan, Hong Kong. In Taiwan, there were many new temples being built.

The Christian Church offers rituals for birth, for marriage, for burials. These are three important events in people's lives. For the

Buddhist, there's no baptism. Then marriage: for the Chinese, you have the tea ceremony. In a Westernised society, it's not legally binding, you go to the Registry of Marriages. It's a legalistic exercise – do you accept this woman, or man and so on. Whereas the Church asks, whoever has any objection, stand up and object now. Then the vows to take this person to love and to cherish, in sickness and in health, in poverty and in wealth, till death do us part. These are comforting words and have a strong psychological impact.

When you die, the priest comes to give the final rites. Hon Sui Sen (former Finance Minister) was a deeply religious Catholic, and so is his wife. The wife sincerely believed that when she dies she will meet her husband. This gives her great comfort.

I don't have that belief. So I got to have other defence mechanisms. I will say well, life's like that. *C'est la vie*, as the French say.

When my mother died, she was not a Christian and we did not want a Buddhist ceremony. We had a simple ceremony. I gave her a eulogy. So did my brothers, but it was not as comforting as the resonance of a church with chants and organ music.

The music has developed over the centuries to match the mood. I was at Hon Sui Sen's funeral rites at the Cathedral of the Good Shepherd. The priest gave the sacrament to the family. Everybody took this wafer. I didn't because I'm not a Catholic so I just sat back. Everybody else took it. It gave the family great comfort. When they went home, they were at peace.

Now I am faced with what to do with my wife because she's not a Christian. I have to give her a final eulogy, so will my sons, so will my grandchildren.

I'm not likely to meet my wife again in heaven or elsewhere. For sentimental reasons, she and I would like our ashes to be near each other. That's about it.

Q: *So where do you get your spiritual sustenance, if at all?*

A: I don't know. I've survived all kinds of crises. There must be something that helps me bounce back. I don't need to believe in the supernatural to bounce back.

Q: *On the number of ministers who are Christians...*

A: They're not aggressive Christians. They know how to live and let live. You want to swear on the Bible, so be it, whether the Old Testament or the New Testament. They read out their oath of allegiance, the formula varying with one's religion. No, if we get a Cabinet full of Christians, we may have an intolerant Cabinet, we'll not allow that.

Q: *I think some people worry that the other religions will also respond.*

A: The Buddhists have responded. They must respond, they must defend their flock from diminishing. It will settle down.

We've studied Korea and Japan. Whenever there's a crisis in Japan, new religious sects develop, not necessarily Christianity, but new deviants of Shintoism and other sects.

In Korea, they chose Christianity. In Taiwan, temples proliferated. In Hong Kong, more Christians but not as many as in Singapore or Malaysia.

Q: *Do you see it becoming a challenge to maintain a secular, multireligious core to lead the country?*

A: No. I don't see any sign of that in any of our MPs. We had the free vote on the Human Organ Transplant Act, HOTA.[8] Christopher de Souza voted against it. He felt strongly, so let him. He's a Catholic. I don't see him proselytising. But he feels strongly. Because the Pope disagrees with HOTA, he should not agree with this. I believe the Pope is wrong.

Q: *In the 1980s, the government reacted to the involvement of the Catholic Church.*[9]

A: Yes, they were interfering in politics. If we had allowed it, then the other religious groups would also enter the political arena. We're going to have political parties divided by religions. We stopped it. The Catholics were caught up with the Latin American Catholic movement of social action to raise the conditions of the poor when the Catholic Church was not doing the job.

I put a stop to it. When the Pope came here, I explained that "this may be all right in Latin America but we're multiracial, your Catholics start this, other religions will respond, we will have trouble between religions. All religions must stay out of politics. So we'll remain harmonious."

You look at Malaysia. They will never resolve the problem. I used to ride with Tunku Abdul Rahman in his car. He treated me as a courtier. I had to follow him to weddings and all social functions. Everywhere, they had new mosques. I said, "Tunku, why don't you build clinics?" "No, no," he said, "Kuan Yew, you don't understand these things. This is a Malay society. They need to pray. You just give them the right prayers and a little bit of better life and they will be happy, they will work with you."

That was the beginning, the early beginning. That was the early beginnings of using Islam as a political factor to rally all Muslims so that no non-Muslim can muscle in on Muslim society and win votes. When we went into Malaysia, having won over some Malays to voting for the PAP, he said, "You stay out. PAP can be here but stay within the Chinese community." I said to him, "Then we're going to have a divided society." He said, "No, try with the Eurasians and Indians, but leave the Muslims alone." Now it's deeply entrenched. PAS is going to have unity talks with the UMNO leaders. You can read that in the Malaysian press. It was bound to come to this. Why should Malay-Muslims give up their special rights? Because Anwar Ibrahim has a platform on this? I don't see PAS agreeing to it.

Q: *Just now you mentioned that the core of the ministers tend to be fairly moderate, nominal Christians. How do you make sure that they stay that way or that the people making policies, like the permanent secretaries, aren't too inclined in one way?*

A: No, the population as such will not vote for such persons. If you don't go and join the Seventh Month Festival you will lose votes. That's one simple test of your flexibility. There are certain Chinese virtues which will not change. And the lower-educated still believe in the old pantheons of Chinese gods and goddesses, Kuan Yin, Matzu and all the rest. If you are a strict Christian, you shun temples, you shun the Seventh Month Festival. They react that this MP is no good, he's not a part of us. So you will lose votes.

Q: *But that's of course every five years, right?*

A: Yes, surely.

Q: *But in the interim, as you, let's say, observe a colleague, and let's say he's moving in one way?*

A: If he moves that way, he will lose his election. The acid test is, whether you can carry the population with you. If you can convert the whole population, we will have enormous trouble. But I don't see that happening. I visited Augustine Tan's[10] constituency. There was a sacred tree with lots of candles and wishes. The people prayed for four-digit numbers. I said to Augustine, "This looks like a fetish." He's a Christian but said, "No, no. It gives them comfort.

We must leave it be."

If you go and demolish a sacred temple or whatever, but somebody believed, "I prayed here and I got a baby," you demolish that against his wishes. You're going to upset the whole community.

The Chinese Communist Party was against religion. They suppressed it. Once they relaxed, ancestor worship came back, right? So at Qing Ming, they all go to the ancestral graves to *sao mu*, clear the grass and other growth on the graves. These are deep, millennia-old traditions. The Christians were in India. New civilisations like Fiji, the Christians converted pagans to Christianity. In India, how many Christians are there? They could not dislodge the deep roots of Hinduism, the Hindu pantheon, Ganesh, the elephant god, and so on.

Q: *Within the Singapore Cabinet, when there are discussions on issues, to what extent do the ministers' religious beliefs influence the positions they take, for example, on moral issues – casinos, homosexuality and so on? Does that ever come up?*

A: They're modern thinking people. This is the reality of the society, we decide what is in our interest and how the people will react. Homosexuality will eventually be accepted. It's already accepted in China. It's a matter of time before it's accepted here.

I don't see the grassroots being converted to Christianity. If the grassroots are converted, and it's total, then we become a different society.

Language without tears

Lee Kuan Yew has had to deal with some of the toughest issues involving race and language in Singapore – the closing down of Nanyang University or Nantah and the compulsory learning of a second language in schools, among others. These unpopular measures could not have been implemented without his legendary political will and tested his persuasive powers to the limits. In his interviews with the authors, he was unapologetic about the way he resolved those tricky issues and as convinced as ever that they were the right decisions which have benefited Singapore in the long-term.

Q: *Some of us have noticed that you are quite absorbed these days with this subject – language, learning of the Chinese language or bilingual policy. Can I ask what is your concern over this issue and why are you so absorbed by it?*

A: The concern is, first, a sense of yourself. So we insisted on the mother tongue because I saw the difference between the Chinese-educated and the English-educated. The English-educated were rootless. So in the midst of crisis in 1956, Raffles College students were laughing outside, the roadside, while a great riot was in the making at Chinese High School. I believed there was a sense of total political apathy and just stupidity, no sense or feeling for what's happening in society.

Q: *But you were English-educated and your close colleagues were too.*

A: We understood that to win over Singapore we got to win over the Chinese-educated. The English-educated was a small fraction of the population. So we got in touch with the left-wingers because we wanted to get the Chinese-educated. So I have no doubts that if we lose our Chineseness, our sense of being ourselves, not Westerners, we lose our vitality. So that was our first driving force.

Of course Singaporeans, being what they are, they found no value in it: what is culture? I can read Chinese culture translated in English, which isn't the same. It doesn't give you a sense of self.

And what finally convinced me that it is absolutely important, my two sons who went to Chinese school when they had crew cuts, they went to Cambridge at a time when everybody had long hair, and they just kept their crew cut. They were not overwhelmed by conforming to Westerners. I am me, you are you and I talk mathematics like you, I compete with you but I'm me. I mean they've full self-confidence.

Q: *And if they had gone to an English school?*

A: Oh, they would have been different. The English-educated students kept long hair because they felt that was part of the world that they belonged to, whereas my sons felt that they were part of the world that's different. It was part of a revolutionary Chinese generation, not today's China but China of the 1950s and '60s where huge upheavals were taking place.

But in recent years, parents thought learning Chinese was a waste of time, no value, etc. Then, suddenly China's rise. Unless we have more people mastering this language, we will lose our opportunities because they're going to come here, their English will not be very good, they will know very little Malay, they will need Singapore counterparts who can work with them, speak English, speak Malay, take them around the region.

All our people who do business in China know that if you can't speak Chinese, you're out. How do you operate? So I've had any number of e-mails from English-language school students with Chinese as a second language (CL2), not Special Assistance Plan schools (that give special focus to Chinese), to thank me for forcing them to pass the CL2. They say thank you, because of that background, I caught up.

I mean the world's biggest economy can use us and help us grow but we need that language to connect with them. We need the English language to connect with America and Europe and the English-speaking world. That's how we progress. Why can't we master this and connect with China and grow with China? They're going to be the fastest growing economy in the next 20, 30, 40 years. Look at the level they are at. It will take them 60, 70, 80 years to reach the American per capita.

Q: *Looking back, do you have any regrets over the development of our bilingual policy?*

A: No, not at all. Had I known how difficult it was to teach children from English-speaking homes Chinese using Chinese as the first language, which was what we were doing because the Chinese school teachers were teaching them Chinese without any knowledge of English and refusing to use English because the children were Chinese. The teachers thought, I speak to you in Chinese like I do in a Chinese school and you learn it. And the children are confused, they don't understand. So I changed that. I discovered that many parents were sending their children abroad to avoid learning Chinese as a second language.

Then I met Goh Yeng Seng who is now head of the National Institute of Education's Chinese section. And he had taken his PhD in Linguistics at London's School of Oriental and African Studies, but he had to learn English. He passed his Linguistics PhD. And he said he learnt English the way I learnt Chinese – with the help of Chinese. He looked up the dictionary, this English word means so-and-so. If he looked up the English-English dictionary, he might have spent years and never caught up. He looked up the English-Chinese dictionary, he learnt.

I learnt Chinese by looking up the Chinese-English dictionary. So I decided to try out in the schools, teaching the children from English-speaking homes Chinese using English. It succeeded. We tried it in four schools. All four schools reported progress from children and parents. So we overcame resistance from the

Chinese-educated groups and spread the practice to more schools.

Now the position has altered because the teachers are now bilingual. The younger teachers who replace those old teachers speak English as their first language and they were specially trained in Chinese to boost their ability to teach Chinese. So now, there's no problem. And we've also learnt to have modules, so you learn at the pace that your home background allows you to learn. If you can make two, three modules in one primary year, go ahead. You can make only one module, okay, next year we do the other module. So the problem is solved, but it took 40 years to get there, because of ignorance.

What to do? If I knew as much then as today, how much pain and heart-rending frustration I would have avoided. That's life. You learn and become wise after the event.

Q: *Actually there was a lot of feedback from English-educated parents but I think much of their feedback was dismissed as their lack of interest in the language, therefore they had no motivation to learn or to encourage their children to learn.*

A: Which is partly true. They would have no motivation to learn if it's a case of I've got to pass this to get to university. After that, I forget it. Now, China rises, it's a matter of I've got to master this. You're a lawyer, an accountant, whatever your profession, if you also speak Chinese, the multinationals hire you, pay you expatriate pay, expatriate housing, expatriate education for your children. You save money, you come back, you're a richer man, you've got a big CV. So they're taking it seriously. Now the motivation problems are over.

Q: *You mentioned the different responses of the English-educated and the Chinese-educated communities to the language policies and the changes that had to be made. How deep is the divide today* *between these two groups?*

A: I will say with the younger generation, the divide is marginal because they are all English-speaking and Chinese-speaking as a second language. I was in Hanoi and *The Straits Times* sent their journalist from Beijing to cover me. And I looked at her CV. She didn't do Chinese at university. She went to the London School of Economics. She studied Chinese as a second language in school. Our ambassador told me that when she first started working in Beijing, she found it difficult to cope. Within six months, she caught up because she had Chinese as a second language. So I asked her, how did you catch up in six months?

She said because I speak Mandarin at home. So although she did not reach a high standard of examination Chinese in reading and writing, she has the fluency of the language and she could easily expand. And now, after two years she's completely part of the Chinese-speaking community there.

Now it is an economic imperative. Look, where are our engines of growth? The English language for America, Japan, Europe, Britain, Australia, New Zealand. Where will growth now come from?

We're not giving up the old; we want free trade agreements with all of them. And we are adding new growth engines to our economy: China, India, the Persian Gulf states. I think we should get some of our chaps to learn Arabic again to connect with them. So we must have an Arabic quarter, hookah pipes and so on, so they feel comfortable. The Arabs were here from the beginning of Singapore. They all came from Yemen. There's Arab Street. We should recreate a little Arabia there. And that will help us link up. They speak English. But when you do business there, you got to control workers, you got to speak a little bit of Arabic.

As for doing business with India, learning Tamil is not much use. It's only spoken in Tamil Nadu. If you want to learn an

Indian language, it has to be Hindi because there're about 300, 400 million speakers in the north of India. But the people who do business all speak English, so that's okay. But in China, you can't speak Chinese, you can't operate. Only a small number of the highly educated speak good English. Everyone was learning furiously for the Olympics but they learnt a few words and phrases, that's all.

Q: *The closure of Singapore's only Chinese university, Nantah, in 1980, has left a lingering sense of loss among Chinese-educated people of that generation. Could it have been avoided? Would it have been a plus today if there was a Chinese university in Singapore?*

A: If we have one, who's going there? You're going to send your son to a Chinese university in Singapore when they can go to Beijing or Shanghai?

I've offered Wee Cho Yaw (banker and Chinese community leader): we will revive the old Chinese school, you fill it up. He turned it down. He knew he couldn't do it. No Singapore parent who wants his son to succeed in Singapore wants his son to have a schooling that does not give him a command of English.

Q: *With the rise of China, do you see a need to further refine the bilingual policy? Because of late, you've been talking not just about bilingualism but also biculturalism.*

A: No, no, that's only for a small group. You want everybody to reach that level – not possible. You'll go mad. Cannot be done.

Q: *So for the majority, the bilingual policy will remain as it is today?*

A: Yes of course, but we must try and get 100, 200, maximum

300 who can go deeper. The trouble is the bright ones who can go deeper will want to be accountants, lawyers, architects, etc and not be language specialists. But with that, eventually they can go to China and be architects there, like Liu Thai Ker.[11]

Q: *Given the economic imperative of learning Chinese, do you think it might be useful to liberalise the bilingual policy for the minorities and let them learn Chinese if they want to and not take mother tongue in school?*

A: For the Chinese who speak English at home, it's already so difficult. Senior Minister S. Jayakumar sent his children to do Chinese. They've succeeded, but they are bright and they made the effort. Some Malays can make it because they put in the effort. But they want to do English, Malay, Arabic in the Quran and Chinese.

Q: *But if you allow them to pick a second language of their choice, my suspicion is that the better off Malays might choose Chinese.*

A: If they're prepared to risk their children's educational burden, I think no reason why we shouldn't allow it. But if there are difficulties, please don't blame the government. This is your choice and you come in knowing full well it's not an easy language.

Q: *Could you foresee the world would turn out this way, when you decided to make English the working language of Singapore 40 years ago?*

A: No, 40 years ago, I knew English would give us the best entree into the developed world: America, Britain, Canada, Australia and New Zealand, probably large parts of Europe because their companies would use English. And the Japanese coming here would use English. So it gave us the best advantage. I did not foresee that French and Russian would just disappear, nor that the Internet would overwhelm the world with English. That was a stroke of luck.

Had we gone Russian, we would be sad, sorry for ourselves. I told my son to learn Russian. I said the Russians are good in mathematics so you have English and you have Chinese and Malay. Since you can do it, learn a bit of Russian. He passed his Russian O levels with distinction, went to Russia on his way to Cambridge and could make a speech in Russian. But what for? Now, he can barely understand when he speaks to Russian leaders.

Q: *He has more than your average number of neurons.*

A: But what for? He can use his neurons for other more useful things. Look, I have learnt six languages. Can you keep up six languages? I have to read the economic news around the world, Dow Jones, S&P, Singapore, and Indonesia, Malaysia, exchange rates. That's all taking up neurons. You got to note the economic trends, analysis of the economic situation, whether we are getting out of the crisis and how soon. Can you keep up six languages? Rubbish. You'll go mad.

You need one master language where you work fast in that language, get your information and set out your thoughts through that language. That language for me is English.

Q: *You've had to deal in the past with people who have worked the ground politically on language. Are these issues way past? Is the question of which language should be used in Singapore settled?*

A: No, language usage in the world will always evolve and shift. In the next 50 to 100 years, for us, the dominant languages will be English and Chinese in that order. But who can tell what languages are dominant in the world in 200 to 300 years?

Latin was the language of Europe. Up to the 16th century, many scholars, including Erasmus, wrote in Latin. The Church used Latin. By the 18th century, they were switching into their own languages. Gradually Latin disappeared. Latin is a dead language except for liturgies in the Catholic Church. No one can say English will be dominant forever.

I do not believe Chinese will ever take over as the world's main language. It's too difficult for non-Chinese who do not speak it from very young. There's no phonetics, or pinyin. They will never do that because then they can't read old tombstones and old bamboo inscriptions in their own ancient literature. As long as they don't give up the written character, to learn the language is a double problem. First you learn to speak and listen, which is difficult because the words are monosyllabic with five tones, four and one light tone. Second, you've got to recognise more than 3,000 characters. You can guess the pronunciation of some because there's a relationship between the radicals in the character, but the same word can have several different meanings. The same word can have different pronunciations. It's complicated.

Mai is to bury, *man yuan* is to complain. It's the same character. So for a long time, I wondered why. My teacher said, the word changes pronunciation when its meaning is different. I looked up the dictionary, found it does. But when I looked up the dictionary, I was looking for just one meaning. I did not know the history of the word and how it evolved. It's a real problem. And when you combine two words together, the meaning changes. It's a very difficult language.

Q: *But do you see the possibility that one day, with the rise of China, there would be Chinese in Singapore who would want a greater place for the Chinese language here?*

A: No. We are part of Southeast Asia. Where does Chinese get us? Who is going to support our economy? Trade with China alone? If you are Hong Kong, China will support you. We are Singapore, and independent. China will not support us.

They have told us when we negotiated for a free trade agreement, that we are not Hong Kong. Hong Kong is a part of China. They gave good terms to Hong Kong. But we are a sovereign country, what they give to Singapore they must be prepared to give to the others. Of course if you join China as a special administrative zone, that may be different. You want to do that? But we don't have the proximity.

Hong Kong now is about to link up more thoroughly with the mainland. A bridge will connect Hong Kong, Zhuhai, Aomen (Macau) and all the cities in the Pearl River Delta.

Q: *But the emotional pull may be quite strong, especially the soft power of China.*

A: No. What emotional pull? You know the Plen.[12] His son was sent as a baby to China to be brought up. So Eu Chooi Yip met Goh Keng Swee. They were old friends. He said the son has given up ideology. Will we allow him back? The Plen's son was in Tsinghua, bright, not a communist and he's married a Malaysian Chinese. So we allowed him in and I met him at dinner. I was curious, so I asked him, "Tell me how you grew up in China."

Singaporeans and Malaysians were put together in a village in Changsha. They grew up separately from the China Chinese, went to different schools, with different treatment. He went to Tsinghua with the China Chinese. Although he grew up there, spoke like them, he was treated as different.

Q: *But that's the old China, I mean, the China 30 to 50 years ago.*

A: I went to Xiamen in the 1980s, and they brought me to a place where Singaporeans and Malaysians who have gone back live in part of Xiamen. They live separately. They have not intermingled. Maybe after two, three generations, their children may be accepted, going to the same schools but you are Huaqiao (Chinese citizens residing in countries other than China). Huaqiao is one grade lower. Huayi (ethnic Chinese residing outside of China) is two grades lower. It won't happen.

These were fears we had when the communists in Singapore were so powerful. Many banished pro-communists wanted to come back, we said no. We were stupid. We did not understand that they were never accepted in China. Did not understand that in China, they found that instead of being embraced by the motherland, they were treated in a different category.

When the time came, the Chinese made friends of Asean. They fixed the Vietnamese. So all the guerrilla movement stopped getting arms, radio facilities and money. I had told Deng Xiaoping that as long as China supported them, there could be no cooperation with China.[13] He stopped it. They were abandoned.

I met the Plen twice in Singapore after he surrendered to the Malaysian government. Deng told the Plen, it has come to an end. He gave them money to buy their own radio equipment and go to Thailand. He told the Plen to stop, otherwise Lee said no cooperation. He blamed me. But he brought it to an end. China's interest is first or that of the Malayan Community Party? You believe that they will sacrifice for you? Of course we talk of friendship. We talk of similar cultures, but really our cultures are different. We are more Western.

LEE AND
LANGUAGE

Imagine, if you can, Lee Kuan Yew struggling to speak English, and with a Chinese accent to boot. That picture seems far-fetched today because his mastery of the English language has become an essential part of who he is as a person and as a leader. But at the close of a two-hour interview on race and religion one evening in April 2009, Lee allowed himself to muse about how differently his own life, and Singapore's history, might have turned out if he had been educated in Chinese, rather than in English.

"You repeat after me, then you write this, you read out aloud. I thought, it's crazy. I learnt nothing."

When he was six years old, his maternal grandmother insisted he be enrolled in Choon Guan Primary School, a Chinese-stream school in Joo Chiat. Since his family spoke English and Malay at home, Lee found classes in Mandarin tough going.

"She wanted to send me to a Chinese school. Like a fool, I thought, what a silly way of teaching. You repeat after me, then you write this, you read out aloud. I thought, it's crazy. I learnt nothing. So I said, transfer to an English school. I persisted in not staying six years of primary school in Choon Guan School, then a Chinese school. I would have had a grounding (in Chinese). But my English would not be so good. I'll be speaking English with a dialect accent."

He convinced his mother to transfer him to an English school. That was how he ended up studying at Telok Kurau English School for six years, followed by Raffles Institution, after which he read law at Cambridge University. Singapore's history might well have turned out differently if his life had taken a different course, and Chinese had been his first language, he said.

"Yes, I think so. I became more Southeast Asian as a result of doing it in English and going to Telok Kurau where I met a lot of Malay boys from the Telok Kurau Malay School, who transferred over. They were two years ahead and they transferred into English and they were overaged by two years.

"But I got to know the latter well in the playing fields, and in classrooms. There was easy interaction. When I worked with the unions, postal workers, PSA, there was easy rapport. I spoke their language, they understood me. And if I could not speak Malay, in Malaysia I would not have been effective."

Singapore was part of Malaysia for two years, from 1963 to 1965. Lee was then Prime Minister of Singapore and an opposition politician. He stood out because he was an English-educated Chinese who was also fluent in Malay, the native tongue of Malaysia. He championed a Malaysian-Malaysia, in which people of all races would enjoy equality.

On 27 May 1965, Lee delivered a passionate speech in the Malaysian Parliament, which was to be his last. Speaking in Malay, he criticised the policies of the UMNO-led Alliance government. He stressed that while he accepted Malay as the sole national language of the federation, he failed to see how that would lift the rural Malays out of poverty.

That speech was to play a crucial role in Malaysian Prime Minister Tunku Abdul Rahman's subsequent decision to boot Singapore out of the federation, he said.

"The last speech I made in Parliament, I decided to use Malay. I explained in Malay why making the Malay language (the sole national language) is not going to change the standard of living of the farmers. What they need is irrigation and better crops," Lee recalled.

"All the old heads with white Haji caps on the Alliance side were nodding. Tunku and Razak (Deputy Prime Minister) decided this fellow should be out.

"But at that time, I spoke Malay fluently. You ask me to make a speech now, I have to prepare for it because it's disused. Language loss. But it's easy to pick up again because I spoke it fluently as a child with the Malay boys."

But the path he chose came at an "enormous price" because it meant he knew no Chinese until age 32, when he struggled to learn the language as an adult. As a young man of 23, he went to England to further his studies. That was when he realised that though he spoke their language, his values were a world apart from those of his English peers. But his ignorance of the Chinese language meant he had no way to access the treasure trove of literature based on the Chinese values which his family had passed on to him.

"When I went to England for the first time, in 1946, I realised that I was different from them, I will never be a part of them. I can speak like them, I can even behave like them if I want to but I am not them. I have a different set of compass points in my mind because those were transmitted to me by my family. They were not scholars in Confucianism but the values that were implanted in me were low culture, not high culture Confucianist values. As I learnt my Chinese, I suddenly realised how very Chinese my basic values were," he said.

He decided to send his three children to Chinese schools so that they would not suffer the same loss that he had because he had failed to master the Chinese language earlier in his life.

"I would have felt more self-confident of my Chinese values and my Chinese heritage. When in England, I would have been more self-confident and said, 'Well, that's you, I'm me.' But at the same time, I would pay a price in not speaking as fluently in English because it's bound to affect my English pronunciation and I couldn't do Chinese and Malay at the same time. I would have lost my Malay. Supposing I'd been in Choon Guan School, I would not have had that advantage of six years with Malay students as a young boy.

"So if I look back on my life, well, I made the best use of the position I was in. It's a lot of good luck, but language capabilities were critical. So I have no regrets. Anyway, regretting is no use. Because of my suffering, I made sure my three children will not suffer. So they have Chinese as their first language, then English, then Malay. Today English is their first language because they are not using their Chinese. They're using English at home, at work. Ask the Prime Minister to write his Chinese speeches. He has to get it translated, then he can correct it to reflect his meaning."

Endnotes

1   This interview took place in July 2009. Mrs Lee Kuan Yew died on October 2, 2010.

2   Ahmad Ibrahim was a member of Singapore's first Cabinet in 1959. He held the portfolios of Health and Labour before his death, in office, in 1962. Rahim Ishak was the youngest brother of Singapore's first head of state Yusof Ishak and held various government posts in the Education and Foreign Affairs Ministries from 1963 to 1981. Othman Wok joined the PAP a few days after the party was formed and became Social Affairs Minister from 1963 to 1977, and then ambassador to Indonesia until 1981.

3   Tang was sued for calling PAP leaders liars and criminals during the January 1997 general election. He fled the country after the election.

4   Saudi Arabia subscribes to the more austere and conservative Wahhabi version of Islam; women are not allowed to go out without guardians, unrelated men and women cannot go to restaurants together and are separated in offices, and women are not allowed to drive.

5   In a March 2006 column titled "Volatile Mix of Oil, Islamism and WMD", Lee argued that Jordan's King Abdullah II was a force for moderation.

6   Tao Li emigrated to Singapore from Wuhan, China.

7   Mohammad Aslam Yar Ali Khan, a Singaporean of Pakistani descent, was arrested by Northern Alliance forces in Afghanistan in November 2001. He was a member of Jemaah Islamiah and implicated in plots to attack targets in Singapore.

8   The party whip was lifted over a vote in March 2009 to change the Human Organ Transplant Act. Christopher de Souza opposed the amendments to allow living donors to be reimbursed for expenses related to the transplant, because he felt such provisions could be abused.

9   The interviewer was referring to Operation Spectrum in 1987, in which 22 Singaporeans were detained and accused of being part of a Marxist conspiracy to overthrow the government and establish a communist state. The core group of detainees included many who were involved with the social work of the Catholic Church.

10   MP for Whampoa 1970–1991.

11   Liu Thai Ker is an architect and urban planner who headed first the Housing and Development Board and then the Urban Redevelopment

Authority. He has helped to re-plan many cities in Asia and the Middle East, such as the Nanjing eco-island and Qufu in China.

12 "The Plen" is short for "the plenipotentiary", a nickname coined by Lee for Fang Chuang Pi. Both he and his superior Eu Chooi Yip were leaders of the Malayan Communist Party in Singapore. Eu was allowed to return to Singapore in 1991 on compassionate grounds; he died in 1995. Fang's son, Guan Shao Ping, was offered a job at Singapore Technologies Holdings in 1990 after being talent-spotted by Goh Keng Swee. Fang met Lee in 1995 to negotiate the return of former insurgents to Singapore; he did not succeed. He died in 2004 in Hat Yai, Thailand.

13 This was in 1978.

7
FROM
STRANGERS TO
SINGAPOREANS

EACH DAY AT lunch, Lee used to sit down with a group of nurses. They were stationed in his home at Oxley Road to take care of his bedridden wife, before she died in October 2010. He used to have his meals with her, but when she no longer could, he spent the hour chatting with the nurses, as he practised his Mandarin and quizzed them on their life in Singapore.

One was from China, married to a fellow Chinese immigrant from Shandong who was in IT. She had been in Singapore for 15 years and has become a citizen. They have a five-year-old son in Singapore. Her worry: whether her son could catch up in English-speaking Singapore. She grumbled to Lee, "My son can write 60 Chinese characters but he can't write five English words."

Lee recalled, "I said, you speak to the Singapore nurses, they will find you a retired teacher and she might want to charge you several hundred dollars a month, twice a week, one-on-one. He'll soon pick up English once he goes to school. She says, no, when he goes to school, he's at a disadvantage because the other children can already read and write in English."

Lee was struck by how Singaporean her worldview was. Like many other Singaporean Chinese parents, she worried about whether her child's command of English would be good enough for him to excel in Singapore – not whether he would retain his command of his native Chinese language.

"So you see, the orientation is already shifted. And there's no intention of going back. New immigrants like them will lose their sense of being foreigners because they want to fit in. They may not fully integrate, but their children will grow up and become Singaporeans by attending our schools and mixing with other Singaporean children."

From that encounter, Lee drew two lessons. One is the sheer insurmountable fact of Singapore's scarce labour force and the need to open its doors to foreign workers and new immigrants, especially as the population ages.

The other lesson: It is not the presence of foreigners that should be the issue, but how they are to be managed to minimise social tensions and allow for integration.

Stark facts

To Lee, the demographic facts are so simple and stark, he wonders how anyone can fail to see the obvious. Singapore's tiny resident population of 3.7 million had a total fertility rate of 1.22 in 2009, well below the replacement rate of 2.1.[1] This means the population will decline in no time. Fertility rates are unlikely to reach 2.1 even with all the marriage and procreation incentives in place. The only way to stop this: Top up the population with high-quality immigrants.

Lee put it bluntly: Without immigrants and foreign workers, and at the dismal rate Singaporeans are reproducing themselves, there will be 1.5 working-age people to support two elderly people by 2050. "Not tenable. The whole economy will collapse," he said.

Today, there are eight adults aged 15 to 64 to support each elderly resident aged 65 and above. With fewer babies born each year and the fertility rate remaining far below the replacement level of 2.1, the proportion of older people will just go up. By 2039, if there are no migrants, there will be two working-age people to support each elderly person. With migrants, the number goes up to 3.2.

"If the economy is growing because you've got these migrants, then at least you've the resources to cope. If you don't have the economy growing, like Japan, then you've had it. Japan can't get the economy to grow. Old people don't spend, they do part-time work, they get lower pay and the productivity is low. Despite one stimulus package, another stimulus package, third stimulus package, they just can't get it started."

Lee is deeply disturbed about the impact of a rapidly ageing population on Singapore's future. It is an issue that strikes close to home. He is, after all, keenly aware of the personal limits of being an octogenarian.

During one of our meetings on this subject, he strode into the room wearing a pair of trainers which he called pumps. About four weeks earlier, he had fallen from his exercise bike and sprained his thigh. "It's four weeks and I'm still not fully recovered," he said plainly. "I'm not all right but it's getting better, so I got to wear these pumps because they are more comfortable. It'll eventually recover. But as you age, it takes longer to recover."

Already, many elderly people were wheelchair-bound, bedridden or need 24-hour care, he said. "We're going to have many more such people.

We can't have all of them in institutions. At home, you've got to provide home care, home nursing, visit every day or every two, three days, help the family to look after him, change dressing or medication, whatever. It's going to be a very huge problem."

Indeed, it is already very difficult to get enough people willing to work in the eldercare sector. There will be a need to supplement the numbers with foreign nurses, allied health professionals and healthcare workers.

Lee, a pragmatist who likes to test his theories of the world against real-life observations, has only to look around his neighbourhood to see at first-hand how dependent Singapore is on a foreign workforce.

"Look, around my house are all the old buildings being demolished and being rebuilt. Every morning, the Malaysians come out on their motorcycles. When the house is up, the roof and so on, the Singaporean appears.

"I watch it with a kind of resignation because if I were the Singaporean, I would do the same. I ask myself, would I do what the other fellow does? Wake up at about 5 in the morning to beat the traffic jam?

"But it's still worth his while because one dollar is two and a quarter ringgit and he's got no job on the other side anyway. So he buys his motorbike and he rides every day to work.

"When he goes home, he multiplies his earnings two and a quarter times and his cost of living is low except when he's here and I'm quite sure he brings his lunch along with him."

As Singapore develops, it is becoming a high-cost city. On the other hand, located in the heart of Southeast Asia, Singapore has access to a hinterland of cheap labour – both skilled and unskilled – from neighbouring countries. The government's policy of opening its doors to foreigners to work in Singapore helps keep the cost of living low – and helps Singaporeans afford convenient services like domestic help.

At one point during our interview, as the writers asked Lee for his response to Singaporeans' worries about foreigners taking away their jobs, he turned to each writer and asked, "Do you have a maid? You? You?"

Most did. As Lee admitted, he himself has domestic helpers who cook and clean at his home. He also had a team of nurses, foreign and Singaporean, to care for his wife. His point: Singaporeans are the main beneficiaries of the government's open-door policy, as costs of services are kept low with the presence of a large pool of low-cost foreign workers.

The last 10 years in particular have seen a dramatic shift in the population, as the number of foreigners in Singapore grew visibly. In 2000, there were 754,524 non-residents. In 2009, the number was 1.25 million, an increase of 66 per cent. These are foreigners on work permits or employment passes of a few years. The majority are work permit holders, such as domestic maids from the Philippines and Indonesia, or construction workers from China, India and Bangladesh. A smaller number are skilled and professional workers in the technical, service or financial industries. Some are foreign students or dependants of employment pass holders.

Their presence has been all too visible – and grating to some Singaporeans. Buses, MRT trains, beaches and parks are noticeably more crowded. There have been complaints of Chinese nationals in the service industry who cannot serve Singapore's non-Chinese population as they do not understand English.

Dormitories for large numbers of male workers sited in residential areas have drawn a backlash from those in comfortable middle-class estates such as Serangoon Gardens. When large numbers of Indian expatriates moved into some private condominium estates, some Chinese Singaporeans moved out, complaining of curry spice smells and loud Bollywood-style parties. Reports of hardworking foreign students winning academic honours in national examinations and taking top awards in school competitions have caused worried parents to wonder if their Singaporean offspring could cope with the foreign competition. A 2006 *Sunday Times* survey found that 86 per cent of those polled objected to the government's open-door policy because they feared losing their jobs to foreigners. Two-thirds also said they believed that skilled foreigners, often referred to as "foreign talent" in local parlance, enjoyed all the benefits of being Singaporean without the responsibilities.

Lee sympathised with some of these sentiments. He said he understood the unease that parents felt when they saw hardworking immigrant children top the school. But he felt that the right response should not be resentment, but a resolve to try harder to beat the foreigner.

"One of my doctors has a neighbour who has sublet parts of his house. So the smallest part was a back end let out to a PRC couple with a son. And the son has put up a canvas or a plastic roof and put a naked bulb and is reading at night. So he told his daughter, who's in secondary 3 or 4, he says, 'You look at that.'

"The boy knows that if he doesn't succeed in mastering English, he will get nowhere. That drive is enormous. This doctor understands, he doesn't complain and said it makes his daughter work harder. And it's not just working harder. Some of them come from the smartest schools, and they end up winning the prizes in school and scholarships. So Singapore parents know that their children are going to meet fierce competition.

"But my answer to that is, in a tug of war, do you want this bright chap on our side or the other side, pulling for the Vietnamese or the Chinese team?"

To Lee, the presence of foreigners is a spur to Singaporeans. He has no truck with the view that foreigners take away locals' jobs. He referred to a memo from the Manpower Ministry which listed job vacancies, to make the point that even midway through the 2009 recession, there were 20,000 jobs still available, but Singaporeans did not want these jobs.

"Singaporeans say, service jobs are not available – that's rubbish. They don't want to work in the retail sector or make beds in the hotels. They want the easy jobs. There are 20,000 jobs available at this moment, which they don't want to do. There are many construction jobs but they'll wait until the building is completed and the roof is on, then they'll go in and fix the electrical fittings and the pipes for the sanitation.

"You know, if I were them, I would also, as a citizen, say: 'Well look, you find a better job for me', because they can see that we're getting in these jobs. But to take on such jobs, we have to upgrade their skills and their education. For those above 40, it's not so easy. Unlike the younger workers, many of the older ones did not receive post-secondary education in our ITEs, polytechnics and universities. But we must all try. If they try hard enough, they can make it.

"The jobs are there. The claim that they are being squeezed out of service sector jobs is a fallacy. You go to any hotel, they'll tell you they are short of people. Same for the restaurants, they don't mind students doing part-time jobs there two, three times a week and get paid for it. But many Singaporeans are unwilling to do these jobs. That's part of the new Singaporean and we have to accept the inevitable rising aspirations of our people."

To Lee, such complaints about foreigners taking away jobs are just "grumbles". Singapore needs to retain its open-door policy so the Republic continues to attract new immigrants and foreign workers to boost the population and support the economy.

Without migrants, the population will decline and the economy will slow down. The government's own studies of migration's impact on economic growth and public expenditure rates in the three decades between 2010 and 2040 bear this out. During those years, Singapore will have to contend with a triple challenge of a very low birth rate, an ageing population and a maturing economy. There are two scenarios:

Scenario 1: Migrants continue to come in significant numbers. The flow slows in later years as development and standards of living in China and India catch up with Singapore's. Some outflow is expected every year as a number of citizens and permanent residents relocate overseas. But with a healthy inflow of immigrants, the workforce is dynamic enough to allow Singapore to maintain robust economic growth. There are enough young people to defend the country and look after the elderly.

Scenario 2: No migration. The labour force contracts overnight. Economic growth slows down straightaway and even becomes negative in subsequent years. The economy shrinks. The working population feels squeezed by higher healthcare and social costs rise as the number of older people goes up. Talented Singaporeans leave for greener pastures.

Singapore may never recover once trapped in this downward spiral.

"Thus we cannot be diverted from this course, which has been carefully calculated," Lee said categorically, "just because of a recession and the grumbles."

In staying the course, the government has also sought to integrate foreigners into Singapore society, principally through housing policies. Singapore imposes ethnic quotas in its public housing estates, which house more than 80 per cent of the population. The aim is to ensure a good interracial mix in residential areas, a lesson learnt from the 1960s when racial riots flared up. In those days, some villages were exclusively Chinese or Malay. These days, all races mingle in government-built Housing Board estates.

The government remains vigilant in making sure that new citizens and PRs (permanent residents) do not congregate in certain areas. As Lee acknowledged, the instinct to congregate among those of one's own kind is deep. At the same time, the state also wants new immigrants to integrate into the mainstream. This requires active management, such as imposing quotas on public housing. In March 2010, the government introduced a separate quota for PRs buying resale flats to prevent them from forming enclaves in public housing estates.

"I'm told in Australia, Sydney, there's one area which is a Vietnamese village where you can almost believe you're in Vietnam ... All the Vietnamese mafias are in that area, you go in at your own risk. We have not allowed that to develop here," said Lee.

But Lee also takes the long view. The first generation of immigrants will have some problems settling into Singapore. But the next generation will settle into Singapore and learn Singaporean ways. The important thing is to prevent immigrants forming their own enclaves which would impede the integration process.

Schools also play a vital role in the mingling between foreigners and Singaporeans. Here, Lee revealed that there are plans to cap the number of branches of the Global Indian International School which now has three campuses in Singapore, along with a rule requiring those who want permanent residency to attend local secondary schools.

Beyond policy, Lee considers it very important for Singaporeans to help integrate new immigrants. This way, they can imbibe the values of Singaporeans. He has little patience for those who want to keep Singapore closed to foreigners. The one trait he considers most Singaporean, he said, is the ability to accept others into the family of Singaporeans: "My definition of a Singaporean, which will make us different from any others, is that we accept that whoever joins us is part of us."

"My definition of a
Singaporean is that whoever
joins us is part of us."

Q: *You have been one of the strongest advocates of opening Singapore up to foreigners. Will Singapore be dependent on foreigners forever?*

A: At the rate we're reproducing ourselves, yes. Otherwise we'll end up in 2050, with 1.5 working persons to support one elderly – it's not tenable. The whole economy will collapse. And because the burden will be so great, bright young ones will emigrate rather than bear those heavy burdens. Why do you think we are asking Singaporeans to have more children? Because we are not reproducing enough to replace ourselves, we have to depend on the children of the migrants to become Singaporeans so that our population will always comprise a majority of Singaporeans. We are making sure that they are spread out and their neighbours are Singaporeans and their children are mixing with Singaporeans and going to school with them.

You cannot change the present generation of immigrants, whether Indians, Chinese or whatever, but you can definitely absorb the next generation because either they're born here, or they are very young when they come. They go to our schools, they begin to talk and behave like Singaporeans.

Without the foreigners, we will not have the manpower to maintain our growth. It's as simple as that. We don't have the numbers. How many babies are born every year? About 30,000 to 35,000.[2] It should be double that number, right? At the time I took office, there were 62,000 babies every year and that's with a population of less than 2 million.

Q: *Is there a limit to opening up? You mentioned once that you didn't think we should allow the population to go up to 6.5 million, as some government development plans provide for.*

A: No, I think for space reasons, you want to have a certain optimum environment, so you've got to have green lungs, the recreational places and make this a livable, pleasant city. But they believe they can go to 6.5 million by reclaiming more land. They said they can reclaim another 15 per cent.

But after that, what? So you have reclaimed to the maximum, to our maritime boundaries, then what? We will then have to upgrade our quality. We're trying our best. We can't change the genetic composition of our population. But we can maximise their potential with education and training, like what we're doing now with SPUR (Skills Programme for Upgrading and Resilience)[3] and taking advantage of the recession to upgrade their skills and qualifications, to prepare them for the new industries that will come in when the economy recovers. The old industries will not return. They have gone to cheaper countries.

Q: *Are you surprised at the level of resentment among some Singaporeans towards foreigners?*

A: No, I'm not surprised. This is something new. We've brought in large numbers, as you can see from figures in the last few years, because the economy expanded and we needed them in various sectors. Then we had this recession and during this recession, we have not mandated that the work permit holders or the employment pass holders go first because then it sends the wrong signal to the employers and the foreigners.

What we've done is give up to $300 worth of "Jobs Credit"[4] per month for every Singaporean employee and the employers decide. If they decide to keep the foreigner and forgo the $300 subsidy, there's a reason for it, right? We need a solution that gives a certain amount of flexibility to the employers to decide who they will retain and who they will let go. It depends on the contribution and productivity of the worker.

As a government, we have got to consider the total position

so that when recovery takes place, there's minimum difficulty in increasing our production. These are not things done at random. They have been carefully thought out, discussed, not just by the Ministry of Finance and the Ministry of Manpower but discussed by the whole committee, including the Ministry of National Development, Ministry of Trade and Industry, and then brought to Cabinet for a decision.

Why do you think there's no panic in Singapore as there is elsewhere? Because we have created these opportunities: training incentives, subsidy for each Singaporean worker employed, giving the employers the option of keeping him or sending him on training and getting back somebody better trained. We have the resources, which we built up over the years, so we are able to respond decisively during the crisis, and there's no panic.

The government cannot be diverted from its course, which has been carefully calculated, just because of a recession and the grumbles around. Our focus is on the long-term survival of Singapore.

Q: *Given the sudden rise in influx of foreigners and the simmering resentment that has caused, is it time now to pay attention to soothing the feelings of the citizens?*

A: We're trying our best to integrate them. First, we are spreading them out in the HDB estates. But when the Indian immigrants buy condos in the East Coast, we can't stop them. So there will be a disproportionate number of North Indians among condo dwellers in the East Coast.

But in the HDB flats, where the majority of them are, we're trying – without actually forcing integration – to offer more opportunities for integration and mutual understanding. The People's Association is forming integration committees in each constituency.[5] But the process will take time.

At an internal PAP dialogue in the lead up to this year's party convention, one of the new immigrants spoke in Mandarin. When she was scolded by other speakers for not having mastered English, she broke down. How could she master English and speak as they speak? You have to give her time. She wants to integrate, she took part in this panel and she got scolded. We need to be more understanding and considerate. She's making an effort. She wants to reach out and tell us how she feels. Let's give her time to integrate. Both sides will need to put in effort, it's a two-way process.

If we were back in the 1960s, four children per family, this matter will not arise, we won't have to do this. But then we would never have the accumulated capital to create the infrastructure and the schools and educational institutions, because we'll be always trying to catch up with the population growth. Today, we could have 6 to 7 million people from our own people. But in all the developed countries where the women have got equal education and job opportunities, the birthrate goes down.

New immigrants are becoming like our citizens. I've got a nurse who comes from China and she's got one child. So I said, "Why not have two? Better still, three." She said, "No, no, very costly. You know how much the kindergarten charges are? And now he's about to enter school, I've chosen the best neighbourhood school and every week, I've got to guide the children across the street to do my share of the volunteer work for at least one year before my child is taken in."

She said, "Two children, I'll be broke. By the time I get back to work, I've lost my position while others have gone up."

So her thinking has become exactly like Singaporeans'. They thought that the new migrants will behave as they did before, but they're going to behave exactly like us, calculating and rationally working out options. We've not found a sustainable self-growth equation. Maybe never. Only Sweden and France have managed to reach a total fertility rate of about 2. The others have not, especially the more developed countries in East Asia.

America is different because they still have ample open spaces and they are an optimistic people. I think in time, they will also get to that stage. Japan and China's main cities have gone that way – many unmarried women in the media, in business. So this is a problem that's worldwide. It's a structural social change. When you educate women with equal job opportunities, the social structures permanently change.

Q: *How do you see Singapore society changing with this large influx of foreigners?*

A: I see them as a spur to make Singaporeans strive harder to compete, which is a good thing. If we're able to spread them out, they cannot influence us more than we influence them. The change will not be that great. Their children become Singaporeans.

I don't see how they will not become Singaporeans. Many China Chinese parents are complaining, "Look, my son doesn't want to do Chinese in school because he wants to concentrate on his English and to do well."

He will speak Mandarin at home but he's not going to go to a SAP (Special Assistance Plan) school and put in the effort. He wants to win a top position. He sees how the Singaporean children are calculating, and he says, "Okay, if I over-do Chinese, I will lose to them. To win, I must concentrate on the key subjects – English, Science, Maths, Additional Maths, Physics, Biology. Then I score."

Q: *How about the issue of integrating foreigners into Singapore society?*

A: It's an issue we have to face and it's one which is fraught with very difficult transition problems. The China Chinese and the locals don't quite get along, so they stick to themselves. The Indians come from the north and even those from Tamil Nadu consider themselves superior to the Singaporean Indians. So again there's no mix.

The next generation, because of our schooling, will be all the same. But the present generation come at 40-plus, 50-plus, so they will live for 10, 20, 30, 40 years. We have to help them assimilate. I was listening to a channel 95.8 radio programme in Mandarin and they were interviewing I think a middle-aged Chinese from China, new citizen. And he said, "How can I assimilate? I try. But I eat different food, different cooking, my life habits are different. My children are going to local schools, they'll become Singaporean naturally. But overnight, how can I change?" He was speaking the truth.

So we cannot get them to change overnight, but we must try and spread them. If they congregate, they buy secondhand homes, resale homes and stick together, that will be a problem. They will speak to one another in their own languages, and not speak English. So we've got to watch the HDB resident profile and spread them all over. Then their neighbours are mostly Singaporeans. Being outnumbered by Singaporeans, their children will mix with the Singaporean boys and girls, multiracial, and they will grow up differently.

This has now become a very important exercise in social engineering. If you leave them alone, they will all gather together. It's a big problem for this generation. But if you don't handle it well, the next generation may not be totally integrated because they would stick together. We want to have a quota of not more than so many per cent of what they call those who are not *tu sheng tu zhang de* or not locally born and bred per estate.

Q: *You've talked about the need to spread out the new migrants but on the ground, there are areas, including in the public housing* *estates, with higher concentration of foreigners.*

A: What we cannot prevent are rentals. We've allowed homeowners to rent out their HDB flats to earn some money. To keep track of all the rentals is a massive effort. Some rent out the whole flat, some let out rooms. How do you control them? We can control them when they buy a flat and they live there as a permanent resident or as a citizen but not as a temporary lodger. We cannot control them when they rent flats from present occupants. These are probably transients. If they intend to stay, they would in this downturn buy a resale flat or a new flat.

What is the alternative? Have your economy go down? The most important thing for any country is to have economic growth. If you have no economic growth, you stagnate and decline.

If you want to keep your people rooted to your country, you must offer them economic opportunities. You look at Hongkongers who have migrated to Canada in large numbers (in the years leading up to the handover to China in 1997). But there were no economic opportunities in Canada. So they returned to Hong Kong but kept their families and children in Canada, Toronto, Vancouver. Hong Kong is where the money is. They're called "astronauts".

Q: *Singapore has allowed so many foreigners in, in a fairly short time, for economic and demographic reasons. How do we balance that with the social costs that are becoming quite obvious?*

A: Well, there's a sense of discomfort. Suddenly you hear a different twang when they speak in Mandarin or you hear Indians speaking not Tamil but Hindi and they look somewhat different, and sometimes very different. It's unavoidable. I asked some expatriates I met, "Where is your ultimate destination? Where are you going to stay when you finish work?" One who came from Britain said, "I think I'll go to Australia." I said, "Why?" He said,

"Well, better options there." And he added, "In London where I come from, when I go home, I do not recognise the place. There are so many new people there: Poles, Asians, Arabs, Africans and so on. I feel like a stranger when I go home." But the British economy has been booming until this recession, and countries in the European Union who've blocked migrants did not boom as much as Britain.

Of course Britain has tanked because of excesses in the housing sector, and buying these toxic assets. But the economy was booming. London was the centre of the empire. So they had the metal and other exchanges. How could they keep it up after empire? By bringing in new firms and talents from all over the world to locate there, especially American banks.

They created the euro dollar. The American banks located in London. London built up a huge financial sector. They were English-speaking, English-speaking lawyers, accountants, the whole supporting structure of the banking system. The American lawyers and accountants also located in London. Now there's a setback. But they hope to recover. I watched this, and concluded they grew because they went global.

Q: *One concern that Singaporeans have about foreigners is that so many of them come here, take up permanent residency and see very little incentive to become citizens.*

A: That is true. That is a concern for us too.

Q: *And then they worry whether the second generation will do the same.*

A: No, no, no, the second generation cannot do the same. You may be a PR but if you are male, when you reach 18, you have to do national service or lose your PR status.

Q: *I've spoken to Indian PRs who tell me that when their children hit 18, they will just leave and go to Australia.*

A: They go, then they can't come back.

Q: *They have a choice of citizenship at that point in time, and they intend to come back as PRs and work under employment passes.*

A: No, no, they will not be allowed back. We have a rule that if you as a PR leave without doing national service, you cannot come back. You're a PR, you spend your childhood in our schools, benefiting from our system, you have to do national service. If you leave before doing national service, you're not allowed to come back. We've had to tighten our rules because people will try to get around regulations to take advantage of the position. But only some of the wealthier Indians believe that they can go home and maybe after 20 years, we will forget their past and let them in. They are mistaken.

Most of our immigrants are quite happy for their sons to do national service. They know the conditions. They see their neighbours' children. For them it is a standard of living and a quality of life that their country of origin will not be able to give them for another two or more generations. They are quite happy to stay here.

Q: *Why do you think there's this resistance among PRs to take up citizenship?*

A: Take the Malaysians, many have not given up Malaysian citizenship. It's because they have properties in Malaysia and family is still there. It's easier to go back and forth. When their parents are gone, then they take up Singapore citizenship.

I have a personal doctor who's in that position. His wife and children are here and they're Singapore citizens. If we give dual citizenship, it will make the position worse. We're not a big country like the US.

Q: *As we allow more foreigners in, how difficult will it be to maintain the racial composition of our population?*

A: The difficulty will be to find the equivalent number of Malays or Muslims to get those numbers up because the number of Muslims from Malaysia and Indonesia who come here are far and few between. Of course if you let in the labourers, we will be flooded. For the well-educated professionals, they have less competition and more privileges in Malaysia and Indonesia. Why should they come here?

A few Arabs come, married to our Muslim women who've been working in the Gulf. They've decided Singapore is not a bad place. We've not prevented women from bringing their educated spouses back. But their numbers are small.

The Malay leaders know the situation. I have encouraged them to find more Malay-Muslim immigrants. Some of the Muslim professionals who have been transferred to Singapore by the MNCs here, their children attend school here and they intend to leave their children here even after their postings have ended. We welcome them, and hope that more will come.

The percentage of Indians is going up because of the number of bright Indians who come in. You look at the source: it's a billion people and the educated ones are about 200 million. They are English-educated, play cricket, they add to the variety of our skills in sports and otherwise.

There are three Indian schools here. There were going to be more but I said no. You either go to a Singapore school or you go back to India, because in the Indian school, even if they stay on as

PRs and do national service, they are not readily absorbed because they've been orientated towards Indian culture.

So in fact we're thinking of making a subsidiary rule that if you spend your secondary years in an Indian school, you won't qualify for PR. You'll have to go back to India because the textbooks in these schools are all India-orientated, the knowledge is Indian, the sentiments and everything. That's the problem.

Q: *At a recent event organised by Chinese newspaper* Lianhe Zaobao, *many new immigrants spoke about how grateful they are to you for your leadership and the opportunities made available to them in Singapore. And you remarked then that many Singaporeans do not feel that way.*

A: That's normal. The simple reason is they are from a different base – a Chinese base or an Indian base. It's a sudden upgrading when they are in Singapore. For the adult Singaporean, it's been incremental, so he doesn't feel it. For his children, they think our development is a natural course of events, which unfortunately it isn't. I can think of circumstances where all our achievements could disappear rapidly, and we've nothing to fall back on.

We sing (the national anthem) *Majulah Singapura*, we say the pledge but we're not yet a nation. We're still in transition, hoping to become a nation, maybe in another 100 years. America has been around for 250 years and I do not believe they are fully a nation. Yes, they go to World World II in Europe together, the blacks and the whites. They fought together in the Vietnam War. When they went back, the blacks lived a separate life. Even now, most of them live separate lives.

We are trying to succeed under very difficult conditions. We took some drastic decisions at the beginning and shuffled the people together. Had we not done this, it would have led to a different Singapore.

They took a different route in Malaysia. They have completely separate ethnic communities. Chinese, Indians and Malays, even at the top of the economic social group, are not interacting as equals. They've become separate communities. Are they a nation? No.

Are we a nation? In transition. When will we arrive? I cannot tell you.

A leader can only settle his succession. After that, it's up to his successors. Stalin goes, Khrushchev dismantles the Stalinist system. Khrushchev goes, Brezhnev starts on a different framework. Brezhnev handed over to Andropov in his late 80s, nearly about to die. When Chernenko died, Gorbachev came in and dissolved the Soviet Union.[6] They were not a nation, they were an empire.

Are the Chinese a nation? Yes, the Han, who are 90 per cent of the population. They have 5,000 years of history. But Xinjiang and Tibet? They hope to make it a nation by mixing these regions with Hans. Every heterogeneous nation faces this problem.

Nationhood is an artificial creation, it's an artifact of how you divide peoples of different races into countries that govern themselves. Will Malaysia always remain as it is? I do not know.

Q: *The flipside of immigration is emigration, an issue that you had to handle when you were Prime Minister and a phenomenon that continues to be a source of problems. How do you see it panning out, especially in a more globalised world?*

A: I don't think we can stanch the outflow because it is a global problem. So what will keep our students rooted to Singapore when they go abroad? Job opportunities equal to what they can get abroad. Then they will come back.

What will deter them? The prices of homes and cars? In America, the home is cheap, the car's cheap but there's a glass ceiling and you are not within the magic circle and will never be accepted. It's a white man's country. Maybe President Barack Obama can get by. He's an exceptional man in exceptional circumstances, but socially the blacks generally don't mix with the whites. You have to weigh that.

Our bright students in the US are offered jobs before graduation. The students start off saying, "Okay, I'm going to get this experience before I go back to Singapore." Will they come back if we don't have a vibrant financial centre? I don't think so. If we do, then their own companies will send them back here because they will network better here. So what does it depend on? Economic dynamism and job opportunities.

If you ask me, loyalty, bonding, camaraderie in national service, camaraderie in school, yes. But if the economic and job opportunities are not here, talent will not return. When there is a recession overseas, emigration drops.

Q: *Do you see new threats to our multiracialism from immigration and from, for example, Indian nationals bringing over their caste prejudices and the Chinese nationals their disdain for darker skinned people?*

A: I don't think so. Those who want to stay here know that they are the minority. The Indians know that Hindi will get them nowhere, they have to master English. They can keep their Hindi but that's for sentimental reasons. They can go back to India and do business, fine, but you can do business in India with English. They must make sure their children fit into this place, otherwise they won't get on.

Caste will take some time to wear off, because the new immigrants are still caste conscious. The second generation, growing up in the schools, when they get married, will face pressure from their parents who say, "I'll get you a wife from India." But that will disappear eventually because a wife from India doesn't fit in. The son has already found a woman here, he will resist. You have so many Indian doctors marrying Chinese doctor wives.

For the Chinese, I see fewer difficulties. There's no caste. They speak with a different accent but their children are going to speak like Singaporeans because of schools. In fact, I hope that their accent will improve our accents. They speak a more correct Mandarin, we speak with a Nanyang accent.

Q: *One other threat to social cohesion is when wealthy foreigners indulge in ostentatious displays of wealth, which goes against the grain of what Singaporeans are used to.*

A: That display of ostentatious wealth is mainly with the Indian women. If you have it, you want to wear it, that's your business. Does it make our people envious? You already see such displays in magazines like the *Tatler*, right? I am not in favour of building up a social elite culture, but we decided to leave it be. Every society has this sprinkling at the top who like to be leaders of fashion, party-goers in society. Let them be. They are a minority. They don't set the standards. The standards are set by the ministers, MPs and CEOs.

With waterfront homes and F1s, they'll come in. We're trying to attract them. Ong Beng Seng is trying to get more of the jetsetters to attend the F1.

With the integrated resorts, we'll have more conventions and big shows. People will fly in, wealthy Indians and Chinese. The shows are being subsidised by the casinos.

So you're going to have the wealthier people come here. It's all right. You see them on television, you see them in real life. You want that? Strive hard. You, too, can buy the jewels. But I don't think Singaporeans will want to wear loads of jewellery to display their wealth. It's not in good taste.

Being Singaporean

Lee grew up singing *God Save the Queen* as a British subject. He learnt to salute the Japanese flag during the Japanese occupation of Malaya in World War II. As a grown man, he was pivotal in the Malayan anti-colonial struggle.

Growing up in Neil Road in Singapore, he used to travel up to the Malayan peninsula where his father worked for the Shell oil company. "You just drove through in a car. No customs, no immigration. I thought of myself as a Malayan."

Then Singapore left the Federation of Malaysia and became an independent country, with Lee as Prime Minister.

It is intriguing to ponder: At what point did he consider himself Singaporean? Lee pauses, and replies wryly, "Accidentally I created this entity called Singapore and that resulted in the Singaporean."

But if Singapore became a nation by accident, becoming Singaporean is a matter of choice. As Lee sees it, people choose to stay in a country, or return home, when there are good opportunities.

Ask Lee what makes a Singaporean and he is clear: Someone who accepts others into the nation, regardless of race, language or religion.

Q: *You described Singapore as a nation in transition, given its young history where we do not have a common language, culture or geography. What must Singapore be like before you consider it a nation?*

A: There must be a sense of self, a sense of identity, that you are prepared to die for your country, that you're prepared to die for one another. Just look at the Chinese, how many times they've been invaded, but they have recreated themselves when the invaders got weak because there is that cohesiveness: same language, same culture and the same Han race.

Are we the same language, same culture? No. We have adopted one language which is a foreign language, like the West Indies or some African countries which have adopted English but they are not one nation. If we lose our second language, we lose all sense of our identity, not just the Singaporean. You don't create a nation in 45 years.

Q: *Is there a worry that the influx of foreigners into Singapore will further dilute the national identity we're trying to build?*

A: Maybe, but what's the choice? I keep on saying to Singaporeans, please have two children at least, if possible three. They have not responded. What's the choice?

Q: *At the risk of sounding sentimental, is there anything emotional about being Singaporean?*

A: I went to Perth and met the Singaporeans who have settled there. They fondly remember Singapore. The man who organised the gathering has kept his son's passport as insurance. The son graduated from a university in Perth and was working as an accountant for one of the big firms. I said, "Why do you keep the Singapore citizenship?" He said, "Well, he went back to do his NS, he wants to make sure he's got an alternative in case there's a downturn here."

He came back and did his NS but his family is there. If he marries an Australian girl, if they're jobless there, he'll bring his Australian wife here. Supposing Perth became dry, with climate change, they may decide to come back. We are in a world of transition. The old patterns no longer hold.

Q: *What constitutes the Singapore identity? How would you pick out a Singaporean in a crowd?*

A: Let me give a broad view of what identity means. Identity varies with circumstances. So British identity during the period of the empire, the Welsh, the Irish, the Scottish all identified themselves as British. And British Empire was dissolved and then they said, "I'm Welsh, I'm a Scot, I want a separate legislature, and the oil which is off Aberdeen belongs to me."

So the Labour government allowed them their own local legislatures. That further accentuates the divide. So now they have parties supporting independence for Scotland. Identity shifts. If you ask me, is there a Malaysian, I don't think so. There's Malaysian Malay, there's Malaysian Chinese and Malaysian Indians.

In Singapore, what will identify a Singaporean with the changing circumstances? An acceptance of multiracialism, a tolerance of people of different races, languages, cultures, religions, and an equal basis for competition. That's what will stand out against all our neighbours.

The Indonesians did not consider the Chinese their citizens for decades. The Chinese had to change their names to *pribumi* names and they were still not accepted. Now because of the rise of China, they have allowed Chinese schools to reopen and Chinese TV stations. But remember Jusuf Kalla got only 12 per cent of the vote as a presidential candidate because he was not a Javanese. Is there an Indonesian identity? Yes, they all speak Bahasa Indonesia now. What else? They belong to one administrative regime, same defence force, and whether you're a minority in New Guinea or elsewhere, you are part of Indonesia and you can't break away. So it is an identity in the making.

Whereas with Japan, with China, old nations, they are established. The classical definition of a nation is, one race, one culture, one religion, one people. Which are the countries with those attributes? Today I would say Japan, inland China, not the coast which has become different, and Germany before the war, where nobody else is acceptable except Germans. But today the Germans have to accept the Turks, they are forced to give the Turks German nationality although they are not being integrated.

The Swedes have had to accept refugees, Somalis, Sri Lankan Tamils and many others. Will they become Swedes? It will take many generations. Will they be accepted as Swedes? Legally, yes. They are entitled to unemployment benefits, welfare support. But they are outside the inner circle.

My definition of a Singaporean, which will make us different from any others, is that we accept that whoever joins us is part of us. And that's an American concept. You can keep your name, Brzezinski, Berlusconi, whatever it is, you have come, join me, you are American. We need talent, we accept them. That must be our defining attribute.

If we don't have that attribute, are we going to have only those who are like us, Chinese from China like us? Indians from India like us? Malays from Malaysia are different from us now. In time, people from China, India or elsewhere come here, they change. That's a defining attribute. English will be our working language, and you keep your mother tongue. It may not be as good as your English but if you need to do business with China or India or Malaysia or Indonesia, you can ramp it up.

Q: *Many Americans are willing to die for their country, which they believe is a land of opportunity for people of all kinds. Is that how you see Singapore?*

A: No, it's more than that. This is a near miracle. When you come in, you are joining an exceptionally outstanding organisation. It's not an ordinary organisation that has created this. You're joining something very special. It came about by a stroke of luck, if you like, plus hard work, plus an imaginative, original team. And I think we can carry on. Singapore can only stay secure and stable, provided it's outstanding.

Q: *When you were growing up, you were first a British subject, then a Japanese subject and then you were Malayan. At what point did you see yourself as a Singaporean and what does being Singaporean mean to you?*

A: I'm not a typical Singaporean. Accidentally I created this entity called Singapore and it resulted in the Singaporean. I grew up, yes, as a British subject. My father was working first in Singapore. My grandfather was a purser onboard Heap Eng Mo Shipping Line, belonging to Java's Sugar King Oei Tiong Ham, and he became the agent and power of attorney in Singapore. He made a fortune out of trade. He married my grandmother in Semarang and brought her here. My father was born in Semarang. As a child he was brought here. Because his father was a British subject, he was born a British subject. So when I was a child in Neil Road, which was then a posh area, we had Javanese servants in the house because they're harder working than the Malays. My grandmother spoke Javanese. Did I consider myself a Singaporean? No.

Then my father worked for Shell and he was sent to Johor and Batu Pahat and Kuantan. During school holidays, I used to go up, and you know, in those days, it was all one administration. You just drove through in a car, no customs, no immigration. I thought of myself as a Malayan.

But the Malays in Malaysia did not think of the Chinese and the Indians as belonging to Malaya. You are *orang tumpangan*, lodgers, so we can be turfed out. When we got turfed out, we had to create a Singapore identity. You've asked me what are the key attributes, I said those are the basic attributes. Without those attributes, Singapore cannot survive. If we are at odds with each other, we won't survive.

Q: *So in the beginning, being Singaporean was a conscious choice, a decision. At what point did that move from the head to the heart?*

A: I cannot psychoanalyse myself that way. All I know is that we were put in circumstances that required us to identify ourselves as Singaporean. We became Singaporeans when the Malaysians put up the immigration and customs at the Causeway, and we had to do likewise. You had to show your identity card. Before that, you just passed through.

In a way, we welcomed it. Otherwise, the whole of the Malayan Railway land would be flooded with Malay squatters. Jobs here paid higher. That's how history is made. We were dealt this pack of cards. We must make the best of it. We've not done too badly.

HISTORY OF
OPEN-DOOR POLICY

The open-door policy has roots in Singapore's own history. Migrants have been the backbone of the country's growth and prosperity since it was established as a British trading post in 1819. The British maintained a liberal, open-door policy for over a century. The first influx of mainly male workers from China, India and the Malay archipelago came in droves to work tin mines, rubber plantations, and as coolie workers. Women came after the 1930s, and Singapore became a settled rather than a transient society. The population began to grow organically through births, rather than through inflows of migrants.

> *Migrants have been the backbone of the country's growth and prosperity since it was established as a British trading post in 1819.*

The first citizenship law came about in 1957. The Singapore Citizenship Ordinance gave automatic citizenship to all those born in Singapore. Those born in the Federation of Malaya and citizens of the United Kingdom and its colonies could become citizens if they met residence requirements. Other migrants could become naturalised once they met residence requirements.

Singapore separated from Malaysia in 1965. Its first decade of independence held a largely stable population, with the overwhelming majority being citizens and permanent residents. Figures from 1970 put the population at 2 million. There were only 2.9 per cent who were non-residents, that is, those here on employment passes or work permits.

Over the decades, the non-resident segment of the population grew the fastest. There were just 60,944 such people in 1970. Ten years later, it was 131,820 as Singapore's economy industrialised. It continued to double every decade.

By 2009, the total population was 4.99 million. Of these, 1.25 million or 25 per cent were non-resident. Another 0.53 million were permanent residents. If you add the PRs and the non-resident population, non-citizens together made up 36 per cent of the total population.

Endnotes

1   Singapore's resident population grew from 2 million in 1970 to 3.7 million in 2009 according to the Department of Statistics. Over the same period, the fertility rate fell from 3.07 to just 1.22.

2   There were 39,570 total live births in 2009.

3   The Skills Programme for Upgrading and Resilience (SPUR) was an initiative started to help Singapore companies and workers through the 2008–2009 recession. The government supported companies to send their workers for training to upgrade their skills. It ended in November 2010.

4   The Jobs Credit scheme was another initiative started during the 2008– 2009 recession, with the aim to encourage companies to preserve jobs in return for cash grants. Each employer received a 12 per cent cash grant on the first $2,500 of each month's wages for each employee on the CPF payroll. The scheme was scaled down in 2010 and ended in June 2010.

5   In 2007, the People's Association started the Integration and Naturalisation Champions initiative where volunteers help immigrants integrate with locals. In 2009, a National Integration Council was formed, chaired by Community Development, Youth and Sports Minister Vivian Balakrishnan.

6   Joseph Stalin was the leader of the Soviet Union from 1924 till he died in 1953. Nikita Khrushchev then came to power but was impeached in 1964, relinquishing power to Leonid Brezhnev. Following Brezhnev's death in 1982, the leadership vacuum was filled by Yuri Andropov and then Konstantin Chernenko who both died on the job, their rule lasting just over two years in total.

8 STANDING AMONG GIANTS

A S THIS CHAPTER was being written in November 2009, Lee
Kuan Yew was a much-debated figure among Chinese netizens.
They were up in arms over Lee's candid comment that it was
better for Southeast Asia if the United States were to remain engaged in
Asia, to act as a balance to the growing might of China.

Addressing the US-Asean Business Council's 25th anniversary dinner
in October 2009, he had said, "The size of China makes it impossible for
the rest of Asia, including Japan and India, to match it in weight and
capacity in about 20 to 30 years. So we need America to strike a balance."

This was translated in Chinese press reports as Lee wanting the US
to "counteract" Chinese influence in the region, rather than to "strike
a balance". The suggestion of using the United States to "counteract"
Chinese influence sparked a cyber-storm of protests and a string of
editorials from Chinese papers. Some criticised Lee for siding with the
West against China, especially those elements in the West wary of China's

rise. Some expressed disappointment that Lee viewed the Chinese as outsiders, arguing that Chinese mainlanders viewed Singaporeans as compatriots.

The outcry obscured the fact that Lee has never been reticent about his conviction that it is better for Singapore if the United States remains the dominant power in Asia. With a resurgent China – an unknown entity which, in Lee's view, seems to protest too much about its non-hegemonic ambitions – it becomes even more imperative for the United States to remain engaged in Asia, he has long declared.

Lee's views attract attention because he is unusual among international statesmen for daring to speak home truths. He values candour, almost to a fault. In 1992, he told Filipinos that a country needed discipline more than democracy, and in 1988, he told Australians that it should change its anti-Asian immigration policy. On both occasions, he sparked furore in both countries which were then hosting him. In an interview published in *Time* magazine in 1994, he diagnosed America's social ills, laying the blame squarely on America's lax culture at home, in schools and towards crime. "How can you carry on with this? Your work force is ill-disciplined and ill-educated. How can you compete with the Japanese?" he asked.

During these interviews in 2009, he similarly eschewed political correctness to speak his mind. He questioned if America would retain its vigour once Hispanics and other ethnic minority groups make up the majority of the country, a demographic change expected mid-century. He wrote off Europe as a strategic player in Asia. He dissed India's politics for obstructing economic progress, and dismissed Myanmar's prospects of modernising in his lifetime. And he boiled down geopolitics into a startling basic worldview that human tribes are engaged in a fight for supremacy.

But he is not merely provocative. World leaders listen to him because he has something of value to tell them. For one, his depth of experience is nearly unrivalled.

Like others of his generation, he saw the brutality of power displayed in World War II. His charisma and leadership were forged in the stirring milieu of anti-colonial, revolutionary fervour of the 1950s. His worldview may be described as pragmatic realist, grounded in a realistic assessment of power play between great nations and a clear-eyed view of just how insignificant Singapore is as a player on the world stage. While Lee's views may have been shared by others of his generation, he is unusual in remaining in public life into the 2010s. He can tap a reservoir of insights and experience garnered from 50 years in public office, when he negotiated the terms of self-government with the British and steered Singapore through ups and downs; through armed Confrontation with Indonesia, through its tempestuous relationship with its closest neighbour Malaysia, through eight changes of American presidents, through the Cold War, through hiccups with the Chinese and through various Asean initiatives.

But years of experience alone are no guarantee of depth of insight. Lee has the added advantage of having exchanged views and worked with leading statesmen of his time. These included leaders who were not exactly friendly with each other, but who would separately make time for Lee Kuan Yew, such as Taiwan's Lee Teng-hui and China's Jiang Zemin in the 1990s. Lee also met China's paramount leader Deng Xiaoping, the first time in 1978. In his memoirs, Lee described Deng as "the most impressive leader I had met". He recounted how he had made an impression on the latter with his frank feedback that Asean was unlikely to back China's regional policy at that time for a united front against the Soviet Union and Vietnam. Asean had serious misgivings about China allowing radio broadcasts to be beamed from south China by the Malayan and Indonesian Communist Parties, which appealed directly to the ethnic Chinese in their populations. The broadcasts were stopped eventually.

Back in July 1982, George Shultz became America's 60th secretary of state. Shortly after, he invited then Chancellor of West Germany Helmut Schmidt and his good friend Henry Kissinger, as well as Lee, to a gathering.

As Shultz recalled, "We had the weekend, and afterwards on Sunday, we went down to my house on the Stanford campus and the four of us sat around the kitchen table: Helmut Schmidt, Lee Kuan Yew, Henry

Kissinger and me for about three hours. Finally our wives came in and said, 'We're going to get lunch, you've got to get out of here.'

"It was an intense discussion among that group. Can you imagine a seminar where a new secretary of state is sitting around for three hours listening to Kissinger, Schmidt and Lee Kuan Yew? Man, was that an education."

Former British Prime Minister Margaret Thatcher once said that when she was in office, she read and analysed every one of Lee's speeches. "He had a way of penetrating the fog of propaganda and expressing with unique clarity the issues of our times and the way to tackle them. He was never wrong."

Former US Secretary of State Kissinger, with whom Lee kept in touch over the decades, had this to say: "I've not learnt as much from anybody as I have from Mr Lee Kuan Yew. He made himself an indispensable friend of the United States, not primarily by the power he represented but by the quality of his thinking.

"Over 40 years, when Mr Lee Kuan Yew comes to Washington, he gets to see an array of people that almost no foreign leader gets to see in such a grouping and in a mode which is unique, because he does not come as a supplicant.

"He comes as a comrade, in common efforts, from whom we can learn, who can tell us about the nature of the world that we face. He gives us insights into the thinking of his region."

While many value Lee's views on the changing world, in fact his geopolitical ideology is very simple. He filters everything through the lens of what is best for Singapore. Every fact, every nuance, every meeting, every new information, he acquires during his numerous meetings with world leaders, is stored away in his capacious brain and processed through the lens of how it would affect the Republic.

What kind of balance of power in Asia will most benefit Singapore? Lee's conclusion is straightforward: Better the devil that is known than the one that is not. America has proved a benign power with only ideological and not territorial ambitions – it wants to spread democracy and human rights, not grab land. Japan has a past history of aggression in Southeast Asia. China may not repeat its history of establishing vassal ties with Southeast Asian kingdoms, but the memory of the unequal relationship may colour expectations despite China's assurances that its rise will be peaceful. Therefore, it is better for Singapore for the United States to remain deeply engaged in Asia.

Will the rise of China create conflict? Lee believes the change in the balance of power from America to China will be gradual, with the United States remaining dominant for decades, perhaps half a century, to come. He surmises that the shift in balance to China will not be as peaceful as that from Britain to America, but that there will be no full-fledged war.

On the trajectory of US influence in the Asian region, Lee said, "I do not see them retreating. But I see Chinese power growing. The Chinese attitude is: We're not against you; we welcome an American presence – because they know they can't substitute for the Americans and the countries here welcome the Americans. So they just wait and grow stronger. Economically and militarily, they may not catch up for 100 years in technology but asymmetrically, they can inflict enormous damage on the Americans."

Is there a tipping point when Chinese influence will prevail? Lee: "I'm prepared to hazard a guess for 20, 30 years, Americans will remain the dominant power. They're not going to retreat. Economically, they may have a lower GDP than the Chinese, but militarily they are the technologically dominant power. We are with them. In 50 years, I think China will be – if there're no internal upsets – a considerable power."

But he added the caveat: "I cannot look 50 to 100 years ahead. Many things can happen, in China and in America too. America's demographics will change. By 2050, they'll have the Hispanics and other ethnic minorities form the majority.[1] Will Hispanics become American in culture or will Americans become more Hispanic in culture? Can Americans make the Hispanics become hard-driving, let's-go-for-it Americans? If not, they may slow down."

Meanwhile, what are the prospects of an armed skirmish or conflict in those 20, 30 years while America remains on the ascendance with a rapidly growing China?

Lee: "Very small. Both sides know they got nothing to gain. What territory are you fighting over? Taiwan? Can the Americans win against China over Taiwan? No.

"I met an American senator yesterday and he said now the problem is being resolved. Trade and investments are growing, the two economies will be seamlessly interlinked. They will not have to confront China over Taiwan. Reunification will take place in a peaceful manner."

Lee is also sanguine about the prospects for China developing peacefully, without social tensions erupting: "For 10 years, no trouble. Their control is complete. Everywhere life is improving, including the backward provinces. Maybe 20 years, no problem. What will happen when 70 to 75 per cent of the population is in the towns, which will happen by 25 years? All will have cell phones, PDAs, laptops or Netbooks, with Wifi to stay connected. The government cannot suppress news and information.

"They are trying to block dissenting opinions from gathering momentum so they take down the website. But it's like cleaning up the Augean stables (from the Greek myth about the labours of Hercules). You can't quite succeed. But they will try. And they are smart and pragmatic.

"In 20 years they'll have a group who are Western-educated in charge. They will know what has to change if they are going to maximise their potential. They may be smart enough to play by the rules."

Will China become democratic? "Partially. In a pyramidal fashion, small town, small villages, they allow free play. Communists, non-communists can stand. It's a check on corruption. Big towns, they will control the elections to make sure that reliable people are candidates, and the big towns will elect CCP (Chinese Communist Party) members as provincial leaders, and together from these provincial leaders, the politburo will select the next politburo and Central Executive Committee. This is my guess of the manner they will be more open in the selection process. At every level, they will ensure reliable cadres who will uphold the Party principles. I am sure they have thought out this and many other ways. They must have a controlled and less risky outcome."

Lee has met some of these senior Chinese leaders on a regular basis: "The present leaders are pragmatic and realistic. There's less talk of communism, but they have a deep-seated commitment to look after the poorer people and have a fair and more equal society, caring especially for those in the deprived areas."

When it came to analysing relations among countries, Lee's views were typical of his unvarnished, provocative self. We asked Lee if there was an overall theme, or underlying philosophy, behind his worldview on strategic and geopolitical affairs. This, after all, is a man sought after by world leaders for his insights into global, especially Asian, affairs.

His answer was startling for the way it went back to basics. He bypassed talk on human society, politics, or geopolitical concepts of cooperation or competing spheres of influence. To Lee, the will to power is the dominant drive for humankind, pushing each group to reach beyond its own borders to expand its territory. And how do groups determine who their enemies and allies are? To Lee, such calculations are rooted in self-interest and degrees of genetic proximity.

As he summed up the World According to Lee Kuan Yew, some among the group of journalists interviewing him felt bemused. He had expounded at great length on his beliefs in the genetic transmission of intelligence and his Darwinian view of human society in an earlier interview which touched on social welfare and income distribution, and which is covered in another chapter. This interview, months later, was supposed to be a conversation on Lee's geopolitical views. Yet on this topic, too, it turned out that his views are driven by his belief that genes shape human behaviour.

This involves two core convictions. The first is his belief that relations among individuals, and among groups, are determined by genetic factors. People and societies tend to help those closest to them genetically. With that genetic lens firmly in place, Lee predicts that the shift of power from America to China will cause more disruptions than the transfer of power from white British to white Americans after the mid-20th century.

His other key conviction stems from the belief that groups are engaged in a battle for supremacy. Power is the underlying theme in Lee's view of nation-states. Each nation seeks access to resources to maximise its own power base. It cooperates with others out of self-interest. Altruism in Lee's worldview derives from a cool calculation of two things: whether an act will help advance one's own self-interest as a nation; and whether an act will advance those of similar genetic makeup. If one or the other interest is advanced, a nation may proceed. Where there is a conflict between the two, self-interest rather than kin-interest will prevail.

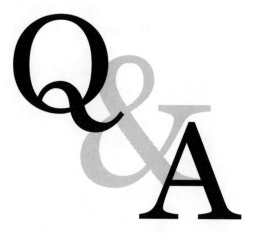

"We just want maximum
space to be ourselves."

Q: *We're going to ask you about your views about world events and geopolitics. Is there an overarching framework which you depend on to explain the behaviour of countries and how they interact with each other?*

A: It's always been the same from time immemorial. A tribe wants more space, wants to take over the territory of other tribes, they fight and they expand. Even when it is part of them and they become a different unit, they still fight, for supremacy.

(Sociobiologist) Edward Wilson says when two tribes fight, the third tribe will join the tribe that shares more of their DNA. He described it as an innate, inherited gene that seeks to multiply itself.[2]

In China, you will see that over the centuries, as they got invaded, the Han absorbed the others – Manchus, Mongols – and they all became Han. The only tribes they can't assimilate are the Uighurs and the Muslims in Ningxia. The other group which they have not been able to assimilate are the Tibetans, because the Tibetans live on a high plateau with less oxygen, and many Han people sent there have come back, because their lung capacity cannot adjust.

Look at the whites. They fought each other. Then they fought each other for empires. First the British captured large chunks of India, Southeast Asia, Africa, occupied North America but lost it to the American colonies, Australia and New Zealand, South Africa.

Although the British fought the Boers in South Africa, when it came to meeting the blacks, they joined up. They thought they shared more DNA because they are whites and the Boers came from Holland.

I think this is an inevitable evolving of the human species because now the whole globe is related and the whites in charge in America and Europe now face a world where the Chinese and next the Indians will be dominant. So it'll be interesting to see how they adjust. For Britain to hand over power to the Americans was relatively smooth and pain-free. The British slowly declined, the Americans slowly took over. Same language, similar civilisation and the Americans just took over the English language.

I'm not sure how it will go when the Chinese become gradually more and more equal to the Americans, which will be by the end of the century. By the next century, you would have learnt that either you coexist or you destroy each other.

Q: *So this view of yours, it is quite Darwinian.*

A: It's not quite Darwinian, it's something that I've observed empirically. I didn't start off with any theory. I didn't start off with Edward Wilson. Wilson just gave me an intellectual basis and an example, but I've observed this.

This is an inevitable part of human evolution. As you form nation states, you have the resources of those who are not of your stock but you can use them as part of your strength. So the British used African Rifles, Indian Army and fought many wars. And the Afghan situation is the same, different tribes fight for supremacy but confronted by the Russians, they all joined up together and beat the Russians. Now confronted by Nato (North Atlantic Treaty Organisation) forces, they will join up together and beat up Nato.

Q: *You said you did not set out thinking this way. How did you come to this worldview and what were some specific events that led you to this conclusion?*

A: This is the result of a gradual growing up from a child to adolescent to a young student to a mature adult.

The Japanese, when they came into Singapore, did exactly what the British did, divide and rule. So they treated the Malays with kid gloves, they co-opted the Indians who had surrendered and they whacked the Chinese. Genetically, the Chinese are nearest to them but the Chinese have posed a threat to them in the past and they wanted to conquer China and dominate China. Then they'll have the resources of the Chinese to conquer this part of the world. It was biting off more than they can chew. They lost. But they were especially cruel to the Chinese because the Chinese in this part of the world donated to the nationalist government in Chongqing to fight them.

So you come to your own conclusions. Why is he beating me up? Because I'm Chinese. Why is he gentle to the Malays and winning the Indians over? So there the genetic link is overcome by another ambition, to be the boss of East Asia. You got to do your own calculations; you can observe these things.

Q: *You don't believe, as human society progresses and modernises and with globalisation, that there will be moderating influences on this particular view?*

A: Have you got any daughters?

Q: *Yes.*

A: Supposing an African black were to marry your daughter, what is your reaction? You will cheer or you will tell your daughter, look, think again, right? I have no qualms in telling you that I'll tell her "you're mad".

In fact a Jewish doctor wanted to marry my daughter, when she was working in MGH (Massachusetts General Hospital, where she trained as a neurology resident). So my wife said, are you sure that will last, an American Jew? She thought over it and she said, "Yes, that's true." It will last for a few years, then move on.

Supposing it had been a Chinese doctor from China or from Taiwan. Well, my grandson, the PM's son, brought home this young lady. She was on her way to Japan on a scholarship, so it's more or less committed, you know, coming to Singapore to meet the family. He brought her to meet me. She's an MIT graduate, a mainlander whose father was a professor. They live in America now. She was brought up there since the age of 7. There's no unhappiness. We say, "OK, that's not bad." He's found a Chinese girl, to begin with, and she's bright and she's very agreeable, pleasant, and she's bilingual so maybe he'll become bilingual over time.

Supposing he'd brought home a white girl. Are you sure you want to do that? But what would my reaction be? I'd say well, think it over carefully. It's so much of a struggle. Right? I mean, it is an instinctive reaction.

Q: *Are you saying that all these deep-seated tribal instincts are as relevant on the international arena as in the personal arena? What does this mean in terms of the rise of China with the transition of the Anglo Saxon-based power to a Chinese base? So, is conflict inevitable?*

A: At this moment I think the American outcome is best for us. I don't see the Chinese as a benign power as the Americans. I mean, they say *bu cheng ba* (won't be a hegemon). If you are not ready to be a hegemon, why do you keep on telling the world you are not going to be a hegemon? You're just not a hegemon, all right? But I know the Americans are a hegemon but a gentle one. I've got on with them. Why not leave the present hegemon in place?

Q: *What about the economic imperatives? Surely nations would not fight if there's an adverse effect or cost on trade, investment, business confidence? Aren't those factors relevant in the geopolitical order today?*

A: They thought so as Germany entered the European system and grew strong. Germany was late in having an empire. She decided to go for it. The others combined and beat her, including the Americans. So now they've decided okay, let's settle for Europe.

I do not believe that trade and economic relationships are decisive. It is one factor but if you believe you can win and take over, why not? You suffer for a while but after that it's all yours. But I do not believe that outcome is possible when both sides have hydrogen bombs. You will both destroy. So the competition will be at the edges.

Q: *But don't you think at least on the state-to-state level, there has been more use of international organisations, more cooperation – don't you think these urges to dominate one another can be contained by institutions?*

A: How old are you?

Q: *I'm 26.*

A: Well, if you ask the same question when you are 46, that means you haven't learnt very much. You ask Kishore Mahbubani, you ask anybody who's served in the United Nations. Yes, between small countries you have no choice, right, because you can get UN Security Council saying stop fighting and if you don't, we'll take action. But when it involves a major power, when it involves another Security Council member, or even when it involves two non-Security Council members, say India and Pakistan, they just ignore exhortations and fight on.

Q: *How does this view of yours about self-interest and kin-interest inform Singapore's foreign policy or shape our approach to dealing with other countries?*

A: It does not. But it's one of the factors. You take the Malays in Malaysia. They thought: *serumpun* (same stock) towards the Indonesians. The Indonesians now have more hatred for the Malaysians than for us because they are quarrelling over oil fields in Ambalat (a sea block in the Sulawesi sea). We are not quarrelling over that. And they nearly went to war when their ships clashed near Ambalat.

It cuts no ice with the Indonesians. I'm the big brother. They say *serumpun*, that means you surrender to me as the elder brother. And the Malaysians do not want to surrender these oil fields and they say, let's go to arbitration. Why should they? And the Malaysians claim that now Sipadan and Ligitan belong to them, the boundaries are different.

So it's not a done deal, it's not a finite position. It shifts. But if we threaten either one of them, then they have to combine together and fix us because then we are a thorn in their side. So we just keep quiet and leave them be. We'll be friendly to both but don't push us around.

Big powers in the neighbourhood

To Lee, the fundamental principle that should guide Singapore through the changing strategic landscape remains the same: to maximise economic and political space. Ever the realist, he sees the rise of China and India, and the restive Southeast Asian region, through the lens of Singapore's interests. One pressing issue for him is how to share his experience and insights with younger leaders.

Q: *We're in the middle of a tectonic shift in the global order. What are some underlying fundamental principles that should guide Singapore's foreign policy?*

A: It's the same. We just want maximum space to be ourselves. And that is best achieved when big "trees" allow space for us, between them we have space. You have one big tree covering us, we have no space.

Q: *Can you flesh out what Singapore needs to do to create space among giants for itself?*

A: Supposing we had not created the ties we have created with America and Japan. This is before China and India, where America, Japan and Europe were players in the strategic world. Britain still had considerable military forces and was interested. That gave us space, we were not boxed in by the Asean countries. You don't want to trade with us, that's your choice. We bring in the multinationals, export to the world. In the end they also joined us in getting multinationals. We get more and better quality investments, higher value added. So we've broken free from them.

Supposing we hadn't done that and we listened to all those who say: let's be friends with them. What is the purchasing power of Indonesia? What is the purchasing power of Thailand as against Japan or America? Even Australia and New Zealand? They may be 25, 27 million or even three million but they have high standards of living. That's economic space.

And because we provide a secure, stable base in the centre of the region, they can sell fruit, butter, eggs, frozen chicken, frozen pork or whatever. They base themselves in Singapore and then slowly feel their way into the region where the demand is. We started as the hub, we made it a hub. We were already partially a hub under the British, we just improved it.

Q: *There's a point of view that things could get tougher for Singapore because of two factors. One is the rise of a less benign superpower – China versus the US. And the other factor is because a statesman of your stature would be not around. What's your response to that view?*

A: No, no, no. The second one is ephemeral influence and larger forces are at stake. If the US completely withdraws from East Asia and China becomes the only dominant power, then I say we are in a tighter position because supposing you do something to displease them, they don't have to invade you.

Our ties with them are growing day by day economically even though we're trying very hard to diversify into India and to other parts of Asia. But they are the big market. All they do is squeeze us economically. Hong Kong now knows its place. The economy goes down, they might say, okay, I allow my chaps to go buy your properties and the stock market immediately goes up. Do Hongkongers realise who butters their bread? Yes, of course. Do the anti-Chinese, pro-democracy groups increase their power or those groups that say let's work with China? So Anson Chan (Hong Kong's chief secretary, 1993–2002) has decided to give up. She took a position which is not tenable right from the beginning. She opposed China. She thought British system, democracy, American support, they can maintain 50 years. Rubbish. The day the flag came down, Chinese flag went up, that day China was the sovereign power.

The British understood it. I understood it. I've seen it happen across the world, all the colonies decolonised and I'm a trained lawyer. The imperial system of preferences has become meaningless. Every independent country goes its own way. We have trade agreements with America, China, India and the region. We don't have a trade agreement with Britain.[3] What for? How much can they buy? But during imperial days when you're part of them, they made sure that we're part of their economy.

Q: *You talked about how the US is a benign power and how it's to our benefit to have close relations with them but are* *there costs to that relationship?*

A: The costs are we are not liked by our neighbours. But our neighbours want to be friends with America, but we are better friends, so they are unhappy with us.

No, anything we do makes them unhappy. Right? What are the costs of that? And we allowed the American logistics base here, great umbrage, anti voices from Malaysia and Indonesia. Then when the South China Sea became a dispute, Ali Alatas (then Indonesian Foreign Minister) says we have always been in favour of America having naval logistics forces in Singapore. Oh, that's very good. We didn't let it be known at that time and now the Philippines have regretted closing down the Subic Bay American naval base.[4] They are just short-term thinkers. Now it's too late. They should never have closed that base, then they won't have lost the South China Sea islands under dispute. The American navy would be there helping the Filipino navy. If the Chinese navy engages the Filipino navy, the alliance will be invoked. But they've chased the Americans away. The Americans are not going to go back from Singapore. What for? It's taking on an unnecessary burden for nothing.

Q: *In terms of the balance of power in the region, you've spoken at some length about the US and China. How does India fit into this balance?*

A: India does not geographically fit in the Pacific. But the contest will be in the Pacific and the Indian Ocean. China has moved naval forces into the Indian Ocean to protect its oil supply from the Gulf, and commodities from Africa. That's where the Indians are a force. If the Indians are on the American side, the Americans will have a great advantage. So the Chinese have to have a counter, and have developed ports in Myanmar and in Pakistan.

Q: *Sometimes you appear more optimistic about China's growth than India's. In your memoirs, you said that in the '50s China and India were both models of development and you wrote that you hoped India would succeed.*

A: Because China was communist. Their economic system could not make it.

Q: *At what point did you come to that conclusion?*

A: By the 1970s. There are fundamental differences. Edward Luce of the *FT* (*Financial Times*) wrote *In Spite of the Gods* (subtitled *The Strange Rise of Modern India*). It's interesting and decisive in the comparison.

First, India is not one nation but many nations. The British made it one nation with their railway and one administration. And then it broke up into India and East and West Pakistan, that later broke into Pakistan and Bangladesh. The British allowed rulers of the princely states to decide which country to join. The ruler of Kashmir, a Hindu, decided to join India. The majority population in the state were Muslims. This decision of the Hindu ruler was never accepted by the Pakistanis. The peoples of India speak many different languages. Hindi, 40 per cent in the north. English, maybe 35 per cent across the whole subcontinent. Tamil, 10 per cent in Tamil Nadu. You speak in Malayali, 3 per cent.

In China, 90 per cent are Han Chinese and speak Mandarin. And they've simplified the Chinese characters and educated almost everyone to master Chinese. So CCTV is understood throughout the whole country.

Compare the cultures. The Chinese are doers. The Indians are contemplative and argumentative – (Nobel Prize-winning economist) Amartya Sen entitled one of his books *The Argumentative Indian*. When the Chinese decided to make Chongqing a prosperous centre in the western region, they gave it the necessary resources. Then you find Chongqing swiftly blossoms.

I was in Bombay. The Deputy Chief Minister of the state government of Maharashtra asked if I could have a dialogue with him and his ministers and the chief officials on how to make Bombay like Singapore. So I spent three hours with them.

I said, "Your airport: if you want to be a financial centre, study Shanghai and you see the difference. Your roads are scruffy, cows, trishaws, potholes, hawkers, squatters. When you reach Bombay eventually, you see the sea and you see a few high-rises but higgledy-piggledy." I asked where does Bombay get its revenue from? He said, from the Maharashtra government. Where's the Maharashtra government getting its revenue from? From the whole of Maharashtra, but Bombay is the biggest source of revenue.

I asked, "How much of what Bombay earns goes back to it?" He said, "Well you can't say, but the majority goes to the whole state, farmers." So to win the votes of the farmers, they use the revenue from Bombay. So I said, look, you want Bombay to be a financial centre like Pudong, the Chinese made Shanghai an independent city with provincial status. So it deals direct with the centre. Why not make Bombay the same? No, he said, "We can't do that. If we do that we lose our revenue." So I said, "Then you will always have Bombay as it is."

Two days later I had lunch with Prime Minister Manmohan Singh and his security adviser. So I recounted this to Manmohan Singh. I said, "Look, if you're serious about Bombay becoming a financial centre like Pudong or London or New York, you make it an independent province dealing direct with the centre."

He replied, "I'll never get it passed through Parliament." To get it passed, all 30 states must agree and all the votes and so on. He said it's just not possible. So it will never be done.

And every state consists of coalitions from different parties. And you get the Communist Party as part of the Congress government, but in Calcutta and Kerala they follow different policies. They invite investors to their states. But they prevent the centre from privatisation. They're playing politics all the time. And there are 10 parties in the coalition. It's not one country, it's many countries.

The Chinese are one government: do it and you'll be promoted. Don't do it, you will be sidelined. It's done.

The systems are not comparable. Both their GDPs were the same at the time of independence and when China started its open-door policy, it was a China stuck in the old system. Today, China's GDP is three and a half times that of India. India is growing at about two-thirds the rate of China. But they're a big country and they're a counterweight in the Indian Ocean. And we want them to be part of the Southeast Asia balance of forces.

Our sea routes go west and east, so we're friends with both. There's no contradiction. They will not make it at the same pace. The West played India up at the beginning. A *Financial Times* article brought the Indians back to earth. Do not talk about India and China in the same breath. They are two different countries. But does that make India a non-player? No. It's a bigger player than the whole of Asean put together.

Q: *When we talk about Asean, increasingly people are saying that it must be successful as an economic grouping, 550 million people, a market that's half the markets of China and India each. How do you see that prospect of Asean as an economic grouping?*

A: The logic of joining markets is irrefutable and it will happen. This is going to be a slow process. So let's go for individual FTAs (free trade agreements). So you don't move, we're moving.

Q: *Are you personally disappointed at the slow pace of Asean's integration?*

A: No, I'm surprised that we've made this amount of progress. The reality has sunk home. But between sinking home and actually responding to it, there's a time lag. It makes little difference to us. We're not depending on the Asean market. We're concentrating on US, Japan, South Korea, China, India, the Gulf. We have structured our economic ties that way because our neighbours were unable to move quickly. Had we followed them and gone at that pace, where will we be today?

Q: *Many societies in this part of the world are in a state of flux, as the politics have not been settled, Thailand, Malaysia, maybe even Indonesia. Do you worry about this region? You're quite sanguine about Asia as a whole.*

A: They will not collapse but they will not do as well as they could. When the tide rises, all ships rise. Their ships are not in the best of conditions but they will still rise. We will do better because we keep in trim. The investments will come into the region.

Q: *How widely shared is this point of view that there must be a balance of power with the US presence continuing to be strong here? Because some worry about parts of Indochina falling under China's influence. So where does that leave the rest of Southeast Asia?*

A: No, the Vietnamese will not fall under China's influence. These people talk without an intimate knowledge of the history, the culture, the Vietnam and China relationship and the present condition. Yes, the Vietnamese are chary of the Chinese but are they going to be dominated? No. They're already changing attitudes to Americans. Cam Ranh Bay could be built into a naval base for the American navy. They will have a balance of powers. China gives more aid to Cambodia and Laos than any other country. Thailand is friendly to both US and China. Myanmar welcomes the Indians and the Chinese. They balance one against the other.

Q: *What is your best guess about Myanmar and whether you see major changes in that society over the next decade or so?*

A: You either have revolution by consent or revolution by violence. How long can this leadership stay? How long can the next leadership stay? It will pass on to a younger group of colonels. They are isolated, they can see Thailand progressing. Yes, they are getting richer personally, but the country is getting poorer: poor doctors, no medicines, no education, you want your country to be like that? So if they've got any brains they will open up. And when you open up, you got to educate your people. When you educate your people, certain consequences follow. So I don't see them getting on.

I've given up with this lot. Any American comes, I say, look, speak to the younger ministers. I was speaking to Khin Nyunt, he's the most intelligent of the generals, he was in charge of intelligence and I persuaded him to go the Indonesian way, take off your uniform, form a party, go for elections and present yourself as a political force. They were heading that way. Then Suharto fell. They said this is wrong advice. Don't talk to me about Myanmar. I've already written them off for my lifetime.

Q: *PM Lee Hsien Loong and Malaysian Prime Minister Najib Razak came to a landmark agreement on the Points of Agreement to move the railway station and free up Tanjong Pagar for development. Next up is a Mass Rapid Transit line to Johor Bahru. The Iskandar region is trying to attract more Singapore businessmen. Are you optimistic about economic cooperation going forward? How much closer can both sides get economically?[5]*

A: Singapore is economically vibrant. If Malaysia wants to plug into Singapore's growth, especially for southern Johor, it must welcome Singapore's investments and businessmen. Prime Minister Najib understands this. He wants the Iskandar region in southern Johor to grow. The economic imperatives are strong. I doubt if irrational political issues will be allowed to stifle the economic cooperation from going forward. How much closer both sides can get economically depends on how Malaysians in the peninsula welcome Singapore businessmen. Singaporeans must feel that their investments are safe, and that they are welcome.

Q: *If there were any conflicts between the US and China, or China and India, would Singapore have to pick a side?*

A: China and India, I don't think there'll be a conflict. What are they going to conflict over? The Himalayas?

Q: *They share a long border.*

A: What is that long border worth, mountain fortresses? What is the point of invading India and occupy one billion people and be responsible for them? Are the Indians going to conquer Tibet? No. Will the Indians ask the Dalai Lama to leave his Dharamsala residence near the Tibetan border? No. The Chinese are unhappy that the Dalai Lama is so close to Tibet. China and India cannot fight a big war because they both have nuclear weapons. What are they going to fight over? And what's the outcome?

What are the Americans going to fight China over? Control over East Asia? The Chinese need not fight over East Asia. Slowly and gradually they will expand their economic ties with East Asia and offer them their market of 1.3 billion consumers. They are already amongst the first three countries for imports and exports in seven out of 10 Asean countries. This is since they opened up and began to buy and sell in the 1990s. Extrapolate that another 10, 20 years and they will be the top importer and exporter of all East Asian countries. How can the Americans compete in trade?

Q: *You've ruled out conflict between China, India and US in the region at least for the next 20, 30 years but is there a particular conflict or flashpoint in the region you think is likely to happen over the same period? What should Singaporeans be most worried about if there are regional conflicts?*

A: First, if we don't have a defence capability, we are at risk both from the Malaysians and the Indonesians. They'll knock us about. They will not openly invade us, because, you know, the Security Council will say you have to leave and so on, they can see all our international connections. But they will harass us but if they know that they harass us, we can harass them back, ah, that's a different matter.

And other than that, all right, the Philippines fights with Indonesia or fights with Vietnam, which I don't think is likely, so what? I don't see Indonesians fighting the Burmese. Anyway they haven't got the weapons of high calibre. We have the most modern weapons of all the states in Asean. We have the best-educated workforce. No other Asean country has a population like us: well-educated and computer-literate. You read the *Pioneer* magazine on "3G SAF" (third generation Singapore Armed Forces) and it gives you a glimpse of what kind of different battle scenes we train for.

Who can do that in this region?

Not only must you have top people, people who have established the systems but the people out in the field will have to operate it. What kind of lieutenants, sergeants do you have?

Q: *Do you foresee a day when those weapons will be put to actual use?*

A: If somebody miscalculates. Supposing a general says, look, Sir, Singapore is not a pushover. He says never mind, hit them. Then? They know they can't occupy us and we will hit back. So their generals must be thinking: They will hit back, then what happens?

Q: *What's the likelihood?*

A: Not if they're rational. However, as you know, not all leaders in our neighbourhood are rational all the time.

Q: *How do you navigate relations in an environment with a big power pressing on you and the US distracted and neighbours who may be unfriendly?*

A: But unfriendly does not mean they will attack us. We've a balance of forces. Americans consider us a very powerful and strategic logistics base for forward placement of weapons and ammo. I've just met a US senator, he said, "Thank you very much." He's on the armed services committee. We're helping them in Afghanistan. We helped them in Iraq. So they sell us weapons, we train our air force new fighter planes in Arizona. We have joint air force exercises with their squadrons – we're training with the world's top fighter pilots.

Q: *It's interesting, just now when you listed the countries you didn't really mention Europe. They're still one of our biggest trading partners and one of the early investors here.*

A: As a trading partner, yes.[6] But they are fading away as a strategic partner.

Q: *Is our relationship with them or the region's relationship* *with them going to be purely economic, do you think?*

A: Yes, of course. They can't even settle the Balkans without American assistance. They're not spending money on defence. They haven't got one defence policy. They haven't got one foreign policy. It's 27 different countries, full stop.

Q: *So is there a need to engage them at all?*

A: There's a need to engage them because, well, we've got old lines with the British. It's foolish to lose them. They are members of the Security Council.

France is another Security Council member. We've cultivated France; we've cultivated Germany. But we know that increasingly their interests are in Europe, in Africa, in North America and Latin America. That's their economic future. And they don't see themselves competing against the Chinese and the Americans in this part of the world. If you were them you'll come to the same conclusion – what's your cost base? What's your strategic interest? So, those are the facts of life.

The drift away from them was relentless and the British saw it, too. That's why they withdrew from east of Suez.

Q: *Can we discuss the Middle East?*

A: What do you want to know about the Middle East? What's going to happen? Nobody really knows. The Middle East is kept together in this configuration because of the American presence. If there's no American presence, who's the dominant power? Iran now, right? After the invasion of Iraq, Iran has become stronger. So Abu Dhabi has forged an alliance with France and France has put some forces there, they give Abu Dhabi confidence and get benefits from Abu Dhabi. But can France take on Iran? But anyway, it's some comfort because if Iran gets difficult before a war, they have to consider the French reaction.

The only power that can counter the Iranians are the Americans and I don't think the Americans are going to leave that area. The oil will prevent them from leaving that area because you can't allow that region to go into the hands of Iran. So they are stuck there.

The British were there as protectors. When they withdrew from east of Suez in 1971, the Americans filled the gap. The Americans leave, who fills the gap? Nobody. So a regional power will take over. Who? Iran. All the other states are Bedouins except Iraq, they have a long civilisation among the Euphrates. And the Iranians are fully aware that they are the only civilisation in that region of that size. And the Arab, Bedouin Arabs, yes, they have money and all the oil, but they know that this is a very big power. And the Iranians are producing nuclear scientists, they are bright people, brighter than the Bedouin Arabs. It's finally the quality of your people, not just numbers.

Q: *Do you see a major confrontation between Israel and Iran?*

A: I cannot say. I doubt it. Israel has not got the military technology to blast the bunkers to get at the nuclear sites. They may be able to get through without all their planes being shot down but only the Americans have the blockbusters. Americans would give it to the Israelis but, you know, then you got a real big war. So if you have to do it, better the Americans do it. It's open, I am done. So the Arab world will not become more anti-Jew. Whether they will do it is another matter. (US Secretary of State) Hillary Clinton says, we will arm the other states correspondingly. How? With nuclear weapons or anti-missiles? But they're not going to let go.

So the mistake was really not to deal with Iran before they went into Iraq. But it's done. The last eight years have changed the global picture.

And whatever the faults of Saddam Hussein, he was anti-Iran. He had attacked Iran, made a mistake. He thought Iran will weaken, he attacked them, the Iranians were prepared to send in their suicide squads and fought on. So he brought out biological weapons which is against human rights, but he was dead scared. And according to the interrogation (by the FBI after his 2003 capture), he said he was always ambiguous about having weapons of mass destruction because if he admitted he had none, Iranians would know that he was weak and would wallop him. So he wanted the Iranians to believe that he had weapons of mass destruction. So the right, cynical strategy, which a person like Henry Kissinger would do, is to support the Iraqis and prevent the Iranians from ever getting their influence across into the Arab world. But George W. Bush's advisers were not of that quality. Democracy, Paul Wolfowitz, mad dog![7] A country with 4,000 years of history had never anything other than rulers who were autocrats. So that's a total disaster.

Then we are in Afghanistan. Obama, during the campaign, talked of Afghanistan, well, that's a popular war, Iraq unpopular, we will fight in Afghanistan. At the time he said that I winced because I said, "Oh God, we'd be in Afghanistan for a long time." So how do they get out of Afghanistan without losing face?

Q: *You have also spoken about the Middle East as a source of militant Islam. I remember when you spoke to some of us soon after 9/11 you were very pessimistic about the world and how global terrorism would change the face of the world as it were. Are you less pessimistic now looking at how it has turned out?*

A: Well, I think the militants made a mistake when they attacked Saudi Arabia and started blowing things up. The Saudis started drawing back from it because now they're involved, because they thought this was going to happen outside. This is their pact with the Wahhabi leaders. Can they completely withdraw? No. Then the Wahhabi religious leaders may not back them and the royal family may collapse.

So I see this pendulum moving backwards and forwards. Where it will stop, I don't know. They just want to survive as a dynasty and have this wealth. So they share their wealth with the Wahhabi leaders and the Wahhabi leaders go on this crusade.

Q: *What's the quality of our leaders here, and what do you do to download your databank on geopolitics to the younger ministers?*

A: Amongst the present leadership, I would say PM (Prime Minister Lee Hsien Loong), Teo Chee Hean, George Yeo. Going down younger, Khaw Boon Wan. He speaks Chinese, he speaks English, he understands where we are heading, who's who, what's what. He speaks Chinese but he has no doubts at all that he is not Chinese when he is dealing with them. Who else? I'm not sure, maybe Ng Eng Hen, but because he doesn't speak Chinese, he hasn't quite got that same exposure. But they are not fools, they will catch up.

Q: *What do you do to download your databank?*

A: We sit down, we got to make decisions. I either support or oppose, and if I oppose, I give my reasons; if I support, I give my reasons. And I said look, here's the direction you have to go.

We have to go to Afghanistan. Shall we or shall we not? They want us to send a medical team to support the Australians and the Dutch in a dangerous area called Uruzgan. I said look, it's part of the insurance premium we are paying, we got to pay. You want the Americans to stay here, you want a strategic framework agreement with them, known to our neighbours, you want the logistics base to stay here, you got to pay this price. Go.

I mean, you calculate. If America were going to be out in five, 10 years, do we need to pay this price? No. The British – we knew they were going to leave. But we know the Americans cannot leave. If they leave, they've lost their global influence. They know that the Pacific is the biggest area of contention in this century, not the Atlantic. And they are going to go up Japan, and if they can, South Korea, Australia and New Zealand, and if they can, us and the Philippines. The Philippines will play both sides. Chinese are giving the Philippines a lot of help.

You cannot say, look, I predict this will be the trajectory. No. I predict this will be the trend. The trend may change, the tide may change, as of this moment I say 20, 30 years I do not see the Americans disengaging from a contest which they had fought for since Admiral Perry opened up Japan, and they have the superior technology. Yes, the Chinese are building an aircraft carrier, but can they build one which is nuclear? Can they pilot those kinds of aeroplanes? It will take them 50 years, by which time the Americans would have other improvements. It's not easy.

Being Chinese

Lee has always had an ambiguous relationship with his ethnicity. He grew up in a Peranakan or Straits Chinese family speaking Malay and English. He struggled to learn Hokkien, then Mandarin, to communicate with Chinese-speaking Singaporeans. In England as a student after World War II, he found he had more in common with non-Chinese Malayan students than with the Chinese from mainland China. In post-independence Singapore, he steered Singapore's bilingual policy, making it compulsory for ethnic Chinese Singaporeans to learn Chinese in school, and making mother tongue languages a must-pass subject for entry into local universities, a policy he later admitted was a mistake which caused hardship to several generations of students from English-speaking homes who struggled to master Chinese.

He has always separated ethnicity from nationality. He is Chinese ethnically, but does not identify with the values or identity of those from the Chinese mainland. In fact, as this extract from one of the interviews for this book shows, he has no qualms declaring that it is sheer romanticism for Chinese Singaporeans to think of mainland China as a kind of motherland.

Q: *You spoke earlier about how you're very clear about what being Chinese means. You are Chinese ethnically but you're not Chinese like the mainlander Chinese.*

A: Yes.

Q: *I wonder how informed are other Chinese Singaporeans on that score, because in the 1990s when you wanted to sprout a second wing, you talked about* guanxi *(connections) and value of* guanxi. *What do you make of all that fixation?*

A: Look, you got to look at the Chinese at different levels. The older generation, they are romanticists, like my uncle-in-law who says, "I want my bones to be buried in China." He married my mother's sister. Utter rubbish. His bones are now in Kuala Lumpur somewhere. He has this romantic idea that, you know, this is a land of my forefathers. I have no doubts that the land of my forefathers would have brought me down in the world.

That's why he came out here and made good, went back and bought himself a mandarinate[8] of the lowest class and he got a picture drawn up. And he built himself a manor house which they have now refurbished and made into a historic tourist site and they sent me a CD. I said thank you very much. First they wanted me to contribute. I said no, no, I'm not Chinese, I'm Singaporean, I'm not going to visit the place, my brother can go and visit the place. He has, I'm not going to. They took a picture of the occupants, they all looked like country bumpkins and I'd be one of them.

So I have no romantic ideas about where I sprang from. I'm very grateful that my great grandmother who was born here of China-born Chinese decided she's not going to go back with her husband because she doesn't know China and so kept the children, including my grandfather here, so that's why I'm here. I'm a lucky fellow. Yes, we are all lucky fellows.

But the older generation has this romantic idea. So they say okay, we owe an obligation to send money back. So Tan Kah Kee[9] built schools, built universities and he went back. That was the dream of every Chinese emigrant: I will make good, I'll help my fellow clansmen. Very few did.

Then you have the younger generation, English-educated, learning Chinese language, finding it tough and meeting Chinese and others, so troublesome. I discovered this when I was a student in England, that I had more in common with the Singaporeans and Malaysians of other races than with the Chinese from China because they are completely different. Their dress, their manners, their language. They are a different lot, that's all. They come from a different society. Of course, at the end of the day they are Chinese. If my son and my daughter wants to marry over there and they can even incorporate them, I say, well, okay, I mean because there will not be a sudden change in their features and so on.

Q: *But as China increasingly flexes its soft power, I can imagine that as a young Chinese person growing up in Singapore you will begin to look to China?*

A: If you go to China regularly you'll know you are wrong.

You can go anytime and the more successful they are, the less they will think of you and the more they will treat you with condescension.

Look at Lim Sau Hoong – she is in public relations, helped them in their Olympics, completely conversant in two languages. In fact, Chinese is her first language, although she went to a bilingual school. She did a catchy logo for CCTV, she did the ad for Bank of China, she helped in the Olympics preparations. I believe the Bank of China pays a retainer, so she won't do it for any other Chinese bank. Well, they asked her to set up a branch in Beijing. She doesn't want to. When you want me, you phone me up, give me what you want and I'll make a special visit, and we'll talk it over.

Never open an office there, you become one of them, she said. They'll just order you around. She stays in Singapore. When they need me, she said, they have to write to me or phone me, then I will consider whether I will go for this assignment. She is smart: I am a Singaporean, I'm not your subordinate and these are my terms. You have an office there, and their office makes no differentiation between you and the China Chinese, *ma shang zuo, kuai dian* (do it immediately, hurry up). She says no, I need a few days, I need a few weeks, let me think it over.

That romantic idea of going back to the bosom of your motherland is a delusion. We have become different, that's all. You can go back to China, you're still different. Your children are born and bred there, then they may be reabsorbed. Their inputs will be Chinese inputs.

Q: *Will this attitude of the Chinese towards Singapore change as they become even stronger and influential?*

A: Of course. They expect us to be more respectful – you must respect me. They tell us countries big or small are equal, we're not a hegemon, *bu cheng ba*. But when we do something they don't like, they say you have made 1.3 billion people unhappy. *Shi san yi* – 1.3 billion. When they make us unhappy? You know it is *bai wan* – million – unhappy. So please know your place.

Q: *Some people believe that you can be a global citizen, and you can be Singaporean and still go back to your roots in China. What's your view?*

A: There is no such thing as a citizen of the world. You are a citizen of some country and you have a choice: you can be a citizen of Singapore or Malaysia, you choose. Or you can go back to your Chinese roots, maybe you will go into Hong Kong or Taiwan and eventually be Chinese.

If you go to China, I don't think you will belong. They'll say okay, we'll accept you. But look at even the Malayan communist cadres who sent their families and children there in order to free themselves to continue to fight in the jungle in Malaya – nevertheless, they were treated differently. They were all kept in Changsha, capital of Hunan Province: in a special group, they went to special schools, special unit. They did not mix with the ordinary Chinese. I met the son of the Plen (Fang Chuang Pi, head of the Malayan Communist Party). He was bright, he got into Tsinghua University and he married a Malaysian Chinese girl. He didn't marry a Chinese from China.

You think you're Chinese, and that you will blend in, but you will not. You are already different. We are already different. Just like the American and the British people, or for that matter, the South African whites, Australians, New Zealanders and the British.

The Taiwanese mainlanders and Chinese mainlanders, who have not stayed in Taiwan, yes, they are same stock, same heritage but had different exposure, different standpoints, different views of the world. Are we Chinese? Yes, ethnically. Can we sit down with the Chinese and really feel part of them? Not possible. Because you speak Chinese? No. Your major premises are in your mind.

Endnotes

1 According to a Pew Hispanic Center report in 2008, white non-Hispanics will form just 47 per cent of the population in America by 2050, down from 67 per cent in 2005. Latinos will form 29 per cent of the population, up from 14 per cent in 2005. Asians' share will be 9 per cent, up from 5 per cent. Blacks will remain constant at 13 per cent.

2 This was in Edward Wilson's book *On Human Nature*, which won a Pulitzer Prize in 1979.

3 Since 1993, Singapore has signed 18 regional and bilateral free trade agreements (FTA) covering 24 trading partners. It signed an FTA with the United States in 2003, the India-Singapore Comprehensive Economic Cooperation Agreement (CECA) was signed in 2005 and an FTA with China was sealed in 2008. While it does not have an FTA with Britain, it is currently in negotiations with the European Union for a free trade deal.

4 The US Naval Base in Subic Bay, the Philippines, was the second largest overseas military base of the US Armed Forces. It was closed down in 1992 under President Corazon Aquino.

5 This question was sent as a follow-up email question in 2010 after the deal was sealed as Lee played a pivotal role in the Points of Agreement of 1990 which he signed with then Malaysian Finance Minister Daim Zainuddin. The POA covers the ownership of Malayan Railway land in Singapore. The land in Tanjong Pagar, Kranji and Woodlands was occupied by Malaysia and would have been returned to Singapore. Three parcels of land in Bukit Timah were later added to the deal. Negotiations, however, hit a deadlock until May 2010, when both sides agreed to a land swop. The swop was finalised in September 2010: Malaysia would exchange the six parcels of railway land for six parcels of land in the Marina South and Ophir/Rochor areas. The new land parcels would, in turn, be jointly developed by Malaysia and Singapore.

6 The European Union is Singapore's largest trading partner with S$86.8 billion of goods traded in 2009. Europe accounted for 11.6 per cent of Singapore's total external trade.

7 Wolfowitz was a deputy secretary for defence in George W. Bush's administration and a leading advocate of military action against Iraq to topple Saddam Hussein and to force regime change towards democratisation.

8 A high-ranking public office in the Chinese empire.

9 Chinese businessman, community leader and philanthropist who emigrated to Singapore from Fujian province, China in 1890. He made his fortune mainly in rubber plantations and founded many schools in both Singapore and China. Tan later became a communist supporter and returned to China in 1950.

9
SINGAPORE
GREENING

WHILE IN BOSTON on a sabbatical in 1968, Lee Kuan Yew noticed something odd. The leaves, the bushes, the trees, the foliage were all a verdant green.

In Singapore, bushes by the roadside were covered with grime from the diesel of cars and lorries. Boston was no less an industrialised city. But trees and leaves maintained their emerald sheen. Why was this so?

On a drive in Boston one day, he saw cars going into the petrol station, queueing up for something. The ever-inquisitive man asked what was happening.

"The driver of my car explained that every six months, you have to get your car exhaust and other polluting parts checked. They give you a label to put on your car after it has been checked. So they do not have exhausts that polluted these trees and shrubs."

When he returned to Singapore, he followed up on that idea, requiring vehicles registered in Singapore to go for emissions inspections. To this day, cars between three and ten years old must be inspected every two years, and cars over ten years old have to be checked every year. As lorries from Malaysia carrying goods into Singapore were particularly bad polluters, the Singapore government introduced a fine on polluting vehicles.

"The buses used to give out enormous volumes of smoke and the exhaust from lorries, particularly those from Malaysia, continued to do so even after we got control of our own (vehicles). We then put a levy on their lorries that belched smoke and that forced them to jack up standards."

He added, "The condition of our plants gave me an indication of the pollution levels. Then I installed pollution-measuring machine meters. That's how we tightened up on the diesel lorries and buses."

From the word go, Lee was way ahead of his time in being determined about making Singapore a clean and green city-state for everyone. He believed strongly that it was not just the rich who were entitled to clean streets, good plumbing and fresh air. The environment had to be pleasant for all, rich and poor. A squalid environment for the poor would be a breeding ground for disease. It would also allow political resentment to creep in and fester. The solution was to clean up the whole city.

In the context of 1960s Singapore, with its crowded urban tenements and rural areas with no proper sanitation, the task was easier said than done. Lee took a personal interest in environmental issues to make sure other ministries and government officials took this monumental challenge seriously.

He continues with his personal interest in green issues to this day and has kept up to date with the environment debate in its current form, with its emphasis on climate change issues.

When it comes to global warming and climate change, Lee is a complete realist. He dismisses the reservations of climate change sceptics and accepts the general consensus that emission of greenhouse gases, especially carbon dioxide, causes global temperatures to rise, triggering environmental changes that will result in sea levels rising, rivers drying up and mass migrations of peoples in search of water.

He does not believe that self-interested nation-states will be able to get together to agree to binding cuts in emissions. He thinks the impasse between developed and developing nations on this issue will remain, as developing nations resist curtailing their emissions so they do not need to slow down their pace of development, and developed nations resist having to transfer billions in wealth to developing nations to pay the so-called "climate debt".

Instead, countries like Singapore just have to assume that countries will continue in their drive for development, that emissions levels will not fall to any significant degree, and the world will continue its ride pell-mell on its way to dwindling renewable energy resources and rising sea levels. Smart countries will have to do their sums and do their best to cope with the fallout from such catastrophes.

To Lee, Singapore's options in this area are limited. Solar energy isn't viable yet. Nuclear energy remains a high-risk option. Energy-deprived Singapore will just have to continue relying on fossil fuels. In any case, whatever it can do to reduce its own carbon emissions will not make any impact on the global environment. In the trade-off between the environment and a nation's economic growth, Lee is hard-headed. If Singapore is pressured to achieve emissions cuts targets expected of developed countries, it will point out that much of its carbon emissions spring from activity to produce or service other countries' products, since Singapore has an export-heavy economy.

"We tell them: Look, who are the end-users of that energy? How can I reduce my carbon footprint and still make a living, it's not possible. You ask me to die. Then you take over responsibility of 5 million people. Can you?"

"Why should I throw away something which I'm comfortable with? I'm not interested in impressing anybody."

Q: *Even in the early years, you were a very strong advocate of a clean and green approach to Singapore's development. How did you come to this position?*

A: We are a city in a compact island. An elected government cannot have certain sections of the city green and clean, as when the British were here, and leave the rest to fester. And they were festering: squatter huts, Malay villages, no drainage, no sewers, no lavatories, open earth drains, flooded.

If we did not create a society which is clean throughout the island, I believed then and I believe now, we have two classes of people: the upper class, upper middle and even middle class with gracious surroundings; and the lower middle and the working class, in poor conditions.

No society like that will thrive. We were going to have national service. No family will want its young men to die for all the people with the big homes and those owning the tall towers. So it was important that the whole island be clean, green and with everybody owning property. It was a fundamental principle on which I crafted all policies, and it's worked.

This is a priority which was very high up on my list. Apart from finance and defence, it's a sense of equalness in this society. You can't have this sense without giving all Singaporeans a clean and green Singapore. Today, whether you are in a one, two, three, four or five-room flat, executive condominium or landed property, it's clean. You don't live equally, but you are not excluded from the public spaces for everybody.

Q: *Singapore was industrialising during this time, and some industries coming in were polluting. How did you strike the balance between development and environment? Were there some projects that had to be called off or delayed because of environmental pollution concerns?*

A: We would consider what were the anti-pollution measures that could be installed to diminish or eliminate it.

When we started the Jurong petrochemical refinery and petrochemical plant with Sumitomo, they used Japanese standards. We had a terrible row because we wanted German standards, the highest in Europe. I had seen Kaohsiung (in Taiwan) – played golf on the Kaohsiung golf course, quite some distance away from their petrochemical plants. As we play, we can smell the fumes from the petrochemical plants.

We had a fierce argument because the cost would go up. We insisted on Sumitomo doing it the German way, otherwise we'll stop the project. If you installed all the necessary equipment and cut down the pollution, we'll give them all concessions on labour like cancelling work permit fees. A bargain was struck and they carried on. Today at Jurong Country Club or Raffles Country Club, you don't smell it. Had we allowed it, the retrofitting would have been most expensive.

The Germans were the ones with the highest standards because they had their refineries and petrochemical works near their towns. Americans became more stringent as time went by but they had huge areas like Houston where winds and hurricanes would blow them away. As they increased homes around these plants, they have jacked up standards. But we are just one small island. If we were to spoil it, we've had it.

Q: *Did your thinking on how Singapore ought to be greened change and shift over the years?*

A: No, on all fronts we have to change. We have to keep up with world standards. If we want to be a first-world oasis, we must produce first-world conditions, not just the environment but facilities, health standards, services, connectivity, security. We just have to keep up with the highest benchmark that exists at any one time. Then you are in the game.

We were called a sterile, lifeless island, but safe and pollution-free. We went for the basics. Now that we have entrenched the basics, we can go for the "buzz": whole-night drinking along the Singapore River, around the marina, and with nightclubs, karaoke bars, discos, whatever. The integrated resorts with casinos will bring new problems. Wong Kan Seng (Home Affairs Minister from 1994 to 2010) and the police, after careful consultation, said they were confident to control drugs, money laundering and prostitution. What they can't guarantee is the gambling addiction. So we set up safeguards. If we don't go for the integrated resorts, a large chunk of the high spending tourists will not come here.

It's like F1 (Formula One). In the 1970s, I didn't think it was a good idea to have cars racing around and instigating our young to drive recklessly. But seeing how F1 has developed a jet set following, whole jet setting groups would come in, paid for by the banks that they patronise, we're missing something. So I changed my mind. We're not going to do a special track. We fence up the road sides and let them race in the city, like Monaco. Monaco's a success.

$Q:$ *What trade-offs were made between economic development and environmental considerations?*

$A:$ One mistake we made was to allow the refinery (at Tanjong Berlayer) near the Tanjong Pagar harbour. I was against it. But we were short of investments. A Japanese company (Maruzen Toyo Oil Company) said if we gave them this site which is near the harbour, they would build a refinery. Goh Keng Swee urged me, go for it. It was against my better judgment. He said we needed the investments, we needed to signal to the Japanese that they are welcomed so I agreed – 30-year lease. We had to wait until the lease expired. They handed it over to (oil multinational) BP.[1]

Q: *Some people are saying that Singapore's petrochemical industries are going to be a stumbling block because they emit a lot of carbon, and they stand in the way of Singapore adopting certain protocols on carbon emissions. Do you think that's true and will Singapore have to give up its petrochemical industry?*

A: Our total carbon output or footprint is 0.2 per cent of the world's footprint.[2] Our refineries do not serve us. Probably 5 per cent of our oil refineries and petrochemicals serve us. The rest are for export, bunkering and other countries in East Asia. The multinationals have invested in Singapore because of our security. They supply the end products to all countries in the region, as far as Alaska in the north and to New Zealand in the south.

We've told the United Nations' Intergovernment Panel on Climate Change, "You got to look at this aspect. China, when accused of pollution, replies that it is manufacturing all these products to send to the West that have pushed pollutive industries to China."

But in China's case, they use coal-fired power plants. We use gas for our power plants. We've done everything possible to minimise the pollution.

Because we fear that our gas suppliers from Malaysia and Indonesia may break their contracts, renege – from time to time they talk about, they need the gas more than we, Singapore, when they want to sell it to someone else at a higher price – so we're setting up an LNG terminal to store gas and getting gas from Qatar and other places.

We will not be held hostage. We have to constantly adjust our position. Nothing stays static.

Q: *When you say the world has to adjust to the consequences of not having the stomach to make a change, what exactly do you mean?*

A: Australia has felt it in the south. The north is getting more rain. However, that's the first phase. If the trend continues then I think it's not too bad for us and we'll get more rain. But it could well end with the currents changing direction, we get more El Ninos and less rain in Singapore. That is troublesome.

We have to prepare for different scenarios and nobody can predict what will be the outcome for Singapore. The trend at the moment is, we are getting wetter not drier. Australia in the south is getting drier, in the north wetter. They have to pump the water down to the south. But they have endless supplies of coal, gas and uranium and can desalinate and recycle water like we do.

Q: *Are you completely persuaded by the people, for example Al Gore, who argue about how climate change has changed the world? Are you persuaded by the evidence that they have brought forth?*

A: My assessment is, the governments do not have the will to do what is necessary and lose votes. We must be prepared to adjust to a different world.

The Americans want China to stop using coal or to reduce their pollution. China says, "You have been the great polluter all these years accumulatively." Now the negotiators from China and India say they want the US to reduce pollution by 40 per cent on the 1990 standard. However, the American Congress has passed a Bill to reduce greenhouse gas emissions by only 4 per cent from 1990 levels. The Chinese are not going to move. China has not been responsible for earth warming, the US has.

Every country is trying to grow because if they don't grow, they will face internal problems. So my gut assessment is, better prepare to adjust to the consequences. By the time China and India realise earth warming's devastating effects on their own environments, they will begin to act decisively.

Our problem is that if the Polar ice caps melt, the forecast is that sea levels will go up one metre or more.

We've had the Dutch study the building of dykes for Singapore. But it is not feasible. They concluded that we have to build a seawall. We can build a seawall. Then our port will be outside the seawall. What's going to happen to the surrounding island archipelago? We become a centre of a diminished archipelago. The consequences are not clear.

If the sea level rises one metre, we can lose part of our beaches and still survive. But if, let's say, it goes up to 6 metres, then without a seawall, one-fifth of Singapore will be under water.

Q: *How likely do you see that eventuality?*

A: I'm not a climate expert. I cannot calculate these probabilities. I have to accept what the experts tell us.

Q: *Can we be a model of an advanced tropical city and not be so reliant on air-conditioning?*

A: We can't change our climate. In fact, all cities become hotter because of the heat retention of the concrete and the roads. If we had constant breezes and land for homes, maybe you can do with less air-conditioning but not all homes are able to catch the breeze. Many will be blocked by other tower blocks.

How can we stop offices from using air-conditioning without loss of productivity? In the 1950s, working as a lawyer in Laycock & Ong, only the lawyers had air-conditioners because they were expensive. The clerks and other employees were out in the open office. Every afternoon, the fans go at full speed and they'll have paperweights to prevent the papers from scattering. Typing mistakes increase after a meal and as the afternoon heats up. Productivity goes down.

So when I had my own law office from 1955, I air-conditioned the whole office. A small office, on the first floor of 10 Malacca Street. Productivity did not go down in the afternoon.

The wafer fab plants and other delicate jobs, where all wear gowns and plastic headwear to keep hair and other particles from upsetting and degrading the products, will not be able to work without air-conditioning.

There's no other way. We have only one choice, that's to build high-rise. We cannot go back to two, three-storey buildings. This Istana building, completed in the 1860s, is orientated to face the northeast and the southwest monsoons. It has long corridors to keep the sun out.

When I used to be invited by the governors in the early 1950s, there was the Indian-styled punkah. These were a long stick and a cloth banner that somebody, an Indian orderly called the punkah-wallah, would tie to his toe and pull back and forth and you get air moving. In India during the hot summer months, the Muslims had this latticework on windows and verandas. They will throw water on it, hot air will blow through and the water will cool the rooms and get cooler.

We are not a naturally breezy place, except by the sea. How did people live in the old days? How did the Malays cope? They built houses on stilts with an attap roof and wooden structures, open doors and windows. Attap roofs are better than zinc roofs or tiles. You don't need a ceiling, it's a non-conductor of heat. But if there wasn't a breeze you feel the still air. Both men and women wear sarongs. Air goes up their legs. The men are in singlets or stay bare-chested. That's our climate.

Q: *What about new concepts like electric cars and electrifying our transport system? Would that help our city?*

A: That will come. It's starting with hybrids. Companies are deep into R&D for the electric car. They are almost as good as a petrol or diesel car for acceleration and speed. The problem is: how long can it last before you need a recharge of the batteries? Buses can use gas. Even cars can use gas. We have to study these options.

Q: *How about solar power? Do you see a potential there for a tropical city like Singapore?*

A: I have been on the advisory board of Total, a major French oil company, since 1992. Over 17 years, each time they put their histogram – oil, coal, nuclear, is like that (raising his hand); and wind, solar, tide and renewables are like this (lowering his hand).

The Germans have done research on solar panels. One proposal is if they place them on the Sahara desert that has sunshine the whole year round, it will supply the electricity the EU needs. But (laughs), how much will it cost? And then the sand storms will come. Your solar panels are covered with sand, then who has to blow off the sand?

But if we have solar panels on all our rooftops, we can have battery storage of electricity for halogen lamps and hot water and if it is raining and cloudy, you may not have enough.

But it will come. The Chinese are making these solar chips cheaper and better than the Germans. Also wind powered fans.

Q: *What about nuclear energy for Singapore? Is that a possibility?*

A: There's a possibility of a small nuclear unit that is quite safe, so they report. It's like the power unit of a nuclear submarine. But no nuclear unit is totally safe. We can put it on a floating platform, and try the smallest unit available. If it works, we go to a medium-sized unit. Then we can add more small-sized units. Our problem will be what do we do with the energy in the evenings when the factories, offices and homes don't need electricity? When you have a hydro station, then you pump the water back to generate more power.

I saw one in (the former) Yugoslavia. They pumped the water back at night when consumption of energy is low. This pumps the water back into the top reservoir. Then there's more water to push through and generate electricity from the turbine dynamos turning. But we must have such a disparity in height between our reservoir and the ground. We are energy deprived.

Q: *Looking at Singapore today, are you satisfied with the balance that has been struck between making it livable and sustainable environment-wise, and making it a globalised city?*

A: I would not want a big population because high density of population makes for tight living conditions. However skilful we are, whether ingenious in creating park connectors, or keeping green spaces, or reclamation – if we bump up our population to, say, 6.5 million, including those on work permits because we require them to keep the economy going, the high density will be uncomfortable. When I go to Hong Kong, even without the pollution I do not enjoy it, due to the density of people. Or old Shanghai. In 1976, we stayed in their best guest-house. I went downstairs to walk around, there were masses of people like a river in flood. You got to keep on moving or they will push you on. And it was dark. The shops were dark, the street lamps were weak.

In Hong Kong, their homes are so cramped that they spend almost all of their leisure time outside; they entertain outside. In Singapore, people have big TV sets, all the latest gadgets, dressed up their comfortable homes. Most of the revellers late at night are foreign tourists.

My personal preference is less population density. But I'm not in charge. The government will go the way they believe is necessary for Singapore.

Q: *Coming back to your comments earlier on global warming, the point that the world doesn't have the stomach to tackle it head-on: are you pessimistic about the long-term outcome?*

A: Yes. So I've said at the outset we must prepare to adapt rather than to hope that we don't have to adapt. How much we have to adapt depends on how excessive the warming is.

Q: *What needs to change for the world to have a different mindset and resolve to tackle this problem?*

A: The day the Chinese and the Indians find that hundreds of millions of farmers along these river basins and small traders in the towns face a water shortage, ah, there'll be huge problems. Where do these people go to when there is not enough water? How do they feed themselves? They will move to any place that can support their lives. There will be international turmoil.

Q: *Given your pessimism, you don't think that the world will come to any realistic multilateral agreement?*

A: No, I don't think so. You watch Copenhagen.[3] The Chinese have said: You want me to cut down, you give me clean technology free. You've got it, you give it to me and you cut down by 40 per cent below 1990 levels. And Congress has passed a Bill to reduce by 4 per cent.

Q: *Is there a lack of global leadership in this?*

A: I don't think it's a lack of global leadership. What leader of any big country or even a small country like Singapore can say, "Okay, we give up growth, even have negative growth to save global warming"? I don't think the Singapore government can afford to listen to you. Every leader, every government is thinking about its own difficulties.

Q: *If and when we become an Annex 1 country (industrialised country or economy in transition which has committed itself to reducing greenhouse gas emissions) under the United Nations Framework Convention on Climate Change, how would this affect Singapore?*

A: No, we will tell them: Look, we are unable to comply. All these emissions are for products that you are using, that the world's airlines are consuming.

We are a hub for trade, logistics and a refilling station for ships and aircrafts. How can we comply because they say so?

We export, we don't manufacture products for our consumption. Aircraft refuel, ships refuel. How can we cut without destroying our hub status, which is the reason for Singapore's existence?

We tell them: Look, who are the end-users of that energy? How can I reduce my carbon footprint and still make a living, it's not possible. You ask me to die. Then you take over responsibility of 5 million people. Can you?

Q: *Unless there's a way that they can separate the imported components versus the domestic components.*

A: They must do that. Yes, of course.

Q: *We have this perennial problem with the burning and the haze in the region, the result mainly of smoke from slash-and-burn farming in Indonesia. Can nothing be done to tackle this problem?*

A: Even if they had the will, Jakarta was under the haze and Jakarta airport was closed, they would move but only insofar as

Jakarta is affected. Jambi, Riau islands, Balikpapan, it's okay, just wear masks and carry on.

Q: *Are you personally frustrated that there's been very little progress on this?*

A: No. I live with the reality that they have not been able to stop the burning to clear forests for plantations or farming.

What is MM's carbon footprint?

Lee is known in Singapore for his simple, down-to-earth lifestyle. He and his wife live in a house which has not been renovated for decades at Oxley Road, prime real estate in the central city area. He wears the same worsted wool suits when travelling on planes to go overseas. He was, in a sense, an ecologically conscious consumer long before such a concept became fashionable. Never in favour of the disposable society, he believes in the value of thrift, not over-consuming resources. The day this interview took place, he was wearing a jacket so old, he confessed the man who tailored it for him had died. His lifestyle is so spartan, he considers it an extravagance for the Prime Minister to wear a new shirt each year for the National Day Rally.

Q: *How about your own lifestyle? How environmentally conscious are you? Do you try to reduce your carbon footprint? You sleep with air-conditioning?*

A: I do but what can I do? Without air-conditioning I will not get a good night's sleep.

Q: *Do you try to recycle?*

A: We haven't got the system of different dustbins for different items. Our people have yet to understand and would not be able to do it: Bottles, tins, food, go into different chutes and bags. We'll get there sometime.

Q: *Another part of being environmentally conscious is not to consume so much, and you're not particularly a great consumer?*

A: No, I'm not. I eat less, I travel less. I wonder whether I'm right in buying my car. Even if I travelled by the best Mercedes Benz taxi limousine, it'll cost me less than what my Lexus is costing me every day. Except that I don't know what time I'm going to wake up, and take the one kilometre to office, one kilometre back. My car is five years old and it's only done 20,000 km.

Q: *In photographs we can see that your wardrobe, your shirts, seem to have been kept for years, decades. You don't throw away your stuff.*

A: Why should I throw something away which I'm comfortable with? I'm not interested in impressing anybody.

I had a supervisor who taught me criminal law. He used to be a lecturer but, you know, he became old, so he only did supervisions and he had a fireplace that did not give out any smoke because he was gassed in the First World War, and he had a lung problem. He also had a large family. He had leather patches on his coat elbows, knees of his trousers. One student was bold enough to ask him, "Sir, are you lacking in clothing?" He took it gracefully. He laughed and said, "That college porter at the gate has to be dressed well. He wears a top hat, always to look smart. I don't have to dress to impress anybody."

As I listened to that, I said, "It's inverted snobbery." But it makes sense. I see no reason why I should impress people by having a big car or changing my suits every now and again to keep up with the latest styles.

The trouble is my wardrobe is now full up. I've got many new suits that are absolutely in good condition because I seldom wear them. I don't go to office every day wearing a suit, except for formal functions or when I am abroad. They are of finest worsted wool. In fact, the older I get, the less willing I am to spend time putting on a suit and tie. I just have a blouson or a buttoned-up Chinese jacket, and it saves a lot of trouble. I have had them for many years and they are very comfortable.

Q: *Isn't it a virtue though?*

A: No, it is not. You may say it's a virtue, others think, why is this chap that thrifty? Watch other prime ministers. They always have new ties, new shirts and suits to look good on TV.

I mean, you look at our Prime Minister. He wears a new shirt every year for the National Day Rally. Look, I have no reason to want to impress anybody.

Q: *May I ask, how many years have you had your jacket?*

A: This one? It's a very comfortable jacket. The man who tailored it for me is dead.

Q: *How many years have you had it?*

A: I can't remember now. Nearly two decades or 15 years. And it's very comfortable.

Q: *That applies to your house as well. I mean MM, I haven't been there but people who have been there say you've not done much to renovate and to upgrade it.*

A: I've told the Cabinet, when I'm dead, demolish it.

Q: *Why?*

A: Because I think, I've seen other houses, Nehru's, Shakespeare's. They become a shambles after a while. People trudge through. Because of my house the neighbouring houses cannot build high. Now demolish my house and change the planning rules, go up, the land value will go up.

Q: *But isn't that part of Singapore history?*

A: No, no, no. You know the cost of preserving it? It's an old house built over a hundred years ago. No foundation. The cost of maintaining it, damp comes up the wall because there's no foundation. So the piling in the neighbourhood has made cracks in my walls. But fortunately the pillars are sound.

Q: *By your comment then, you don't place great store on preserving old buildings? It's like the old National Library, no architectural significance but when it was torn down I think a lot of people still bemoan its loss today.*

A: I don't think my daughter or my wife or I, who lived in it, or my sons who grew up in it will bemoan its loss. They have old photos to remind them of the past.

Endnotes

1   Maruzen ran a refinery at Tanjong Berlayer from 1960 to 1964. BP took over then and continued running it as a refinery till 1995.

2   2007 figures.

3   The Copenhagen Summit, more properly known as the 2009 United Nations Climate Change Conference, attempted to draw up a road map for countries to moderate greenhouse gas emissions and mitigate the effects of climate change beyond 2012, when the Kyoto Protocol expires. The Summit resulted in a US-backed deal, the Copenhagen Accord, which includes a recognition to limit temperature rises to less than 2 degrees Celsius and promises of US$30 billion in aid to developing nations from 2010 to 2012. It also agreed to raise US$100 billion a year in climate aid by 2020. The Accord is not legally enforceable and was seen as too weak by developing nations, environment activists and political commentators. A year later, in Cancun, Mexico, countries agreed on adopting a more balanced package of measures, including keeping temperature rise to below 2 degrees Celsius by reducing emissions.

Lee addresses a crowd at a PAP rally calling for independence, at Farrer Park on
17 August 1955.

Protesters take to the Padang during the Maria Hertogh incident on 11 December 1950.

Police battle students and strikers in Alexandra Road and Tiong Bahru during the Hock Lee Bus riots of 1955.

Police trying to maintain order during the Chinese school student riots on 13 May 1954.

Lee Kuan Yew and members of the
Cabinet after the swearing-in
ceremony on 5 June 1959.
(L–R) Goh Keng Swee, Toh Chin Chye,
Yong Nyuk Lin, Lee Kuan Yew,
Ong Eng Guan, Ong Pang Boon.

Finance Minister Goh Keng Swee,
Deputy Prime Minister Toh Chin Chye
and Prime Minister Lee Kuan Yew in
September 1962 at the Singapore
Badminton Hall counting centre for the
referendum on merger with Malaysia.

Lee hoses down
Cheng Cheok
Street as part
of a week-long
campaign in
November 1959
to spring clean
Singapore.

A fiery Lee rallies the crowd before the Tunku leaves for London on 16 November 1961 to meet with British ministers on Malaysia.

Lee going door to door to campaign for the PAP during the Hong Lim by-election that was held on 29 April 1961.

Lee on a "problem-probing" tour of the vast Jurong farmlands on 24 November 1962.

Lee visiting Kampong Kembangan during a constituency tour on 12 January 1963.

Lee Kuan Yew and Lim Kim San viewing a model of the Cantonment Road housing estate in 1963.

Lee at the launch of his pet project, the tree planting campaign, in 1963.

Lee at a tree planting ceremony in Queenstown in 2007. He makes it a point to attend tree planting events in his Tanjong Pagar ward every year.

Lee shakes hands with young children and their parents during his tour of Siglap on 28 July 1963.

Lee on a tour of Kampong Kembangan in 1963.

Lee about to give a stern message to Singapore Harbour Board workers not to "play" with communists, on 10 September 1963.

Lee being sworn in as Prime Minister on 19 October 1963, following the September General Election.

Lee and Othman Wok, Minister for Home Affairs and Social Welfare, visiting the site of a Geylang fire that left 2000 homeless on 16 November 1963.

Lee looking into the needs of the economy as he visits the up-and-coming site of the Jurong Industrial Estate on 10 May 1964.

Lee gives a speech during a five-hour tour of the Southern Islands on 7 August 1964.

The kampong crowds greet Lee during his tour of Punggol constituency on 24 January 1965.

In one of the iconic moments of Singapore history, Lee breaks down during a televised press conference to announce the separation of Singapore from Malaysia on 9 August 1965.

Lee, Mrs Lee and E.W. Barker open the PAP's Tanglin branch at Balmoral Road on
23 October 1965.

Lee pays a visit
to house-proud
residents at the
opening of the
Everton Park
housing estate on
8 November 1965.

A protest by Ngee Ann college students in 1966 stops traffic along Chulia Street.

Lee visits a Buddhist temple on his tour of the Sepoy Lines constituency on 7 August 1963.

Lee attends Founder's Day parade at St Joseph's Institution on 15 May 1967.

Lee sharing a meal with Malay residents of Geylang Serai in 1967.

Once an avid golfer, Lee tees off with former British Prime Minister Harold Wilson near Wilson's country home, Chequers, in April 1966.

Lee with (from left) Rajaratnam, Toh Chin Chye and Goh Keng Swee meeting British Commonwealth Secretary George Thomson to discuss the British military withdrawal from the region at City Hall, 9 January 1968.

Lee inspecting the guard of honour at the Singapore Armed Forces Training Institute at Pasir Laba Camp, Jurong on 18 June 1968.

British Conservative leader Edward Heath meeting Lee at City Hall on 7 January 1970. He became British Prime Minister in June that year.

During a mid-morning tour of the polling centres in his constituency, Lee is greeted by J. Ramakrishnan of Gan Eng Seng School, who asks for his autograph on 2 September 1972. He readily obliges.

Lee Kuan Yew, PAP candidate for Tanjong Pagar in the general election, waves to his supporters as he arrives at the Singapore Polytechnic nomination centre on 23 August 1972.

Lee meets Mao Zedong at his residence in Beijing on 12 May 1976.

Lee meets one of his most-admired statesmen, Deng Xiaoping, then senior vice-premier of the People's Republic of China. It was their first meeting, in November 1978, during Deng's official visit to Singapore.

(Top) Prime Minister Lee Kuan Yew speaking to a packed lunchtime rally crowd at Fullerton Square on 20 December 1976, during the General Election campaign of 1976.
(Bottom) Laughter rocks the PAP stage as Foreign Minister S. Rajaratnam takes a dig at the opposition.

Indonesian President Suharto gives Prime Minister Lee Kuan Yew a warm handshake at Jakarta airport on 7 September 1982.

Malaysia's new Yang di-Pertuan Agung, Sultan Mahmood Iskandar of Johor, and the Queen leading the Lees and other members of the royal family into the banquet hall at the Istana Besar on 26 November 1984.

US President Ronald Reagan, Prime Minister Lee Kuan Yew, Mrs Reagan and Mrs Lee, on their way to a state dinner after posing for photographs at the grand staircase of the White House in Washington, on 8 October 1985.

Lee delivers his address to a joint meeting of the US Congress in Washington on 9 October 1985, during an official visit to the United States. Behind him are George Bush, then US Vice-President and President of the Senate, and Tip O'Neill, speaker of the House of Representatives.

Lee greets good friend and former US Secretary of State George Shultz, on 12 October 1992.

Iron Lady Margaret Thatcher, Prime Minister of Britain, dines with Lee and Deputy Prime Minister Goh Chok Tong at the Istana on 31 July 1988.

More than 30 press photographers and television cameramen wait to capture Japanese Prime Minister Yasuhiro Nakasone and Prime Minister Lee Kuan Yew shake hands at the Prime Minister's official residence in Tokyo, 16 October 1986. Lee was on a seven-day visit to Japan.

Prime Minister Goh Chok Tong with Senior Minister Lee Kuan Yew in 1992.

Where it all started: The PAP was conceived in the basement dining room of Lee's Oxley Road home. It was here that the founding members, comprising a small group of trade unionists, teachers, lawyers and journalists discussed setting up a new left-wing party.

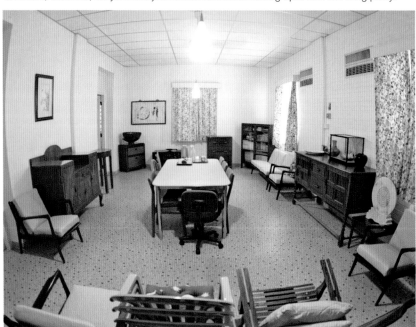

Senior Minister Lee Kuan Yew speaking at the lunchtime rally at UOB Plaza on 30 December 1996. Behind him are, from left, Lim Hwee Hua, Tony Tan and Lee Hsien Loong.

Minister Mentor Lee (fourth left) at Prime Minister Goh Chok Tong's last Cabinet meeting as prime minister, 11 August 2004. From left: Cabinet members Yeo Cheow Tong, Teo Chee Hean, Tony Tan, Lee Kuan Yew, George Yeo, Mah Bow Tan, S. Jayakumar, Lee Boon Yang, Ng Eng Hen, Balaji Sadasivan, Lim Swee Say, Yaacob Ibrahim, Vivian Balakrishnan, Lee Hsien Loong, Goh Chok Tong, Wong Kan Seng, Lim Hng Kiang, Lim Boon Heng and Khaw Boon Wan.

PAP members are showered with confetti as they celebrate the party's 50th anniversary at a rally in which Prime Minister Lee Hsien Loong delivers his maiden speech as secretary-general after taking on the post in November 2004.

Lee, the architect of the bilingual policy, speaking at the launch of the inaugural Speak Mandarin Campaign on 7 September 1979.

Deep in concentration, Lee is sending an SMS in Chinese to Yatiman Yusof, then senior parliamentary secretary at the Ministry of Information, Communications and the Arts, as Wee Chow Hou, chairman of the Promote Mandarin Council, looks on, 13 December 2004.

Lee calling on former Malaysian Prime Minister Mahathir Mohamad on 27 April 2005, at the Perdana Leadership Foundation, a library and research centre of archived material on Malaysia's Prime Ministers.

A garlanded Lee, 1965.

A garlanded Lee waves to the crowd at a PAP rally in Yishun during the 2006 General Election campaign.

Lee and Tanjong Pagar GRC MP Indranee Rajah on a victory parade to thank supporters on 7 May 2006, a day after Polling Day.

In a sign of strong bilateral ties, Singapore's three top leaders were present at the wedding ceremony of Brunei Crown Prince Haji Al-Muhtadee Billah and his bride Sarah Salleh on 10 September 2004. From left: Prime Minister Lee Hsien Loong and his wife Ho Ching, HRH the Duke of Gloucester, Prince Richard, Minister Mentor Lee Kuan Yew and Mrs Lee, Malaysian Deputy Prime Minister Najib Tun Razak and his wife Datin Seri Rosmah Mansor, and Senior Minister Goh Chok Tong and Mrs Goh.

Lee with Nadarajah Kamalanathan, 54 (left), a retired teacher, and the
family of Sinnappu Kanapathipillai, 92 (in wheelchair), on 5 November 2006,
during a house visit to Block 107, Spottiswoode Park.

Lee, accompanied by Mrs Lee, touring SIA's new Airbus 380 superjumbo on 22 October 2007.

Minister Mentor Lee Kuan Yew greeting constituents as he arrives at the annual Tanjong Pagar GRC Lunar New Year celebration dinner at Henderson Secondary School, on 6 February 2009.

Minister Mentor Lee Kuan Yew finds the time to mingle with the crowd at the Istana garden party, on 7 February 2009.

Lee meets Singapore Traction Company bus driver Ali Ahmad for the first time since the 1950s, during a house visit to Henderson Heights on 8 November 2009. As a young lawyer, he had helped to mediate a dispute between employees and the company.

Old friends: US elder statesman Henry Kissinger and Lee greet each other before Lee was awarded the lifetime achievement award by the US-Asean Business Council on 27 October 2009.

Lee is greeted by Goh Chok Tong as he arrives at the 44th National Day Parade at Marina Bay on 9 August 2009.

Lee meets US Secretary of State Hillary Clinton at the State
Department on 26 October 2009.

Lee calls on 44th US President Barack Obama at the White House on 29 October 2009.

Lee calling on Malaysian Prime Minister Najib Razak on 9 June 2009 at the administrative capital of Putrajaya. Lee was on a week-long visit to Malaysia.

Russian President Dmitry Medvedev conferring the Order of Friendship, Russia's highest civilian award, on Lee at the Istana on 15 November 2009. The Order recognises those who have made a significant contribution in strengthening friendship, cooperation and relations between nations.

Lee on the skybridge of the iconic public housing development The Pinnacle@Duxton on 13 December 2009.

Lee, flanked by Tan Hee Teck (left), chief executive officer of Resorts World Sentosa and Lim Kok Thay during a private visit to Resorts World Casino at Sentosa on 13 January 2010.

Lee met former Chinese President Jiang Zemin on 13 May 2010 at the latter's hometown in Yangzhou, Jiangsu province. The private meeting was at the invitation of Jiang, who hosted Lee to dinner before accompanying him on a tour of the scenic Shouxi Lake. (Photo © Yeong Yoon Ying)

Minister Mentor Lee Kuan Yew penning his wishes for a young generation at the opening ceremony of The Pinnacle@Duxton PCF Education Centre. MM Lee had written "Wish all of you a bright and happy future" during the ceremony held on 15 August 2010.

Lee lights the cauldron to signal the start of the first Youth Olympic Games, on 13 August 2010. He is with Minister for Community Development, Youth and Sports Vivian Balakrishnan (left) and Ng Ser Miang, chairman of the Singapore YOG organising committee, at the Promontory@Marina Bay.

Minister Mentor Lee Kuan Yew acknowledging the standing ovation from a group of Singaporeans at a reception organised by the Singapore Chinese Chamber of Commerce and Industry in China, 16 May 2010. Lee, who had visited China 32 times since 1976, shared with the audience the early problems which the two countries faced with the Suzhou Industrial Park project during the 1990s.

Lee pauses to take in the view of the Singapore skyline from atop Marina Bay Sands' SkyPark Observation Deck during his visit to the integrated resort on 22 June 2010, the eve of its official opening. With him are Sheldon Adelson, chairman and chief executive of Las Vegas Sands, and his wife, Miriam.

Lee at the River Hong Bao festival at Marina Bay, 15 February 2010. During his visit, he toured the exhibits, watched performances on stage and tasted some Szechuan cuisine.

Members of the Sikh community help Lee wear a turban during the reopening of the renovated Bhai Maharaj Singh Memorial Temple on 3 July 2010.

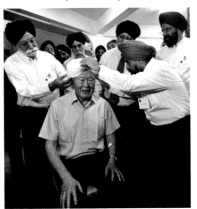

Lee stops for a break amid a tour of The River Vista@Kallang on 21 July 2010, part of the Active, Beautiful, Clean Waters programme.

Lee waves to the crowd at the 2009 National Day Rally.

PART 2
INSIGHTS
FOR
THE YOUNG
AND CURIOUS

10
NOT YOUR AVERAGE GRANDAD[1]

I WAS NOT looking forward to this at all. The atmosphere in the Sheares Room in the Istana was tense, despite my teammates' small talk and encouraging words from my colleague, Robin Chan. Across the wide mahogany table from us, the empty seat was a constant reminder that, in a few minutes, Minister Mentor Lee would stride in and sit down in that chair for the last in a series of heavyweight Q&A sessions held with panel members of this book over the preceding months. I was directly opposite that chair. And I was going to ask Singapore's founding father and global statesman what his favourite movie was.

Lee's press secretary sensed my nervousness. "Talk to him like you would talk to your grandad," she said. "With respect, but no need to be too stiff!" Robin and I exchanged a rueful glance. He said, "Can you imagine going, 'Hi, grandad'? Whoa." I had to agree. My grandfathers would never have written memoirs endorsed by Henry Kissinger.

---

1   This chapter was written by Rachel Lin, 25, the youngest member of our team of seven writers.

Before that afternoon, I'd had an easy job. I joined the team behind this book right at the start as an all-round Girl Friday. The writers told me what material they wanted for their chapters. It was my job to hunt down the sources, read up on climate change and Scandinavian welfare and national income statistics and whatnot, ring up experts, organise focus groups and tie it all together in countless briefings and emails. There were even a few arduous weeks spent sifting through 27,000 National Archives photos of Lee.

But this was something completely different. I should have realised at the start that Robin and I – the two youngest members of the team – had been recruited for a reason. The dreadful truth only emerged during a planning discussion a couple of months into the project: the writers wanted to have a chapter on youth and Robin and I were in charge.

"Think of yourselves as the sacrificial la... I mean interlocutors," my boss told us. "Ask him questions that young Singaporeans want to ask."

It was a tall order. There were only two of us journalists and a multitude of young Singaporeans out there with opinions. Looking at ourselves, the prospect seemed even dimmer. How could they possibly expect two overseas-educated *angmoh pai* (Hokkien for "Westernised folks") – including myself, a frequent wearer of black clothes and sporting jewellery studs pierced into the skin near an eye – to represent young Singaporeans?

The first thing to do was to consult the experts.

Surveys that we checked out by National University of Singapore academics and also the National Youth Council gave us a rough picture of the average young Singaporean – well-educated, fundamentally traditional and materialist, but shifting subtly away from the older generation's conservatism.

These surveys did not tell us what they would say in their own words, though. So Robin and I set about collecting questions from as many people as possible. Okay, one of the things we used was Facebook. And no, we didn't just ask our friends. We tried to get questions from young Singaporeans of diverse backgrounds. Essentially, this was what we posed: "If you could ask MM Lee any question at all, no matter how weird or trivial or irreverent, what would it be?"

After two weeks of begging, we came up with a list of almost 70 questions. They gave us a pretty good insight into the issues that fire up young people: sexuality, gender, culture, the environment, politics, disability.

Other questions, however, gave us pause. Early on in the process, we had decided not to edit the questions at all, apart from correcting spelling and grammar mistakes. We wanted the questions to reach Lee in the same shape as they were in when they were submitted to us. We also promised that all the questions would find their way to him, except for anything that was just too insane or, as in the case of one particularly hilarious one written half in Hokkien, a rhetorical question.

Personally, I was delighted with how people responded to the "no matter how weird or trivial or irreverent" bit. I could almost imagine the wide grins and raised eyebrows behind some of the more light-hearted suggestions:

"Do you believe in fengshui and astrology?"

"Does your food go through a tester before you eat?"

"Who's your favourite child or grandchild?"

Those are the kinds of question I'd ask my grandad, as a bit of fun. Okay, maybe not the "favourite grandchild" one, in case I opened a massive can of worms.

But putting them to Lee? As I sat waiting for his entrance, I was starting to have doubts. Quite a number of the young Singaporeans that I'd contacted – especially those aged below 20 – said they had questions, but didn't want to reveal them. They feared retribution of some kind. Some of them mentioned "things" that had happened to their relatives after some anti-government slip of the tongue, or a non-PAP vote.

Their fear was beginning to rub off on me, though not because of those "things". I had other reasons to hesitate. Lee had given me sleepless nights ever since I started work on this project, and it wasn't because I'd read about him so much that I'd started dreaming about him, too. As for most Singaporeans, he'd become a kind of political celebrity to me, someone to put up on a pedestal or shoot down in flames, depending on whether you liked the PAP or not. I was curious about his personal life, but turned off by some of his political views. Even though, having already taken part in several Q&A sessions for this book, I now had a more nuanced understanding of his ideas, and even though I had come to know that a human heart does beat under that white uniform, I was still in deep conflict.

In earlier interviews, Lee had held forth about Singapore's vulnerability, how we had little margin for error. It depressed me. I wanted something to fight for that didn't sound freakishly like a castle under siege defended by dogmatic, extremely irritable knights.

The Singapore I loved, the one I had grown up in and where my childhood memories were formed, was a place of warmth and friendship. The Singapore I doubted, the dysfunctional bits, I hoped we could change. But now, I felt like I was being told that this country was so fragile that relaxing just for a moment meant disaster, that it was his way or the highway.

There was even one point when I felt upset enough to consider feigning some serious imaginary illness, thus achieving both a silent protest and enough medical leave to skip all future interviews. Racial equality, both as an ideal and in practice, is fundamental to my worldview. I have also tried to keep myself informed on developments in science and genetics. So I really could not agree with Lee's Social Darwinist beliefs and his hierarchy of races. I was not persuaded that some ethnic groups were more blessed with certain gifts than others, or had a larger raw intellectual capacity. Neither was I sure that those views were entirely scientific. It was a struggle to have to sit through that. It marked my lowest ebb in the course of the entire project.

But Lee is far, far more than his fears for Singapore or his racial philosophies. His views are more fluid and sensitive to historical context than I have represented them so far. I agreed with many of his views on democracy, such as its cultural preconditions and its chequered past. He knew that Singapore had changed massively since he was in charge and that his finger was no longer on the pulse.

Listening to him, I was conscious all the time of his formidable mind and his immense grasp of facts. But those two elements – race and vulnerability – really seemed to be fixed points in his ideology. I could not shake off the feeling that I was confronted with a leader who was, at once, very impressive and very obstinate.

The turning point came during the interview on immigrants, when we were discussing the Singaporean identity. For him, he said, being Singaporean had been a conscious choice. The rest of us, who were born here, just had to live with it. "That's not entirely the point," I thought. The experience of the past interviews had left me jaded. "We don't choose to be born here, but it can be a badge that we wear with pride or shame. Right now, I'm edging towards shame."

Then the penny dropped. I can still remember the exact statement that gave me a change of heart. Did Lee see Singapore as a land of opportunity, one teammate asked.

Lee replied, "No, I think more than that, more than that. This is a near miracle. When you come in, you are joining an exceptionally outstanding organisation. It's not an ordinary organisation that has created this ... It came about by a stroke of luck, if you like, plus hard work plus an imaginative team, original team. And I think we can carry on. It can only stay as it is, secure, provided it's outstanding."

I paused. I had never seen it in that way before: that Singapore was a near miracle, an accident of history. All those national education lessons had drawn some sort of a narrative thread through our past, as if where we are today was the natural result of a chain of dominoes that led back to Raffles. That's not really true, I thought. There's nothing natural about how we got here. It took decades of development, choices made over generations, at all levels, to reach this point. There were always options, always paths that we could have taken. For the one set of paths we've taken, we've got this result. It's a result that is, in some respects, really miraculous.

Neither is there anything inevitable about the direction Singapore will take. "No system," Lee said in a later interview on politics, "lasts forever."

Well, that struck home. It meant that the door to change was open, and to hear it from Lee himself, the man who embodied the principle of taking charge and steering a course through history, was moving. Somehow, seeing him as the man who had the courage and dedication to get his hands dirty in the political arena, who gave up his private life back in 1954 to realise his ideal of equal opportunities for all – that actually filled me with awe. Few of us can say that we were motivated by the same sort of courage and steely singlemindedness. Okay, so it didn't really remove my earlier misgivings. But it made me feel as if a grappling hook had been thrown across the gulf that separated me from his ideas. It tipped the balance a little away from ambivalence and a little more towards admiration.

Back in the Istana, I composed myself. Robin checked his voice recorder. Through the grand double doors that opened into the Sheares Room came a sudden buzz of activity and the collective footfalls of an entourage of security officers. We exchanged a glance: Let's Do This.

Lee was all of 86 years old, but his stride – at least, for this interview – was still purposeful, his voice deep and assured. As he took his place across the table I was reminded of my own grandfather, who even in his 80s went for long brisk walks at dawn, sometimes carrying sacks of rice as weights. He seemed to belong to some past, more formidable generation, one that had stared hardship in the face unblinkingly.

But he was not hidebound by that generation's conservatism – or even the conservatism of society today, for that matter. "I'm not liberal and I'm not conservative," he said. "I'm a practical, pragmatic person, always have been and I take things as they are." Of course, the label of pragmatism can often conceal ideological biases. When Lee's particular brand of pragmatism was applied to the issues raised by young Singaporeans, however, the results were a mix of the traditional and the progressive.

He believed that women, for example, had a different biological makeup that gave them a special role as mothers. "Women become mothers, women have responsibility to bring up their children. Men will have to share a part of that responsibility but they're not women, they haven't borne the child," he said.

Thus he could see a lesbian couple as effective parents, for example, but not gay men. "Two men looking after a child? Two women looking after a child, maybe, but I'm not so sure, because it's not their own child. Unless you have artificial insemination and it's their own child, then you have a certain maternal instinct immediately aroused by the process of pregnancy. But two men adopting a boy or a girl, what's the point of it?"

This stemmed in part from his own experiences as a father: "I never had to change diapers for my children." It was a far cry from his own son's approach to fatherhood. Prime Minister Lee Hsien Loong is a past master at nappy-changing. He had never poked any of his babies with a safety pin and it was a skill he urged other fathers to take up as well, according to a newspaper report in 2010.[2]

Diaper duties aside though, Lee felt that women could, and had, attained equality in employment opportunities, pay and promotions. The government gave them equal status as citizens, he said. Foreigners who married Singaporean women can now become Singapore citizens.

Facts seem to bear this out: The World Economic Forum's 2009 Global Gender Gap survey found that Singapore was above average in terms of wage equality, ranking ninth out of 134 countries, and in terms of the number of women in senior and managerial positions.[3] The gender wage gap has also been narrowing,[4] and in the 20–29 age group, more women than men are taking up professional and managerial jobs.[5]

The reality, however, is that inequality still has some grip on society here. The World Economic Forum study ranked Singapore 33rd out of 44 high-income nations, with particularly poor performance in the area of women's political participation.[6]

Another study, conducted by the consultants Watson Wyatt in 2008, found that out of the 100 largest companies in Singapore, 72 had no women non-executive directors on their board.[7] The average gross monthly earnings of men exceeded that of women across all industries.[8] Women are still expected to pull their weight in the workforce and perform their duties at home, or, if they can afford it, hire a foreign domestic helper.[9]

The challenges extend to more insidious, psychological realms. The number of teenagers treated for eating disorders at the Singapore General Hospital rose sixfold between 2002 and 2006. More than eight in ten Singapore girls surveyed wanted to change their looks, while six in ten had self-esteem problems over their weight or appearance. The majority of teens with body image issues were women aged 17 to 25.

The trend in both the United States and Europe, of legislating for equality, however, was not Lee's solution of choice. New laws would just collide with society's conservatism and result in unintended negative consequences, a dilemma that was thrown into stark relief by the question of encouraging a more family-friendly social environment.

"We want to be family-friendly," Lee said. "As far as the government is concerned, we are having crèches in the offices, rooms set aside for breastfeeding of children; we're encouraging the private sector to do likewise. We just need to face up to the fact that women are now working and if we don't accommodate their needs as mothers, then they'll have fewer or no children."

What about subsidies, I asked, like in the Scandinavian countries, which have among the highest fertility rates in Europe?[10] Too costly, he answered. We'd break the bank. My reply: How about more modest measures, such as paternity leave?

"How old are you?" came the response.

"I'm 24."

"Well, you haven't thought of the problems that you would face if you were the employer," Lee laughed. "Paternity leave means the man is absent from work. We can legislate, but each company will do its calculations: How much of a chore it is, what it'll cost and what time will be lost. You can legislate and then they won't employ married men with children, then you have repercussions. I think this has got to take its course. We are basically a conservative society."

He believed, then, that policy-making was constrained by society's values. There was no point in forcing change unless society itself had reached a new consensus, even if Lee believed that new approaches were needed. He raised the example of a single mother in Teheran: "A young woman got pregnant, she thought of abortion, then she saw the movement of the baby on the ultrasound and she decided to keep it. In the eighth month she told her brother and he said, 'You're a shame on the family, abort now.' She fought and refused, her parents refused to recognise her, so she was alone."

"Do you think she made the right choice?" I asked. Single mothers are left out by many of Singapore's pro-family policies. They are not eligible for Baby Bonus payouts, tax relief or maternity and childcare leave.[11] Some social welfare schemes, such as subsidised Housing Board flats and Home Ownership Plus Education, are targeted exclusively at married parents or divorcees.[12]

"That's a personal choice," Lee said. "I mean, from Singapore's national point of view, I think we ought to keep the baby. But the family may think otherwise and she may think otherwise because it's more difficult for her to get married if she has a child. There are pros and cons but, from a demographic point of view, I'm in favour of more babies, especially from educated women with educated partners. It may sound rather pragmatic and practical but that's the way life is."

It was a reality that Singapore had to face. The question was one of coming to terms with it and working with the trend. But the room for manoeuvre was constrained by social values. "This is a very conservative society. If we move in that direction, I think many of the older generation will be outraged because they say, 'What will happen to my daughter? You're encouraging this.'

"I believe in facing trends, and this is a trend. If we don't face up to it we're going to have a social problem later. But how we face it is important. The British way, which encourages single women to have more children for more government subsidies, and leads to more irresponsibility, that's another matter. But our belief is that case in Teheran was an extreme case. It shouldn't happen to anybody anywhere."

I asked if he felt frustrated by how society's views were diametrically opposed to his own. Again, Lee took the practical view: Singapore's conservatism was a fact of life. "If I were the prime minister, I would hesitate to push things through against the prevailing sentiment, against the prevailing values of society. You're going against the current of the people, the underlying feeling. What's the point of that, you know? Breaking new ground and taking unnecessary risk?"

Instead, he was confident that Singaporeans would eventually change their minds, that acquiring knowledge and exposure would lead them to new ways of seeing and doing things. "It will evolve over time, as so many things have. My own sort of maturing process will take place with other people. I can't change them overnight; I think their own experiences, their own reading, their own observations will bring about the change despite innate biases."

I suppose it's the same kind of evolution that is taking place to some extent with the issue of disabled people and their integration into society. According to Lee, "We are now at a point where people say, we should do more. I said okay, let's improve. If you can make them useful or make their lives more bearable, why prevent it? Let's help them to enjoy life as much as they can." Now buses and MRT stations are being retrofitted to be more accessible to disabled patrons. Mrs Lee herself had employed a blind telephone operator at her law firm.

His daughter, Lee Wei Ling, has dyslexia, and he suffered from a mild form of dyslexia himself, Lee revealed. He had learnt to overcome it early on and it was only detected in his late 50s, when his daughter brought a dyslexia specialist in to see him. The disorder manifested itself in spelling problems and during a speed-reading course. "I did not succeed, because I usually have to run my eye back to make sure that I've got the right word. So that slows me down. But because I read more slowly I read only once and it sticks. So there are compensations. The important thing is not to be discouraged and feel I'm disabled."

And Lee told us again of his grandson, who had Asperger's and is an albino (see chapter 11). He took a longer time because of his learning difficulties, but he went on to university at NUS, graduated and now aspires to teach English.

"Supposing we had abandoned him, said 'Hopeless', today he'd be, I think, just a discard in the corner," Lee said. "But we spent time, got him into this special school where he learnt to read and write. Finally he joined a mainstream school." And when we asked Lee, later in the interview, who his favourite grandchild was, he replied, "All of them are favourites. But I would say the most likeable fellow is my disadvantaged grandson. He's turned out very polite, well-spoken, well-behaved."

I was still waiting for that inevitable "young people nowadays" speech that my grandfather would make whenever he talked about how times were a-changin'. And I wasn't disappointed when Robin posed the next question, about political apathy among young people.

He had seen his fellow students in university get fired up about politics, campaigning for their candidates in the US primaries in 2008. Both Democrats and Republicans had joined battle. Wouldn't allowing political activism on campus combat apathy back home as well?

Lee's answer was simple: Young people nowadays aren't apathetic because there's no political activism in the institutions. They're apathetic because they're too comfortable. Campus activism was just theoretical posturing, immature debates between youth who were high on idealism but low on experience. He said, "I was at the London School of Economics for one term and there was political activism. Pretty British girls were handing out communist pamphlets to me. And in Cambridge, they had a debating society. They got ministers to come down to debate and they tried to pretend that they were aware of all these issues but, looking back, I think they were not really mature. In their early 20s, what experience have they got?

"You have to have a certain amount of experience in life to understand the difficulties large groups of people face in life," he said. "Then you become an activist. I was not an activist in Raffles College or in Cambridge. I just listened, I watched, I learnt. But when I came back and wanted to go into politics, I worked with the unions and I decided we had to do something about this. I mean, they were underpaid. Their children had no future. So I formed my ideas, discussed it with my friends."

No amount of university debating, Lee thought, could substitute for the biggest spur to his political career, and one that he felt today's young Singaporeans lacked: the prospect of losing everything. His generation had lived through the panicked evacuation of the British during the Second World War, a brutal Japanese occupation, and communist insurrection. In 1965, they were left with a small country to defend. Political engagement had only emerged against a backdrop of conquest and crisis.

It was exactly the same thing with entrepreneurship, he thought. He attributed the commercial success of Jewish businesses to their persecution and deprivation in the ghettos. They learnt to be enterprising after having been barred from other professions. Singaporeans, by contrast, had it easy. "We have too many people who have comfortable lives and comfortable jobs. Why should they take the chance? You've got small capital, you might lose everything. You've got to start again. You've got to restart your life."

What did today's young Singaporeans have which compared to such experiences? Not much, he said. Life's too comfortable. We've become victims of our own success. The foundations for a thriving Singapore had already been laid: cleanliness, greening, law and order, the economy. The taxi driver or hawker of today, Lee said, has an asset – in the form of an HDB flat – that would get him at least $150,000 to $200,000, "if he doesn't spend it going to Batam". And Singapore has been going beyond the basics to liven things up: the integrated resorts, Formula One and so on. The government had beefed up the existing infrastructure well enough to minimise the impact of the new liberalising measures, he said.

"What are you going to change in Singapore? What do you want to change in Singapore, fundamentally? What they want is more growth, better homes, cars, more travel, better schools, better nurseries, better kindergartens. That's it they are fringe items." Lee was adamant.

"If we had difficult social and educational conditions, we're going to have political activism all the time, as you have in Thailand. Or now in Malaysia or in Indonesia ... They will get interested in politics the moment it hurts them. The moment the shoe pinches, they will be jumping around. They're unemployed, they'll get interested in politics very quickly. They'll vote for the party that says, 'I'll get you re-employed'."

Then the classic courtroom Lee appeared. "All right," he said, turning to Robin. "You start a party today. What are you going to sell? Where's your platform? How are you going to change people's lives?"

"I'm not talking about starting a party," Robin replied.

"When you say 'interested in politics', you must have something you want to do, right? Economics, social policies, whatever it is. You put up one and see whether you can survive six months." Lee then gave the example of the Workers' Party 2006 election manifesto, "You Have A Choice": "Low Thia Khiang put up his manifesto, which the voters did not buy. We just tore it to pieces. What are the alternative choices for Singapore?"

But surely, I thought, there was something else. I wondered if the students Robin knew on campus had been "too comfortable". Certainly they must have been fairly well-off, intelligent, with good prospects. Did that preclude them from activism? And I remembered the young people who had questions, but were afraid of voicing them. Wasn't this keeping people back, and wasn't part of it the creation of his political style?

Lee certainly didn't think so. It was an ingrained thing, one that could be overcome in times of adversity anyway. "It's part of Singapore's culture and it goes back to a very patriarchal society, especially with the Chinese. Look, why did we form the People's Association? Because during that period (in the 1950s and 1960s) nobody would join a political party. It's too dangerous. If the communists win, they will fix you. But join the People's Association and do social work, yes. In Malaysia they started off that way, the same as us. The Malaysian Chinese Association was a rich men's club. But now they've got real difficult politics because the minorities have been disadvantaged in education, jobs, licences, everything."

But didn't he think that, just maybe, the climate of fear was partly his doing? I asked. "Come off it! Are you fearful? If you're fearful why do you ask me this question? Is anything going to happen to you? Utter rubbish!" Lee said, irritation rising in his voice.

"We may not personally be fearful but we did encounter quite a few young people who were," I persisted.

"I cannot explain that and I'm not interested whether they're fearful or not fearful. I think it's better that they're fearful and they take me seriously, than if they think I'm somebody they can brush off. That's all. And if you're the prime minister and you're brushed off, you're in trouble," was his response.

Even the phenomenon of young Singaporeans emigrating was taken in stride. New Zealanders emigrate to Australia; Australians emigrate to the US, the UK, elsewhere, he said. It was a fact of life in a globalised world. "If you believe it's because of fear and so on that they leave, utter rubbish! It is the attraction of greener pastures in the other paddock. That's all."

So what's left to young people? I was starting to get pretty discouraged. The "no choice" argument had made a reappearance. Feelings of fear had been dismissed.

Finally, Lee turned around. "A hundred years from now, will there be a Singapore? I'm not sure. We don't have good people with us, with thinking capabilities, talent and organisation abilities, we die.

"Then what will happen to Singaporeans? Those who are well-educated, they can migrate. But what about the majority of people who haven't got those qualifications? They will just go downhill and start becoming other people's maids and labourers. You say it's not possible? I say, think again carefully. Where were we in 1959? Where were we in 1963? What did we face in 1965? Singapore will always be like this, naturally progressing on autopilot? You must be nuts if you believe that."

Well, I wasn't nuts. I don't believe that anything runs on autopilot. And I suppose that was as good a call to action as any. Many things have become better since 1959; I'd be hard-pressed to deny that. Singapore doesn't have much in the way of natural blessings, after all. We're an act of political will as much as we're a near-miracle. Keeping what progress we've made, improving people's lives, ironing out the kinks in the system – that's up to us to figure out.

"Right. Finished?" Lee asked, brusquely. We were running out of time. The serious questions that we'd decided to use as a safe opening gambit would have to make way for the more irreverent ones. After that pep talk, however, I wasn't sure if I was up to asking him about that favourite movie of his.

"We have a section on personal questions," Robin said.

"All right. Proceed."

I tried my best to sound relaxed. "If you could be a statesman at any point in the world history, which one would you be and why?"

"That's a parlour game. I would not be a statesman at all. It was circumstances that created me," he said. "I don't think, 'I want to be a statesman'. That's rubbish. You don't become a statesman.

"I do not classify myself as a statesman. I put myself down as determined, consistent, persistent. I set out to do something, I keep on chasing it until it succeeds. That's all. That's how I perceive myself. Not a statesman. It's utter rubbish. Anybody who thinks he wants to be a statesman needs to see a psychiatrist."

Lee certainly wasn't one of those head cases. He would rather have been a lawyer than a statesman. But if he had not chosen politics, what kind of law would he have practised? With the country in turmoil, he said, where would his law office even stand? It was what drove him into politics.

That question set the tone for the rest of the interview. As the questions grew more personal, more humorous, a curious interplay of public and private perceptions of Lee emerged. On the one hand, people clearly wanted to know about him and his personal life. He'd been an undisputed leader of Singapore for so long that all sorts of rumours had been flying around about him, and young Singaporeans wanted to know the truth directly from him.

It was almost surreal to see the man confronting the myth. It was pleasant to see him reminisce about past times. He seemed to relax more. He laughed every time some oddball question was posed. When a question fired him up, he sparked with energy. For a moment we got a glimpse into his more personable side, and I actually started enjoying the interview immensely.

Was Lee a closet sentimentalist? During his last trip back to London, he had gone to visit the Compleat Angler, a beautiful hotel in the town of Marlow, on the banks of the River Thames. It was his 86th birthday celebrations, but he had dined at that hotel for the first time 47 years ago, under very different circumstances: the merger negotiations. Surely, my teammate Zuraidah said, his return marked some kind of emotional connection.

Lee waxed lyrical for a moment. "I remember one of the best meals we had. We were having a very difficult time with the Malayans at that time. So we broke off. Let's go down this place on the Thames, Marlow, Compleat Angler. Wonderful meal. Beautiful setting. Quite relaxed. So that was 1960-something.

"This is 40-plus years later. The weir is still there. And as befits the British, they kept the surrounding buildings also. And it's probably a heritage site or whatever, so you can't alter the place. It's part of old England, which they've modernised inside, but still with the ambience. It's not sentimental, it's just harking back to my youth!"

Then he added, ruefully, "My tastebuds were different, so it doesn't taste the same, although I'm quite sure the quality of the food could not have gone down since the last time. But my tastebuds now are blunted!"

Did his food go through a tester before he ate? This question evoked a long chuckle. "What do I need that for? Who's going to poison me? I'm not a defector from the KGB."

Did he believe in fengshui and astrology? "A lot of Singaporeans suspect that you do," my teammate Ignatius said.

Lee was genuinely shocked. "Utter rubbish! Utter rubbish! I'm a pragmatic, practical fellow. I do not believe in horoscopes. I do not believe in fengshui. And I'm not superstitious about numbers. But if you have a house which other people think has disadvantaged fengshui and numbers, when you buy it, you must consider that when you resell. So again it's a practical consideration. Not that I'm interested in it. But if I buy that, I must get a low price because when I sell it I will get a low price. You believe I go for fengshui and horoscopes?" he asked, laughing with incredulity.

"You know, there are all these stories about how our one dollar coin has got eight sides to it," Ignatius explained. "Maybe you thought that it was a good idea and it was auspicious."

"People spin these yarns! It doesn't bother me," Lee said.

What did he miss most about pre-independence Singapore? "The wider open spaces," he said. "I used to cycle down from Siglap to Raffles Institution. And it used to be called Grove Road. Now it's Mountbatten Road. It was all empty land. And Kallang River was where the British Overseas Airways Corporation flying boats used to land once every few days.

"But then, at the same time, there were fewer people. There were about less than a million people when I was growing up. So there was a lot of space. I could go down to the sea. The sea was not polluted. There was a good satay man by the sea. So my friends and I would swim and then we'd eat satay. But if I go and eat satay now I'll get a stomachache because I cannot take peppery things in the same quantities. My internal processes will rebel against it!"

Cycling was definitely something close to his heart. Pedalling to school early in the morning and back late in the evenings left a young Lee sweaty and he sometimes caught cold. When it rained, he simply donned a raincoat and shook out his damp hair before starting class. Later, in his early days in England, he had a dim view of London's public transport system, and when a friend, Cecil Wong, told him about the bicycles of Cambridge, he was a convert. "I said, 'Well, that's the place for me. I'm from a small town.' So I got myself transferred and for three years I cycled. Of course it's cooler there, so you don't sweat. Kept me fit. I used to have to cycle about five miles uphill to go to Girton to see my girlfriend." The "girlfriend" was Kwa Geok Choo, his wife of more than 60 years.

Of course, there was a policy point behind this particular memory. "I think we should really consider special tracks for cyclists. Encourage it, then instead of this LRT (Light Rail Transit) and so on you have bicycle racks at MRT stations. It's better for everybody's health, it's better for the environment and it's certainly better than having the place or having the roads overcrowded with cars, taxis, buses. Doesn't make sense to me."

He approved of the Vélib' system in Paris, where subscribers can rent bikes 24/7 from one of the 1,450 automated kiosks across the city and return them to another kiosk at their destination.[13] Still, the "softness" of the younger generation made him doubt that the scheme would catch on here. "But, you know, the modern generation: even to go to the bus stop, they want shelter," Lee said. "I think girls may not like it, they'll be sweaty. The boys will say, 'No, I'm doing my national service later, why you make me do national service now?' We are rearing a generation that wants to be in comfort but I think cycling is good for them. It did me good, anyway."

The answers Lee gave to personal questions were poignant, but it was his reflections on his political career that struck me the most. Over all those decades, he'd seized the reins of Singapore, cut down his opponents, earned high praise and bitter criticism. How did he feel he had performed, as a man looking back at the politician? In his quieter moments, did he have his doubts?

Apparently not, was the answer. Questions about what his regrets were, what he felt he needed forgiveness for – those were "parlour game questions", as he called them. It was pointless raking over past failures and triumphs. He had done his best. There were moments when I could almost hear Frank Sinatra's voice singing "My Way" as he spoke.

He had been wrong about some things, he admitted. Malaysia was one of them. He did not believe, back then, that Malaysia would become a Malay and then an Islamic country. He had expected the Tunku to resurrect the sultans and the old court rituals, but did not know it was to assert total Malay supremacy. Separation had been a tremendous blow.

But mistakes did not mean regrets. Lee said, "I did what I thought was right, given the circumstances, given my knowledge at the time, given the pressures on me at the time. That's finished, done. I move forward. You keep on harking back, it's just wasting time.

"Do I regret going to Malaysia? No. It was the right thing to do. Did it fail? Yes. Do I regret pressing for a Malaysian Malaysia and making it fail? No. It was all part of a process of growing up."

This threw me, I'll admit. Suddenly, after all those happy memories and anecdotes, the political core of the man re-emerged. For a moment I had almost begun to think that I was indeed having a conversation with a grandfather, lured into a false sense of intimacy. I had wanted to believe that the grappling hook across the gulf had widened into a bridge that at least permitted some kind of sympathetic understanding.

But I could never look at Lee as a wise grandfather-figure. The gap between us was more than generational, more than intellectual: it was visceral. I've never known anyone with such single-mindedness.

I could grasp people who looked back and said, "I was wrong." But it takes no small amount of conviction in the essential rightness of one's own enterprise to regard one's history with a cold, clear eye and say, "I have no regrets." About as much conviction, perhaps, as it takes to say, "I do not care what people think of me."

And to all intents and purposes, Lee really didn't care. Now that the cut and thrust of electoral politics was no longer a necessity, that conviction shone through. "I'm no longer in active politics. It's irrelevant to me what young Singaporeans think of me," Lee said.

"What they think of me after I'm dead and gone in one generation will be determined by researchers who do PhDs on me, right? So there will be lots of revisionism. As people revised Stalin, Brezhnev and one day now Yeltsin, and later on Putin. I mean, I've lived long enough to know that you may be idealised in life and reviled after you're dead."

With that, the interview ended. His conscience was clear, no matter what the history books would say. He had done what he thought was right and that was good enough for him.

Still, what about regret? This kind of passionate intensity was beyond my comprehension.

A couple of days later, a friend of mine from the United Kingdom came to visit. He wanted to go to the National Museum so I padded along. I hadn't seen the new history exhibits before, so we hooked ourselves up to the audioguides and went on the tour.

Somewhere in the tour there was what I can only describe as a "Lee Kuan Yew Room". On the walls hung old black-and-white photos of Lee on the campaign trail, going on walkabouts, or hard at work. A small TV set had been suspended in front of some benches, playing clips of his speeches on loop.

I pushed buttons on the audioguide until it started playing the soundtrack to those clips. There were speeches in English, in Malay, some at rallies, some at what seemed to be either press conferences or in Parliament. The calm, assured, colonial-accented voice spoke of Malaysia and the future of Singaporeans. There was even a speech in Hokkien, with Lee persuading strikers to back down. For someone who had picked up Hokkien from scratch as an adult, his delivery was deeply impressive. Heck, my parents speak Hokkien at home and I'd be hard-pressed to make a speech in that dialect.

So I found myself looking at a man who had gone from his posh bungalow home and his Cambridge education to the attap huts and shanty towns of old Singapore, who swept the streets and shook hands with labourers and farmers and shopkeepers and maids. He'd jumped into the political fray, an English-educated bourgeois, and somehow picked up Chinese and Hokkien to reach the masses. He'd had the nerve to tell them, in their languages, that he understood their problems and that they and their children could have better lives, if they would trust him. He had put on knuckledusters against enemies who had the real strength to crush him. Conviction.

"Did that room help your project?" My friend asked me later, as we left the museum into a rainy afternoon.

"I suppose. I now know I can admire something I can't understand."

"I don't believe
in love at first sight"

Homosexuality – It's in the genes

As in many societies, the issue of homosexuality is controversial in Singapore. From the heated parliamentary debates in 2007 over whether to retain or repeal Section 377A of the Penal Code, which prohibits sex between men (it was eventually retained), to the unease over homosexual content in student sex education manuals, the subject polarises the public. It was no surprise then that we received questions on this topic from both sides of the conservative-liberal divide, including one that asked how Lee would feel if one of his grandchildren were gay.

Q: *What is your personal view on being gay? Do you think it's a lifestyle or is it genetic?*

A: No, it's not a lifestyle. You can read the books you want, all the articles. There's a genetic difference, so it's not a matter of choice. They are born that way and that's that. So if two men or two women are that way, just leave them alone. Whether they should be given rights of adoption is another matter because who's going to look after the child? Those are complications that arise once you recognise that you could actually legally marry, then you say I want to adopt. Vivian Balakrishnan says it's not decisively proven. Well, I believe it is. There's enough evidence that some people are that way and just leave them be.

Q: *This is more of a personal question, but how would you feel if one of your grandchildren were to say to you that he or she is gay?*

A: That's life. They're born with that genetic code, that's that. Dick Cheney didn't like gays but his daughter was born like that.[14] He says, "I still love her, full-stop." It's happened to his family. So

377

on principle he's against it but it's his daughter. Do you throw the daughter out? That's life. I mean none of my children is gay, but if they were, well, that's that.

Q: *So what do you see is an obstacle to gay couples adopting children? You said, who's going to look after the child?*

A: Who is going to bring them up? Two men looking after a child? Two women looking after a child, maybe. But I'm not so sure because it's not their own child. Unless you have artificial insemination and it's their own child, then you have a certain maternal instinct immediately aroused by the process of pregnancy. But two men adopting a boy or a girl, what's the point of it? These are consequential problems, we cross the bridge when we come to it. We haven't come to that bridge yet. The people are not ready for it. In fact, some ministers are not ready for it. I take a practical view. I said this is happening and there's nothing we can do about it. Life's like that. People are born like that. It's not new, it goes back to ancient times. So I think there's something in the genetic makeup.

Q: *It took time for Singaporeans to be able to accept single women MPs. Do you see Singaporeans being able to accept a gay MP? It's already happening in a fairly widespread fashion in Europe.*

A: As far as I'm concerned, if she does her work as an MP, she looks after her constituents, she makes sensible speeches, she's making a contribution, her private life is her life, that's that. There was a British minister, I shouldn't name him, a Conservative. He was out of office but he was hoping to become the leader of the party and we had dinner with a few friends.[15] He thought he had to come out upfront that when he was at university at Oxford, he did get involved in same-sex activities. But he's married now with children, he's quite happy. So he came out with it. He didn't become leader of the party, and that's Britain. He thought he had come out upfront and it'd protect him from investigative reporting. It did not help him. But had he kept quiet they would have dug it out, then it's worse for him. So there you are. You know, there are two standards. It's one thing the people at large, it's another thing your minister or your prime minister being such a person. I mean Ted Heath[16] was not married. I shouldn't say who the ministers were who said he's a suppressed homosexual. So the opposition party leaders were telling me because it's very strange. Here's a man in the prime of life and getting on, 40, 50, still not married, single, and he was that way at Oxford. So they said, suppressed homosexual. That's the opposition talk by very reputable leaders who tell me that seriously. So? And with it of course is disapprobation, that he's unworthy to be a leader. But that was in the early 1970s.

Q: *Did you come to this view on homosexuality just through scientific reasoning alone?*

A: No, by my observation and historical data. I mean, in the Ottoman empire, they had a lot of it. And there was one story that T.E. Lawrence was captured in Arabia and they sodomised him. The Ottomans had their share of homosexuals and I'm sure there were also women in the harems. So? So be it.

Q: *What about your acquaintances or your friends growing up throughout life, were any of them gay as well?*

A: I'm not sure about acquaintances, but not my friends. I mean, they were all married. But I'm sure there must have been. This is not something which is recent, it goes back into historic times. And you have animals sometimes acting that way. So it's not just human beings, there's something in the genetic code.

Q: *So this is one aspect where the conservative views of society are diametrically opposed to your own practical view?*

A: I'm not the prime minister, I told you that before I started. If I were the prime minister I would hesitate to push it through against the prevailing sentiment, against the prevailing values of society. You're going against the current of the people, the underlying feeling. What's the point of that, you know, breaking new ground and taking unnecessary risk? It will evolve over time, as so many things have, because after a while my own sort of maturing process will take place with other people. You don't just live and then you cut off your ideas after a certain time. You keep on living and you watch people and you say, "Oh, that's the way life is".

Q: *But are you, personally speaking, frustrated by this conservatism?*

A: No. I take a purely practical view.

Q: *But are you frustrated by how this conservatism is perhaps opposed to the practical view?*

A: No, that is life. I can't change them overnight. I think society, their own experiences, their own reading, their own observations will bring about the change despite their innate biases.

Love and the pragmatist

Poets and philosophers know all there is to know about love, but what about a pragmatist like Lee? Does he believe in it, a young Singaporean asked us. A tenderness creeps into his voice, as Lee talks about the one love of his life – his wife of 63 years – and dishes out some practical advice.

Q: *Do you believe in love, and love at first sight?*

A: I don't believe in love at first sight. I think it's a grave mistake. You're attracted by physical characteristics and you'll regret it.

Q: *But love, surely?*

A: Yes, yes. I married a woman whom I knew for a long time. I had no interest in her when she was a student at Raffles College with me because I was too young and preoccupied with my work. But she told me later that she was interested in me. During the war, I was making gum mucilage. Yong Nyuk Lin was the chemist, so one production was at my home, the other production was at his home.[17] I went to see him, and there she was. There was time on my hands, I was cycling. So I said, "Oh, she's a nice girl." We became friends. Then it gradually developed and I carefully considered the problem. I think I made the right choice. And with every passing year we adjusted to each other, until now even our habits become the same. That's life.

An Indian man who was an experienced lawyer – I've forgotten his name – and I had a meeting on how to promote marriage. This was way back in 1980-something when I made my speech about graduate women not getting married. He came with a very profound statement. He said, in the West, you marry the woman you love, and then you unlove her. In India, you love the woman you marry. When you marry, you don't know her, but after years it can build up. I thought this was a profound statement. And Jayakumar[18] told me his marriage was done that way. It was arranged by the parents and it's a happy marriage. He's a lawyer, the wife is a doctor. They carefully studied the horoscopes, carefully studied family backgrounds, social backgrounds, financial position. So, yes, ok, it's a fair match. And I think that's much better than saying, oh, she's a pretty girl, I'll marry her. You'll regret it. Beauty is skin-deep. You're just attracted to her physically. And after one, two years of familiarity, you say, oh, I made a great mistake. (Laughs) And she may also come to the conclusion she made a great mistake too. Then you part company.

Q: *If I may be allowed a personal confession, speaking of encouraging marriage, it was your memoirs that encouraged me to get married in the first place.*

A: That's good! I'm very happy to hear that. Which part of my...

Q: *It was your secret marriage in Stratford.*

A: Well, she's an old-fashioned girl with an old-fashioned family, and so was mine. We did not want to have an illicit liaison. It would have been wrong. So we got married. But she was on scholarship, and my tutor would not have been very pleased to hear that I got married, so we just kept it quiet. She wore the wedding ring on a chain. All that I could afford was a platinum wedding ring which I bought at a famous shop. Anyway it's still around, the engraving inside the ring still exists, dates and so on. I think it was the right thing to do.

But these days, I read, the Health Promotion Board and Education Ministry did a poll on teenage boys and girls. Now, more than 7 per cent already have active sex. I don't think that's a good idea. I'd be very sorry to see my grandchildren or my granddaughter do that. I mean, after a while it becomes just a physical commodity, that's all. It doesn't make sense to me.

Finding the time for books and films

Singaporeans love the movies. Singapore has the highest rate of movie-goers in the world, with each person hitting the cinemas about eight times a year on average. In 2009, a record 22 million movie tickets were sold, the highest in two decades. So, yes, young Singaporeans were curious about Lee's film viewing, and also his book-reading choices. His picks are classics from long before they were born.

Q: *Do you have a favourite film?*

A: I don't watch films these days. I don't go to the cinema. No time. It takes a lot of time. But I can remember the best comedy I watched was when I was a student. And I was in London when I watched Danny Kaye. I've forgotten the title, but really he was funny. He could act, he could sing, he could do many things. And for a serious film, *Pygmalion*, and later on a version put out by Warner Brothers. What's the title? I've forgotten the name but it was one of the best musicals on film. Rex Harrison and Audrey Hepburn.

Q: *My Fair Lady?*

A: Yes, because the speech was perfect and the woman was very good because she could speak like a flower girl and she could speak like a duchess. And she could go back again and it's code switching of a very high order. Those stick out in my mind. Longest one I ever saw was *Gone With the Wind*, an American epic. But I don't watch them anymore. So when I read the book, the film reviews mean nothing to me.

Q: *Who are your favourite authors or thinkers? Is there a book that you will recommend that all Singaporeans must read?*

A: What are you interested in? If you are interested in literature,

I would read Shakespeare. I think they're classics. The way he's able to express himself in iambic pentameter, it's superb, the words he uses. If you're interested in economics, I would read Hayek. I think he's right – if you have a planned economy, you will fail. You're interested in politics? No such book. You learn the hard way. You can read Kennedy, *Profiles in Courage*, or Obama and his life story and see how he performs.

Q: *There was an interesting question that was submitted. It said, "I heard that, like Sherlock Holmes, you do not read, watch or hear anything that is irrelevant to your work."[19] Is that true?*

A: By and large, yes. Where is the time? But I read *Don Quixote* for relaxation when the new translation came up, which is well translated. I was in Spain and I got a copy in English. It's not relevant to my work but it carried me back to a different century. Cervantes imagined his knight-errant and Sancho Panza. Quite an interesting read.

Q: *Did you find any lessons in it?*

A: You might mean well but don't tilt at windmills, it's a waste of time. But it was a comedy, it's a story. I don't tilt at windmills.[20] I got mortal foes to fight against.

Subcultures – of Goths and tattoos

If Lee were growing up in Singapore today, would he relate to a hip-hop dancing b-boy, emo rock singers with dark eyeliner or a goth clad all in black? Or could he even be one of them? The list of youth subcultures is endless. Some of the youths we spoke to wanted to know to what extent the government tolerated their distinctive creative and artistic expression that is different from the mainstream. Lee's message to youths is practical: do what you want as long as you don't annoy the general public. Oh, and absolutely stay away from tattoos.

Q: *One of the questions I was asked was about youth subcultures and the person who asked it was a member of a goth music band.*

A: A what?

Q: *A goth music band.*

A: What's that?

Q: *That's where you all dress in black and you play extremely gloomy music.*

A: Why is it goth?

Q: *It's a reference to gothic, like Victorian gothic.*

A: Oh, I see – goth. Okay, so?

Q: *He had problems registering his group as a society. Well, he has more than six people in his group, and he did submit the appropriate documents and he has had problems getting himself registered as a society so that he can comply with the law when he holds his music events. He's also tried to publicise his band by getting into magazines and he's had problems doing that because some agencies have censored or been unhappy with the image that his band projects.*

So he was kind of concerned: Will we become more open to these forms of art or expression?

A: Unless it offends public taste I would just leave it be. You want to dress in black and play gothic music, so be it. But if it is offensive to the general public, then I say we should hesitate. Why annoy the public? Don't misunderstand me, I'm not liberal and I'm not conservative, I'm a practical, pragmatic person, always have been and I take things as they are. That's that.

Q: *Well, one other example is the local tattooing community which is trying to get tattoo accepted as a form of art.*

A: I don't think that's a good idea. I'm very strongly against it because when you want to erase it, it's a very painful process. That's rubbish. Why not paste something which you can wipe off? It's madness to put something permanent and then you think about it later and say it's a mistake and you got to remove it. So I discouraged it. I rang up MICA (Ministry of Information, Communications and the Arts), I said, "Tell the press don't be stupid. Enough problems, why create more problems?" I can see the benefit for people who are doing the tattooing because there's more business.

Q: *So you're against people publicising this?*

A: Well, maybe it goes back to secret society days. I mean no decent man or woman has a tattoo. If you go to a concentration camp then you get a number tattooed on you as a kind of slur on a person.

Q: *But assuming the cultural context changes over time, there would be no problem with it, that's what you're saying?*

A: If people think it's a good idea and they bring their teenagers to be tattooed, that's their business. But I don't think any parent would want to see, especially his daughter, having tattoos. You get into a swimsuit and you immediately reduce your attractiveness. People say, "What's going on? (Laughs) What have you put there? Don't touch me?" It's madness.

Q: *Because it actually has become very popular among young people.*

A: Young people do silly things which they regret when they come to middle age and if my children were going to tattoo themselves, I'd say, "Are you nuts?" (Laughs) People will mistake you for a secret society gangster. You know, the yakuza in Japan has beautiful tattoos all over them. So it's connected with something not socially to be admired.

Q: *This may be a bit shocking but many young Singaporeans are specifically getting yakuza-inspired tattoos now, which is quite unusual.*

A: Well, they will regret it in a few years' time, and the people who erase tattoos will make a lot of money. How does that help them in life? Anybody who comes for employment and I'm the employer, I look at him, I say, "Ah, there's something wrong with this chap's mind. Out with him." No, on that I do not go with any such fad. It's not a trend, it's a fad.

Statesmen who roll their own cigarettes

A seminal figure, an extraordinary man, a statesman who achieved impossible things. These are just some of the accolades heaped on Lee Kuan Yew. What inspired him to become the statesman he is today and what kind of statesman did he think he was? Young Singaporeans wanted to know. Lee's answer: He has no interest in such navel-gazing.

Q: *If you could be a statesman at any point in world history, which one would you be and why?*

A: That's a parlour game. I would not be a statesman at all. It was circumstances that created me: the defeat of the British, the complete collapse of morale, the Japanese brutality, the reoccupation, the struggle for power between the communists and us as the British were withdrawing. That's what created what I am. I don't think I wanted to be a statesman, that's rubbish. You don't become a statesman.

Q: *So what did you want to be?*

A: I wanted to be a lawyer.

Q: *And would that have been what you'd have ended up becoming had you not chosen politics?*

A: Except that had I not chosen politics, who would run this country and what law will you apply? That's what I told Eddie Barker, my partner. I said, "Eddie, if we don't stand for elections and we have duds, you think your law office would be running?" He thought it over and said I'm right. So he came out. But once it got steady, he said, "Well, okay, I haven't paid my mortgage on my house." So that's how I started changing the salary scheme. You don't start life, and say "I want to be a statesman". Rubbish. Next question.

Q: *Or perhaps, which statesman do you most admire?*

A: De Gaulle, Deng Xiaoping, Churchill. De Gaulle because he had tremendous guts. I mean, his country was occupied. He was a one-star general and he represented France. But the British and the Americans supported him and he stood his ground. I watched him. I don't understand French, but I saw the passion with which he spoke. And I read his biography.[21] And when the British and the Americans recaptured North Africa, he went to Algeria and Algiers and he saw a French general there, a four-star general. He said, "Giraud,[22] you're a general of France. What is the American soldier doing outside protecting you?" He's a very tough-minded fellow. And when the British and the Americans were about to march to Paris, he said, "You stop, I march to Paris." No, he had guts and gumption.

Deng Xiaoping is a great man because he changed China from a broken-backed state, which would have imploded like the Soviet Union, into what it is today, on the way to becoming the world's largest economy.[23]

Churchill, because any other man would have given up. But he said, "We'll fight on the beaches." I heard this on radio: "We'll fight on the beaches. We'll fight in the fields and in the streets. We'll never surrender."[24] To say that when your troops have been defeated and were scurrying back from Dunkirk in little ships, any ship that can carry them, required an enormous amount of will and verve and determination not to yield to the Germans. And he had it. But alone he could not have won. So he waited for the opportunity. Finally the Japanese attacked Pearl Harbor, and the Germans declared war on the Americans. He was saved. But he's a great man. He stood by his men. Dunkirk was 1940. And the Battle of Britain, also '40. Saved by the skin, by their Spitfire pilots. Or the Germans, had they commanded the skies, would have crossed the Channel and occupied Britain. The army had been defeated in Dunkirk.

And any other leader, like Chamberlain,[25] would have accepted his terms. Hitler had offered them a partnership of the world. You keep your empire, I will build one in Europe. He said, "No. You're fascist. I'm going to fight you." A very bold man.

I mean, if you ask the Americans, they'll say Roosevelt. But Roosevelt had power and the industrial might of America. And Roosevelt once said to Harriman,[26] he said, "Churchill makes such rousing speeches. Why can't my speechwriters do that?" So Harriman told him, "He rolls his own cigarettes." That's the difference. He rolls his own cigarettes, like de Gaulle. So when he talks, it's deep from within, and not written up by a polished scriptwriter.

Q: *You mentioned several statesmen that you really admired. Do you hope to be remembered in the same way as them by Singaporean youths?*

A: No, I don't. First of all, I do not classify myself as a statesman. I put myself down as determined, consistent, persistent. I set out to do something, I keep on chasing it until it succeeds. That's all. That's how I perceive myself. Not as a statesman. It's utter rubbish. Anybody who thinks he's a statesman needs to see a psychiatrist.

Homeless in Cambridge

For many young people, deciding where to spend the three or four years of their university life is one of the biggest decisions they will ever make. In many ways, the college you choose to go to will define you. For Lee, it was no different.

Q: *What were your fondest memories from your time in Cambridge?*

A: First, I went up one term late and the tutor said, "You're already one term late and I got no rooms for you." So he turned to Cecil Wong whom I knew in Raffles College and he said, "If he's prepared to share his room with you, I'll take you in." So I looked at him and said, "Are you?" He said yes. So two men shared one small bed for one or two terms until I found new digs for myself![27]

It changed the course of my life because in London I would have gone bonkers – the noise, the bustle and so on.[28] I was a small-town boy landed in this big city. But in Cambridge, there were bicycles all around. The town was there to cater to the students, at that time, 10,000 students. It was a very placid, serene society. It encouraged academic pursuits. Of course you got the drama clubs and debating societies, but on the whole it's a quiet place. If you want any excitement you go down to London.

And the other thing was the summer when you can go to the Backs,[29] laze around in the sun because you have so little sun in Britain. And you might find a photograph of me and my wife. Yong Pung How[30] took the photograph. Those are memories that stick in my mind. But you can't relive that. Not possible. We went back in 1990-something but it was a different Cambridge and we were different persons, and it was a rainy day. So that's that.

Endnotes

2   "PM Lee once changed diapers too", *The New Paper*, 15 February 2010.

3   R. Hausmann, L.D. Tyson and S. Zahidi, *The Global Gender Gap Report 2009* (Geneva, 2009), p 164.

4   "Gender gap closing: survey", *The Straits Times*, 27 February 2009.

5   Ministry of Manpower, Singapore Yearbook of Manpower Statistics 2009, http://www.mom.gov.sg/publish/etc/medialib/mom_library/mrsd/yb_2009.Par.19034.File.tmp/2009YearBook_LFtable1_6.xls (accessed January 2010).

6   Hausmann, Tyson and Zahidi, *The Global Gender Gap Report 2009*, pp 14, 164.

7   "Women on board? Not quite", *The Business Times*, 7 March 2009.

8   Singapore Yearbook of Manpower Statistics 2009, http://www.mom.gov.sg/publish/etc/medialib/mom_library/mrsd/yb_2009.Par.44204.File.tmp/2009YearBook_Wtable2_2.xls

9   P. Chew and C. Singam, "Modern Women, Traditional Wives", in A. Chin and C. Singam ed., *Singapore Women Re-Presented* (Singapore, 2004), pp 275–85.

10 "Population paradox: Europe's Time Bomb", *The Independent*, 9 August 2008; K. Howley, "What's the Matter with Everywhere other than Scandinavia and the United States?", http://reason.com/blog/2008/06/30/whats-thematter-with-everywhe (accessed 8 January 2010).

11 "Single mum's plea: Don't ignore us", *The Straits Times*, 15 April 2005; "All they want is to be treated like other mums", *The Straits Times*, 18 April 2005; "Give maternity benefits to unwed mums too", *The Straits Times*, 30 August 2009.

12 "Single mothers need more help", *The Straits Times*, 27 February 2009.

13 "Bicycle rental a hit in Paris", *The Straits Times*, 29 December 2008; Vélib' – velos libre-service a Paris – official site, http://www.velib.paris.fr/ (accessed 8 January 2010).

14 Former US Vice-President Dick Cheney's second daughter, Mary Cheney, is lesbian.

15 Lee is referring to Michael Portillo, who was secretary of state for employment 1994–1995 and for defence 1995–1997.

16 Prime Minister of Britain from 1970 to 1974.

17 Yong Nyuk Lin is the brother-in-law of Lee's wife, Kwa Geok Choo. Lee met Yong during the Japanese occupation, when they both made stationery gum marketed under the name "Stikfas".

18 Senior Minister and former Coordinating Minister for National Security.

19 Reference to the Holmes novel, *A Study in Scarlet*, when the detective reveals that he doesn't know the earth revolves around the sun. The brain, he says, is like an empty attic: "A fool takes in all the lumber of every sort that he comes across, so that the knowledge which might be useful to him gets crowded out, or at best is jumbled up with a lot of other things … Now the skilful workman is very careful indeed as to what he takes into his brain-attic. He will have nothing but the tools which may help him in doing his work."

20 *Don Quixote* is a 17th century novel by Spanish writer Miguel de Cervantes. The main character, Don Quixote, attacks windmills, thinking that they are giants. The phrase "tilting at windmills" – attacking imaginary enemies – comes from the book.

21 Charles de Gaulle was president of France from 1959 to 1969 and, during the Second World War, a leader of the Free French Forces that resisted the Nazi occupiers in France.

22 A reference to General Henri Giraud. During the Second World War, Giraud and de Gaulle were co-presidents of the French Committee of National Liberation.

23 Deng Xiaoping was leader of China from 1978 to 1992. He is widely recognised as the statesman who modernised China's economy.

24 Winston Churchill was Prime Minister of Britain from 1940 to 1945 and 1951 to 1955. Lee is quoting from a famous speech that Churchill made in June 1940 in the House of Commons, shortly after being elected Prime Minister.

25 Neville Chamberlain was Prime Minister of Britain from 1937 to 1940. He carried out a policy of appeasement with Hitler, attempting to avoid war by accommodating Germany's expansionist goals.

26 Averell Harriman was special envoy to Europe.

27 These rooms were in 36 Belvoir Road, Cambridge.

28 Lee had transferred from the London School of Economics to Cambridge University.

29 The Cambridge term for the banks of the river Cam behind the colleges.

30 Yong later became chief justice of Singapore in 1990. He stepped down in 2006.

Private moments

Lee Kuan Yew and Mrs Lee looking happy as they pose for a portrait at the State Room of the Istana in 2004. By then, Mrs Lee had recovered from her first stroke that she suffered in 2003.

Lee Kuan Yew as a student at Fitzwilliam College in Cambridge during the winter of 1946.

A young Lee Kuan Yew in 1930.

The Lees take a family portrait in 1946 before Lee Kuan Yew sailed for England. Parents Lee Chin Koon and Chua Jim Neo are in front, and at the back, from left, are Monica, Dennis, Lee, Freddy and Suan Yew.

Two of a series of photos Lee got his cousin Harold Liem to take of him and his girlfriend Kwa Geok Choo in September 1946 so that he could bring them with him to Cambridge. "We took those photos for me to display in my rooms," said Lee.

Lee and his wife Kwa Geok Choo at the Bridge of Sighs in Cambridge in 1948.

Back in Cambridge for Lee Hsien Loong's convocation in 1974, the Lees pay another visit to the Bridge of Sighs.

The couple return to the Bridge of Sighs in 2000.

Yong Pung How, Mrs Lee and Lee Kuan Yew on the banks of the River Cam in the summer of 1949.

The happy couple, cutting their wedding cake at a reception at Raffles Hotel on 30 September 1950.

Lee and his family outside their Oxley Road home.

The Lees at the
Taj Mahal on
3 September
1970.

Lee with his daughter, Wei Ling, then aged seven, on 22 July 1962.

Lee Kuan Yew and Mrs Lee carrying elder son Hsien Loong.

Lee with Mrs Lee and elder son Hsien Loong upon Lee's return from London, on 22 May 1956.

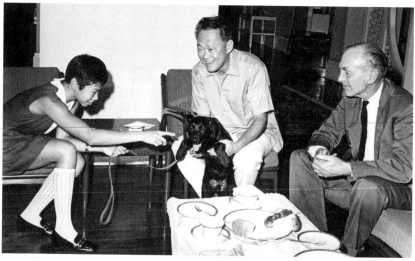

Lee holds on to a puppy labrador retriever, Bonnie, given by British Conservative leader Alec Douglas-Home to daughter Wei Ling when he visited Singapore as Foreign Secretary for a Commonwealth conference in January 1971.

Lee's children, from left: Hsien Loong, Hsien Yang and Wei Ling.

Mrs Lee with Toffee, a cocker spaniel that loved the Sri Temasek grounds.

Bonnie, the Lees' labrador retriever, was "the most intelligent dog" Lee said he had.

Lee Kuan Yew with his father and siblings in 1988. From left: Suan Yew, Dennis, father Lee Chin Koon, Monica, Lee and Freddy.

The Lee family takes a stroll in winter along Henley-on-Thames, January 1973.

The Lees at elder son Hsien Loong's convocation at Cambridge University in June 1974.

The Lee family in September 1973

Lee with Master of Eliot House at Harvard University, Professor Alan Heimert, and his wife, Arline. Lee stayed at Eliot House during his sabbatical at Harvard in 1968.

A beaming Lee Hsien Loong with his parents at a reception to mark the end of his basic military training at Holland Road Camp on 24 March 1971.

The Lees inspect a two-in-one back scratcher and massager while on a visit to Yashima, Japan on 18 October 1986.

Lee joins Ministers and Members of Parliament for a singing rehearsal at Parliament House on 28 July 1987.

Lee braves the cold for a jog along a railway platform in Chengde, China during a two-week state visit in November 1980.

Mr and Mrs Lee at the picturesque West Lake in Hangzhou, China on 21 November 1980.

Lee ready for a hunting trip in Kazakhstan in 1991.

Mr and Mrs Lee with Xiuqi and newborn Yipeng in November 1982.

Lee Hsien Loong with wife Ho Ching and children Yipeng and Xiuqi at the National Day Carnival at East Coast Park, 10 August 1986.

Lee Hsien Loong with wife Ho Ching and children tuck into hawker fare at Serangoon Gardens.

Grandpa and Grandma Lee with their grandchildren. From left: Haoyi, Shengwu, Huanwu and Hongyi.

Prime Minister Lee Hsien Loong
with Ho Ching at a May Day
concert on the Marina Bay golf
course on 23 May 2009.

Lee Hsien Loong and Ho Ching with son Hongyi at
his OCS Commissioning Parade in 2006.

Lee Hsien Loong gamely
takes his wife Ho Ching for a
ride on a trishaw at Nanyang
Technological University's
50th anniversary celebrations
in 2005.

Father, mother and son pose happily for a photo in
July 2006.

Lee Kuan Yew at the National Day Parade in 1997.

SM Goh Chok Tong, PM Lee Hsien Loong, and MM Lee Kuan Yew with other Cabinet ministers at the 2007 National Day Parade.

Dr Kanwaljit Soin, founder of the Women's Initiative for Ageing Successfully (Wings), gives a surprised Lee Kuan Yew a kiss at a dinner in July 2007 to mark the 10th anniversary of the Singapore chapter of the International Women's Forum.

Proud father Lee
congratulates his
son, Lee Hsien
Loong, after he
is sworn-in as
Prime Minister of
Singapore in August
2004.
Below, 18 years
earlier, Lee greeted
his son, then the
Acting Minister for
Trade and Industry,
during a state visit
to Brunei.

Lee is given a book of portraits and quotes by his granddaughter Xiuqi at his 80th birthday celebrations in 2003.

Lee and his granddaughter Xiuqi tour Peterhof Palace in St Petersburg in 2007, while on a week-long visit to Russia.

Three generations of Lees at a family gathering on 4 February 2000: Front row: Lee and Mrs Lee. Back row: Lim Suet Fern, the wife of Lee Hsien Yang, Shaowu, Lee Hsien Yang, Huanwu, Ho Ching, the wife of Lee Hsien Loong, Hongyi, Haoyi, Lee Hsien Loong, Lee Wei Ling, Shengwu, Yipeng and Xiuqi.

The families of Lee and of his silblings at a family reunion on the eve of Chinese New Year on 4 February 2000.

Which is the real Lee Kuan Yew? Lee unveils a wax figure of himself created by sculptors of the London wax museum Madame Tussaud on 6 March 1998.

The Lees celebrate his 77th birthday and the launch of the second volume of his memoirs on 16 September 2000.

Lee and Mrs Lee at his 80th birthday celebrations at the Shangri-La Hotel on 16 September 2003.

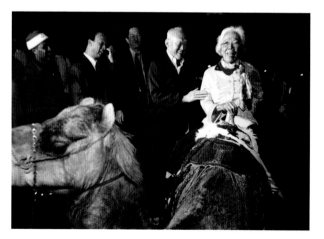

Mrs Lee rides a camel during a four-day trip to Saudi Arabia in March 2006, as Lee looks on.

The couple cover their ears from the sound of exploding firecrackers to mark the beginning of Chinese New Year in Chinatown on 7 January 2006. Jalan Besar GRC MP, Dr Lily Neo offers them ear plugs.

It's love everlasting as they pose for a photo on Sentosa Island on Valentine's Day in 2008. (Photo © Kwa Kim Li)

Mrs Lee comforts Lee during the funeral service for S. Rajaratnam, 2006.

The couple taking a walk at a park in Prague in 2005.

Lee bidding a final farewell to beloved wife Kwa Geok Choo who died on 2 October 2010. Standing by the casket during her funeral on 6 October 2010, he brought his fingers to his lips and reached down to touch his wife's face.

Grandson Yipeng comforts his grieving grandfather during the service at the crematorium.

A portrait taken by the Chinese National Government's official photographer Zhang Jianshe on 5 May 2008.

PART 3
PRIVATE
MUSINGS

11

HUSBAND, FATHER, GRANDFATHER, FRIEND

WHEN MRS LEE KUAN YEW died on October 2, 2010, one question many Singaporeans had was what her death would do to her husband. They had been together for more than 60 years. She had been his wife, soulmate and political confidante for so long, no one was sure how Lee would take her departure. How would he cope without her? Would it change him personally and as Singapore's foremost political leader?

These questions spring not merely from idle curiosity. Lee still wields enormous political influence and his views are widely sought by foreign leaders. If his wife's death were to result in any change to his well-being or his capacity to function, it would have important consequences for Singapore and its people. For now, it is too early to tell.

But Singaporeans had a glimpse of just how close he was to his wife when he spoke at the funeral. When he reached out to plant a last kiss on her forehead, the act of tenderness moved many to tears. Photos capturing it were reproduced in the newspapers, images broadcast on TV. For a moment, the inner life of the private politician became public. That kiss brought to light a side of Lee that many had never seen before: A softer, more sympathetic side, one capable of grief and affection – and love.

When this chapter was first written, Mrs Lee was still alive. Our material came from an interview we had had with Lee in June 2009: seated around a small round marble table and drinking Chinese tea, we had given our curiosity about the Lee family full rein. It was a curiosity shared by many others, we knew. Most people had the basic facts – who his wife and children are, whom they married, how many kids they have and what jobs they do – but very little had been said publicly about how they interact as a family.

Lee's answers gave us what was then an unprecedented glimpse into his personal life. What emerged was the image of a devoted husband and family man. Mrs Lee, he told us then, was unable to move or speak after a series of strokes had struck her down. She was bedridden and drifting in and out of consciousness. Nurses tended to her round the clock, but Lee, too, kept a vigil by her side. He saw her before he went to work, and the first thing he did after returning every night was to go to her bedside and talk to her. He told her what he had been up to that day, whom he had met and what they had discussed. He told her what had been in the news. Then, he took out *Palgrave's Golden Treasury*, an anthology which contained some of her favourite poems, and read them to her. When he went abroad, he spoke to her on a webcam set up by their daughter-in-law, Ho Ching.

He said he tried not to think about the "empty blank spaces" he had to fill now that his wife was unable to accompany him for the lunches, dinners and walks they used to enjoy nearly every day. Instead, he had shifted his focus – concentrating, for example, on brushing up on his Mandarin by talking to his wife's nurses and his staff officers and doing this book with us. "You have to psychologically make adjustments and I've adjusted," he said. "But there will be another adjustment when she finally isn't there. Then this big house will be empty."

It was an image that we had seen in his daughter Dr Lee Wei Ling's columns. Since she first began writing those columns in December 2008, she had lifted the veil ever so slightly on the life of the Lees. "The partnership may not have been exactly equal at particular points in time. But over the years, especially after my mother's health deteriorated after she suffered a stroke, my father was the one who took care of her," she wrote. Being the eldest son in a typical Peranakan family, he "cannot even crack a soft-boiled egg … But he readily adjusted his lifestyle to accommodate her, took care of her medications and lived his life around her. I knew how much effort it took him to do all this, and I was surprised that he was able to make the effort."

It came up again in a rare interview with *The New York Times*, where Lee spoke openly about ageing. "When is the last leaf falling?" he said. "I can feel the gradual decline of energy and vitality. I mean generally every year when you know you are not on the same level as last year. But that is life."

He told *The New York Times* that he had learnt to meditate from a Catholic, Laurence Freeman. The mantra he uses to meditate is Ma-Ra-Na-Ta, "Oh Lord, come". The meditation gave him a certain serenity, he said. "I find meditation helps me go to sleep. A certain tranquillity settles over you. The day's pressures and worries are pushed out."

In that interview, too, the loving husband emerged. He had this to say about Mrs Lee's illness: "I can't break down. Life has got to go on. I try to busy myself, but from time to time in idle moments, my mind goes back to the happy days when we were up and about together.

"My daughter fished out many old photographs for this piece she wrote in *The Sunday Times* and picked out a dozen or two dozen photographs from the digital copies which somebody had kept at Singapore Press Holdings. When I looked at the photographs, I thought how lucky I was. I had 61 years of happiness.

"We've got to go sometime. I'm not sure who's going first, whether she or me. So I told her, I've been looking at the marriage vows of the Christians: 'To love, to hold and to cherish, in sickness and in health, for better or for worse, till death do us part.' I told her I would try and keep her company for as long as I could. She understood."

As a father, Lee was proud of his children and their achievements. Throughout our interview, he brought up example after example of his son Prime Minister Lee Hsien Loong's brilliance, both during his university days and even now as he grapples with the complex problems facing Singapore. He once told a People's Action Party (PAP) conference in 1990 that even Hsien Loong's mannerisms were uncannily like his. "I did not know how much like me he was until I watched him on television one day. He did this (tugged at the shirt sleeves of his shoulders), exactly the way I do." In his interview with us, he said with obvious pride that Hsien Loong had scored 31 alpha questions – questions for which a distinction is given for excellent answers – 12 more alpha questions than the second-ranked student in his year at Cambridge. Hsien Yang also scored a First in Cambridge and could have been appointed head of the civil service had he not left for the private sector.

And there was a twinkle in his eye when he spoke about his grandchildren and a potential Lee dynasty. Hsien Loong's daughter Xiuqi made a short film about the Seletar area losing its old-world charm and is now studying film at the satellite campus here of the famous Tisch School of the Arts. His son Hongyi, who was in the news for publicly blowing the whistle on his errant army officer, has taken a scholarship to study at the Massachusetts Institute of Technology (MIT). Hsien Yang's son Shengwu recently topped his class of 240 Philosophy, Politics & Economics (PPE) students at Oxford, and was named Best Speaker at the World Universities Debating Championships. But he said his grandchildren had shown no signs of wanting to follow in his footsteps and quipped in a booming voice: "If they do, I hope they're of the quality to go into politics or they will degrade the Lee name!"

Back then, it was his candour and the intimacy of his revelations that struck us. But Mrs Lee's death added a new dimension to our interview. Suddenly, the spotlight fell on the Lee family more brightly than it had done before. The Lees' marriage, their political partnership, their private life became public fare. Lee Hsien Loong, Lee Hsien Yang, Lee Wei Ling, Li Xiuqi and Li Shengwu spoke about their family in their eulogies, which were reproduced in the media for countless readers.

After Mrs Lee's stroke, Hsien Yang said, "Papa helped, cajoled and encouraged her in her rehabilitation. He continued to care for her with an infinite amount of patience, love, kindness and good humour. He adjusted his routine to accommodate her changing circumstances and physical condition. His abiding love, devotion and care must have been a great comfort to her, and an inspiration to Fern and me on how to manage a lifelong partnership, through good health and illness.

"When we married in 1981, Papa wrote Fern and me a letter with advice on marriage. Of his relationship with Mama he said: 'We have never allowed the other to feel abandoned and alone in any moment of crisis. Quite the contrary, we have faced all major crises in our lives together, sharing our fears and hopes, and our subsequent grief and exultation. These moments of crisis have bonded us closer together. With the years, the number of special ties which we two have shared have increased. Some of them we share with the children.' Papa has lived this love and commitment throughout these last difficult years."

Xiuqi added her own reminiscences: "Now, my grandad had to peel his own fruit, peel her fruit, pack his own suitcase and make his own Milo. For the first time in a while, he had to handle money so he could pay the maids. My granny locked the money in one place, and kept the keys to the lock in another totally unrelated place. My grandad complained that she needed a system but she retorted that she had a system. And that was that."

The most moving eulogy, however, came from Lee himself. "My wife and I have been together since 1947 for more than three-quarters of our lives. My grief at her passing cannot be expressed in words ... I have precious memories of our 63 years together. Without her, I would be a different man, with a different life. She devoted herself to me and our children. She was always there when I needed her. She has lived a life full of warmth and meaning. I should find solace in her 89 years of life well lived. But at this moment of the final parting, my heart is heavy with sorrow and grief."

Thousands of Singaporeans went to pay their respects to Mrs Lee, inspired by her life and example. Hundreds of column inches went into newspaper articles about her story and special programmes went on air. *The Straits Times* ran an excerpt of this book, blurbed on the front page.

What we had in this chapter, then, was no longer an exclusive, some kind of sentimental scoop. It was something else entirely: a poignant snapshot of a husband coping with the illness of his beloved wife. A portrait taken from happier, less lonely days, when Lee could still feel his wife's presence and she, his. "I'm the one she recognises most," he said. "When she hears my voice she knows it's me."

Now, Mrs Lee's passing has made the "big empty house" emptier. "It means more solitude," Lee said in an email interview in November 2010. "No one to talk to when the day's work is done." Other than those laconic few sentences, Lee is loath to reveal more about his life without Mrs Lee. His private life fades once again from public scrutiny, though speculation about his state of health is rife. But one is left with a lingering impression of loving devotion and fatherly pride that persists long after the spotlight has shifted – an impression that first came across to us when we sat down with him in 2009.

"All my friends in Singapore
and all my political colleagues
are either in wheelchairs, or
gone, or about to go."

Q: *Can we start by asking how is Mrs Lee and how difficult is it for you coping with her illness?*

A: Well, at the beginning it was. When it happened in May 2008 it was traumatic because she had a second stroke then. She had recovered from her first stroke in 2003, reasonably unimpaired. We dashed her to hospital – the National Neuroscience Institute (NNI). There they found a new bleed (in the brain), this time in a more difficult position where it affects the movements. But there was still hope that she would recover with some physiotherapy, although maybe the quality of life would not be as good as before. Then while she was undergoing therapy, within the first two weeks she had two more strokes, one after another. The doctor said it's no use, physiotherapy cannot do anything because it was traumatic. So we brought her home, and I had to shift into my study room, which is next to my bedroom, because she had to have nurses round the clock. All the trauma meant I could not sleep. I developed a heart flutter and all sorts of problems that may have come on a few years later but came on earlier because of the stress.

After a while you adjust yourself mentally. I can do nothing except provide good nursing, so I've resigned myself. So have my children. She's gradually losing more and more of her faculties. There must have been more minor bleeds. Now she has cognition but she can't speak. But that's life. I was thinking to myself when I fell off the bicycle recently – had I knocked my head against the floor, I would be in a similar condition. We can't choose how we go. It's a difficult way of going but life is like that. So I've adjusted and accepted the inevitable. The doctors say even though you expect it when it happens, it's still a blow. I can only wait and see, and I've mentally sort of prepared myself.

It also reminded me of my own mortality and how quickly it can change in the flicker of a second if there's an internal bleed. That's life. I cannot choose how I'm going to go. I just carry on my life and that's that. If you start thinking about it, you will go downhill. Every day is a bonus, so let's carry on.

Q: *Is she conscious of what's happening around her? Can she recognise?*

A: I'm the one she recognises the most. When she hears my voice she knows it's me. This is after 62 years together, which makes it more difficult for her and for me. Because there's full cognition – when I tell her, look, our daughter is in hospital with some problem, she's suddenly alert and listens. But the hours of cognition are becoming less and less because she's sleeping more and more. Energy levels go down.

Q: *How have you adjusted your daily routine as a result?*

A: Well, I used to sit down (with her) for lunch, dinner and take walks. So I decided to have a counter-focus and am now polishing my Mandarin. When I walk I speak to my security officers more in Mandarin now, making up for the vocabulary I never learnt – simple everyday words like tables, chairs, drawers. I used to learn the political, economic and social words and phrases. The nurses also speak Mandarin. When I have lunch or dinner, if my wife is asleep, I talk to them in Mandarin. As a result, my Mandarin has improved tremendously. I was able to carry on two meetings with the Chinese leaders without interpretation. One was with the state councillor Liu Yandong – the only female member of the state council. The other was Hao Ping, Vice-Minister for Education. It gives me another focus of activity, otherwise those are empty blank periods.

I have to psychologically make adjustments. I've adjusted. But there will be another adjustment when she finally isn't here. Then this big house will be empty. Fortunately I'm able to concentrate on my other work, so life goes on. I travel and do all the things I have been doing. If I don't carry on with life, I will degrade. If you think you're going to sit down and read novels and play golf, you're foolish – you'll just go downhill. Every day is a challenge. Every day has problems to be solved.

Q: *What about your own health?*

A: After the heart flutter, (installing of the) pacemaker and (taking) Plavix, I now have a different risk. Plavix is a blood thinner, and you get internal bleeding if you fall. That's very difficult because sometimes they don't even know where the bleed is. If it's in the brain it's a sure disaster. If it's elsewhere in the body, they've got to stop the Plavix and hope it will dry up. The important thing is not to fall down and have internal bleeding. Hence I've changed my bicycle to one that will not easily topple over.

Life means constant adjustments as your physical conditions alter. Up to 30 years of age, you're vigorous. At 40, you begin to slow down and at 50 you slow down more. I decided to fight this and started aerobics. First, jogging; that carried on for about 15 or 20 years until my hips began to give trouble. Then I switched to cycling, which I still do.

Q: *Do you still swim?*

A: Yes, every day. That's to loosen up the joints. At the end of the day, it's also to freshen up – a sort of refreshed feeling – for dinner and the evening's work. You've got to make the best of the rest of your life. If you start pitying yourself and say, oh why can't I go back to what I was, then you're creating misery for yourself.

Q: *Can you describe to us what a typical day is like for you?*

A: Now?

Q: *Yes, now.*

A: Well, I work till late. I've always had a tendency to stay awake after dark and I work late. In 1959, I used to go to the office at City Hall at 8 o'clock in the morning. Then gradually it became 9 o'clock, then 10 o'clock. Now I go in the afternoons, and with the physiotherapy I go in the late afternoon. I just had physiotherapy – one and a half hours – then lunch, wash, change, clear e-mails and now I'm here. After this I don't know what will be on my tray but I've to clear my tray, answer more e-mails, send out some, then cycle, swim, go home, have dinner, chat with the nurses, keep my Mandarin alive, and work. I don't waste time.

Q: *Many people would say that for a man of your age, you pack in a lot in a day. Your recent trip to Malaysia, for example.*

A: That's partly because of my genes – I think 70 to 80 per cent is in the genes. My father lived till the age of 94. My mother lived till 74, then she had a heart problem. But in that period they didn't have angioplasty. At 72, I had a heart problem. But I had an angioplasty and overcame the blockage of the coronary artery. So I'm halfway between my mother and my father. How long it will last, I don't know. I just carry on. That's life.

All my friends in Singapore and all my political colleagues are either in wheelchairs, or gone, or about to go. I can't complain. As for my contemporaries in England, most are dead. Now I only meet one who was an ambassador in Beijing. He is a very brilliant fellow – Percy Cradock. He's got diabetes and lost both legs. I have visited him – a very able, very powerful mind. We kept in touch from college days and renewed contact when he was in the British High Commission in Kuala Lumpur. He mastered Mandarin there and went to China and became the ambassador. Together with Margaret Thatcher, he settled the Hong Kong problem with Deng

Xiaoping in 1984. When I was there in China, I used to see him and he gave me the rundown of who's who and what's what. He's very well informed.

When he came back from home leave, he would stay here for a few days and we would meet. When I go to England, I meet him and he used to come and meet me for lunch and dinner. When I last visited him, I found the whole house had been refitted. I used his toilet, which had been fitted with bars – because for him to go to toilet is a major gymnastic exercise. And all he's got is his wife. No help. Maybe once or twice a week, the owner would come in and clean up the place. That's it. So I think I'm a lucky man. He's the same age as I am. As far as I can remember, he's the sole survivor of my generation. (Sir Percy Cradock died in January 2010. See also page 422.)

Q: *Apart from genes, would you attribute it to other factors, like the food you eat?*

A: I've always exercised regularly. I used to play golf, but found it did not give me vitality because it's a slothful game. My daughter gave me a book by a senior medical man of the US air force (Dr Kenneth Cooper) called *Aerobics*, where he quantified which exercise and how many minutes give you how much aerobic activity. One day she saw me deep breathing at Sri Temasek lawn and said, "What are you trying to do?" I said, "I'm trying to get more oxygen into my lungs." She said, "That's not the way. You walk faster or run." She does that herself. So I read this book she gave me and said, "Well, let's try." So in between golf shots, I started to walk faster, and I found myself feeling better. And then, in between golf shots I started to run. Eventually I said, why am I wasting time with the golf? Just run! Nine holes of golf will take you one and a half, two hours. I run in 20 minutes, I feel better off. So the cost-benefit made me drop golf.

Q: *What else do you do to completely relax? How do you take your mind off things?*

A: Well, after (former Speaker of the House) Yeoh Ghim Seng had cancer, a doctor called K.K. Tan (Dr Tan Kheng Khoo), a Buddhist, saw Yeoh Ghim Seng in hospital and taught him how to meditate. You develop a certain serenity instead of just fretting "I'm going to die, I'm going to die" all the time. I said, "That's interesting. How about teaching me?" So Dr Tan came to the office and gave me about six lessons. At first I had some difficulty. Then after a while I found that if you concentrate on your breathing and slow down your breathing rate – you can have a mantra or not, it doesn't matter – you can find yourself suddenly serene. Your pulse rate and blood pressure go down. And I can feel it as my pulse rate goes down. I've still got the notes somewhere. Still the mind … empty the mind, relax. Look at yourself as a third eye from above and be aware of where you are in this cosmos – that you're just a little particle. Get a sense of proportion that you're just a little bit of this huge universe. Ignore your face. Ignore your body, and when you are deep in meditation, forget everything.

I haven't reached the level he has reached, but I can reach a certain level where under stress, if I find myself grouchy, I go to a quiet corner to sit down. Within 20 minutes to half an hour, I bring my tempo down. He also taught my son Hsien Loong when he had lymphoma.

I met (former Burmese Prime Minister) Ne Win one day. He was here for medical treatment. I said, "Oh, you look fine!" – the last time I met him in Burma he looked as if he was going to die. He said, "Yes, I spend all my time meditating." I said, "Oh, is that so? How do you meditate?" I asked, "Supposing your daughter died (the daughter was outside the room with the son-in-law), will that trouble you? Will that get you down?" He said, "Well, for a short while but I meditate and ask, what is this life? I'm just but a tiny speck. Another tiny speck has been lost." So he mentally puts himself into a more detached position. I wouldn't say it's a trick; it's a psychological method.

I find that useful. Look at yourself as if you're a different person looking at yourself, then you suddenly think, well, I have to put things in perspective. I believe we should teach meditation in schools because that will save going to the doctors, taking Valium or whatever.

Q: *Is meditation easier for you because you are more predisposed to Buddhism as a set of beliefs? I think you once said you were a nominal Buddhist.*

A: Yes, yes, I'm a nominal Buddhist. At most Buddhist temples you have monks and disciples sitting down lotus fashion with the hands cupped together and deep breathing – eyes wide open but seeing nothing, relaxing. I'm not able to do that. I close my eyes but I get some similar effect, not the same as the monks. Former Japanese Prime Minister Yasuhiro Nakasone spent one hour at a temple once a week sitting lotus fashion and meditating. He told me this a long time ago when I gave him dinner in Singapore: "I just sit down in peace and cut out the world." I've not been able to sit down lotus fashion. I had left hip dysplasia when I tried that.

Q: *What else did you do, especially in the earlier days, to relax?*

A: I used to play chess with my children.

Q: *That's nice. Did you let them win or did you beat them?*

A: No, I didn't let them win. I would give them a handicap but as they grew up they needed no handicaps. After a while I said, okay, we'll have to stop it! (Laughs)

Q: *Actually, did you make it a point to spend a lot of time with your children as they were growing up?*

A: Yes, I used to make sure once a year at least, sometimes twice a year, to take the whole family to Cameron Highlands or Fraser's Hill for two weeks and play golf. My children would walk around the golf course with my wife and me. We talked to them. Because of my political activities, I asked, "Do you want to follow me?" My elder son said, "I'll follow you."

So when I went out on my *fang wen* (constituency visits) in '63, he followed me most of the time. He was old enough to remember the 1964 riots (he would have been 12 years old, and in Catholic High School).[1] I remember a car was sent out to bring him home (when the riots broke out) but couldn't contact him because it was such a confused and chaotic situation. He walked home alone. My two other children were younger, so it didn't hit them the way it hit him.

Q: *Why do you think it was PM who entered politics and not the younger son?*

A: Our younger was born in '57 – five years younger than PM.

Q: *Wouldn't he also have some of the same exposure to your constituency visits, even if not as much?*

A: No, he didn't come with me. He was too young.

Q: *Even in the '70s? Late '60s?*

A: No, in the '70s he was already preparing for his 'A' levels.

Q: *So you think it was the exposure rather than the personality?*

A: It was exposure, and particularly the riot when Hsien Loong was trapped on the chaotic roads. At that time my younger son and daughter were at Nanyang Primary School. It's out of town, near King's Road, so the car could get them back. But Hsien Loong was at Catholic High School in Bras Basah Road, where suddenly curfew was announced by acting PM Toh Chin Chye. Everybody went out of school and traffic got jammed because all the offices were closed up. It made a tremendous impact on him because he realised that this place could just go upside down. And what happened in '65 he would remember, being 13 years old. He would have been cognisant of what was going on. I remember that night we stayed in Sri Temasek on 8 August before the announcement of separation on the 9th. We did not know how the Malays would react. From the strident majority they now became a frightened minority, especially the UMNO bigwigs who were lording over the whole population. Suddenly they were vulnerable.

Q: *At which point did you have your first inkling that PM would go into politics?*

A: My first indication was when Trinity College in Cambridge offered him a fellowship to become a mathematician and teach maths there. He wrote to his tutor and said, "I must go home. I've joined the Singapore Armed Forces, my father's the PM, and for me not to go home and do what I have to do would be bad for the country and bad for me." So I knew he was going to come back whatever happens. He was not going to be attracted by the glamour of becoming a great mathematician. He had said he was going to read maths to satisfy himself. He satisfied himself and that was enough, so he was coming back.

That was a most decisive letter. I met his tutor (Dr Denis Marrian) years later at Prince Charles' wedding and he said, "You know, your son wrote me a letter that was most impressive – very decisive." I said, "Oh, show me the letter." He said, "No, I cannot. You must ask his permission." The British are very correct. So I wrote to my son and said, "Can I see your letter?" He said yes and the tutor sent me the letter written in Loong's own hand. His commitment to Singapore was total. "I'm going to go back," he wrote. "I do not want to be a spectator and I'm going to play a part in Singapore." The riots, the campaigning, coming down from Cameron Highlands the night before independence was declared and staying at Sri Temasek – all these have left a mark on his mind.

Q: *If your younger son was too young to be exposed to politics, what about your daughter? She's in between.*

A: Well, I never took her out, because she's a girl. How can I be looking after her when she's running around among many other people? Daughters have got to be protected.

Q: *How would you describe your relationship with PM over the years and now? Has he met your expectations, or even exceeded your expectations?*

A: They are two different questions. The relationship grew as he grew up. By the time he was 16 or 17, he had made up his own mind. I didn't tell him to take the SAF scholarship, he decided it. He had already got the President's scholarship the year before. But I think he decided since he was going to come back and if there's trouble he'll have to fight, he might as well become an officer and fight as an officer, not as a private. So he took the SAF scholarship and came back every vacation for training.

Q: *Was there any discussion that you had with him as to what he will do after 'A' levels?*

A: No, the discussion was that he could not go to university straight after taking his 'A' levels at Catholic High in Chinese. I said, "No, better don't go away. Spend another year here and do some economics and mathematics, and in English, before you go." So in that one year he repeated his 'A' level exams in National Junior College and he also did Russian, which he got a distinction for. I don't think he remembers much of it now, but it can come back. He tried to do classical *wen yan* Chinese but found it too difficult. That one year I think (former economics professor) Lim Chong Yah gave him tuition, two or three times a week, which is now proving useful.

Cambridge is a snooty place, especially Trinity College because Isaac Newton was there. I knew Iain MacLeod, then shadow chancellor, was a close associate of Rab Butler who had been Deputy Prime Minister and was the master of Trinity. So he helped my son get admitted to the university. Hsien Loong said he wanted to do mathematics. They said, "You got to take an examination first before we will consider you for mathematics." So he did the exam. And as a result they said, "You can skip the first year, you go straight to the second year." So he had an extra year to do because you have to reside three years in college before you get a degree. He decided to do computer science. He expected it to be a growing science. A year after that, when (another SAF scholar) Teo Chee Hean got a First in Manchester doing engineering, I told PSC to send him to London to also learn computing. This was useful. We had two members in Cabinet who were aware of what was happening in the computer world and introduced it into the government and the SAF.

Q: *Would you have been disappointed if none of your children went into politics?*

A: No. Why should I be disappointed? They do what they are good at and what they are interested in. To force them into politics when they do not have a political interest would have been a disaster. Why should I do that? What's the point of it?

Right from the beginning, my wife and I agreed. What are they good at, what they like doing, what will earn them a decent living – that's what they should do. My daughter wanted to be a vet, but her mother told her, "You think you'll be looking after dogs and cats? You'll be in the abattoir checking pigs, cattle and sheep carcasses!" Go and have a look, her mother said. She went to have a look, came back and said, "I'll do medicine." There are times when she would say, "I wish I'd been a vet because vets are making enormous sums of money, more than the doctors."

Q: *Do you hope any of your grandchildren shares the same passion as you and the PM for politics?*

A: They've shown no such signs. They are they. They are the responsibility of their fathers and mothers, not of my wife and I. I have no interest in anyone of them going into politics. If they do, I hope they're of the calibre and character to go into politics, otherwise they will degrade the Lee name! (Laughs) Yes, surely! You've read about (British statesmen) Pitt the Elder and Pitt the Younger.[2] There was no follow up after the younger Pitt. No, I am not interested in that, not interested in dynasties. Nor Singapore. We want the best people in charge. Then our chances of success are at the highest.

Q: *What do you make of Hsien Yang and how his career and life have panned out?*

A: He decided to follow his brother and wanted to go to Cambridge too. I said you know your brother was quite exceptional and you are going to the same college. They will expect you to live up to his standards. He said, "That's all right, I'm not doing mathematics, I'm doing engineering." He was not abashed. He was not under his brother's shadow. He went up and got a First. He wanted to get a Starred First, but he didn't get it. He also wanted to do electronic engineering. Halfway through, he decided that electronic engineering would be out of date by the time he finished with the SAF. So he did civil engineering which would not go out of date. He's a sensible and practical man.

(In the SAF) he went to the armour brigade. Eventually he wanted to leave for SingTel. The Defence Minister told Goh Chok Tong, look, this chap will make head of civil service. They told him that, but he said, "I don't want to be in the civil service, I don't want to spend my whole life in it. I'm going to go out into the commercial sector." So he left.

He's good at investing, very shrewd. His mother would give him her money to invest. Most times, he invested wisely. After SingTel, he said, "Enough of this, I've proved himself." James Wolfensohn from the World Bank[3] knew him and knew he was smart in investments. He asked me to get him to join with his two children who were starting a boutique investment bank. I put it to him and he said, "No, they want to make use of my contacts in this part of the world." Instead, he took up this job at Fraser & Neave. I said, "That's not a full-time job." He said, "Yes, but I'm also going to manage my portfolio." So he went to Fraser & Neave and managed his portfolio.

Q: *There's a certain perception in the public that he's somewhat rebellious. Would you agree with that?*

A: No, no, no. Why should he be rebellious? What is there to rebel against? We're not trying to force him to do anything. As I said, we decided that by 17 or 18, they had minds of their own. They are highly intelligent people. They read, meet people and will decide for themselves.

When they were young, we planted a few basic ideas. We said these were basic values. Don't do that, that's bad. Even if you make money doing that, it's wrong to do. So they grew up with solid moral values. My wife and I are proud that they are what they are. They are not spoilt, they won't cheat. They'll do good. They are good honest people.

Q: *When you look back over your life, your political life and your personal life, what gives you the greatest sense of satisfaction?*

A: That I've lived my life to the fullest. Given the circumstances, I did my best in politics. I did my best to bring up a family, which I could not have done alone. My wife did most of the nurturing. She'd go home every day for lunch. In those days traffic was light. So from her office in Malacca Street to my house was about five or seven minutes. My children were brought up as normal ordinary children.

When the car was busy, some of them would go to school by bus. They grew up expecting to be like other people. That was most important for them. They did national service, both boys, with no favours and no special treatment. We made sure that they were exposed to what they were going to face in the world. I couldn't have done more.

In 1967, after a gruelling trip to America, I took them to Phnom Penh and then Siem Reap where Sihanouk let me use his villa. We've still got a picture of my son Hsien Yang putting his head behind a statue where the head had been removed – both he and his sister! They rode elephants. Those are perks which they enjoyed that very few at that time could because Siem Reap was not opened to tourists as it is now. Not so many of the statues were stolen, and the bas reliefs on the walls had not been chipped off. I don't want to see it again. It will sadden me to see it. It's now touristy and degraded.

Q: *Would you consider yourself a strict father, in the upbringing of your children?*

A: Yes and no. My wife did most of the disciplining. She had the cane, I didn't. I never hit them.

Q: *You did not need a cane to discipline them?*

A: No, I didn't need a cane and didn't have one. My wife's cane was not used very often but she has caned them. The children knew that there are certain things you must not do. I would support my wife so that there's no bickering between the husband and wife, where the children say, "Oh, my father is right!" (Laughs) I gave my wife full support. I would back her. On the whole I would say it's a harmonious family.

Q: *Did you discuss very much with your wife how to bring up the children?*

A: Yes, of course. The first thing we decided was to send them to Chinese schools. That was a major decision in those days because we feared their English would suffer. But we said it's too vital a part of their lives, if you look into the future, you must know Chinese. And they will learn English at home, because the mother speaks to them in English. I practised my Mandarin with them until they finished primary school. Then the matters I wanted to discuss were complex concepts, so I had to switch to English. My eldest did 12 years in Chinese up to 'A' levels. The other two did 10 years, up to 'O' levels. One wanted to do medicine, the other engineering. How do you learn medical phrases in Chinese and then switch to English? So they switched to English at 'A' levels. But because of the early years, their Chinese is deeply implanted.

There was a Mrs Dinness who was teaching in the armed forces school, probably Tanglin barracks. She would come to the house for them to get the rhythm of English speech. Then when she went back to England, I got a British voluntary service officer – first a young man, then a young woman – to come and read poems and novels. They got the rhythm and flow of the language, so learnt to speak properly, not Singlish. As a result, there was no trouble when they switched to an English-language university. In the end, English became their master language because of constant use in life. Chinese became their second language, but easily revived.

Looking back, I think if Singapore parents had been more bold, I could have run a special course where in the primary stage some would learn more Chinese than English – for the Chinese to sink in, particularly those from English-speaking homes. Then it is embedded in them. As it is, it's a constant struggle all throughout school, in their careers and later in life. But Singapore parents and students wanted English because they want to score well. In a way they are right, because your Chinese can be first-class but if your English is second-class, you're disadvantaged.

Q: *Did you and Mrs Lee have certain expectations of the children or did you pretty much allow them to be the person that they were going to be or wanted to be?*

A: No, as I said earlier, we did not try to shape their careers. We were both lawyers, but we did not think it was good to encourage them to be lawyers. Instead we asked: what are you good at? What are you interested in? What will give you pleasure and satisfaction, and you're good at it?

My son was good in mathematics. I asked, "What will you do after that? You're going to teach?" He liked mathematics. He's got a special bent – a problem-solving mind. In his final year, when the Oxbridge University Club in Singapore asked the university who was the best student in Cambridge to give a prize to, a tutor replied, "Lee Hsien Loong scored 12 more alphas than the second man in the Tripos. Never in the history of the Tripos – 12 more alphas." An alpha is one problem solved. Loong had 12 more problems solved than the second fellow who also became a wrangler (a student with first-class honours in mathematics). I subsequently met his professor, Peter Swinnerton-Dyer, who told me, "Your son is quite remarkable because usually a mathematician is concentrated on mathematics, but he's got a diversity of interests." We knew that he was exceptionally gifted. I think he got the best combination of our two DNAs. I was good in mathematics. My wife was good at literature. He got both. The others have also combinations of both but not in as advantageous a way as he has. It's the luck of the draw. The dice is thrown, the two DNAs got mixed up and he got the best of one and the best of the other. That's his luck.

Q: *How about in terms of temperament? Would you say Hsien Loong also had the best of both from you and Mrs Lee?*

A: I've read this British psychologist Hans Eysenck, who said in his book that boys tend to follow their mothers because the X gene is bigger than the Y gene, the male gene. So they have more of the mother's qualities than the father's. Girls have double Xs from the mother and the father, so they tend to have more of the father's qualities. Empirically I would say that's not far off the mark. The differences may not be very great but I think there's a difference. Loong is a different personality from me. He's more, how would I say, equable – less intense than my daughter who takes after me. Ling is very intense. She's got no children, so she writes this and does many things outside neurology. She gravitated to an activist role. Her extra energy made her run "The Tent" to get girls who've been led astray. She raises money for this purpose. She should have married and had two children, then things would have happened differently. (Laughs) But what to do? She was happy as she was, so that's that. They lead their own lives.

Q: *Did you, like other parents, have strong feelings about their friends or who they loved and married?*

A: Once they are 17 or 18 you cannot control your children, but before that, you try to implant certain values. So I used to tell them that when they marry they ought to read George Bernard Shaw. If you think your child will be as pretty as your wife and as clever as you, you're mistaken. It's a combination of both – Mendel's Law (a theory underlying much of the study of genetics).

So if you want less trouble in life, especially about getting extra tuition for your children and sweating over whether they will pass their exams well, just choose somebody who is in the same category as you are and the chances are your children will be in that category and you don't have to worry. Who they chose finally depended on whom they met. My elder son met a Malaysian girl who was a doctor in Cambridge. The other married Lim Chong Yah's daughter because Chong Yah taught him economics and he got to know his daughter. That's his choice, but the result is, as I've said, no trouble for me or my wife!

Q: *What do you think of your grandchildren?*

A: Loong's daughter is very talented. She's got talent in music, painting, art, and she can write. She used to write for a women's magazine in *The Straits Times*. I once read a piece she wrote about a luggage bag. I didn't know you can make a luggage bag sound so very attractive! She's got a skill with words. Then she moved on to something else and did architecture. She could have done interior decoration. Because she doesn't have to earn a living, she's making shows, and she made a successful film about how Seletar will lose its old-world charm. She's undergoing an intense course – three years – by (famous art school) Tisch School here. She's already finished one year and she's exhausted. Now she's got to prepare a script to do a film for herself to produce. I said, "After this, are you going to really go into films or are you going to switch to something else?" She's multifaceted, but I think she will stick to films. I said, "Are you going to do this in English or in Chinese because if you do this in English, where's your market? In the West you compete with Bollywood and Hollywood, so you're out. Better to do it in Chinese because you have Taiwan, Hong Kong and China, and also Southeast Asia." She said, "No, no, I will do it in English." Although her Chinese is not bad, she prefers English. I said, "All right, you carry on."

The boy is an albino. The father had the gene and the mother had the gene. Unfortunately he got both genes combined in him, so he's albino and shortsighted. But he's turned out well. He took his time in school because he can't see clearly, what's written on the blackboard and so on. He has to use the binoculars to see but he took his own time. Now he's got his degree at NUS. He can score a maximum of five merit points and he scored four merit points. So, not bad.

The other two boys – Ho Ching's children – are both bright. One has taken a scholarship at the Massachusetts Institute of Technology (MIT). The other doesn't want a scholarship even though he could easily get one. But he's going to do IT (information technology) and he wants to stay there first, get some experience and take a further degree. Then he will come back. It's a different world because his father can pay, and so that is not important. If I were the father, I'd say, no, you better take that scholarship and come back. Why should I spend $300,000 or $400,000 for nothing? I can put down half the payment on a house for you! But they are not my responsibility. My wife decided early on that she will not quarrel with her in-laws or her daughters-in-law. The children are their responsibility. We just take them out for outings.

Q: *Do you have many friends?*

A: I keep life-long friends. There's a Chia Chwee Leong who was with me in Raffles College and Raffles Institution. He became a chemist and went on to be the chief government chemist. We shared one room in Raffles College, a double room which faced the setting sun that was very hot. So we moved out after one term but became friends. He's a Singaporean. During the Japanese occupation, we would meet and chat. I still see him. He ran foul of Toh Chin Chye who was in charge of the Ministry of Health back then. Toh Chin Chye more or less forced his resignation. [Mr Chia clarified in a 19 January 2011 *Straits Times* interview that he retired optionally in 1972.] I did not interfere. I didn't want to because it was Toh Chin Chye's ministry. So he resigned and joined a chemical factory in Jurong – Lim Soo Peng's chemical factory (Chemical Industries Far East). He's a friend of (former Public Service Commission chairman) Phay Seng Whatt who had invested in this chemical factory. I still visit him and he visits me. I was interested to know how his children are doing – two sons and one daughter. His daughter's unmarried and keeps cats. One son is teaching at NUS, another son is a lawyer.

You know something interesting? My wife told me Chwee Leong was watching to see whether my daughter would get into school one year earlier. Because she was born in January, she'd have to wait 11 months to be enrolled. Chwee Leong was watching because if she got in and his son didn't get in, he was going to kick up a fuss. Well, Ling didn't get in. She waited one more year but then when she got in, they gave her a double promotion. I think after primary 1 they pushed her up to primary 3. We are friends to this day.

Percy Cradock is a friend to this day and in fact I'm hoping to write to him. Perhaps I'll meet him for the last time in case, I don't know, either he or I have reached that point when either one of us may not be here. So, we'll meet again. (Cradock died in January 2010.)

Q: *In your position, is it difficult to keep up with old friends?*

A: My old friends, I still keep in touch with them. They are not friends I make to get advantage out of. They are friends because we spent time together, we found each other agreeable and we maintained the friendship.

Another friend was Dr Fong Kim Heng whom I brought into politics and he became deputy speaker, way back in 1960-something. You can look him up in the Hansard. He developed a drug habit and started taking pethidine (a painkiller). He had pains, but in the end he couldn't get off the drug. As a doctor, he should never have injected himself, but he did. He paid the price for it, which is sad. I keep in touch with his brother who looks after his two sons. For a few years, my wife was seeing them (and advising) about the property and so on. I brought him into politics because I needed people who were reliable and who had the ability. And he was a bright fellow, same year with me at RI (Raffles Institution). He went into medicine and became a doctor.

Q: *Would you agree it becomes more difficult to make good friends, after you became PM especially?*

A: Not necessarily, but you make friends at a different level. I'm friends with Henry Kissinger, George Shultz, Tony Blair ... but they're not just political friends. We got to know each other politically.

I got to know Kissinger in 1968 in Harvard when he was still teaching there and I was spending two months there. He found my views on Vietnam were like his. Then he was appointed national security adviser, so he left Harvard. On my way out of the US, I went to New York and we met again. There, I gave him my views on Vietnam, and he said, keep in touch. As it turned out, Nixon thought well of me and because he had noted all the things that I'd said to him when he came through in pursuit of the presidency, a friendship developed over the years. Even after Kissinger ceased to be Ford's secretary of state, he kept in touch with me. Once a year, sometimes twice a year, we would meet. Now we are both on the same JP Morgan Chase international advisory board.

When I went to the US, I used to stay with him in his country house in Connecticut. He's a friend. When my wife suffered her stroke, he rang me up several times asking how she is. One night he came here with Shultz and I gave them dinner.[4] He said, "Can I see your wife?" I said, "No. She'll be most embarrassed to see you in her condition." When Shultz's first wife was dying of cancer – he lived in Stanford in one of the staff quarters because he used to teach there – my wife and I visited her. They're also close friends.

Q: *So you have a network of friends all over the world. But who are your confidants? Who do you turn to if you're feeling a bit down or you want somebody sympathetic to talk to?*

A: I would say my wife.

Q: *And now? Do you go to her bedside to talk to her?*

A: I do that every night. I read to her, I tell her what I've been doing for the day and the news of the day from *The Straits Times*, *IHT* and *Wall Street Journal*. Then I read her the poems that she likes and has flagged over the years.

Q: *She can't speak. How does she convey how she feels to you?*

A: She blinks. Yes, one blink; no, two blinks.

Q: *What were some of the best times you had as a couple?*

A: Well, my greatest joy was when my wife won the Queen's scholarship and I managed to get her into Cambridge immediately after that, because that meant she didn't have to wait for me for three or four years in Singapore. Had she not got a scholarship, I'd have gone back (to Singapore) in three years and finished the Bar exams as soon as possible. Before I left, she had said, after three years we will become strangers to each other. I said, "No, we won't." In the end, she took a risk and so did I, because we might have drifted apart. She got the scholarship, I got her a place and we got married that December quietly in Stratford-upon-Avon. Then we came back and remarried again in 1950. I don't think that's an offence (laughs), to marry a woman twice, the same woman!

Q: *In your personal life, apart from your wife, what was the most trying and difficult period for you?*

A: (Long pause) I think when my son's wife died. His whole tent collapsed. The pole was struck down. He had a second baby who was born two or three weeks before she died in October 1982 – hence no wife, little albino baby boy and one Filipino maid. His mother-in-law and mother pitched in. The mother-in-law was good enough to stay with him in his apartment in Cairnhill. My wife used to go there and help out. We would take them out for walks around the Istana. The first year was most troubling. He was in a daze. I said, you have to face the future, you can't be grieving all the time. We got him books on grief, including one well-written book by a Cambridge philosopher. I said, at the end of the day you have to move on. Moving on means you have to find a woman who will marry you and accept these two children. I've seen what happened with my uncle (mother's brother) who married my father's sister. They had three children. She died. He remarried. The new wife, the stepmother, ill-treated the three children. So my wife used to give them enough food, and cared for them. I said that was a terrible position.

There was a Taiwanese trade representative here – a general who has now retired and gone back to Taiwan – who was friendly to me. He said that he would try and find a wife for my son. He said that his wife had died and he remarried; he has carried on and started a second family. So he introduced a girl. We met the girl in Taipei and brought her down here. My son said, no, she doesn't fit me. In the end, he decided on a workplace associate. Ho Ching was in the Defence Ministry in the cipher department. Loong was in computers. He was also in ciphers for some time. I suppose they must have known each other then. They must have redeveloped the friendship. I said, "You better make sure that she accepts your two children otherwise it's a real misery. You'll be sad, your mother will be sad, I'll be sad."

Ho Ching came in fully aware that she's walking into a family. She has been a good mother to the children. In fact, she's bent over backwards for them, as a result of which my granddaughter has not enough discipline. She's flitting from one interesting job to another interesting job. If she is turfed out of her father's hotel, and earns a living, she will have to concentrate her mind on what she wants to do. But she's not my daughter. Her father gave her leave and licence, paid for the fees at Tisch – $250,000 for three years. Bought her a secondhand car.

Q: *What would you say is the secret to a long and happy marriage?*

A: First of all, we accommodated each other. There was nothing we fundamentally disagreed on. She knew my quirks and I knew her eccentricities. She's a voracious reader. She read Horace, the *Iliad* and Gibbon (*Decline and Fall of the Roman Empire*). She read books on fishes, on food – the books on her bookshelf at home. I'm not interested in those subjects but she is. I'm interested in what I am doing. In the case of my memoirs, she would read my drafts and would simplify the English to make it easier to read and understand. Because as a conveyancing lawyer she's particular about the meanings of words – they should be clear, they should be simple. As a result, she influenced my writing style. I used to write convoluted sentences, the way I speak. She says, no, no, speaking is all right because you can repeat yourself and you can pick up where you left off. But in writing, you write a sentence and you move on. So you make it clear and crisp. If you look at my writings before my memoirs, my written style has more loops. She cured me of loops. She said, you want this to be read by 'O' level students. Don't use multi-syllable words when you can use a single-syllable word, which is what (British style guide writer) Ernest Gowers advised. It was good advice. One of my doctors told me, I read your book and I found it very simple. So my wife succeeded. We adjust to each other.

Q: *How else did she influence you?*

A: In almost everything. I left the domestic chores to her. She runs the household and the maids. Now I have a problem. I got a man who fixes things up and looks after the maids. It's not satisfactory because he doesn't know what the maids do in the bedroom and it's not cleaned as before. It's a problem. I have to get my sister to teach the cook because my daughter is not interested in these things. She's interested in her work and writing the next article and her Blackberry. Her cooking is to take raw salmon and put it in the microwave. My wife is a good cook and she gave instructions to the maid how to cook.

She'll know when something is not right. She's got highly sensitive tastebuds and sensitive nostrils. She can tell straightaway, oh, you've put too much *lengkuas* (galangal) and so on, reduce it. I would not have known what was wrong. I just knew it didn't taste good. She would know. I miss all that. Life goes on. Now my sister helps to train the cook. She's a good cook. Life means adjustment. We make do after a while.[5]

Q: *Do you have any regrets in your personal life?*

A: I find that unproductive. It's a parlour game. What is there to regret? I made the decisions given the circumstances, given the knowledge that I was able to obtain at that time, and I picked the choice that would give me the greatest latitude if it should fail, to find another way out. What's finished is done. Presented with the same problem, with that same knowledge, me at that age, that was what I would do.

What is there to regret? Do I regret going into Malaysia? No. I believe we had to try. Do I regret making an issue of it during Confrontation?[6] The British high commissioner said, wait until Confrontation is over, then we can settle these things. I thought otherwise; by the time Confrontation is over, Tunku will not be dependent on British, Australian and New Zealand troops and he will just use force. I decided to press the issue then, a Malaysian Malaysia or nothing. What is there to regret? Had I not tried, I think that would be a matter for regret. But we have tried. That was 1965. This is 2009, the same issues are there – is it a Malay Malaysia or a Malaysian Malaysia? Najib says it's "one Malaysia", but that's not the same as Malaysian Malaysia. One Malaysia means all the races are living in one country. But it's obviously paying some dividends because UMNO seems to have got back some support in the Kota Bharu by-election.[7]

Q: *You said earlier that you're not interested in perpetuating a dynasty, yet over the years that's a label or accusation that you have had to live with. Has that been frustrating?*

A: No. There are just certain stereotype subjects journalists want to leverage on, utilise, to bring me down a peg or two. I will not allow that. You prove it – that Loong is not fit to be there and that he's there because I have engineered it. I went out of my way to make sure that I was not responsible for his promotion. I had not the slightest doubt that he would make it anyway. Look, who could better him – mentally, in political experience, in linguistic abilities? Nobody.

The big problem now is the next PM will not be trilingual. He may not even be effectively bilingual, which will be a disadvantage. I did not give only Loong the languages to prepare him for this job. I gave them to all my three children, because I told them whatever you do, you're living in this part of the world and you will require English, Chinese and Malay, so learn them. So when they were young, they learnt them. They haven't used their Malay very much because now only English and some Mandarin are necessary as our Malays now understand English. If they have to, they can revive it. It can be revived. At least they understand Malay so they can go to Indonesia or Malaysia and understand what's said, which is an advantage. Loong can read Jawi too. No, he's got a capacious mind. I'm not trying to boast about his abilities but he learnt the Russian alphabet, he learnt Jawi, Chinese characters and also musical notes. You show me someone else who can do all that. You know, if I were not PM, he might have made it earlier. And I've said so.

No minister has any doubts that Loong can get down to that minister's details of problems and work through them – every angle of it, whether finance, trade or whatever. It's a gift. He's got my mathematical and numerical capabilities and sees alternatives. And he's got his mother's retentive capacity for words and ideas. You test him. Harry Newman Jr, an American from Harvard who went to do a DPhil in Cambridge, was running the *Granta*, a student paper, and we became friends. We went our separate ways from 1950 when I came home, but we wrote to each other. He moved from the east coast to the west coast, near Los Angeles, one of the resorts there. And when an American says "come visit me", they mean it. So when I did my trip in '67, I told the State Department I want to meet him and gave his address. They arranged for me to meet him. When Loong went to the US to do his Artillery course, he travelled to the west coast on his way back to work with Arthur Doolittle. Newman said to Loong, come stay with me. He then wrote to me and said Loong was quite remarkable. Newman's a man who loves words. He's a real estate man and made a fortune there but his love is for language and poems. He writes poems. I've got three books of his. Apparently, he had asked after a difficult word and Loong gave him the answer just like that. He was astounded. And Loong is not into English literature, he's in mathematics. I had not the slightest doubt that he was going to be outstanding. He is what he is, he doesn't have to strive extra hard. He just does it.

Q: *What is your day-to-day professional relationship with the Prime Minister like?*

A: My professional relationship with the Prime Minister is most correct. He writes to me as MM; I write to him as PM. If I have an important matter I will see him, not he sees me. There are times when he finishes the Cabinet meeting and I say I will see you in the office or I'll stop by to have a chat in your office. That's an informal thing. But I make quite sure that the relationship is kept at formal levels in formal meetings. I'll not be talking to him as a father to a son, but as a Minister to the Prime Minister. And that's correct.

I don't worry about ceremony. People stand up, people have guards of honour for me, but it doesn't matter. If you have no guard of honour, I don't mind. Take (former British Labour Chancellor) Roy Jenkins. The French President knew that he liked guards of honour. So whenever he did something which was favourable to France as chairman of the European Commission, they put on a guard of honour. Whenever he did something they disliked, there's no guard of honour. Nobody is waiting for him and he's taken by an aide to see either President Mitterrand or President Giscard D'Estaing ... I think that's a weakness. I'm not interested; it's a courtesy. When I went to Pakistan with (former President) Muhammad Zia ul-Haq in charge, from Delhi to Islamabad in an Indian Airlines plane, when it crossed the border, six F16s followed the plane. I thought we were being attacked! No, it turned out to be a guard of honour for me. Still, it amused me. I thanked him for it.

What does it add up to? Other world leaders see me because I give them ideas. They bounce ideas off me and they get some benefits. That's what it's all about. They don't see me for fun. They've got more important matters to do.

Q: *But have you had any disagreements with him? How do you resolve it with the Prime Minister if you disagree on something?*

A: No, if we disagree, he makes the decision because that's his responsibility. I have said to all Cabinet ministers, when I was active as Prime Minister, I would go by my judgment of what the ground reaction will be because I'm in touch with people. I'm talking to them and I visit the HDB estates, especially the new ones to know what the new tenants are like. They were young people who'd done well, leaving their parents behind in the old estates. So I got a feel for them. I looked at what they had in the fridge, the difference between the Malay household, nicely decorated, and the Chinese household, quite bare mostly, but savings are high. The Malay household will have redone the flooring and curtains, have a huge television screen and so on. I noted all these differences in spending habits, what they think is important.

Nowadays I look at photos and videos. I listen to radio and watch TV. Yes, I go down to my constituency for events like Orange Ribbon or whatever, but they are huge gatherings. I meet a select group of people who are already supporters of that movement, whether it's trade unions or constituency leaders. So I tell the younger ministers, frankly my finger is not on the pulse as it used to be. So you have to judge the ground attitudes.

Similarly, dealing with the Malaysians – I'm going by old vibes on who I trust, who I distrusted, who I will listen to. But the younger generation (of Malaysian politicians), I meet them but not frequently. Nor do I meet them in-depth, not enough to gauge them. So I said (to Singapore's younger ministers), you have to decide whether you think this is a serious commitment (from Malaysia), or not.

I read Roy Jenkins on Jean Monnet. Jean Monnet was the man from the coal and steel community who thought of the European Union and wanted Germany and France to transcend their wars. He was the driving force. Roy Jenkins wrote that when Monnet was old he could not travel. So he would get the people whose judgments he knew to be sound and he would suck out information from them. Well, that's what I try to do. You can only suck out what information is in their minds. And many of them now don't speak Malay. So they don't get the same feel of the situation. Yes, we have Malay ministers who speak Malay but it's different when you're non-Malay and you understand what they are saying to each other and to you. It makes a difference I think.

Q: *Moving on to the PM's wife, are you troubled by some of the things that are being said about Madam Ho Ching, whether it's her performance as Temasek CEO or her relationship to the PM?*

A: Not at all, because all the people in the know in Singapore know the quality of these people. Ho Ching has repositioned Temasek during the time she's been there.

I was talking to Ong Beng Seng[8] yesterday and he raised this question with me. We were talking about how he can develop

Desaru as a resort. He's very good at that. He said, "You know, moving out from Temasek is a mistake. She can do it. We don't need this American."[9] I said, "I don't know what it's all about. She says it's time to move on and change." But he said, "She has changed Temasek and completely revamped it."

So if she's not up to the job, even without it being said, people will know this is nepotism and the PM is risking the country's future by favouring his wife. He did not want to be responsible for her appointment. So Dhanabalan and Chok Tong (Goh Chok Tong was then Prime Minister) appointed her. And she's done a good job of it. She's resigned not because she made a loss on Merrill Lynch. She thinks it's time to go and she probably wants to do something else. But she's remained on the board until October, remaining as chief executive and showing the new CEO what she's been trying to do. At some time or the other, a succession must take place.

Just as Hsien Yang says, all right, I've done enough. I've proved myself, made SingTel go international. He bought into India's Bharti, and it's making money. He went to Australia, and people thought SingTel was going to lose money, but it didn't. He's got a nose for investments. I'm not worried (what people say) but I will not have this nepotism allegation repeated until it becomes believed internationally.

Q: *Some people have been asking what Madam Ho is going to do next and there's speculation that she's being groomed for politics...*

A: No, I have never heard about it. At her age, to go into politics doesn't make sense. You have to develop a whole new different skill set as they would call it, right? You have to go round knocking on doors, talking to people, meeting the people and so on. That's not her forte. If she had done that when she was 30-plus or even in her early 40s, yes. But now, no. If she was contemplating it, I would advise her not to. Her husband will advise her not to because he knows that it's too late to learn to work the grassroots. He's looking for people in their late 30s and early 40s who can adjust and change.

Look, we had invited Koh Boon Hwee[10] when he was in his late 30s and early 40s, but he said no. He's now made his mark in the private sector, but even if he says I'm willing now, it is too late because he cannot adapt at this age. So we asked him to help in DBS, SIA, SingTel. Help us that way, he can.

Q: *You speak about Ho Ching being a good wife and mother, bending over backwards, accepting PM's first two children as her own. But the public doesn't seem to see this side of her.*

A: Why should they? It's not relevant. My style has been that my private life is my business and every politician's private life is his or her business. I do not subscribe to the American or British style of politicking. I'm not sure in Europe today whether they dig into your family affairs, but in America they do. So they play up Michelle Obama, the children, the dogs and so on. Maybe it gives them a better sense of the family, but how does that help them in deciding whether he's a good president and whether he's concentrating on the right things to get the economy going?

Q: *But it does help the public image, in case she becomes the target of criticism?*

A: It makes no difference. I have always been judged on what I've been able to do and what I've promised the people. Whether I have a harmonious family life or a contentious family – that may be of interest to investigative journalists who like to write it up, but it's irrelevant. The question is whether I am able to concentrate on my job. Clinton was able to have all these rows. He must have felt very angry and humiliated but he carried on with his job. But in America, it was unbecoming of the President to do what he did. Nevertheless, to bring it all out and impeach him for that was, I think, in bad taste. And it was also bad politicking to degrade him and so the whole system. The French would not do that. When Mitterrand died, his non-wife came forward with a child. I'm sure the French newspapers already knew about it; the wife knew about it; but that's the French way. They've different attitudes to the private lives of political leaders.

Q: *Well, it is a bit of a shame that the public does not see more of this side of Ho Ching. There are letters to the Forum pages of the newspapers saying she should be more of a wife to PM.*

A: They're a minority. Does she perform in her job? Does he perform in his job? Did he favour her to get into this job? No. All right, then let's go by what they've done. Let's make no excuses about whether you have troubles at home and therefore you can't do these things. If you have so many troubles at home, then you should either take leave or quit.

I was listening to a programme on leaders' illnesses and they interviewed several people. Finally they went to David Owen, who's a former foreign secretary, and they said, "Does it matter? Should the health of the leader be in public?" He said, "Yes." They asked why. He said, "Well, if you've a serious illness, you tend to be indecisive." So he then gave an example: "Mitterrand, for 11 years, he and his doctor kept his prostate cancer low key, when in fact it was a battle for his life all the time. After he died the doctor said, 'For 11 years I had to keep this quiet.'" But they also said there were times when Mitterrand should have been decisive and he wasn't, because he was undergoing radiotherapy and chemotherapy, which must have affected him. I think that's fair. If you're suffering from prolonged or chronic illness, people should know that because that affects your performance.

Q: *You are no longer in charge. How has that been difficult for you?*

A: No. It started in 1990 when I handed over to Goh Chok Tong. I stayed behind because the whole administration had been configured to fit me. All the multiple buttons – I knew which ones to press. So I stayed behind to help Chok Tong double-declutch and change the system to suit himself. You know, like a car, you move the steering wheel, the seats and so on to fit you. You must do this because you may not have the same kind of mind (as the previous driver). But I told him certain things are important – you must read this once a week and know what's happening. The green campaign, you must keep it up. You have to show the committee that this is important and the Ministry of National Development must understand that this is an important part of our strategy – not just to be green but as part of an overall strategy for Singapore's development.

But three ministers resigned in rapid succession because they didn't take to his style – Tony Tan, Yeo Ning Hong and Dhanabalan, three heavyweights.[11] So I called them up and said, look, give him time, he's got to settle down. If after 18 months you still feel the same, then you can leave. So they came back. I helped sort it out and in the end they stayed on. I think had I not stayed on, he would be bereft of some heavyweight ministers and the problems will end up on his desk. I stayed out of the limelight, but I helped him. Loong also did not try to outshine him; he just supported him. After 14 years, he decided to step down. I never suggested to him that he should go. He decided he will go because he calculated that he took over when he was 50. Loong will take over when he's 50-plus. And Loong still had to find a successor. So he resigned. Loong asked Chok Tong to stay on because he had first to concentrate on the domestic issues, while (Chok Tong) had built up a network with the new generation of European leaders at Apec meetings and so on. My links go way back. I don't have the same links with Romano

Prodi[12] and the new EC President Barroso.

They find me of value as a databank. My job is to help Singapore succeed, no matter who's in charge. Consolidate what we have achieved. And there are things which I can do because of my many years experience and my links with world leaders, both in the region and in the world, which the others cannot do. I can pick up the phone and ring up Kissinger or George Shultz and they can ring up whoever is in charge. So during the 1997 financial crisis, I rang up George Shultz, and he says, "I'll speak to Rubin".[13] So he spoke to Rubin. And I spoke to Rubin after that because Rubin knows that I'm a friend of Shultz, so that means he's dealing with somebody who's trustworthy. So now Rubin is a friend, through George Shultz. I mean, that's how you build up, through good references, people whom you trust.

I've had the advantage of making friends with important people. Because of the Vietnam War, they came through here, especially Americans. Loong hasn't got that advantage. He's got to cultivate them but he's got a good start now. After his meeting with Loong, Obama told his staffer, "That's a good man." The staffer told Heng Chee (Singapore's ambassador to the United States). So he is off to a good start. With the younger generation (of world leaders), I do not have that same connection but of course some, like Clinton, wanted to see me, although his staff blocked him. Or Tony Blair, although he knew me before he became PM.

Sarkozy knew me casually before he took over and he met me one or two months after he took over, just to find out more about what I know of this part of the world and China. But he has got his own ideas and he will decide on how he deals with the Chinese. I've also met David Cameron and I'm meeting him again in September (2009). Why does he see me? Because the older Conservative Party leaders know me and must have told him, that this man is worth meeting. So he brought William Hague[14] and three others, his inner confidants, to meet me.

Q: *How do you decide when you want to speak up publicly on an issue? In recent years you've been more active...*

A: I'm not more active in contradicting the policy or veering away from the policy because it's not my business to go and make the jobs of the younger ministers more difficult. It's my business to help them. That's what I'm here for. I'm not here to detract from them or to elevate myself. That's irrelevant.

They're going to carry the torch forward, not me.

In November 2010, after Mrs Lee's passing, we requested one more interview to update the book. Lee agreed to answer our questions through email.

Q: *When we last spoke, you said that you have made some adjustments to your life, given your wife's condition. Now that she has passed on, what is life like in this "big empty house" that you spoke of?*

A: It means more solitude. No one to talk to when the day's work is done.

Q: *What did you think of Singaporeans' reaction to Mrs Lee's death? Were you surprised that she was so well-loved?*

A: Only mildly. She was friendly to one and all. Never used her rank.

Q: *Over the course of the year, you have given several interviews to the Western media – such as* National Geographic *and* The New York Times *– which gave a refreshingly candid view into your private life. Many Singaporeans were struck by the revelations,* *especially of you and Mrs Lee. What has changed for you that you are now opening up to the public in such a way?*

A: Nothing special has happened. My wife's being unable to read freed me to talk to the media. She was a very private person and I respected her attitude.

Q: *Many Singaporeans were surprised that you meditate and were taught by a Catholic. Have you reconsidered your faith since Mrs Lee's passing? Do you see yourself adopting a faith in your twilight years?*

A: No. Learning to meditate, it so happened that my instructor was a Catholic. He did not try to convert me. And at my age it's unlikely that I can be converted.

LOVE
STORY

To the bright, young men and women gunning
to be top student at the prestigious Raffles
College, Kwa Geok Choo must have seemed
quite the adversary. A year earlier, she had
been the only girl to be enrolled in the all-boys
Raffles Institution. And now, after the first-
year college examinations in 1940, she had
topped the school in English and economics
– way ahead of second-placed Harry Lee Kuan
Yew. In his own words, he was "disturbed and
upset" by Kwa, who proceeded
to trounce him again the
following year. How could
he hope to win the coveted
Queen's scholarship and go
to England to study law with
someone like her around? Yet
what 17-year-old Harry Lee couldn't possibly
have foretold was that seven years later he
would be hoping against hope for the prize to go
to the very same girl.

*At a New Year's Eve
party in 1945, he took
her aside and asked if
she would wait for his
return. ... she agreed to
wait for him.*

Fast forward to 1944, as Singapore
prepared to enter its third year of the Japanese
occupation. The two meet again under very
different circumstances. Everyone's studies had
been disrupted by the war. The young Harry,
now juggling a variety of jobs to earn extra
income for his family, had hit upon a potential
new revenue stream. Fellow Raffles College

graduate Yong Nyuk Lin reckoned he could use tapioca flour to make stationery glue, which was in short supply at the time, and Harry Lee decided to fund his experiments. At Yong's house, he ran into Kwa, who turned out to be the younger sister of his new business partner's wife. As business flourished, he visited the Yong household often over the next few months and a friendship blossomed between the two. By September, he had plucked up the courage to ask her out for the first time – to attend his 21st birthday dinner at a Chinese restaurant in Great World.

Her acceptance was an event "not without significance", according to the rules of love at the time, Lee would recall decades later in his memoirs. It set in motion a growing attachment that would face its first test soon after the Japanese surrender in September 1945. Eager to press on as quickly as possible with his education, Harry decided against rejoining Raffles College, where he could only hope to graduate more than two years later. Instead he and his brother Dennis would use the family savings and go direct to university in Britain to study law. But that would mean leaving Kwa – he had begun affectionately calling her "Choo" by then – behind.

At a New Year's Eve party in 1945, he took her aside and asked if she would wait for his return. Choo was frank and asked him if he was sure about making a commitment to her, especially given that she was more than two years older than him. When Harry said he was certain about his feelings for her, she agreed to wait for him. "This was the way we dealt with each other," Lee wrote in his memoirs. Whatever issues they had, he said, "We faced them and sorted them out. We did not dodge or bury them." With only nine months to go before Harry set sail for England, the two lovebirds made the most of their remaining time together. Old photos show a young couple very much in love but uncertain about the future, anxious to record this special moment in their lives.

The winter of 1946 was an eventful time for Harry Lee. After a miserable first term in the London School of Economics frying steaks that stank his clothes and unsuccessfully trying to rub the capital city's soot out of his shirt collars, he applied to Fitzwilliam House in Cambridge University and got in. With catered meals and a more peaceful environment, Harry Lee was happy and soon resumed excelling in his studies. But the happiest news would arrive several months later in the summer of 1947 – an event he now rates as one of the happiest moments of their couplehood. What he had hoped for had come true – his girlfriend Choo had clinched the Queen's scholarship.

But the Colonial Office that gave the scholarship could not find a place for her in any university that year, so he would have to wait one more year – till 1948 – to be with her again. Taking matters into his own hands, he personally went to see the Mistresses of the two women's colleges in Cambridge, in an effort to persuade them to take Choo in that same year. Eventually, Girton College agreed and Choo boarded a troopship in August 1947 headed for Britain.

A couple of months after a joyful reunion at the Liverpool docks in October, he secretly married the love of his life in William Shakespeare's birthplace – the picturesque Stratford-upon-Avon. Talking about it 51 years later in an interview with *The Straits Times*, Kwa refused to cloak the ceremony in an overly romantic hue. They had simply made up their minds about each other. "What was the alternative?" she said. "To cohabit, as they say now, or to live in sin, as they would have said 50 years ago?" To mark the occasion, Harry Lee bought her a platinum ring, and when they returned to school for the New Year, she wore it on a chain around her neck.

From then on, Mr and Mrs Lee Kuan Yew have never really been apart. After graduating from Cambridge, they stayed together in a cottage on the English coast for a year – rogue students who skipped all their lectures and prepared for their Bar examinations in London on their own. When they returned to Singapore in August 1950, they initially worked for the same law firm (Laycock & Ong), but later set up their own firm (Lee & Lee) with Harry's brother, Dennis. As he entered politics and rose through the ranks, becoming Prime Minister in a few short years, Kwa became a working mother looking after their three young children. She worked seven minutes away from the house, Lee recalled in this set of interviews, and she made sure she was home every day for lunch – just as he would be home every day for dinner. Aside from taking care of the house and the kids, she would vet his speeches and polish them before delivery and be a sounding board for ideas and policies he was considering.

When their children were a little more grown up, she travelled extensively with her husband on his official trips abroad. "Would you believe me if I say we never disagree or quarrel? We did not need to agree on any working arrangement. We worked together and complemented each other," she once said. Both well into their 70s then, the two continued to work hand-in-hand on Lee's memoirs in the months before that, staying up until the wee hours of the morning and fiercely debating the finer points of phrasing and sentence structure. It was no surprise when Harry dedicated his memoirs to his "wife and partner Choo". And she told *The Straits Times* in 1998, "Of course I felt as proud as could be when I finally saw it in print."

Once, when she was asked on his 80th birthday in 2003, what was the most misunderstood thing about Lee, she replied, "I read somewhere that 'few elder statesmen can command as much respect and condemnation simultaneously as Lee'. I will leave it to these writers to argue which one has most misunderstood Kuan Yew."

For herself, what she most admired about him were his powers of persuasion. And she recalled at least seven turning points in both their lives when he succeeded against the odds to make things happen their way. These included asking her to wait to marry him even though he was going to be away for three years, and getting the Mistress at Girton to accept her even though the Education Department in Singapore then doubted her chance as it could not get a place for Eddie Barker (the former Law Minister in Lee's first Cabinet) despite his Queen's scholarship. "I also admire his steadiness, resourcefulness, and courage in times of great stress," she added.

It is a testament to their love that many ordinary Singaporeans now know how close Lee and his wife were. Choo kept an extremely low public profile over the decades, but the public somehow seemed to know that she was intelligent and kind, and that the founding father of Singapore is what he is partly because of her. It is the kind of love story that inspires people today, but from long ago the couple steadfastly denied being sentimental. There were no midnight proposals on moonlit balconies, they insisted. And the Hepburnesque quality in the old photos of them as happy young lovebirds was the result of them being posed. "If romantic means sentimental, then the answer is no," Choo once said of the relationship. "Neither of us would care for candlelit dinners."

Endnotes

1   The July 1964 Malay-Chinese riots killed 23 people and injured 454. A second riot broke out in September that year, leaving 12 dead and 109 wounded.

2   William Pitt the Elder was a British statesman and Prime Minister of Britain from 1766 to 1768. His son, William Pitt the Younger, was also a statesman and became the youngest ever Prime Minister from 1783 to 1801. After the Act of Union joined great Britain and Ireland, he ruled as Prime Minister of the United Kingdom in 1804. He died in 1806, unmarried and leaving no children.

3   Wolfensohn was president of the World Bank.

4   Shultz served as US Treasury secretary (1972–1974) and later, as secretary of state (1982–1989).

5   Lee's sister Monica, born in 1929, is the second youngest of the Lee siblings. The others are younger brothers Dennis, who died aged 77 in November 2003; Freddy, born in 1927; and Suan Yew, born in 1933.

6   A period of military conflict between Malaysia and Indonesia. It lasted from 1963 to 1966 and was an attempt by Indonesia to destabilise the new Malaysian state.

7   Lee was referring to Manek Urai, a state seat in Kelantan which PAS retained in a by-election, but with a slim margin of 65 votes over its UMNO opponent, compared to over 1,000 votes previously.

8   Managing director of Hotel Properties Ltd.

9   Lee is referring to Chip Goodyear, who was appointed CEO-designate at Temasek Holdings in March 2009 but quit abruptly in July 2009 before taking office, citing differences regarding strategic issues. Lee's remarks to the interviewers were made before Goodyear left Temasek.

10   Former chairman of DBS.

11   Dr Tony Tan took a break from his post as Minister for Education, leaving the Cabinet in 1991. He rejoined the Cabinet in 1995 as Deputy Prime Minister and retired 10 years later. Defence Minister Yeo Ning Hong stepped down in 1994 and Trade and Industry Minister S. Dhanabalan left in 1993.

12 Former Prime Minister of Italy and President of the European Commission.

13 Robert Rubin, then US Treasury secretary.

14 British first secretary of state and secretary of state for foreign and Commonwealth affairs.

Select Bibliography

Acharya, Amitav. *Singapore's Foreign Policy: The Search for Regional Order.* Singapore: World Scientific Publishing, 2008.

Barr, Michael. *Constructing Singapore: Elitism, Ethnicity and the Nation-Building Project.* Copenhagen: NIAS Press, 2008.

Barr, Michael. *Lee Kuan Yew: The Beliefs Behind the Man.* Washington: Georgetown University Press, 2000.

Bhaskaran, Manu. *Re-inventing the Asian Model: The Case of Singapore.* Singapore: Eastern Universities Press, 2003.

Chew, Melanie. *Leaders of Singapore.* Singapore: Resource Press, 1996.

Esping-Andersen, Gøsta. *The Three Worlds of Welfare Capitalism.* Princeton: Princeton University Press, 1990.

Ghesquiere, Henri. *Singapore's Success: Engineering Economic Growth.* Singapore: Thomson, 2006.

Gould, Stephen Jay. *The Mismeasure of Man* (Revised Edition). New York: W.W. Norton & Co, 1996.

Han Fook Kwang et al. *Lee Kuan Yew: The Man and His Ideas.* Singapore: Times Editions, 1998.

Harrison, Lawrence E. and Huntington, Samuel (eds). *Culture Matters: How Values Shape Human Progress.* New York: Basic Books, 2000.

Herrnstein, Richard J. and Murray, Charles. *The Bell Curve: Intelligence and Class Structure in American Life.* New York: Free Press, 1994.

Huntington, Samuel. *The Clash of Civilisations and the Remaking of World Order.* New York: Simon & Schuster, 1996.

Huxley, Tim. *Defending the Lion City: The Armed Forces of Singapore.* St Leonards: Allen & Unwin, 2000.

Lai Ah Eng (ed). *Beyond Rituals and Riots: Ethnic Pluralism and Social Cohesion in Singapore.* Singapore: Eastern Universities Press, 2004.

Lau, Albert. *A Moment of Anguish: Singapore in Malaysia and the Politics of Disengagement.* Singapore: Times Academic Press, 1998.

Lee Kuan Yew. *From Third World to First: The Singapore Story 1965–2000.* Singapore: Times Editions, 2000.

Lee Kuan Yew. *The Singapore Story: Memoirs of Lee Kuan Yew.* Singapore: Times Editions, 1998.

Leifer, Michael. *Singapore's Foreign Policy: Coping with Vulnerability.* London: Routledge, 2000.

Lim Chong Yah and You Poh Seng (eds). *Singapore: Twenty-five years of Development*. Singapore: Nan Yang Xing Zhou Lianhe Zaobao, 1984.

Lim, Linda. "Singapore's Economic Growth Model – Too Much or Too Little?" Paper prepared for the Singapore Economic Policy Conference 2008; accessible at http://www.fas.nus.edu.sg/ecs/scape/doc/24Oct08/Linda%20 Lim.pdf

Low, Linda. *The Political Economy of a City-State Revisited*. Singapore: Marshall Cavendish Academic, 2006.

Lu Yuanli. *Why Can Singapore Do It?* Nanchang: Jiangxi People's Publishing House, 2007.

Luce, Edward. *In Spite of the Gods: The Strange Rise of Modern India*. London, Little, Brown & Company, 2006.

Mahiznan, Arun, and Lee Tsao Yuan (eds). *Singapore: Re-engineered Success*. New York: Oxford University Press, 1998.

Mauzy, Diane K. and Milne, R.S. *Singapore Politics Under the People's Action Party*. London: Routledge, 2002.

Minchin, James. *No Man is an Island: A Portrait of Singapore's Lee Kuan Yew*. Sydney: Allen & Unwin Australia, 1990.

Neo Boon Siong and Chen, Geraldine. *Dynamic Governance: Embedding Cultures, Capabilities and Change in Singapore*. New Jersey: World Scientific Publishing Company, 2007.

Rahim, Lily Zubaidah. *The Singapore Dilemma: The Political and Educational Marginality of the Malay Community*. Kuala Lumpur: Oxford University Press, 2001.

Rose, Steven, Lewontin C. Richard and Kamin, Leon J. *Not in Our Genes: Biology, Ideology and Human Nature*. New York: Pantheon, 1984.

Sandhu, Kernial Singh and Wheatley, Paul (eds). *Management of Success: The Moulding of Modern Singapore*. Singapore: Institute of Southeast Asian Studies, 1989.

Shiraishi, Takashi (ed). *Across the Causeway: A Multi-dimensional Study of Malaysia-Singapore Relations*. Singapore: Institute of Southeast Asian Studies, 2009.

Trocki, Carl A. *Singapore: Wealth, Power and the Culture of Control*. London & New York: Routledge, 2006.

Vasil, Raj. *Governing Singapore*. Singapore: Mandarin, 1992.

Wilson, E.O. *On Human Nature*. Cambridge: Harvard University Press, 1978.

Zakaria, Fareed. *The Future of Freedom: Illiberal Democracy at Home and Abroad*. New York: W. W. Norton & Co, 2003.

Zakaria, Fareed. *The Post-American World*. New York: W.W. Norton & Co, 2008.

Index